Operation Goodtime and the
Battle of the Treasury Islands, 1943

Operation Goodtime and the Battle of the Treasury Islands, 1943

The World War II Invasion by United States and New Zealand Forces

REG NEWELL

McFarland & Company, Inc., Publishers
Jefferson, North Carolina, and London

LIBRARY OF CONGRESS CATALOGUING-IN-PUBLICATION DATA

Newell, Reg, 1954–
Operation Goodtime and the Battle of the Treasury Islands, 1943 : the World War II invasion by United States and New Zealand forces / Reg Newell.
p.   cm.
Includes bibliographical references and index.

ISBN 978-0-7864-6849-2
softcover : acid free paper ∞

1. World War, 1939–1945 — Campaigns — Solomon Islands.   2. New Zealand. Army. Divison, 3rd. Brigade, 8th.   3. United States. Marine Corps. Marine Amphibious Corps, I.   4. World War, 1939–1945 — Amphibious operations.   5. World War, 1939–1945 — Regimental histories — New Zealand.   6. World War, 1939–1945 — Participation, New Zealand.   I. Title.
D767.99.T74N49 2012   940.54'265931—dc23   2012027795

BRITISH LIBRARY CATALOGUING DATA ARE AVAILABLE

© 2012 Reg Newell. All rights reserved

No part of this book may be reproduced or transmitted in any form or by any means, electronic or mechanical, including photocopying or recording, or by any information storage and retrieval system, without permission in writing from the publisher.

On the cover: *Landing from L.S.T.s Near Falamai, Second Wave Coming In*, by Russell Clark, circa 1945, watercolor, 502 mm × 684 mm (Archives New Zealand/Te Rua Mahara o te Kāwanatanga, Wellington Office [AAAC 898 NCWA 54])

Manufactured in the United States of America

McFarland & Company, Inc., Publishers
Box 611, Jefferson, North Carolina 28640
www.mcfarlandpub.com

To the Treasury Islanders, and all the Kiwis and Yanks who together made Goodtime a success— one more step towards the end of the Great Pacific War.

And especially to Bert Cowan, one of New Zealand's quiet warriors.

Acknowledgments

I WOULD LIKE TO THANK all of the people who have helped and contributed to this work. In particular I would like to thank the veterans who so generously provided me with their recollections and guidance: Bert Cowan, Jesse Scott, Campbell Davie, Bob Dunlop, David Williams, Ron Tucker, Allan Rogers, Trevor Whaley, Peter Basil Renshaw, George Luoni, Ray Otto, Andy Lysaght, Bernie Harris, Ashley James, Thom Sen, Jeff Tunnicliffe, Forbes Greenfield, George Hodgson, Harry Bioletti, Charles Barlow, George E. Tschudi, Clair Charles and Wilmer Easley.

I would also like to thank the veterans' families who have helped — Joan Clouston, the Thomas family, the Nash Family, the Wickham family and David Estep. My typist, Kirsty Nolan, has tirelessly aided this work. Finally, I would like to thank my wife Heather and my son Michael, who have put up with my obsession with Goodtime.

Table of Contents

Acknowledgments vi
Preface 1

ONE • Meeting on Mono 3
TWO • The Opposing Forces 13
THREE • The Gamble 41
FOUR • The Downed Aviators, the Treasury Islanders and
    the Japanese 64
FIVE • The Cowan Patrols 82
SIX • Invasion: 27 October 1943 96
SEVEN • Goodtime—The Air Aspects 139
EIGHT • Loganforce at Soanatalu—Desperate Defense:
    29 October to 3 November 1943 144
NINE • Consolidation and Elimination of Japanese Defenders 150
TEN • Aftermath and Legacies 187

• APPENDICES •
A: Composition of 8 Brigade, 3 NZ Division 201
B: United States Forces: The Land Component 202
C: The Allied Naval Component 202
D: The Japanese Order of Battle and Weaponry 203
E: Distances to the Treasury Islands in Nautical Miles 204
F: Beaching Times 204
G: Weapons of 8 Brigade, 3 NZ Division 205
H: Uniforms and Personal Equipment of 3 NZ Division 207
I: Amphibious Operations Vessels 207
J: Order of Battle: Goodtime Assault Landings 208

Chronology 209
Glossary 211
Chapter Notes 221
Bibliography 233
Index 237

Preface

ON 27 OCTOBER 1943 a force of New Zealanders and Americans invaded the Treasury Islands and retook them from their Japanese occupiers. Atypically in an American-dominated theater, the New Zealanders provided the fighting men and the Americans the support troops, although both found plenty of fighting to do. The invasion was the first time New Zealand forces took part in an opposed landing since Gallipoli in 1915. On this occasion they were under the overall command of the United States Navy and reliant on American air, naval and logistic support. The invaders faced severe risks but, nonetheless, succeeded in their tasks with relatively slight casualties.

Back in New Zealand, the invasion, code named *Operation Goodtime*, received little publicity, mainly because of the need for operational secrecy. The invasion, together with the other contributions made by 3 NZ Division, have faded into obscurity and few, apart from the islanders, surviving veterans and specialists in the Pacific War, are aware of it. For the Americans who participated there was little publicity, and what there was, was overshadowed by the seizure of Tarawa and the horrific casualties that followed there.

The efforts of the Allied soldiers, sailors and airmen have been unfairly forgotten and deserve recognition. Likewise, the heroic actions of the Treasury Islanders who hid downed Allied aircrew and provided guides and military intelligence to the Allies have been overlooked. For the Japanese defenders of the Treasury Islands there has only been the dust of oblivion, as they were merely a minor footnote in Japan's war in Asia and the Pacific. Their story also deserves to be told. Overall, a blanket of obscurity descended on these groups and it is the intent of this book to provide them with some recognition.

Operation Goodtime was a small part of a titanic struggle which the Japanese call "the Great Pacific War." For those involved, however, it was a pivotal moment in their lives. The Great Pacific War was made up of many such small struggles on islands, atolls and archipelagoes temporarily lifted out of obscurity by their sudden strategic significance and whose names never achieved popular resonance. As John Rentz, a U.S. Marine Corps historian, put it, "Operations on the Treasury Islands, Choiseul, Bougainville, Green and Emirau were additional markers on the highway that led to the quarterdeck of the *Missouri* in Tokyo Bay"[1] where the Japanese formally surrendered.

My awareness of Operation Goodtime came about as a result of doing a course on the Pacific War through the American Military University. I used a text by John Lorelli on amphibious operations and was intrigued by a reference to the Americans and New Zealanders undertaking amphibious operations in the South Pacific in World War II. I prided myself on being knowledgeable about the Pacific War and my country's role in World War II. I realized that this was a forgotten story. The more I looked into matters the more fascinated I became by it. Ultimately this led to my undertaking a doctorate through Massey University, Palmerston North, New Zealand, which examined the role of 3 NZ Division in the war in the South Pacific. During my research I came across veterans who had participated in Goodtime and who generously talked to me. Although a relatively small operation, I was impressed by the human dimensions to the story, and this book is an outcome of that.

A Note on Sources

This work is primarily based on records contained in Archives New Zealand, Wellington and the interviews with veterans that I had conducted during my doctoral research. I had the good fortune to obtain copies of the diary of Major General Harold Barrowclough and at the other end of the command spectrum Bombardier Gordon Thomas. The Web site of the USS *Cony* was particularly helpful. David Estep was very generous with providing family records relating to his father's time on Mono. Iulia Leilua helped by providing photographs and information on the modern Treasury Islands. Maori Television assisted by making available interviews conducted for their ANZAC Day specials.

One

Meeting on Mono

IN THE EARLY HOURS OF 25 October 1943, Ensign Jesse Scott, U.S. Navy, strained his eyes to make out two figures approaching the native hut on Mono Island where he was hiding from Japanese soldiers. He nervously raised his pistol and aimed it at the approaching figures. Scott and two of his fellow aviators had been shot down and had been hidden by friendly natives. As the figures got closer, Scott relaxed. He could see that the one in a green uniform was a European accompanied by a native. The European was a New Zealander, Sergeant William A. (Bert) Cowan, the leader of a reconnaissance patrol consisting of two Solomon Islanders and an American who had been stealthily delivered to the island by a U.S. Navy PT boat.

For Cowan this was simply yet another unexpected turn in a dangerous mission behind enemy lines. For Scott and his companions Cowan represented the hope of freedom. For the natives of Mono Island, Cowan presented the hope of liberation from the hated Japanese occupiers. The genesis of this providential meeting took place many months before and would come under the singularly ill-named Operation Goodtime.

The Strategic Situation

On 7–8 December 1941, the Japanese Empire launched strikes at the American fleet based at Pearl Harbor, Hawaii, and British Commonwealth forces in Malaya. In the following weeks the Japanese in a brilliant series of thrusts overran Malaya, the Dutch East Indies, Burma and the Philippines. For the first six months of the Great Pacific War, the Japanese, with almost contemptuous ease, eviscerated Allied naval, air and ground forces. They created the myth of the invincible Japanese super soldier and seemed unstoppable.

With the sinking of HMS *The Prince of Wales* and HMS *Repulse* on 10 December 1941 and the fall of Singapore on 15 February 1942, the British Commonwealth's Far Eastern defense strategy evaporated and with that went the security of Australasia. A flippant remark of a British representative at the 1939 Pacific Defense Conference, held in Wellington, New Zealand, that in the event of the fall of Singapore New Zealanders should seek the protection offered by the Waitomo Caves seemed to be coming to fruition.[1] There were no British naval forces in the South Pacific capable of stopping a determined Japanese invasion of Australia and New Zealand. The only force possibly able to do this was the American Navy commanded by an Anglophobe, Admiral Ernest King, the chief of naval operations. American planners had decided that the retention of Australia was desirable but not essential for the American war effort.[2] Strategically, it made little sense for the Americans to defend Australasia. Their War Plan Orange was based on the idea of a thrust across the central Pacific, the seizure of advanced bases for provisioning of warships, a climatic naval battle which would secure naval superiority and the strangulation of Japan by way of naval blockade.[3] King, however, believed that Australia and New Zealand were "white man's countries" and thus had to be protected from the Japanese barbarians.[4] He made the extremely risky, even foolhardy, decision to commit American aircraft carriers to the defense of Australia. The gamble paid off at the Battle of the Coral Sea in May 1942, which, although an American tactical defeat, was a strategic victory in that it turned back Japanese troop transports bound for Port Morseby in Papua–New Guinea, a precursor to any invasion of Australia. This American victory and the subsequent destruction of Japanese aircraft carriers at the Battle of Midway in June 1942 meant that the war in the Pacific would be an American-dominated one.

For New Zealand, the relationship with the Americans was one of discomfort mingled with a powerful sense of relief at imminent Japanese invasion being repulsed.[5] Pre-war, there were doubts whether America would fight Japan if the Japanese attacked British Empire possessions. There was friction between Wellington and Washington over the sovereignty of several atolls in the Pacific which had assumed importance as flying boat bases. In 1939 the warship HMS *Ajax* was dispatched to Christmas Island to deter a land-grab by American personnel. There was no direct pre-war diplomatic representation between Wellington and Washington. New Zealand was assumed to fall within the British sphere of influence and the Americans conducted their diplomacy with Whitehall rather than Wellington. The evaporation of British power in the Far East and the Pacific changed all of that. By agreement between Britain and America it was decided that America would be responsible for the defense of Australasia. For the Americans there was the sense that they were the dominant partner and they saw little benefit or reason to consult indigent, subordinate allies such as New Zealand. The Pacific Defense Council was set up for the Allied nations to have a voice in Pacific strategy. The Americans, however, saw it simply as window dressing, a sop to their allies. The war in the South Pacific would be an American war.

The Americans imposed their own command structure on Canberra and Wellington, ignoring the ANZAC (Australian and New Zealand Army Corps) command structures.[6] Fresh from being rescued from his doomed command in the Philippines, General Douglas MacArthur assumed command of the South West Pacific Area and Vice Admiral Robert Lee Ghormley assumed command of the South Pacific Area encompassing New Zealand and the islands to its north. The division of command areas amounted to the U.S. Army taking over the defense of Australia and New Guinea and the U.S. Navy taking over the defense of New Zealand. Although U.S. Army units would fight in the South Pacific and U.S. Navy units would fight in the South West Pacific, there was a palpable sense of rivalry between the U.S. Army as exemplified by General MacArthur and his U.S. Navy counterpart, Admiral Chester Nimitz.[7] Into this maelstrom of egos and rivalries the New Zealanders found themselves ill-placed.

The Americans soon made their superiority obvious with their demand that New Zealand troops (including those of 8 Brigade) should be returned to New Zealand from Fiji, where they were a garrison, and their replacement by American personnel.[8] The Americans wanted homogeneity of command and it also feared that Wellington would ask American troops to be sent to garrison New Zealand on the basis that New Zealand troops were defending Fiji. Faced with a steadfast American demand, Wellington had little option but to comply. New Zealand's recently-appointed minister in Washington, Walter Nash, suggested that American troops be sent to New Zealand and that New Zealand soldiers train alongside their American counterparts in amphibious operations.[9]

Admiral King, perhaps as a way of softening the blow of New Zealand's ejection from Fiji, responded positively to this. The New Zealanders decided to formally create a division based on the cadres of garrison troops from Fiji. An offer was made of a full division complete with heavy artillery to be made available by 25 August 1942. The Americans thought that this division could be usefully employed by garrisoning Guadalcanal, in the Solomon Islands, recently retaken from the Japanese. However, the New Zealand force, 3 NZ Division, could not be created in time and the idea was shelved. The division, although only partly formed, was too useful an asset to be ignored in the personnel-starved South Pacific. At Ghormley's request, units of 3 NZ Division garrisoned Norfolk Island and Tonga briefly and then New Caledonia.

At the Arcadia Conference in Washington in late 1941 to mid–January 1942, British Prime Minister Winston Churchill and American President Franklin Delano Roosevelt reaffirmed the Allied policy of "Germany First," whereby the defeat of Germany took priority over the defeat of Japan. It had been embarrassing that the first American offensive of the war was at Guadalcanal and that the publicity of this epic campaign enhanced King's quest for resources to be sent to the South Pacific.

The strain of the battle for Guadalcanal broke Ghormley. His replacement, Admiral William "Bull" Halsey, had a much more pragmatic approach to the use of New Zealand soldiers, and he pressured Wellington to complete its commitment to provide a full division of trained troops. Ironically, Wellington also preferred to follow a "Germany First" policy and the cream of New Zealand's manpower was to be directed to 2 NZ Division in the Mediterranean.

After the successful completion of the Guadalcanal campaign the question became one of, where to next? It was not thought desirable to remain passively on the defensive — the Japanese were too unpredictable and too strong in the South Pacific.[10] In particular the Japanese had set up a strong naval, air and land base at Rabaul in New Ireland.[11] Those forces threatened the security of the South Pacific and had to be neutralized.

> The very name — Rabaul — haunted the thinking of Allied leaders in the South and Southwest Pacific. It was the main remaining threat to the American-Australian life-line. No operation in the Solomons or New Guinea, no matter how successful could be considered complete as long as Rabaul remained strong, since it was always possible for resurgent Japanese troops to move from Rabaul and attempt the reconquest even of Guadalcanal or eastern New Guinea.
>
> Neutralization of Rabaul in consequence, was an indispensable condition of the South Pacific planning of the Joint Chiefs of Staff. It was essential that the place either be seized or contained before projected operations in the Philippines or the South Pacific could be undertaken. Thus the Northern Solomons campaign, which consisted of one large opera-

tion (Bougainville) and numerous smaller ones, became in effect the campaign to contain and neutralize Rabaul.[12]

Rather than a direct assault, it was decided by American Joint Chiefs of Staff that Rabaul would be by-passed and neutralized by Allied air and naval forces. American planners gave their plan the code name Operation Cartwheel and subsequent Allied operations in the South and South West Pacific would focus on the neutralization of Rabaul. To do this island bases had to be seized from air and naval power that could be projected. Those bases in turn, needed garrisons to prevent them from being destroyed.

After Guadalcanal the New Georgia Islands campaign had been undertaken. It had been a grueling campaign which had worn out the combat capability of some of the units involved.[13] It was clear that the Japanese were determined, proficient jungle fighters who, if given the chance, would exact a significant toll of Allied lives. Rather than confront the Japanese in a series of grinding, attritional battles, it was decided to pursue an "island hopping" strategy and simply bypass the centers of Japanese strength and allow them to wither away.

The next step up the ladder of the Solomon Islands was to be Bougainville, the biggest island in the Solomons. It offered the advantage of being a large island from which air and naval bases could be created. It was decided at an early stage that it would not be possible to conquer the whole island and that perimeters would be set up and the Japanese invited to dash themselves in futile Banzai charges against well dug-in Allied troops.

There was a potentially divisive problem for the Allies. Bougainville and the Treasury Islands were on MacArthur's side of the line dividing his South West Pacific Area from Nimitz's South Pacific Area. However, given that one of Cartwheel's primary aims was to secure the flank of MacArthur's drive up the New Guinea coast, there was reason for MacArthur to be flexible. The demarcation line was adjusted slightly so that Bougainville and the Treasury Islands came within Nimitz's command area. Halsey as Commander of the South Pacific would establish a remarkably amicable relationship with MacArthur. The Treasury Islands and Bougainville campaigns would be the U.S. Navy's show.

In many respects the timing of Cartwheel operations was influenced by and, indeed, driven by, Douglas MacArthur. MacArthur had an ardent desire to return to the Philippines to liberate its people. However, he faced opposition from King, who favored a thrust across the Central Pacific. In order to convince the Joint Chiefs of Staff that an advance from the South West Pacific was not only viable, but preferable, MacArthur had to speed up the pace of his force's advance,[14] and that meant neutralizing Rabaul and protecting his flank. MacArthur therefore instructed Halsey to speed up Cartwheel.

The Bougainville operation was allocated the pleasant, almost Japanese sounding code name Operation Cherryblossom. Bougainville promised to be a tough nut — it was within range of Rabaul and striking distance of the Japanese fleet based on Truk. Bougainville was well garrisoned and had sufficient forces to counterattack any landings. Furthermore, Bougainville was an obvious target.[15] However, it was hoped that the precise landing place could be kept secret and that the lack of roads would hinder the rapid deployment of Japanese reserves. It was also hoped that Japanese strength on Bougainville could be dissipated by focusing their attention away from the invasion beaches at Empress Augusta Bay. It was decided that two diversionary operations would occur, one on Choiseul,[16] Operation Blissful, and the second, using New Zealand troops, on the Treasury

Islands, Operation Goodtime. Codenames were selected by COMSOPAC,[17] the Commander of the South Pacific Area.

As Andrew Roberts has pointed out "It does indeed seem astonishing that operations in which men's lives were at stake were often given light-hearted and sometimes downright flippant codenames, but war often throws up such like fey, light-hearted jokes deliberately designed to contrast with the lethal reality of the operations they masked."[18]

Codenames were also given to geographical points. New Caledonia, for example, was referred to as "Poppy" or "White Poppy." The Treasury Islands were given the code name "Goodtime," which may explain why the invasion was called "Operation Goodtime." Generally codenames for military operations were chosen that had no connection to their subject matter in order to maintain secrecy. "Goodtime" appears to have been an exception to this rule.

Perhaps it is fortunate that few of the men taking part in the operation knew its name. The codename was known only to staff officers. The Seabees only knew that they were headed to "Island X."[19]

The Treasury Islands

The Treasury Islands received their name from their European discoverer, Lieutenant Shortland of the Royal Navy, allegedly "after the source of his pay" in 1788 whilst returning to England with two convict ships from Australia.[20] The Treasury Islands are part of the Solomon Islands chain and are fairly typical of the smaller islands in the northern Solomons. They consist of two main islands, Mono and Stirling.

Of volcanic and coral origin, Mono is a round shape roughly four miles in a north to south direction and roughly 6 miles in an east to west direction. There are three prominent volcanically-formed peaks. Streams flow from these peaks to the coast providing good drinking water. Thick forest covers the island with a small mangrove swamp on the coast east of Laifa Point. On the northern and western sides there are steep cliffs but on the northeastern side there is a sandy bay. A small boat landing existed at Soanatalu. The southeast coast from Toaloko Point has cliffs 30 to 60 feet high. On the northern coast there are a number of caves. Suitable landing beaches were limited and were mainly on the south coast along Blanche Harbor. The cliffs, vegetation down to the waters' edge and surf conditions all limited choices of landing sites.[21] "The beach at Falamai offered a good harbor with high hills to the rear commanding the area"[22] according to one description. The population made up of approximately 150 to 200 Melanesians was sparse with four villages, the main one being Falamai in the south. Falamai village was located close to the shoreline. The native population was considered to be "canoe people" and consequently pathways around Mono were limited. Native trails were used to connect villages with native gardens. A rudimentary track connected Falamai and Malsi which mainly followed the coastline. Falamai was considered "a good sandy landing beach," albeit rather steep. It was thought to provide good shelter in all seasons. Blanche Harbor was likewise considered to be a good anchorage with both eastern and western approaches being wide, deep and freely navigable.[23]

A view from the heights of Mono Island across Blanche Harbor to Stirling Island (War History Collection, Alexander Turnbull Library, Wellington, F-44769-1/2).

Stirling Island lies less than a mile to the south of Mono, separated by Blanche Channel. Long and narrow and shaped like a hook, Stirling is three miles long by one mile wide and has a maximum elevation of some 200 feet. Stirling is a raised coral island and because of its comparative flatness and less dense forest, it offered the best potential for an airfield. It had the additional advantage of a basic road system which had been created by the owners of a coconut plantation.[24] Although there is a lake in the eastern part, the water is brackish and drinking water supplies are problematic. There are two sheltered bays on the northern side of the island.

Blanche Harbor has a number of small islets including Watson, Wilson and Savo (not to be confused with the island adjoining Guadalcanal). Watson and Wilson are oval-shaped. They were not garrisoned and had significance only as navigational points.

The strategic significance of the Treasury Islands was that they lay 28 miles south southwest of Bougainville. Some 18 miles to their northeast lay the heavily Japanese-garrisoned Shortland Islands. Some 60 miles to the southeast lay Vella Lavella, garrisoned by troops of 14 Brigade, 3 NZ Division. In deciding which islands to seize the American planners had as their essential criteria whether the island could be reached by Allied airpower so that a protective air umbrella could be thrown over the invading force. Also, there was the consideration of whether it was within range of Rabaul. The Shortland Islands were discounted because their beaches and aircraft sites were inadequate. The Treasury

Islands fulfilled the criteria and offered the chance to establish long-range radar, a naval base for PT boats and a staging area for Allied landing craft en-route to Bougainville. Despite its evident benefits the Treasury Islands had one major drawback—they were within a few minutes' flying time of Japanese airbases on the Shortland Islands and Bougainville.

The Treasury Islanders were considered "unusually healthy," no doubt due to the fact that the Treasury Islands were non-malarial.[25] An intelligence report said that they were believed to be pro–Allied, "...disliking the Japs because they receive no medical aid from them as they formerly did from the British. They are relatively well educated and many speak English." The intelligence report went on to comment that "The Treasury natives of course fear the Japanese, and their actions will to some extent be dominated by this fear until a show of force by our troops."[26]

Not all Solomon Islanders were pro–Allied. Indeed, some were actively pro–Japanese and acted as Coast Watchers, informants, guides and laborers for them. It was considered that "...the natives are impressed by a show of strength and force. Many of those who now seem to favor the Japanese do so for that reason. It is likely that these natives will, in the main, reverse their attitude as soon as the Allies have landed in force and demonstrated superiority in numbers and equipment."[27]

As Eric Bergerud has commented, "The war in the south Pacific was a struggle between outsiders." It had come "without warning or invitation to the people of the South Pacific and concerned issues that few understood in the least. With some very notable exceptions, few in the area had a personal stake in the war or the outcome. It was not a national or ideological crusade."[28] The arrival of Japanese soldiers in the Solomon Islands tested colonial relationships to the extreme as the Solomon Islanders found themselves embroiled in brutal warfare and used by both sides.[29]

The Allies did, however, have the advantage that the British had created a basic administrative infrastructure in the Solomon Islands in the pre-war years. The Treasury Islands were administered as part of the British Protectorate of the Solomon Islands' Shortland District. British rule had been established in 1893 and had obtained an aura of legitimacy by virtue of its longevity. The Islanders in the 19th Century had a reputation as headhunters and were considered to be "the most treacherous and bloodthirsty of any known savages."[30] Methodist Christian missionaries had visited the islands pre-war and the Christian influence was strong. The native dialects were Mono, Alu and Fauro.[31] English was taught by the missionaries and some natives were able to converse in English and Pidgin English.

Preliminaries to Invasion: The Special Mission of the USS *Greenling*

Prior to 1942 the Solomon Islands had seemed an unlikely place for industrialized 20th Century forces to fight. There were no resources of great importance, the population was small, the climate was unhealthy, the terrain dense and forbidding and there was little in the way of ports, airfields or infrastructure.

One of the problems confronting American planners was the paucity of accurate maps. Halsey commented, "...Our charts of the northern Solomons were sketchy and far from reliable; hundreds of square miles of the interior were dismissed with 'unexplored.'"[32] A submarine commander engaged in dropping off a covert reconnaissance patrol on Bougainville checked the navigation chart that he had been supplied with and discovered that Cape Tokorina, the invasion site, was seven miles in error.[33]

By 1943 American planners had a number of tools at their disposal for reconnaissance of possible landing sites. The first was photograph reconnaissance aircraft. These planes were dispatched to take photographs of the Treasury Islands to provide information on topography, likely landing sites and Japanese defenses. These sorties were often conducted "down on the deck." By 1943 analysis of photo reconnaissance material had reached a state of considerable sophistication. Sand table models of the Treasury Islands based on photo reconnaissance material were reproduced. The difficulties were that photo reconnaissance could yield only limited information where areas like Mono were heavily forested and photographs could not disclose whether the soil of a landing beach would be strong enough to support the weight of landing craft, especially the large Landing Ship Tanks with their huge cargo bay doors. The American preference was to land specialists and take samples of soil and check out the hydrology—the effects of tides, currents and any other relevant factors.[34] Quite often these specialists were delivered to the sites by United States Navy PT Boats, small high-powered motor boats with limited armament but potential to be stealthy. Despite their speed, such craft were vulnerable to air attack. The third method was to deliver the specialists by means of submarine. This was the method chosen to investigate the Shortland and Treasury Islands.

The boat chosen was the USS *Greenling* (SS-213). *Greenling* had been built by the Electric Boat Company in Groton, Connecticut, and commissioned on 21 January 1942. It had carried out six patrols and its crew was well seasoned. Greenling had experienced torpedo troubles initially but once these had been resolved it sank a sizeable number of Japanese vessels, including destroyers, freighters and even sampans. On its fifth war patrol Greenling had carried out a "special mission," so its crew had experience of covert operations. On completion of a successful sixth war patrol, *Greenling* berthed at Brisbane and was refitted by the submarine repair unit. There, its commander received instructions to carry out a special mission in the Solomon Islands.

On 29 July 1943, the USS *Greenling*, undertaking its seventh war patrol, sailed from Brisbane to Tulagi in the Solomon Islands, where it waited for about a week for the right moon conditions. It left Tulagi for its reconnaissance mission[35] with an unusual cargo of engineering and hydrographic specialists and a British officer, Lt. Colonel David Trench, with Solomon Islanders[36] and an escort of U.S. Marines. The group numbered 26 to 40 men.[37] The *Greenling* was a Gato class diesel-electric powered submarine designed for long range cruising with every inch of space utilized. With a normal complement of 60 men, the discomfort caused by the additional passengers must have been tremendous. Charles Barlow recalled that the rafts were stowed in the empty torpedo "skids" and that the natives spread their mats on the deck in the aft torpedo room. Everyone got on "fine, as most combatants do when working together."[38] On reaching the destination on 22 August 1943, the submarine off-loaded the men into rubber boats which were then divided into two patrols which were rowed to beach areas on both the Shortland and the Treasury Islands.

Charles Barlow, a Greenling crew member, recalls:

> Our orders were to transport them to a point off the selected sites as close to the beach as we could manage and return to the same points to recover them three days later. The Shortland party was to leave in two rafts on the first night and the Mono party in one raft on the following night. To the amazement of all hands and the ship's cook that is exactly what we did.
>
> But things did not go quite as smoothly as the foregoing would indicate—for example: The only available navigational charts had been issued by the German Admiralty in the 1870s and never updated. As a result the Shortland Group went ashore about five miles away from the selected site. This turned out to be the first lucky break since a Japanese shore battery was located where it was intended for them to come in. There was a good sized Japanese occupation force on Shortland Island.
>
> The day after the Shortland landings, as a detachment of the reconnaissance group was proceeding along an island trail approaching a bend around the corner, came a detachment of Japanese soldiers. They stood for a minute or so looking at each other. The Marines were ready to open fire but were refused permission, apparently the Japanese made the same decision and they both turned around and went back whence they came. That night there were lights moving in many places on the island but no contacts were made. When the reconnaissance party left on schedule, having accomplished their objective they were still undetected.
>
> When we returned as scheduled to the point where we had left them we noticed the unusual amount of lights bobbing around on the island but could see no sign of the rafts. They had orders to return to the point where they had disembarked to look for us. They had narrow beam flashlights to attract our attention. Shortly after we arrived at the designated meeting point and still hadn't sighted the rafts. Sonar (ASDIC) picked up the sound of fast screws approaching from the beach. We dove and they passed directly overhead. As soon as they cleared we surfaced and started searching parallel to the beach. In about fifteen minutes we spotted the rafts. We then took them aboard with no-one missing or injured, sank the life rafts and headed for Mono.
>
> The recovery at Mono Island was routine. If there were any Japanese on the island the reconnaissance party did not see them and accomplished all of their tasks with no interference.
>
> The report of the operation was classified as top secret so was not written up with our regular Patrol Report.[39]

Crew member Adam Balzwierczak's recollection was that after the reconnaissance party had been picked up on 23 August 1943, "the rafts could not be deflated quickly enough so some of the crew slashed them to sink faster." He also recalled that on returning to safe harbor the submarine tied up at the dock only to find itself in the middle of an air raid, so "the boat was submerged alongside the dock, so to be hidden from sight. After all was settled down and quiet, the Marines made preparations for going elsewhere.

"Since the camaraderie was there, the hosts and visitors were giving mementos to each other. Some of the Marines even gave their rifles as gifts."[40]

The *Greenling* reconnoitered Nauru and Tarawa and then sailed for Pearl Harbour on 17 September, 1943. Unlike in its previous patrols, no torpedoes were fired, and no Japanese ships were engaged.

The *Greenling* patrol report is particularly laconic and deals only with tonnage of fuel used,[41] vessels and ships sighted and engine difficulties. It refers to the "special mission" being carried out successfully but gives no clue as to what that mission was. It does, however, disclose that the 21 days from 8 August to 1 September were spent on the special mission, that 1670 miles were sailed using up 20,230 gallons of fuel, and that 16 days were spent submerged.

The boat's history of its seventh war patrol records: "A special mission occupied the *Greenling* on the 7th War Patrol, which started on 29 July from Brisbane. This patrol lasted 51 days ending at Pearl Harbour. Combat insignia was awarded. From Pearl Harbour the *Greenling* departed for a very successful two month patrol at San Francisco's Market Street. The base for this operation was Hunter's Point Navy Yard."[42]

The landing party on Mono attempted to be stealthy and buried the canned provisions they had used. These were, however, found by the natives. The reconnaissance of the Treasury Islands was successful. Similar expeditions were carried out by USS *Gato* and USS *Guardfish* around Bougainville.[43]

The patrol produced a detailed report on Mono and noted that although there were signs of enemy patrols, no Japanese were sighted.[44]

Mono Island was not as free of Japanese as it seemed, and the reconnaissance party from the *Greenling* could have run into them.

Two

The Opposing Forces

ALTHOUGH AT THE TIME OF the USS *Greenling*'s visit the Treasury Islands was lightly garrisoned, the Japanese subsequently built up their strength. A force of seven men was initially installed to man observation posts. On 28 September, 1943, 128 Japanese evacuees from Reketa arrived, boosting the garrison to 135. The Japanese steadily built up to about 225 troops. On the day before Goodtime, reinforcements arrived. The Japanese soldiers consisted of troops from 7 Kure Special Naval Landing Force, 7th Combined Special Naval Landing Force and soldiers from 16th and 17th Air Defense Units. They were Imperial Japanese Navy Land Forces and held naval rank. They wore a tropic uniform of green-colored cotton and had anchor insignia on their headgear and uniforms. They could be expected to fight with skill and determination. They were well-equipped with rifles, light machine guns, mortars and artillery. Supply dumps had been created.

The Special Naval Land Forces (SNLF) or "Tokubetsu Rikusentai" were considered an elite organization, at least in the early part of the war. The role of the SNLF troops was to provide naval commanders with infantry troops to guard naval bases and carry out other tasks associated with naval operations. They were trained in amphibious assaults, took part in the Japanese Strike South 1941–42, and distinguished themselves in their bloody defense of Tarawa in November 1943.[1]

The bulk of SNLF troops on Mono were 7 Kure SNLF. This unit was formed in February 1943. It was composed of both conscripts and volunteers from the Kure area who had limited training before being committed to combat. Many of its personnel had been subjected to air attacks before arriving on Mono. The unit can be considered as of lesser quality than the elite SNLF units formed prior to the Pacific War and which were blooded in the Sino-Chinese War. An intelligence report commented:

> Special Landing Forces (KURE #7 and SASEBO #6) have demonstrated themselves as formidable fighters and the most ruthless opponents which Blue forces have engaged in the Sopac area. They are now primarily base defense units, armed with light and medium AA and naval guns of 8, 12 and 14cm. Infantry strength has been increased recently in some units by the addition of two or three rifle companies and mortar and machine gun detachments. The SNLFs have not, however, evidenced thorough proficiency in infantry tactics. Neither the KURE #7 nor the SASEBO #6 has been in combat with troops in this theatre.[2]

A clue to the rapid disintegration of Japanese command and control structures after the Allied landing on Mono is that Commander Mizoguchi, the commanding officer of 7 Kure SNLF, was wounded in an air attack on Santa Isabel. His successor, Commander Yoshino, was wounded when a Japanese convoy was attacked by Allied planes. The convoy diverted to Rabaul and left the commanders there.[3] In early September 1943 some 130 soldiers left Buin on Bougainville by large landing barge and a fishing boat for Mono. About 40 men from the Mountain Artillery unit joined them some time later. The Japanese appear to have been commanded by a Special Service Ensign, a medical lieutenant and two warrant officers.[4] Given that most of the Japanese would have arrived in September, command structures may not have had time to coalesce.

The 16th Air Defense Unit, organized at Kure in April, 1943, was based at Buin and was of company strength. The force sent to Mono was a squad under the command of Special Service Ensign Nakaseko. The squad had arrived on Mono with a group of 133 reinforcements on 8–9 September 1943.[5] The normal distribution of troops was of nine each at the four observation posts. The observation post on Stirling Island was discontinued after the military realized it was too easily cut off. Those troops were then assigned to various gun positions.[6]

Estimates of the size of the Japanese force on 27 October 1943, vary. The estimate given by John N. Rentz, a Marine Corps historian, of about 250 defenders seems accurate.[7]

The Japanese were age 18 and upwards with most of the soldiers being in their early 20s and single. Civilian occupations ranged from carpenter to postal employees. Most had at least an elementary school education. They defied the Western stereotype of being short, weedy and bespectacled. The soldiers were tall, well-built men.

The Japanese did not heavily garrison the island and the impression is created that they were there to act as a trip wire, a warning force. They set up observation posts at Laifa Point, Luia Point, Toaloka Point and Wilson Point and sited mortars and artillery on the obvious landing area on the south of Mono Island. They also built log bunkers which were camouflaged. They did not have any radar installations on the Treasury Islands. There were supply and organizational problems: a 25mm gun had been assembled at the Central Observation Post but this lacked ammunition. By 15 September 1943, the Japanese had built houses in the bush and installed a telephone system.[8] One advantage the Japanese did have was good optical equipment for their observation duties.[9]

The Japanese brought with them to Mono illnesses which were passed on to the local population. Superior Seaman Kohei Mizuno, 7 Kure SNLF, told his captors that a medical report stated that from April to October 1943, 40 natives had died of malaria and 100 from dysentery. He indicated that he had a slight case of malaria immediately after landing on Mono Island.[10] Given that Mono was non-malarial, the Japanese must have been infected before their arrival. An Allied intelligence report noted the susceptibility of Japanese troops to tropical diseases and that those in the Solomons–New Britain area suffered extensively from malaria and intestinal complaints. It was considered that recent arrivals in the Solomons would be in better physical condition than those who had been there for six months or more. Indications were that the SNLF troops were better supplied than their Army counterparts and that "it may be expected that their physical well being will be superior to that of army personnel."[11]

One of the failures of the Japanese military in the Solomon Islands was its inability to provide adequate medical care for its soldiers. One prisoner of war told his captors "that Japanese did not worry much about malaria as it was rarely serious."[12] It is noteworthy that one of the officers on Mono was a medical lieutenant. The Japanese had no qualms about medical officers commanding military operations and it appeared that the Japanese doctor on Mono assumed command of some soldiers. He became a much sought-after target by New Zealand patrols.

Another area of Japanese difficulty was supplying their troops, particularly in the face of increasing Allied air and sea attacks. Army rations were described in an Allied intelligence report as "inadequate in quality to keep troops in condition during active fighting." However, Navy troops were considered as better fed and therefore able to withstand dietary deficiency longer.[13]

The Japanese cemented the locals' dislike of them by raiding the gardens of the locals.[14]

The Japanese Eastern Way of War endorsed ambush, deception and trickery as worthy stratagems. From a Western viewpoint some Japanese practices were viewed as unsportsmanlike, unfair and treacherous. The Japanese forces on Mono stored their ammunition in the church at Falamai — a military use of a religious building that was abhorred by the Allies. From the Japanese viewpoint the structure was largely weatherproof and had the additional advantage that its religious significance afforded the cache some degree of protection. The Japanese practice of feigning surrender and then attempting to kill would-be captors became notorious among Allied soldiers.

By Imperial Rescript and training the Japanese were forbidden to surrender.[15] Surrender was social death and immense shame to family.[16] A senior New Zealand officer observed, "Japanese soldiers appear to be taught that to be taken prisoner is an everlasting disgrace. This is borne out by the fact that prisoners do not desire to write home as their families would be disgraced if it became known that members of them were prisoners of war. More than several have stated that they can never return to Japan."[17]

The Japanese attitude towards Western prisoners during the Pacific War was one of contempt, and frequent atrocities occurred. Soldiers of 8 Brigade, 3NZ Division, who had volunteered to be "soldier companions" to Coast Watchers in the Gilbert and Ellis Islands, were captured by the Japanese and some beheaded at Tarawa. A New Zealand private from 35 Battalion, 14 Brigade, captured on Vella Lavella, was strung up on a tree and bayoneted to death.[18] Fortunately, no Allied prisoners were taken during Goodtime largely due to the small number of Japanese defenders and their disorganized state.

Brutality was prominent in the Japanese Imperial forces with slappings and beatings of subordinates a regular event. Discipline was ferocious. Group rape and the bayoneting and execution of live prisoners to encourage group solidarity were singular features of the Japanese military. Japanese troops could be expected to neither ask for quarter nor give it.[19]

The brutality of the Japanese became known to New Zealand troops. Harry Bioletti, a New Zealand infantry officer, recalled that "The one fear in the jungle was being captured by the Japanese because they would butcher you physically.... You did not want to be captured by them because the prisoner of war conventions meant nothing to them. They didn't subscribe to it."[20]

While it is proper to acknowledge the bravery of the Japanese defenders of the Treasury Islands, there is a darker side. During the course of the Pacific War the SNLF units acquired an evil reputation "stained with the blood of countless victims of the war crimes they perpetrated throughout South-East Asia and the Pacific, from the island of Ambon in 1942 to the streets of Manila in 1945."[21]

In February 1942, personnel from 1st Kure Special Naval Landing Force systematically butchered Australian and Dutch prisoners on Ambon Island.[22] Like their Imperial Japanese Army counterparts, SNLF personnel had a fetish of using swords to behead their prisoners. The massacre on Ambon was eclipsed in the magnitude of its horrors by the depredations of the 31st Naval Special Base Force and other naval personnel at Manila in January 1945. They ran amok behind the front lines burning, raping and murdering Filipino civilians without regard to age or gender. Murders were carried out with utmost barbarity.[23] The Treasury Islanders were not far from the truth in describing their occupiers as "Demon Men."

Although there was only a small garrison on Mono Island, there were some 24,000 to 26,000 Japanese troops on the adjoining Ballale and Shortland Islands, a short barge-ride of only 17 miles. These were high quality SNLF troops. Japanese forces on a number of occasions showed their adeptness at amphibious operations and even counter-invasions. There were a number of likely Japanese reactions to Allied invasion attempts. These ranged from simply defending their positions on the Treasury Islands and Empress Augusta Bay area with the forces already there; reinforcing the Treasury Islands with troops barged from the Shortland Islands and Buin areas or with troops taken from Kolombangara or Choiseul; reinforcing the Empress Augusta Bay area by moving troops overland from Buin or barging them from Buka; carrying out counter landings and striking Allied troops from the flanks or rear using barges, or possibly using a "Tokyo Express" to move troops from Buka or Rabaul; interfering with Allied landings using naval and air forces, or finally harassing Allied supply lines with aircraft, surface units and submarines.[24] The Japanese repeatedly demonstrated their unpredictability and none of these options could be discounted by Allied planners.

In 1943 the Japanese were on the defensive because many of their aircraft carriers had been destroyed at the Battle of Midway, the Eastern Solomons and Santa Cruz Islands. Nonetheless, their air, land and sea forces could still pack a punch. The remaining warships of the Imperial Japanese Navy posed a significant threat to Allied operations. That would remain the case until the destruction of Japanese seapower at Leyte Gulf in October 1944. The Imperial Japanese Army Air Force in particular remained potent and Japanese air power had to be written down by attrition in the early part of 1943. It was noted with concern that the Japanese in the Solomons–New Britain–New Ireland area were holding a heavy striking force of fighters and bombers and were bringing in sufficient replacements to neutralize losses.[25] Japanese troops were heavily engaged in fighting American and Australian forces in Papua–New Guinea and the Japanese commanders were obliged to allocate resources between there and the Solomon Islands. Japanese strategy involved forming a defensive ring around the territory they had seized and to exact such a high price in casualties that the Americans would tire of war and make peace on terms beneficial to Tokyo. Large Japanese garrisons such as those on Rabaul and Bougainville welcomed the prospect of displaying their superior Yamato warrior spirit by defeating the effete Americans. Despite setbacks Japanese military thinking was still dominated by the "victory disease" resulting from the spectacular Japanese victories in 1941–42.

Bougainville dominated the Solomon Islands by virtue of its size and the fact that it was a key advanced base for the supply of Japanese forces contesting control of the Solomons. Air and naval bases on Bougainville, Bulla and the Shortland Islands were mutually supported by airfields on New Britain, New Ireland and Truk. In short, the Allies needed Bougainville to isolate Rabaul and the Japanese conversely needed Bougainville to protect Rabaul.

Tokyo recognized the strategic significance of Bougainville and expected the Americans to invade it. General Hyakutake, the Commander of the IJA 17th Army, and his counterpart at the IJN 8th Fleet were ordered to prepare for this eventuality. The Japanese hoped to destroy the invasion forces before they could land, but if they did succeed then they planned to destroy the beachheads. Hyakutake's 17th Army had 20,000 men and the 8th Fleet had 6,800 men and these forces were deployed in Southern Bougainville and the islands to its south.[26]

There was an intense rivalry between the Imperial Japanese Army and the Imperial Japanese Navy. Normally army and navy units remained separate. The units deployed to the Treasury Islands followed this pattern and were all IJN.

The American Central Pacific drive had yet to begin. Operation Galvanic, the invasion of Tarawa, would occur in November 1943 and would show how determined the SNLF Japanese defenders were. The high American casualties from Tarawa shocked the Americans.

The Allies: The Americans[27]

Prior to the Japanese attack on Pearl Harbor the United States was one of the least militarized of the Western democracies, with strong public sentiment in favor of isolationism. The Japanese attack was popularly perceived as a sneak attack and the outrage resulted in recruiting stations being flooded with volunteers. One of the American triumphs of World War II was the assimilation of civilians into the American armed forces, being equipped with suitable weapons and well trained for combat. The American military had too few trained officers and specialists. It took time for this to be overcome and battle worthy status achieved.

Like the Kiwis, the Americans who fought in Goodtime were essentially civilians in uniform who were only in the military "for the duration." Patriotism often played a key role in the American's decision to enlist. Others were conscripted. The diversity of American society was reflected in its armed forces.

A variety of components of the American armed forces would take part in Goodtime.

The Naval Construction Battalions (N.C.B.) — The Seabees

The one group of Americans their New Zealand counterparts universally respected were the Seabees the Naval Construction Battalions. These men were construction workers, many of whom had worked on massive construction projects such as the Hoover Dam in the United States. The "can-do" motto and attitude and the prodigious and rapid feats of construction carried out by Seabee units impressed their not easily impressed New Zealand counterparts. The Seabees were mainly older, mature men who had been through the hard years of the Great Depression. There was nothing arrogant or pretentious about them and this endeared them to the New Zealanders. By all accounts this respect was reciprocated.[28] A New Zealand officer who encountered them said that they were expert construction workers and he would never dream of giving them orders.[29] The Seabees were required to undertake quite complex work ranging from clearing the jungle to the construction of steel-matted airfields from which bombers could take off to harass the Japanese. A Kiwi commented that "the methods of American Seabees and the vast amount of equipment at their disposal were a source of amazement which only increased with the passage of time."[30]

The Seabees (derived from the acronym "NCB"— Naval Construction Battalion, and featuring the logo of a flying wasp with a white sailor's hat and a machine gun in one hand and a wrench in the other) were one of the most unusual units the American armed forces fielded in World War II. They were the naval equivalent of the U.S. Army Corps of Engineers.[31]

Formed in 1842, the Civil Engineer Corps had been used pre-war as an organization by the U.S. Navy to oversee construction work using civilian contractors and labor. The problem was that once war broke out the U.S. Navy could not continue to use civilians for construction and engineering work on the front line. It was contrary to international law for civilians to engage in military activities, and capture rendered them liable to summary execution.[32] Rear Admiral Ben Moreel foresaw that America would need naval construction workers in the military. He was instrumental in the creation of three Naval Construction Battalions in early 1942. The vexed question was who would command them? Under USN regulations command of naval personnel was the exclusive preserve of Navy officers. Very unusually, Moreel obtained permission for the Seabees to be commanded by men commissioned from the Civil Engineer Corps.

Their purpose was primarily construction rather than combat despite their motto, "Construimus Batuimus" ("We Build, We Fight"). The USN needed skilled construction workers urgently and the criteria for their enlistment was somewhat elastic. Theoretically the enlistment age was between 18 to 50 but it was later discovered that several men over the age of 60 had enlisted. A common jibe by Marines was "Be good to the Seabees, because they might be your fathers." The Seabees tended to be older with engineering, craft and construction experience. As the war progressed and labor shortages bit, things changed. By the end of 1942 men for the Seabees were taken from the Selective Service pool and their average age dropped, as did their overall skill level.[33] Nonetheless, the first recruits had undertaken impressive prewar construction projects such as the Boulder Dam and the skills inherent in the Seabee units were massive. Given their skills there was little purpose in trade-school training, with emphasis instead on military training.[34] The Seabees completed three weeks of boot camp, then were sent to an advanced base depot where they were equipped and given advance training before deployment.

A Naval Construction Battalion consisted of four companies made up of administrators, medical and dental personnel, technicians, stores personnel and other specialists.

The typical NCB numbered about 32 officers and 1073 men. Battalions were organized into regiments and two or more regiments were grouped into a brigade.[35] On the Treasury Islands the 87th NCB acted on its own during the assault and immediate consolidation phase before being joined by further NCB support units.

The Seabees saw action in most theatres and their contribution to victory in the South Pacific was substantial. Very little in the way of ports, loading equipment or airfields existed in the South Pacific. It was the task of the Seabees to change that.[36]

The Kiwis and the Seabees found that they had much in common. Each admired the courage of the other. Both were essentially civilians in uniform for the duration of the war with little tolerance for military bump. They also had a talent for purloining of equipment, food and alcohol. Both had an ability to improvise and to distill alcohol through improvised equipment.

The Seabee force allocated to Goodtime consisted initially of a small detachment of 230 men. On 18 October Company A and part of the HQ Company of 87 NCB were detached and sent to Guadalcanal. Lieutenant Charles E. Turnbull was placed in command. Like most of the Kiwis, the Seabees in this unit had not seen combat before.

Argus Units

Argus units were designed to operate radar sets. In Greek mythology Argus Panoptes ('Argus All Eyes') was a giant with a hundred eyes who was all-seeing. It was therefore fitting that the Americans should use "Argus" in connection with radar. Argus Unit 6 was deployed for Goodtime. The purpose of Argus units was "to provide during the development stage of a United States Naval Base a comprehensive air warning, surface warning and fighter direction organization which will coordinate all radar operations under the area commander."[37] Typically an Argus unit was made up of 20 officers and 178 men. The men were technicians and not expected to be involved in combat.

The U.S. Marine Corps

Operation Goodtime came under the command structure of 1 Marine Amphibious Corps (pronounced 'One Mac'), but nonetheless there would be few USMC troops taking part in the invasion.[38] They were, instead, involved in the planning and command aspects and fighter direction.

Their presence was felt indirectly in that the Tentative Manual for the Conduct of Amphibious Operations had been created out of their experience and the New Zealanders and U.S. Navy personnel involved utilized that doctrine. A considerable amount had been learned about how to conduct amphibious operations since the Watchtower landing on Guadalcanal in August 1942.

The New Zealanders operated in an American-dominated environment and many of the U.S. Marine Corps expressions and acronyms produced befuddlement. At one point the New Zealanders were directed to use the word "impedimenta" rather than "equipment."

Nisei Personnel

The New Zealand Army had few Japanese linguists. Japanese language specialists were needed to translate captured documents, to encourage Japanese soldiers to surrender and to conduct interrogations. Sergeant Harry Shinto, a Nisei (an American born of Japanese parents), and one other Nisei carried out these tasks during Goodtime. Nisei soldiers who had volunteered to fight the Germans and Italians were sent to fight in Italy where the 100th/442nd Regimental Combat Team became one of the most decorated in the American Army. For Nisei, service in the Pacific was voluntary and required the Nisei to overcome any residual loyalties to the land of their ancestors. The Military Intelligence Service recruited Nisei who served with Allied forces in the Pacific. These soldiers faced torture and summary execution if captured.

The dangers to them are illustrated by the experience of Captain John Burden, U.S. Army. A Japanese linguist, he was "...sent with M.I.S. teams to Vella Lavella in the Solomons, where his right-hand man, Tateshi Miyasaki, was almost killed. Miyasaki was stripped to the waist, with no U.S. Army identification on him, when three New Zealanders mistook him for an enemy soldier. They were pointing their rifles at him when Burden yelled: 'He's O.K. He's one of my boys'!"[39]

Because of the need for operational security the activities of the M.I.S. and Nisei in the Pacific were kept secret. The vital contributions made by soldiers like Sgt. Shinto have gone unrecognized.

The U.S. Navy: The Vessels of Goodtime

The crews of the amphibious forces who took part in Goodtime also share in the historic amnesia attached to the operation. As John Lorelli, the author of *To Foreign Shores: U.S. Amphibious Operations in World War II*, has commented:

> Most people know little about the men and the craft used to land the troops. The reason amphibious forces have remained comparatively unsung is clear: amphibious warfare is simply not glamorous. Ships that lift assault forces are large and clumsy, lacking the sleek lines of destroyers or the formidable presence of the aircraft carrier. While combat and news photographers were usually present in droves to record landings, far fewer stayed to cover the mundane task of unloading supplies.[40]

The Americans and Kiwis who took part in Goodtime were delivered to the Treasury Islands in a variety of American vessels, most of which did not exist before the war. The Goodtime invaders were the beneficiaries of a revolution in amphibious warfare techniques and equipment. Understanding these vessels and their capabilities is essential to comprehend how Goodtime was planned and how it unfolded. It is, unfortunately, necessary to navigate a plethora of confusing acronyms beloved by the U.S. Navy.

A Confederate general once summed up the key to battle as "git up thar furst with the mostest."[41] That is certainly true of amphibious warfare — a favorable result requires getting as many troops ashore as quickly as possible with their supporting arms and the necessary supplies to sustain them. Goodtime was to be an assault landing against a small but determined foe. An additional complication was that the Japanese might achieve local air superiority.

The American Navy in 1943 was a burgeoning force. Production lines were turning out ships and equipment at a swift rate. But this was slow to reach units in the front line because of the expanse of the Pacific and the priority given to the war against Germany. Particularly in short supply were the specialized amphibious craft and equipment that would become standard features as the war progressed. Two operations in particular dominated American naval thinking — Operation Cherryblossom, the invasion of Empress Augusta Bay, Bougainville and Operation Galvanic, the invasion of Tarawa in November 1943. There would be a limited supply of landing craft available for Goodtime and these would need to be reused for taking subsequent waves to the beaches. Those landing craft were vital for Cherryblossom and had to be conserved. As Lorelli comments, "if any single transport or cargo ship was lost, the schedule could not be maintained."[42] In many respects the success of Goodtime would be measured in shipping and amphibious craft conserved.

Auxiliary Personnel Destroyers (APD)

The U.S. Marine Corps in the pre-war years envisaged the use of raiders carried in small, fast destroyers. It succeeded in persuading the U.S. Navy to convert some of its moth-balled World War I vintage "four stacker" destroyers into fast troop transports. These Auxiliary Personnel Destroyers (APDs) would embark and deliver reasonable numbers of troops and equipment to their landing beaches. Two boilers and two smoke stacks were removed along with torpedo tubes. Davits, landing craft and troop accommodation were installed.[43] Eight of these vessels would be used to transport New Zealand troops for Goodtime. APD 6, the USS *Stringham* was capable "of berthing and messing 128 men and 5 officers for extended trips."[44] The APDs had, in early September 1943, been used to convoy part of the U.S. 35th Infantry Regiment to Vella Lavella, so they were well practiced in transporting soldiers.

Fletcher Class Destroyers (DD)

Because of the relatively constricted waters of Blanche Channel, it was not envisaged that cruisers or heavier battleships could be deployed. There was a risk of stranding, mines, and lack of sea room to maneuver if attacked. Naval gunfire was integral to amphibious operations and this was to be provided by two *Fletcher* Class destroyers, the USS *Philip* and the USS *Pringle*. Armed with 5 inch guns, these "workhorses of the Pacific" would be able to provide only limited firepower.

Fletcher Class destroyers were among the most numerous produced in World War II. Typically they were of 2325 tons, 376.5 feet long, powered by four boilers and two turbines, and were capable of 38 knots and a range of 6500 nautical miles. They were armed with five 5 inch guns, four 1.1 inch guns, four 20mm guns and ten 21 inch torpedoes. Each had a crew of 273.[45]

Small Coastal Transports (APc)

During Goodtime the U.S. Navy used a number of Small Coastal Transports as auxiliary support vessels. These were built of wood in small American shipyards to fulfill a chronic need for support vessels. They were 103 feet in length, had a beam of 21 feet, three inches and, powered by diesel engines, had a speed of 10 knots. They had a crew of 3 officers and 22 men and four 20mm AA guns.[46]

Auxiliary Motor Minesweepers (YMS)

Built of wood, these 136 foot long vessels were designed to combat the menace of German magnetic mines. They were designated by the U.S. Navy for coastal work but found themselves operating in a variety of theatres including the Pacific. Powered by diesel engines, they were capable of 15 knots. Most of the deck area was taken up with an electric powered drum and winch, twin derricks and stern davits to handle sweeping wires. Armament consisted of a 3 inch Dual Purpose gun and two 20mm Oerlikon AA guns. The crew was 42 men and 8 officers.

In the Pacific YMSs were used for minesweeping, landing craft escorts, tugs, and all manner of duties.[47]

Patrol Torpedo Boats (PT Boats)

Undoubtedly one of the most glamorous of the U.S. Navy's vessels, PT Boats were at their most effective in "barge busting" and covert operations. Small, fast and well armed, the PT Boats were nonetheless fragile. They were wooden and their high performance engines and fuel tanks were unarmored. The PT Boat relied on stealth and speed for its protection.

Specifications varied as the war progressed. Typically they were between 58 to 80 feet in length, capable of 31 to 42 knots, with 2 officers and 9 men and armed with four torpedoes and various 40mm, 37mm, 20mm machine guns.

Tugs (AT)

Tugs may not be viewed as weapons of war but in amphibious operations in the Pacific they proved their worth time and again, often pulling stranded vessels from beaches. For Goodtime the tugs USS *Apache* (AT-67) and USS *Sioux* (AT-75) were allocated.

The *Sioux* had a displacement of 1650 tons, a length of 205 feet and a speed of up to 14 knots. It had four diesel engines capable of generating 4000 horsepower. The ship had a complement of 85 men, and an armament of one 3 inch gun and two 40mm guns.

Launched in May 1942, the Sioux arrived in the Solomons in June 1943, where it carried out "rear echelon activities" in the New Georgia campaign.

Its consort, USS *Apache*, had a similar history, being launched in May 1942 and arriving in New Caledonia a year later. It carried out salvage and towing operations prior to Goodtime.[48]

Landing Ship, Tank (LST)

The really important vessels were the ocean going Landing Ship Tanks. These large, ungainly vessels had the ability to carry huge amounts of tonnage and weapons and had the ability to beach themselves, open their cargo doors at the front, disgorge their cargo and lift themselves off the beaches. Armed with 40mm AA guns, they were nonetheless vulnerable and fully merited their description "Large Slow Targets."[49] Throughout the war there would always be a shortage of LSTs.

Their capacities and capabilities made them an essential part of any major amphibious operation whether it be Operation Overlord, the invasion of France, or the American drive across the Central Pacific. As such these ships were as precious as pearls and not to be risked unduly. They were required for the follow-on invasion of Bougainville. Their ability to transport tanks, equipment and men across oceans and then put them onshore made the LST versatile and particularly valuable in the South Pacific where port facilities were often either enemy held or non-existent. The basic requirement of an LST was a sloping beach on which to land and suitable beach exits for distribution of the material delivered.

The astonishing feature of LSTs was their ability to run themselves onto a beach fully-loaded and retract themselves once unloaded.

Broadside on LSTs looked like conventional merchant ships. What distinguished them were their cargo doors on their bow which split open. Driven by motors, the two bow doors could be opened and closed. Vehicles and equipment could be driven or offloaded onto the beach. It was said: "The LST can arguably be called the most versatile ship in World War II. Being essentially a large, empty, self propelled box with ample above and below deck space made it useful not only for hauling just about anything, but for many other purposes when space was needed aboard a ship, a luxury on most ships."[50]

The LST MK2 measured 327 feet from bow to stern and displaced some 4080 short tons with a full load.[51] The ship (any seagoing amphibious vessel over 200 feet in length is referred to as a "Landing Ship" and anything lesser is a "Landing Craft"[52]) had five levels with a hold divided into 40 compartments. The third deck had provision for vehicles and an elevator-ramp connected the weather deck to the tank deck. The main or weather deck on the top of the ship had clear space which could be used for cargo, vehicles, or in the case of Goodtime, anti-aircraft guns to supplement the LST's 20mm and 40mm guns. The weather deck was crowned by a deckhouse containing a bridge, cabins and gun positions. To the rear of that was a small fantail containing more gun positions. The LST had the capacity to carry landing craft hung from six pairs of davits, hung on both sides of the ship, three apiece.

Its Achilles heel was its comparative slowness, 9 knots. Being large, they were slow and hard to maneuver. Given their size and the tendency for stressed Japanese pilots to equate size with cruisers or battleships, the LSTs became a magnet for Japanese bombs. Therefore they had to be quickly unloaded and out of the area before Japanese planes arrived. Planning for Goodtime was predicated on essential supplies being delivered safely, the LSTs being unloaded fast and the vessels getting underway before darkness fell. Against Japanese warships or submarines the LSTs were essentially defenseless, a fact well appreciated by their stalwart crews.

LST construction began in American shipyards in 1942. The size of the ship's crew varied but was in the vicinity of seven officers and 204 men.[53] Officers tended to be from the U.S. Navy Reserve, many of whom had never previously been aboard a ship. The same was true for many of the crew. Basic seamanship was taught to the men before they were assigned to ships.[54] The flat bottomed and high-sided nature of the ships made them roll horribly in high seas, and there were frequent problems with the electric controls linking the wheel and the rudders. Securing the cargo became an absolute necessity.

For any ordinary ship's captain, beaching their ship was a thing to be avoided at all cost. For LST captains it was a routine maneuver but one which required a considerable degree of skill. LSTs were not considered to be assault craft and were part of a later wave of vessels to be landed once the beach area was considered to be secure. In wartime such hopes often go awry, as they did with Goodtime. Even without the Japanese firing at them, the crew of an LST faced formidable challenges:

> To beach the ship as close to the water's edge as possible, numerous factors were considered: angle of the waves striking shore, wind direction and speed, gradient, bottom conditions and obstacles, disabled vehicles and broached landing craft could damage an LST. If the LST did not approach the beach perpendicular to the waves, and if the surf and/or wind were strong enough, the ship could broach, that is, turn sideways becoming grounded parallel with the shoreline. It therefore might be impossible to unload and could not retract itself.[55]
>
> The procedure for beaching was to approach the beach at standard speed and aim to beach at the pre-designated spot taking into account landmarks, and more especially Beach Masters and guides. The aim was to have a third of the ship in contract with the beach. A stern anchor would be dropped with the goal of laying out 600 feet of anchor line so as to assist with retraction. Retraction was also a complex process whereby the ramp was raised, the bow doors closed and secured, and using a combination of the stern anchor, engines and rudder the LST eased itself off the beach and out to sea.[56]

One of the oddities of U.S. amphibious craft is that they were given a number rather than a name by the Bureau of Ships. An example is LST-339.

Landing Craft Infantry (Large)—(LCI [L])

The Landing Craft Infantry proved to be a ubiquitous part of Allied amphibious operations in the Pacific War. Designed purely as a passenger carrier, the LCI was not intended as an assault craft. It was able to beach itself and retract. With a displacement of 387 tons with a full load and a length of 160 feet, this vessel was capable of carrying 6 officers and 182 troops or 75 tons of cargo. These vessels were intended to deliver infantry quickly to the beach once the beach had been secured. Their unusual feature was ramps on each side of the bow which were lowered to allow infantry to climb down to the beach. Because the LCI lacked bow doors, soldiers had to carry their gear off the LCI by hand.[57]

Much smaller than the LST, the LCI was faster at 15.5 knots and more maneuverable. Nonetheless, sea voyages could be extremely uncomfortable. One soldier declared, "The LCI was a metal box designed by a sadist to move soldiers across the water."[58]

The typical LCI (L) had a crew of 3 officers and 21 enlisted men. As with the LSTs, many were crewed by U.S. Navy Reserve or Coast guard personnel. Armament consisted of four single 20mm guns and two .50-caliber machine guns.

Landing Craft, Infantry (Gun) (LCI [G])

Goodtime saw the introduction of the first LCI(L) gunboats to be used to supply firepower in the crucial moments of the run to the beach. Captain Roy T. Cowdrey, Admiral Halsey's senior ship repair officer, saw the possibilities and had two Landing Craft

Infantry, LCI-24 and LCI-68, modified. Armed with two 20mm, three 40mm and five .50-caliber machine guns, the gunboats were the answer to a "prayer for fire support of assault troops delivered close to shore." Because of their shallow drafts they could follow the landing craft up to the beach.[59] The downside was that they required larger crews and had considerably less troop-carrying capability. The gunboats were converted from ordinary LCI(L)s in Noumea and arrived at Guadalcanal only one day before the departure of the LCI(L)s for Goodtime. They had added armor for crew protection and the quick-firing nature of their armament meant that they packed a heavy punch.

Landing Craft, Tank (LCT)

Another of the wondrous vessels of the amphibious revolution was the Landing Craft, Tank. This flat-bottomed vessel came into production and began to be delivered from American shipyards in late 1942. As with so many other amphibious vessels the crews were largely made up of men who joined the Navy after the Pearl Harbor attack. The LCT was a specialized vessel intended to carry four 40-ton tanks or to transport between 150 and 180 tons of cargo. It had a length of 112 feet and the relatively slow speed of 6 knots. The LCTs used in Goodtime were the Mark 5 version and were part of Flotilla 5. There were no tanks for the LCTs so instead they hauled supplies, including the vital radar units.

Landing Craft, Mechanized (LCM [3])

These craft were designed to load one medium tank (30 tons), motor vehicles or 60,000 pounds of cargo, or 60 soldiers, directly onto the craft. With a normal load it had a range of 500 miles at a speed of seven knots.

Measuring 50 feet in length and 14 feet across, the LCM had a crew of four consisting of a coxswain, an engineer and two crew, and an armament of two .50-caliber machine guns. Like its brethren, the LCM was a flat-bottomed boat which could beach and retract itself. For Goodtime, LCMs would be used to haul and unload supplies.

Landing Craft, Vehicle and Personnel (LCVP)

The LCVP was essential to Allied victory in the Pacific War. Developed by Higgins Industries in the late 1930s these craft have become associated in the popular mind as "landing craft."

Typically wooden, measuring 36 feet, 3 inches in length and 10 feet, 10 inches across, the LCVP was crewed by a coxswain, an engineer and a crewman. The coxswain steered the craft and the other two operated two .30-caliber machine guns on the aft deck. LCVPs had a capacity for 8100 pounds of cargo but usually they transported 36 men and their equipment. They could otherwise carry a jeep and 12 men. The LCVP had two particularly valuable features— its hinged ramp in the front which could be lowered to allow infantry to debark onto a beach, and it could extract itself from the beach and return to its mother ship for further troops. It was capable of up to 12 knots and was quite maneuverable.

LCVPs in theory had a range of 110 nautical miles but generally were carried by host ships and then lowered into the water. Troops would then climb down rope or cargo nets strung over the side of the host ship.

Although there was steel plating on the front ramp and sides of the LCVP, the troops were usually tightly-packed into the craft and there was a strong sense of vulnerability.

Essentials

Technological marvels though the various amphibious craft may have been, they still required some basic essentials to be effective. They needed a reasonably large area of beach of the right gradient on which to insert themselves and retract, a reasonably sheltered area so that they would not broach and, above all, protection against enemy fire. These needs would impel the planners to choose the beach at Falamai as the primary assault landing area. The craft would be at their most vulnerable approaching the landing beach and whilst beached. Vulnerability to enemy fire and aerial attack would have been foremost in the minds of their commanders. Limited sea room and the likely presence of coral reefs limited how close naval gunfire support vessels could approach the beaches.

It should also be borne in mind that the crews of the amphibious craft were often inexperienced in amphibious operations: many had only a short time before been civilians; some had never before been to sea. Goodtime would be on-the-job training.

Allied Airpower

Allied airpower was American-dominated and controlled. The main problems were the limited range of Allied aircraft and the fact that for Goodtime, Allied aircraft would be operating in Japanese-dominated airspace.

Allied aircraft in the Solomons were all American-made — P-40 Kittyhawks, Corsairs and P-38 Lightnings. The squadrons were of RNZAF 15 & 18 squadrons and various U.S. Army Air Force squadrons. The New Zealanders of No. 1 Islands Group worked within the American air command.

Emphasis was on suppressing Japanese airpower rather than throwing an aerial shield over the beachheads.

The Kiwis — 8 Brigade Group, 3 New Zealand Division

Two essential truths are necessary to understanding New Zealand's participation in the land war in the South Pacific. The first is that before World War II, the New Zealand armed forces were minuscule, the land forces consisting of a small Permanent Force cadre of staff officers and specialists backed by a Territorial (militia) force. The outbreak of war would see this force expanded manifold with a consequent dilution of trained officers. The second was that, with the exception of a very brief period of time immediately after the outbreak of war with Japan, the war in the South Pacific was seen as a secondary theatre and the cream of New Zealand's soldiers were sent to fight under General Bernard

Norman Harry Bonsell with unit dog Pooch (War History Collection, Alexander Turnbull Library, Wellington, WH-0155).

Freyberg in the Mediterranean. The force under Freyberg's command known as 2NZ Division would earn laurels in the disastrous Balkan Campaign, the Desert War and the slow slog up the Italian Peninsula. For most New Zealanders, Britain was the focus of their loyalties and the "real war" was in Europe. A commitment to the land war in the South Pacific arose almost incidentally out of the strategic vacuum created by British focus on the Axis powers in Europe.

New Zealand troops were sent to Fiji in 1940–41 simply because Fiji, with its strategic shipping, communication links and airfields was wide open to Axis seizure with potentially catastrophic consequences for New Zealand. The New Zealand government tried to get the best of all worlds by sending raw, untrained and under-equipped troops to garrison Fiji while at the same time using Fiji as a training ground for soldiers to be eventually sent on to Freyberg. After Japan's entry into the war the force on Fiji was built up hurriedly to two infantry brigades (8 and 14 Brigades) of dubious combat effectiveness. Out of these two brigades, 3NZ Division would eventually be created. From its inception 3NZ Division would be denied the glamour and glory of its sister division. It would also find itself in the invidious position of being "an isolated British formation in American theatre of war which is primarily naval!"[60]

The New Zealand or "Kiwi"[61] component of Goodtime was composed of mainly citizen soldiers, men who lacked combat experience and who would, at the end of hostilities, merge back into the societies from which they came. There were only isolated exceptions.

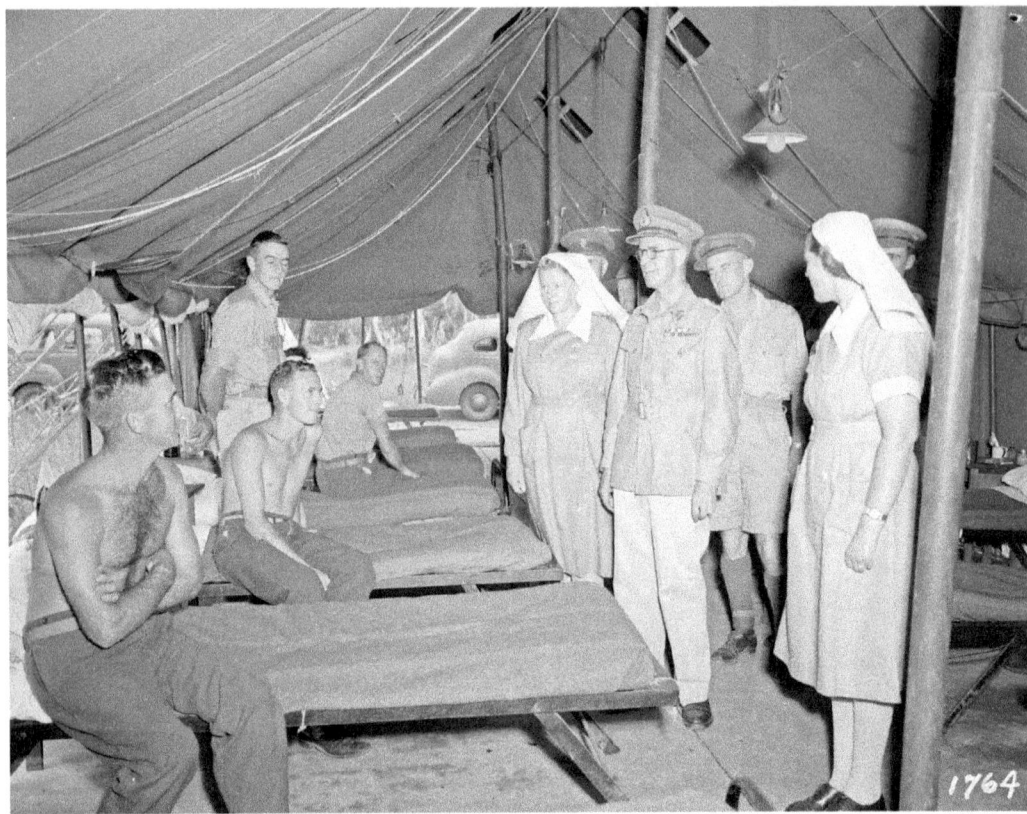

Major General Barrowclough, commander of 3 NZ Division, visiting wounded soldiers (War History Collection, Alexander Turnbull Library, Wellington, F-41530-1/2).

The first was Major General Harold Barrowclough. He distinguished himself on the Western Front in World War I and more recently in the Greek Campaign and Desert War as commander of 6NZ Brigade. When Barrowclough returned to New Zealand he had four other senior officers experienced in modern warfare. Brigadier C.S.J. Duff became his Commander of Royal Artillery. Lt. Col. J.I. Brooke became his G.S.O.1. Col. J. Brooke-White became a Divisional Engineer.

The Deputy Director of Medical Services, Brigadier John Twhigg, had been captured by the Afrika Korps in December 1941, been repatriated and then appointed to 3NZ Division. The Brigade Group commander, Brigadier Robert Amos Row, also had plenty of combat experience but this had been gained at Gallipoli and on the Western Front. Few of the men of 3NZ Division had experience of amphibious operations. None had experience of jungle or tropical warfare or, for that matter, combat against the Japanese. Goodtime would, for many of the citizen soldiers, be their first experience of combat.

The 8 Brigade was returned to New Zealand in July 1942. When Barrowclough took command of 3NZ Division, of which 8 Brigade was a cadre, he commented that the Fijian garrison had spent most of its time building fortifications rather than training, and that exercises at battalion level or above had not been conducted. Barrowclough began his task with a will to ensure that his men were properly equipped and received the training they needed. He purged many of the older men who were unfit for tropical warfare and promoted younger men. Training in bush warfare began with the exercise in the Kaimai Ranges in the North Island of New Zealand with 8 Brigade troops taking the role of the attacking Japanese force at Kokoda. Heavy rain and miserable conditions brought the exercise to an abrupt halt but useful lessons had been learned in regard to logistics and bush warfare.

Vice Admiral R.L. Ghormley, U.S. Navy, requested that 3NZ Division be sent to garrison New Caledonia. By January 1943, 8 Brigade along with the rest of 3NZ Division had deployed to New Caledonia and commenced intensive training, carrying out route marches, live firing exercises, and amphibious warfare exercises. The latter varied from practicing the combat loading of ships and their rapid unloading through to the troops climbing up and down cargo nets and progressing to amphibious landings.

The training began gently enough on dry land on New Caledonia. Cargo nets held up by timber frames were set up and enabled the soldiers to gain confidence and skills. The troops had to master the art of climbing up and down cargo nets slung over the side of troopships. The soldiers had to learn not only to go down the cargo nets but also to climb them so that they could return to the transport ships after a landing exercise ended. For those afraid of heights the process was made even more daunting by the need to traverse the nets in full combat gear including ammunition, pack and rifle. Because of the need to do it quickly a number of men would be on the nets at the same time and there

Troops from the 3 NZ Division undertaking amphibious training on rope ladders at New Caledonia (War History Collection, Alexander Turnbull Library, Wellington, PAColl 5547-039).

Soldiers undertaking boarding practice using rope nets (War History Collection, Alexander Turnbull Library, Wellington, F-20441-1/4).

was always the risk of standing on the fingers of the man below. At the bottom awaited an assault craft which would be swaying up and down with the waves. It required an exquisite sense of timing to make the leap safely from the cargo nets and onto the deck of the landing craft. Failure could result in serious injury or death from drowning or from being crushed against the side of the transport ship. Traversing the nets was "not a job for an unfit man."[62]

> Opportunity was taken for net practice which was the keynote of speedy landings in future operations. The huge rope nets hung over the sides of the transports and personnel, lined in rows of fours, went over in successive waves, dropping into Higgins boats on reaching the bottom. To the soldier loaded like a pack horse with full web and rifle, with the ship rolling in the surge of the sea, and small landing craft at the foot of the net pounding against the side of the ship on the crest of a swell, it was no easy task. Access to the decks again was made in the same manner, but it was many times harder going up.[63]

Measures could be taken for the troops safety—"one could minimize the risk of being squashed between the ship and the landing craft by pulling the bottom of the net into the landing craft."[64]

Gordon Campbell Davie, a signaler with 52 Battery, 38 Field Artillery, recalled,

> We would go over the side of the ship using cargo nets. It required coordination with other soldiers to avoid fingers being trodden on, or falling off the cargo nets. Going up the

nets was difficult and a U.S. sailor told me that the best technique was to grab two parallel ropes and climb. We practiced on cargo nets in full kit which included rifle, gas mask, pack on each side and a big pack on our backs. If you were going down to the landing barge you had to be careful that you were not the last one down. The American sailors had a habit of taking off suddenly and you would look down and the barge would not be there.

Despite the difficulties Davie commented that "after we had done the cargo nets a few times it was cats meat."[65]

A report on amphibious training noted sanguinely: "The best method when on the net is to grasp the vertical ropes with the hands and NOT the horizontals.... There is nothing difficult about climbing up and down the nets and nervousness or lack of confidence is the main obstacle."[66]

This was new for the New Zealand Army and the men took to it enthusiastically. They rapidly acquired expertise in getting on and off the cargo nets, but accidents and injuries were inevitable. Some men froze on the cargo nets during training and had to be removed. Harry Bioletti, an officer in 30 Battalion, recalled that "when that happened one of the crew would go over the side and behind him and help the soldier up." He also recalled that "one of the men got crunched between an APD and a landing craft."[67] The occasional hapless soldier ended up in the drink.

The Kiwis were helped by the American crews of the large American Attack Transports (APA) who had been involved in training American troops and therefore knew the process. The ships of the "The Unholy Four"—so called because in crossing the Pacific dateline they had missed a Sunday and divine service would become very familiar to the men of 8 Brigade. The USS *President Adams*, USS *President Monroe*, USS *President Jackson* and USS *President Hayes* had huge troop-carrying capacity and simplified the logistical problems of amphibious assault. The U.S. Navy provided personnel for the Higgins boats and troopships.

The American method was to sail the transport ships to the target area and then the landing craft would be lowered from davits into the water. The cargo nets would be slung over the side of the ship and the troops would climb down and into the waiting landing craft. Once all the men were in the landing craft it would cast off and travel in a wide circle until all the landing craft were ready. They would then form a line and proceed to the landing area.

There were two aspects to the amphibious training — getting the assaulting troops down the rope cargo net ladders of their transport ships and into their landing craft and, secondly, getting vital gear and equipment unloaded as rapidly as possible. Trevor Whaley, a sergeant in 3NZ Division Signals, X Section, attached to 29 Light Anti-Aircraft Regiment, recorded:

> For our practice assault on Ngaela we were transported from the Canal in an LCI which nosed into the beach and we disembarked by way of two (port and starboard) ramps beside the bow. "Cargo" for LCI's had to be crated and of such dimensions and weight that it could be handled by two men. The procedure was to grab a crate, carry it down the port side ramp/gangway, return aboard by the starboard ramp for a second load and so on. The "cargo" was loaded right up to the bow of the LCI. Prior to our departure from the Canal for the Treasuries, we did a practice load/unload on our LCI (No. 67) on the morning of our departure. The record for the unload was twenty minutes. We did it in eighteen minutes much to the amazement of the skipper and crew. I don't remember the tonnage of

cargo normally allowed. Like the LST, and LCT, the LCI would run aground, bow first. The LST would open the bow doors and drop the ramps and the LCI would lower the twin ramp/gangways. Needless to say, one did not always get ashore with dry feet.[68]

From the perspective of one New Zealand infantryman, the complexities of amphibious assault boiled down to "being at the correct stations on the ships at the right time and clambering down the nets into the landing craft. If there was a swell it was as well to get off the net when you judged that the landing craft was on top of the swell and making sure you didn't get between the landing craft and the ship's side. When the ramp dropped on reaching the shore get off quickly."[69]

Further intensive amphibious training occurred at Efate, in the New Hebrides. In early September 1943, 8 Brigade embarked on the USS *President Jackson* (APA 18), USS *President Adams* (APA 38) and USS *President Hayes* (APA 20) and, escorted by three destroyers, left Noumea Harbor. The opportunity was taken to put the Brigade through intensive amphibious training at Mele Beach, Efate Island, New Hebrides (now Vanuatu). The Intelligence Section prepared detailed maps of the beach area. The convoy anchored in Vila Harbor, Efate Island, on 6 September, 1943, and the troops practiced descending and ascending nets during the morning and landings at Mele Beach during the afternoon.

Barrowclough arrived to see how training was going: "Immediately noticeable was

Soldiers of 8 Brigade in an LCVP training for amphibious operations, 1943 (author's collection, courtesy George Hodgson).

the dense jungle and tropical appearance of the shore line. It was exceptionally hot. Higgins boats were lowered into the water and troops went down the nets with full web and equipment. It was a great sight as the fifty-odd landing craft ferried their 'invasion' complement ashore under the strafing sweeps of attacking 'enemy' aircraft. Coming in from high in the blue sky the planes left vapor trails as they dived at almost 400 miles an hour."[70]

The following day the troops disembarked into landing craft, and combat teams carried out tactical exercises. An orders group conference was held in late afternoon at which Barrowclough highlighted the experiences of 14 Brigade's landing exercises. On 8 September the troops continued landing and tactical exercises.

On 9 September under the watchful eyes of Barrowclough and the American brass Exercise Efate began in earnest. The brigade was hampered by a heavy surf, and a number of landing craft broached; four not being recovered till the following day. Nonetheless, the majority of troops were landed, a perimeter established and the troops dug in. The exercise was concluded the following day with the reloading of vehicles and equipment and re-embarkation of the troops. The exercise was subjected to critical analysis at a conference on board the USS *President Jackson* attended by senior American naval officers and New Zealand army officers. The importance of proper loading of boats

Soldiers of 3 NZ Division on board a landing craft (War History Collection, Alexander Turnbull Library, Wellington, F-19502-1/4).

was highlighted, as was the need to disperse boats during air attack.[71] It was noted that a lot of equipment and supplies not needed in the initial assault had accumulated on the beaches making it difficult to move urgently needed items to the front line. "Many sorely needed Jeeps and Jeep Trailers used to move this cargo inland had arrived at the beach after the cargo instead of before it."[72] Lessons had been learned and valuable experience gained. The brigade earned commendations for the speed and skill of its landing operations.

The 8 Brigade arrived at Guadalcanal on 14 September 1943, rejoining other parts of 3NZ Division. The Kiwis showed their skill and enthusiasm by disembarking and unloading equipment rapidly. The "unloading time and turn around of the ships constituted a record."[73] The tonnage off-loaded from the USS *President Hayes* was a massive 143.2 tons. The brigade established itself in the area between Kukum and the Matanikau River. Further intensive training in jungle warfare by day and night followed with live shoots of field artillery and mortars.

The 8 Brigade Group totaled 4808 men and consisted of three infantry battalions— the 29th, 34th, and 36th together with Light Anti-Aircraft batteries, 25 pound artillery, machine guns, and supporting troops (See Appendix A).

One feature of 3NZ Division was that it was equipped with British-style weaponry and its table of organization and equipment mirrored that of a British infantry division. This meant ordnance and many of its supplies had to be sourced from New Zealand, British or Australian stocks and not from American. The supply line stretched all the way back to Auckland and made the division an American quartermaster's nightmare.

The New Zealand troops outside the combat zone wore a distinctive "Lemon Squeezer" hat, so-called because of its resemblance to the pyramid shaped device popular in New Zealand homes for squeezing the juice from lemons. The headgear was wide-brimmed with the crown pinched by four dents[74] with the forward ridge facing directly to the front of the wearer. It was made of felt and had its origins in the Boer War. In 1916 it became the hat of the New Zealanders, probably as a way of distinguishing them from the Australians who had adopted a slouch hat. In World War II the Lemon Squeezer was worn by New Zealand infantry in Europe, the Mediterranean, and the Pacific. It distinguished New Zealand troops from their Australian cousins who sported a bush hat often with one side pinned up. Although distinctive, the Lemon Squeezer headgear was unsuited to the tropics. It was also hard to keep in shape. The headgear is still worn in the modern New Zealand army on ceremonial occasions.

In the combat zone New Zealand troops wore the British "Tommy" style steel helmet, the so called "battle bowler."[75] The Americans had abandoned this style of helmet for one similar to the German variety, the M1 U.S. Army steel helmet, which provided greater cover for the wearer's head. Steel helmets were heavy, uncomfortable to wear and although providing some protection against shell fragments, were an impediment in jungle warfare because they caught on vegetation.

Appropriate clothing for the tropics was in short supply.[76] The more comfortable American-made cotton twill, green jungle suits were provided to 14 Brigade because they were the first 3NZ Division unit to fight the Japanese. The troops of 8 Brigade had to endure K.D.O.R. (Khaki Drill Other Ranks) heavy drill outfits that were uncomfortable in damp tropical conditions. To add to the discomfort, the uniforms were covered with brown and green paint to provide a camouflage effect — "highly effective for camouflage but uncomfortable when sweating."[77]

An official New Zealand history condemned the New Zealand jungle clothing as "most unsuitable. It is heavier and hotter than its U.S. counterpart and the camouflage paint stops what little aeration there might be in the fabric. It may be good camouflage; as physiological clothing it is very poor."[78] Long-sleeved shirts and long trousers were thought essential for warding off sunburn, skin diseases and malaria. Despite this, the troops often preferred shorts and no shirts. The most lamentable item of Kiwi clothing, however, was the jungle boot. Made of canvas, it rapidly became cracked and leaked to the point of unserviceability.[79]

The New Zealanders were, however, decently supplied with weaponry — .303 Lee Enfield rifles, Mills Bomb grenades, 3 inch mortars, Bren guns and Thompson submachine guns (the only weapon compatible with American ammunition). They also had the Boys anti-tank gun which was universally loathed for being heavy and difficult to move through jungle. Artillery was equipped with the excellent 25 pound gun, which was versatile and able to fire anti-tank, smoke or high explosive rounds to a distance of 13,400 yards. A circular platform beneath allowed it to traverse 360 degrees. Anti-aircraft artillery was in the form of the 40mm Bofors.

Emphasis on Grenades

Grenades were frequently used in jungle warfare. Unlike the flash of a rifle when you fired, throwing a grenade did not give away your position. You could throw a grenade as far as you could throw a cricket ball. The trouble was that in the Solomon Islands in the jungle the trees often have large flanges at the base. A grenade could bounce back at you if you were unwary.[80]

The 3NZ Division had a tank squadron of British made Valentine tanks. These arrived at Guadalcanal for infantry-tank training by the men of 8 Brigade. Tanks had been found essential for destroying Japanese pill boxes and fortifications at Buna in Papua New Guinea, by Australian-American forces. However, they were not used for Goodtime because of limited shipping space, the steep mountainous nature of Mono, and a lack of known Japanese fortifications. The Universal Carrier No. 3 Mark II, more commonly known as the "Bren Gun Carrier," would, however, be deployed. This tracked vehicle had a crew of four or five men, was some 12 feet long and had a maximum speed of 32 mph. They were armed with a .303 Bren machine gun at the front. Although having armor plate, their chief drawback was that they were open topped, which left their crews vulnerable. The Carriers were manufactured in New Zealand.

The troops received C and K rations courtesy of their American hosts. C rations were provided in two airtight containers opened by a tin key. One container contained cold meat and the other ham, sweets, biscuits, coffee, lemon and soup powders, cigarettes and chewing gum. The container could be used as a cup.[81]

At the time of Goodtime the brigade was at full strength, but hanging over its head, as with the rest of the division, was the question of replacements or reinforcements. Despite Halsey's urging, the New Zealand government, struggling to support 2NZ Division in the Mediterranean and other manpower commitments, made it plain that no further men were forthcoming for 3NZ Division. Barrowclough had been forced to disband 15 Brigade in order to maintain 8 and 14 Brigades at full strength. Both Row and Barrowclough were aware that if 8 Brigade sustained too many casualties the brigade would most likely be broken up. The fact that 3NZ Division consisted of only two brigades, 8 and 14, meant that it could not replace an American division in the front line and its tasks would be limited to those able to be undertaken by a brigade. Fortunately Goodtime only required a brigade.

Fear of excessive casualties haunted New Zealand Prime Minister Peter Fraser. He had seen the consequences of British military adventurism in Greece and Crete which had been paid for, in part, by New Zealand casualties. Most New Zealanders at that time identified heavily with Britain. If the British could be cavalier with New Zealand lives, what could be expected of people as distant as the Americans?[82] While there was desire to play a role in the Pacific War and to earn a place at the peace table, this was increasingly outweighed by the limits of New Zealand's resources.

So why were these guys in the funny lemon squeezer hats and the strange way of speaking used in a war dominated by Americans? Simply, they were too significant a military asset to ignore. They were soldiers already in the South Pacific and, unlike American soldiers, did not have to be transported across the expanse of the Pacific to the front line. Admiral Nimitz had lambasted Vice Admiral Ghormley for failing to utilize New Zealand troops.[83] His more aggressive successor, "Bull" Halsey, welcomed the New Zealanders and wanted to use them in combat. Underlying everything there was a scarcity of Allied troops in the South Pacific. Vital points had to be garrisoned because no areas were considered safe from Japanese attack. Units burned out by jungle warfare needed time to recover and fresh units had to be trained.

In early 1943 there were only four U.S. Army and two U.S. Marine Corps Divisions available in the South Pacific area.[84] The war against Germany had priority and American troops were sent to North Africa in 1942 to take part in Operation Torch, the invasion of French North Africa. Later, American troops would be sent to Britain in the buildup for Operation Overlord, the invasion of France. The American commanders in the Pacific were dismayed at this and pressed for reinforcements. These would eventually come, but the reality was that American soldiers were in relatively small numbers in the South Pacific in 1943 and some divisions had become burned out in the grueling fighting for the New Georgia group.

For the Americans there was a profound ignorance of the men of 3NZ Division. They knew that New Zealanders had fought well in the Mediterranean and some, like Halsey, believed that the troops were "desert veterans," confusing them with Australian troops brought back from the desert war to fight the Japanese.[85]

The morale of the men of 8 Brigade Group was high. They had trained hard since leaving New Zealand and were now proficient in weapons-handling and amphibious assault. Most looked forward to the challenge of fighting the Japanese, and would have echoed the sentiment of Frank Cooze, an anti-aircraft gunner. "If we went into action — well anything was better than to stagnate on dreary bug-infested islands!"[86]

For some soldiers, however, the prospect of fighting the Japanese posed a dilemma. Throughout the Pacific War the Japanese universally ignored the Red Cross as a symbol of protection for non-combatants. Hospital ships painted white with Red Cross markings were deliberately targeted and sunk.[87] Hospitals in Hong Kong and Singapore were broken into and medical staff killed. Nurses were raped, and helpless patients bayoneted or shot. Missionaries were systematically killed. The lesson was rapidly learned that although the Japanese had agreed before the Pacific War to abide by the provisions of the 1929 Geneva Convention (even if they did not formally ratify it), in reality they had no intention of doing so.

This posed an ethical and legal dilemma for Allied medical workers and chaplains. If they did not carry weapons they rendered themselves helpless before an enemy unconcerned about killing them. On the other hand, as non-combatants, an essential part of that status was that they remained unarmed. Once armed, they lost the protection of the Geneva Conventions and became fair game.

The nature of warfare in the South Pacific was also relevant. In jungle warfare vision was often restricted and attackers and defenders could be literally feet away yet unaware of each other. They could come across one another unexpectedly, and combat would ensue. There would be little time or opportunity to identify insignia on the other side in a kill or be killed situation.

The Americans on Guadalcanal had experience of what they perceived to be Japanese treachery. Twenty Marines led by Lieutenant Goettge had attempted to take the surrender of a group of Japanese. The Goettge patrol, was a fiasco with the Americans ambushed and brutally wiped out. The incident on 12 August 1942 became widely known "and the psychology of kill or be killed ruled the battlefield thereafter."[88] The Goettge patrol's fate became known to the men of 3NZ Division.[89]

The assistant director of medical services of 3NZ Division asked the Americans and the officers of the South Pacific Scouts about Japanese attitudes towards non-combatants. The answers seemed to indicate that there was no respect for them and that the Japanese aim was to kill as many Allied personnel as possible. John Dower refers to the war in the Pacific as "war without mercy," and that is an accurate summation.

The assistant director decided that the Red Cross symbol was not to be used and was to be painted over on ambulances. Stretcher bearers going into the jungle were to be escorted by Army Service Corps soldiers equipped with Thompson submachine guns. Because firearms would have hampered their work, soldiers of the New Zealand Medical Corps were issued firearms, if they wanted, for the protection of themselves and their patients.[90] Despite the risks, not all non-combatants wanted to carry weapons. 'Bags,' Padre Owen Baragwanath, the popular padre of 29 Battalion, rejected a revolver.[91]

When Brigadier Robert Row received orders from IMAC on 16 October 1943 that his brigade would assault the Treasury Islands, his forces were on the coast of Guadalcanal, 350 miles from the intended target. None of his troops had undertaken an opposed amphibious assault and Row could only hope that the training his troops had undergone would be adequate. Combat is the ultimate audit of a military unit's proficiency. Row had the daunting prospect of not only commanding his soldiers, but also American personnel — a rarity in World War II.

8 Brigade — Row's Command

Brigadier Robert Amos Row was not the first nor would he be the last commander of 8 Brigade, 3NZ Division. Because the land component of Goodtime was essentially Row's "show," it is worthwhile examining the man. As a commander, Row in many respects exemplifies the traits of the men under his command, but differs in some important ways.

Born in Christchurch, New Zealand, on 30 July 1888, of an English mother and an Australian father, Row was educated at Christchurch Boys High and then Canterbury College. He was then a commercial traveler. The military life attracted him and in 1909 he enrolled in the Imperial Rifles as a volunteer. He joined the 1st (Canterbury) Regiment, a Territorial unit, in 1911, and by 1912 attained the rank of major. In World War I, he arrived in Egypt in 1914 as part of the New Zealand Expeditionary Force, and took part in the ill-fated Gallipoli campaign. Wounded at Gallipoli on 20 September 1915, he was evacuated to Malta.

Declared fit for service in early 1916, he rejoined the New Zealand forces on the Western Front in 1917. Row distinguished himself and was mentioned several times in dispatches including those of the British commander Sir Douglas Haig "for distinguished and gallant service and devotion to duty." During the fighting on the Somme in 1918, Row was a liaison officer for his brigade and earned praise for the way in which he carried out his duties. In the critical battles at the end of 1918 Row was a lieutenant colonel and commander of 1 Battalion, Canterbury Regiment. He had ample experience of grueling trench warfare and his courage had been recognized by the Distinguished Service Order and the British War Medal.

The majority of New Zealand soldiers were demobilized in the aftermath of World War I and returned to their civilian occupations. Row, however, had obtained senior rank and decided to continue his army career. The New Zealand armed forces in the post–World War I period shrank to minuscule levels and only officers who were considered to have distinguished themselves and shown potential were retained. Row was initially attached to the New Zealand Army GHQ School in Trentham with the rank of major and became part of the New Zealand Army Staff Corps. Posted back to Christchurch, Row held various staff positions. In the period 1928–1931 the New Zealand Army held a series of amphibious exercises, using British combined operations doctrine. The last one in 1931 involved the Canterbury Regiment in a small-scale raid. Row was not in command but was in a position to observe. Despite the shortage of suitable ships the raid was successful. Together with his Gallipoli experience the exercise would have shown Row, as a staff officer and planner, the potential and the problems associated with amphibious operations.

Row progressed through various unglamorous staff postings gaining experience of logistics and command. From 1933 to 1939 Row was a staff officer at Central Command in Wellington.

On the outbreak of war New Zealand was chronically short of officers and trained soldiers. Row was attached to the headquarters of 2 New Zealand Expeditionary Force on 20 January 1941 and sent to the Middle East. He was returned to New Zealand and posted to Army headquarters on 16 June 1941. At that point the situation in the Pacific was particularly threatening and war with Japan seemed imminent. Row was appointed on 25 February 1942 to command 8 Brigade, 3NZ Division, at a time when Fiji was under

U.S. Army Brigadier General Neal C. Johnson and New Zealand Army Brigadier Robert Amos Row, DSO, observing training (War History Collection, Alexander Turnbull Library, Wellington, WH-0178).

considerable threat of Japanese invasion. He had the unenviable job of commanding an ill-equipped, ill-trained brigade which would have had little prospect of success in the event of a determined Japanese invasion. Row had returned to New Zealand with 8 Brigade in 1942 and had been involved in the re-building and training of his brigade. Goodtime would be the first combat operation for many of his men, including many of his officers.

Row was six years older than his immediate commander, Major-General Harold Barrowclough. Unlike Barrowclough, Row had stayed in the Army after World War I and had gained experience of staff work and command of units. Row would have implicitly understood that, given his age, his prospects for higher command were limited. It must have been disappointing for Row when command of 3NZ Division was given to Barrowclough. There does not, however, appear to have been any friction between the two men.

Bert Cowan, who served as a sergeant in the Intelligence Section under Row, found Brigadier Row "rather snarly," but given the pressures on Row in 1942–43 this is understandable. Cowan also commented that Row was a professional soldier and was demanding in his standards. He was viewed as being a perfectionist in his behavior. He was also building a military unit from next to nothing.[92] An anecdote reveals Row's command style: he issued an order that the soldiers of his brigade were to be limited to one bag as they moved forward into the combat zone. His officers ignored this order. To the delight of the other ranks, Row insisted his officers comply with his order.[93]

Row's Lieutenants

Although Row might have had a considerable role in the planning of Goodtime, the actual implementation of it was to be dependent upon his three infantry battalion commanders—Lieutenant Colonel Kenneth Basil McKenzie-Muirson, M.C., (36 Battalion), Lieutenant Colonel F.L.H. Davis (29 Battalion) and Lieutenant Colonel R.J. Eyre (34 Battalion). Battalion commanders were hugely influential in setting the "tone" for their battalions.

McKenzie-Muirson was a thin, slightly-built man with a peppery disposition, who demanded high standards and commanded respect. "Mad Mac," as he was affectionately known, had a reputation for being a tough, hard man but also caring for the men under his command and of being meticulous with details. One veteran recalled him demanding that his men sing more loudly at the Sunday church service. He was born in Victoria, Australia on 8 December 1894, and his service in both the Australian and New Zealand armies is a testament to the closeness of the ANZAC bond. McKenzie-Muirson served with the Australian Imperial Force between 1914 and 1920. He served at Gallipoli, manning a machine gun and earning a Military Cross. At Polygon Wood, France, in September, 1917, he won a bar to the Military Cross. He later served in Afghanistan.

After the war, he migrated to New Zealand and joined the Canterbury Regiment. In 1922 he was placed on the reserve of officers but maintained a connection with the New Zealand Army. In civilian life he became an inspector of factories. On the outbreak of World War II he was given various training posts. He was appointed to command the Wellington Regiment in April 1942. He commanded 1st Scots Battalion from October 1942 to June 1943. With the breakup of 15 Brigade he became the commander of 36th Battalion.

Eyre saw active service with the New Zealand Division in France in 1917. He served with both the infantry and artillery. He gained a commission but had to relinquish this after the war. He joined the Royal New Zealand Artillery and served at various posts in New Zealand. In 1928 he received a commission in the New Zealand Staff Corps and became adjutant to various Territorial units. He then commanded the Southern District School of Instruction. In 1941 Eyre was sent to Fiji as brigade major of 8 Brigade. When 3 Division was reformed in New Zealand in August 1942, he became the commander of 34 Battalion.[94]

Davis had the distinction of having had recent combat experience with 2NZ Division in the Middle East. He took over command of 29 Battalion when it was located at Ouameni in New Caledonia.[95]

Underneath the battalion commanders were commissioned officers who were mainly young men, not too different from the men they commanded, and who lacked experience in the tropics and combat experience. They had to earn the respect and confidence of the men they commanded, and most rose to that challenge. War against the Japanese was particularly unforgiving of the mistakes of amateurs. Amphibious and jungle warfare also had a low tolerance of mistakes.

Three

The Gamble

Under pressure from MacArthur to advance, Halsey and his staff began drafting plans. Various options were considered but on 22 September 1943, Halsey cancelled all prior plans and opted for two possible alternatives—invade both the Treasury Islands and Empress Augusta Bay on Bougainville, or alternatively, seize the Treasury Islands and the island of Choiseul before invading Bougainville. Based on intelligence gathered, Halsey notified MacArthur on 1 October 1943 that Cape Torokina was to be the main target with invasion set for 1 November 1943. MacArthur agreed and planning began.

It had been intended that the invasion of Bougainville would occur contemporaneously with the seizure of the Treasury Islands. The plan evolved with Goodtime to take place five days before the main invasion went in at Empress Augusta Bay. It would divert Japanese attention to the south of Bougainville, and away from Empress Augusta Bay. Radar stations could be sited to cover Bougainville and a PT Boat base could be rapidly established. The Treasury Islands could also provide a safe harbor for any ships getting into difficulty at Bougainville during Cherryblossom. The success of the invasion of Empress Augusta Bay rested on Cape Torokina being lightly defended and a beachhead being established quickly. One U.S. Marine Corps historian, Joseph Alexander, has described Operation Cherryblossom as

> one fraught with risk for Bull Halsey. He lacked the combat power to seize and defend the entire island. At best Halsey hoped to use his Marines to catch Lieutenant General Haruyoshi Hyakutake by surprise, seize a foothold along the Southern Coast, then defend the enclave desperately while the Seabees carved a pair of landing fields out of the jungle. The rewards would be great. The new airstrips would close the range to Rabaul to 210 miles, making it possible to hit the Japanese nerve center with dive bombers and torpedo bombers as well as Corsairs.[1]

If Operation Cherryblossom was fraught with risk then the diversionary operations on Choiseul (Operation Blissful) and the Treasury Islands both to the south of Bougainville began to look like high stakes gambles. The Choiseul operation was simply a raid and if it failed, American casualties would be limited. Operation Goodtime was a full-scale invasion and for the Goodtime planners there was the risk that if it stalled or the Japanese counterattacked in force there would be significant Allied casualties.

The commander of the 2nd Marine Parachute Battalion, the force that was to raid

Choiseul, Colonel Victor 'Brute' Krulak, was bluntly told by Colonel Gerald Thomas of I MAC: "When you go on this raid, don't expect us to bail you out. We don't have the resources to do it. Do not get involved in a wrestling match. Hit and run! Raise hell! But don't let yourself get drawn into a battle. You're completely on your own."[2]

A similar sentiment could have been expressed in respect to Goodtime. John M. Rentz, the U.S. Marine Corps historian, considers that in assessing the situation Halsey acknowledged the risk:

> From the viewpoint of high level planners, any undertaking in the Northern Solomons involved manifold risks and perils. To embark on the Bougainville venture not only meant an attack under the guns of a well defined objective — Rabaul, but also exposed our forces in the South and Southwest Pacific by committing an important segment thereof to a hazardous operation.[3]

Not only was shipping in limited numbers, there was an "inadequacy of surface forces" to protect supply lines and to cover for forces that were landed.[4]

Prior to Goodtime and Blissful elaborate efforts were made to deceive the Japanese as to where the next blow would fall. Halsey noted that in the Shortland Islands, "Our combat patrols deliberately left evidence of their visit, and almost every day our photo planes made leisurely, low-level flights across the area, followed by, or following our bombers. The Japs fell for it. They began to move troops, artillery, and heavy equipment over from Bougainville, as we were hoping, and we learned from their officers after the war that they firmly believed this would be the scene of our landing."[5]

There was an inherent paradox in the planning of Goodtime: the greater the degree of success in drawing Japanese attention southwards and away from Empress Augusta Bay, the greater the degree of threat to the Goodtime force.

Planning an Amphibious Operation

By 1943 the state of the art in amphibious assault had advanced hugely since the catastrophic Operation Dovetail, the 1st U.S. Marine Corps Division practice landings at Koro Island, Fiji, in 1942, where hydrography was ignored and landing craft were hung up on coral reefs.[6] The Goodtime planners knew that hydrographic factors such as the tidal height, the slope of the beach gradient, shelter from unfavorable sea and weather, water depth and bottom configuration, the extent of mineable water, and the compatibility of the beaches and their approaches to the size, draught, maneuverability and beaching characteristics of the assault ships and the landing craft had to be taken into account of. One thing was certain — ships and landing craft would want to disgorge their cargoes as quickly as possible to get clear of Japanese-dominated airspace. There was limited sea room in Blanche Channel and vessels would remain vulnerable to air and submarine attack.

Terrain impacted invasion planning. A short stretch of beach close to Falamai village in the south of Mono Island was the only place suitable for beaching LSTs, and it had areas where supply dumps could be established. This dictated that the main thrust of the invasion would be at Falamai.[7] The siting of artillery was another factor. Stirling Island was the only position from which field artillery and AA guns could be quickly sited to provide supporting fire and an air defense umbrella. The problem was that LSTs could not beach on Stirling Island, although later engineering work would rectify this.

Unlike ordinary military offensives that start at maximum strength then dissipate as the attackers move forward, an amphibious operation starts with the attackers at low strength as the first wave lands and builds up offensive strength as subsequent waves arrive and the beachhead is secured. As a survivor of Gallipoli, Brigadier Row would have been acutely aware of the vulnerability of the initial landing force. At Gallipoli relatively small numbers of determined Turkish defenders had exacted a significant toll of British attackers and slowed the tempo of the advance.[8]

There are two basic types of amphibious movements—ship to shore and shore to shore. Ship to shore involves the invading troops being transported in large vessels to the area of operations and then offloading, usually by way of climbing down cargo nets to landing craft which then deliver them to shore. Shore to shore involves troops boarding a vessel at a friendly port and being delivered in the same vessel directly to their destination. Goodtime required the bulk of the troops, particularly the assaulting waves, to be delivered ship to shore. The Seabees and their heavy gear in LSTs would be delivered shore to shore.

An amphibious assault is like a jigsaw puzzle: the pieces have to fit into place perfectly and in correct sequence. One of Goodtime's problems was that many of the pieces were in short supply. The number of available landing craft was inadequate to transport more than a limited number of men to the beachhead. The concern was that insufficient strength would be available in the first wave to seize the beachhead. The U.S. Marine Corps Official History records: "...Since only eight APD's (Destroyer Transports), two LST's three LCT's and eight LCI's were available for transportation of the first echelon of the Brigade (which numbered approximately 7,700 officers and men), it was determined that supplies and equipment would be cut to the barest minimum and that only about 50–60% of the troops could be taken in the first echelon."[9]

The reason for this shortage of shipping was due to shipping demands elsewhere. Wilkinson's staff was trying to juggle the shipping needs of Goodtime, Blissful and Cherryblossom as the beginning of the Central Pacific drive was gearing up.

Lorelli comments that while the number of ships available to Wilkinson had never been generous,

> the diversion of amphibious lift to Nimitz meant that these were only eight transports and four cargo ships left in the South Pacific area. The requirement to move two divisions, their supporting units and supplies meant that if any single transport or cargo ship was lost, the schedule could not be maintained. The planners took to calling the operation [Cherryblossom] "Shoestring 2" in memory of the straitened circumstances at Guadalcanal.[10]

Compounding this problem was the American plan to seize an area on the northwest coast of Mono at Soanatalu to set up a radar station facing Bougainville. Having radar able to overlook the designated landing area at Empress Augusta Bay proved to be irresistible to American planners, although it played havoc with logistical and invasion planning. The danger was that the beachhead at Soanatalu would be exposed to a Japanese counterthrust from the Shortland Islands and would be in the path of any Japanese retreating off Mono.

An additional source of discomfort for the Kiwis was that none of the large attack transports—"the Unholy Four," the USS *President Jackson, President Monroe, President Adams* and *President Hayes* on which they had trained—were available for Goodtime. Their absence meant Goodtime would involve smaller craft and therefore more complicated logistic planning.

Goodtime was beach-dependent. There were no port facilities to be seized. The beaches had to be accessible by larger vessels such as LSTs, yet free of tidal currents which would disrupt the passage of smaller landing craft. The beaches had to be wide enough for multiple craft to land, but have the capacity to allow stores and equipment to be landed and accumulated. A close tree line and cover against enemy air attack would be a plus. The assaulting waves had to push inland as rapidly as possible to widen the beachhead. It was also desirable that supporting artillery be landed and emplaced rapidly to provide support in the event of a determined attempt to eliminate the beachhead. Also critical was landing anti-aircraft guns rapidly to protect against air attack. A determined air attack could emasculate the invasion if it inflicted large scale casualties or destroyed critical supplies or shipping. Goodtime was a diversionary operation and the U.S. Navy was not willing to commit more precious resources than absolutely necessary. It was intended that the precious shipping would rapidly disgorge its cargo and retreat out of harm's way. Speed of unloading was essential. Shipping needed to be cleared so that it could be used for Blissful[11] and Cherryblossom.

The invasion sites consisted of Beaches Orange One and Two located on the southern side of Mono Island near Falamai village, Purple One and Two on the northern central area of Stirling Island, and Emerald near Soanatalu. The invading force was divided into three groups— the Northern Force designated to land on Orange One and Two; the Southern Force designated to land on Purple One and Two and Logan Force, which was to land at Emerald.

Resources were limited. Originally the naval gunfire support plan provided for four destroyers for bombardment and anti-aircraft protection until field artillery and AA guns could be set up. On 7 October, Row was informed only two destroyers would be available for the initial bombardment and thereafter only one at call for six hours of fire support.[12]

The U.S. Navy designated the destroyers USS *Pringle* and *Philip* to provide naval fire support. It also designated PT boats from Lambulambu, Vella Lavella and Lever, New Georgia, to set up a picket line from the Shortland Islands to Choiseul with the aim of protecting the invasion force.

American historian Harry A. Gailey raises an interesting question regarding the planning for Goodtime:

> At a time when assault forces were in such short supply throughout the Pacific and the Bougainville invasion was only days away, it is difficult to understand why an entire brigade was to be used to subdue a tiny enemy garrison on one small island. One possible explanation is that Halsey and Vandegrift were reluctant to use untried New Zealand troops in a more ambitious undertaking but were under pressure to allay criticism then current in Australasia that American commanders did not want to use British Empire troops. For whatever reason the Treasury operation was one of the few examples of Allied overkill during this midstage of the Pacific War.[13]

On the face of it the Japanese garrison on the Treasury Islands appeared to have been vastly outnumbered, and the outcome to be a foregone conclusion. However, the Japanese troops were well-motivated and prepared to fight to the death. Unexpected events such as the sinking of transport or supply ships could derail the whole enterprise, leaving it open to a Japanese counter-thrust. God may indeed love the big battalions but that is no guarantee of success, as Allied forces learned from the Turkish defenders on the Gallipoli Peninsula in 1915. As a Kiwi veteran commented on the disparity in numbers: "We didn't think the numbers excessive when going ashore, not all the combat force landed in the same spot and it was impossible to know the size of enemy force we might encounter."[14]

Gailey's assertion that Halsey was reluctant to use untried New Zealand troops in a more ambitious undertaking is simply incorrect. While MacArthur was obliged to use Australian troops in his New Guinea battles because they made up the bulk of his forces, he nonetheless preferred to command American troops and went out of his way to avoid American troops coming under Australian command. Admiral Halsey was a complete contrast. He actively pressed for more New Zealand troops to be sent to the South Pacific and had no qualms about committing them to combat. He allowed American troops to be placed under the command of New Zealanders like Major General Harold Barrowclough. He had no concerns about the combat capabilities of Kiwi soldiers, if only because he mistakenly thought they were veterans of the Desert War. The major limitation for Halsey in using New Zealand troops was that he did not have enough of them. The 3NZ Division remained chronically under-strength.

The use of a brigade for the operation does not seem inappropriate when the potential for Japanese counterattack is considered. Goodtime was anything but a safe, one-sided operation.

The Planning Staff

The Allied chain of command for Goodtime was dominated by the American Navy. It flowed downwards from President Franklin D. Roosevelt and the U.S. Joint Chiefs of Staff through to Admiral Ernest J. King, the Chief of Naval Operations of the U.S. Navy, to the various area commanders. Admiral Chester Nimitz, as commander in chief, Pacific (CINCPAC), commanded Admiral William Halsey, Commander South Pacific (COMSOPAC). He, in turn, had command responsibility for the various naval and land forces that were to take part in Goodtime, principally 1 Marine Amphibious Corps (IMAC). Barrowclough's 3NZ Division effectively came under American command by agreement between Washington and Wellington. Barrowclough was subordinate to Lt. General Edward Puttick, the senior New Zealand military commander based in Wellington. The relationship between the two men was often strained but Puttick resisted the urge to micromanage Barrowclough's division. Brigadier Robert Amos Row, as commander of 8 Brigade, reported to Barrowclough but, in terms of Goodtime, Barrowclough exercised command with a very light hand, trusting to Row's experience and competence. Various battalion and unit commanders of the rank of colonel or below reported to Row. At base the land aspects of Goodtime were to be Row's show.

One of the paradoxes of Goodtime was that although the Americans were in overall command, Barrowclough and Row found themselves commanding American troops.

Admiral Halsey, left, and Brigadier Row share a drink on Guadalcanal during planning for Goodtime, October 1943 (John Rentz, *Bougainville and the Northern Solomons*, p. 94).

This was not the first time a New Zealand soldier found himself in command of American troops,[15] but in the context of World War II it was comparatively rare for Americans to be under foreign command. It is a measure of American confidence in Barrowclough and Row that this was allowed. This should be seen in the overall context that the New Zealanders were subject to American control. The Americans controlled air and naval assets, and only a limited number of American troops were involved.

Although Nimitz and Halsey issued the directive for Goodtime, implementation was at a much lower level. The task was given to First Marine Amphibious Corps but, since no marine units were involved, planning occurred at task force level. The U.S. Navy had a habit of forming formations of ships and men, giving them a force designation number and assigning the Task Force a mission. Once that mission was completed the Task Force was disbanded and fresh ones formed for new missions. The convoluted chain of command and flexibility of organization befuddled the New Zealanders who were having enough difficulty coping with the distinctive cultures of the U.S. Navy, U.S. Marines, U.S. Army and U.S. Army Air Force. For Goodtime, Task Force 31 was formed.[16]

Goodtime was merely an integral part of Cherryblossom, the invasion of Bougainville. In his operation plan of 12 October 1943, Halsey set out his objectives and assigned air and naval commanders to achieve those objectives. Principally, Rear Admiral Theodore S. Wilkinson of the U.S. Navy was in command of Goodtime and its naval aspects.[17] When the historian, Samuel Eliot Morison wrote his volume on the Solomons campaign, *Breaking the Bismarck's Barrier*, as part of his magisterial history of the United States Navy in World War II, he singled out Rear Admiral Theodore "Ping" Wilkinson for praise as an especially adept practitioner of amphibious warfare, and even dedicated the volume to him.[18] Wilkinson is, however, all but forgotten. As the naval commander of Operation Goodtime, Wilkinson bears examination.

If anyone merited the description "straight arrow" it was surely Theodore Stark "Ping" Wilkinson. Born in Annapolis in December 1888, Wilkinson had a stellar naval career and by the end of World War II was recognized as one of the most skilful practitioners of amphibious warfare. Extremely intelligent he graduated top of his class at Annapolis Naval Academy in 1909. Thereafter he held various sea and staff commands ranging from the command of destroyers through to being a director of the Bureau of Ordnance and developing naval weaponry.

By October 1941, he was the director of the Office of Naval Intelligence but managed to avoid the fallout from the Japanese attack on the American fleet at Pearl Harbor. Wilkinson was appointed Deputy Commander South Pacific on 30 January 1943. Appointed commander III Amphibious Force in June 1943, he earned Nimitz's confidence by his skillful command of the naval forces in the New Georgia campaign. Bougainville was to be his next challenge.

Morison considered Wilkinson "the happiest choice in the world for planning and commanding the Bougainville operation.... A scholarly, widely read officer with an excellent combat record, considerate of his staff and everyone who worked with him, Wilkinson went into Bougainville as if he had been preparing for it all his life."[19]

Wilkinson issued a series of orders on 15 and 18 October detailing plans for Goodtime and Cherryblossom. These covered a myriad of intricate operational matters ranging from gunfire support to shipping movements. Wilkinson divided his command into two groups, the Northern Force for the Empress Augusta landing and the Southern Force for the Treasury Islands. Wilkinson retained command of the Northern Force and placed his subordinate, Rear Admiral George H. Fort, U.S. Navy, in charge of the Southern Force.

This division of command created problems because Fort and his staff were not in the Solomons and, in fact, left Auckland, New Zealand, on 26 October 1943, on his flagship, the destroyer USS *Eaton* (DD-510) only a day before Goodtime took place. Much of the confusion and friction that occurred between the Yanks and the Kiwis at a higher command level can be attributed to the pressure under which the operation was put together, the significant changes made by advancing the landing date and that Wilkinson was focused on the larger problem of Empress Augusta Bay. It was essentially Wilkinson's headquarters on Guadalcanal that the Kiwis had to deal with.

Fort, like Wilkinson, is virtually unknown today. He did, however, play a significant role in the war in the South Pacific and, by Goodtime, had become proficient in amphibious warfare. Fort graduated from Annapolis in 1912 and then took the risky and unconventional career path of becoming a submariner. In 1923 he attained the rank of lieutenant commander and command of the submarine S-25. In June 1942, he became captain of the heavy battleship USS *North Carolina*, a prestigious appointment even in a navy where the supremacy of carrier aircraft was evident. He commanded the *North Carolina* during Operation Watchtower, the invasion of Guadalcanal in August 1942, and later at the Battle of the Eastern Solomons. In December 1942, Fort became a rear admiral and served as a deputy to Admiral Richmond Kelly Turner. Fort commanded the landing craft flotillas of Amphibious Force South Pacific when the Russell Islands and New Georgia were taken.

IMAC was given responsibility for land operations in the Northern Solomons and, since 8 Brigade of 3NZ Division had been attached to IMAC, the commander of 8 Brigade, Brigadier Robert Amos Row, had a role in planning. The commander of IMAC, Major General Charles D. Barrett, informed Row on 28 September 1943 that there would be simultaneous landings by 8 Brigade on the Treasury Islands and American forces at Empress Augusta Bay, Bougainville. Row received Barrett's formal letter of instruction the following day and began planning. He tried to gather as much intelligence information about the Treasury Islands as he could. He had the report of the reconnaissance team landed from the USS *Greenling* on 22–23 August 1943, the detailed reports of the American aircrew who had been shot down and spent time on the Treasury Islands, and daily aerial photographs.

Complicating matters, on 8 October 1943, Barrett fell from a building in Noumea and died from a cerebral hemorrhage. Lieutenant General Archer Vandegrift, USMC, at Pearl Harbor was appointed his replacement. He found that Barrett's "staff and commanders were as deeply grieved as I and it took a little doing to return them to the necessary perspective."[20] Nonetheless, Vandegrift was an experienced amphibious warfare practitioner and fully in synch with his naval counterpart.[21]

Row could not land his troops in one wave, so had to choose what to land first, and what to land in succeeding echelons. The shipping allocated for the first echelon, which in effect was the teeth of the invading forces, was "barely sufficient" for three battalions, a field battery, twelve 36mm American light anti-aircraft guns, four American 90mm heavy anti-aircraft guns, one troop of 6 pounder anti-tank guns for harbor defense and one light radar.

Row saw a second echelon containing four 90mm AA guns, a field battery, an anti-tank troop, a medium machine gun company and a heavy radar arriving six days after the initial landing. He foresaw a third echelon arriving 11 days after initial landing and a fourth echelon arriving 16 days after initial landing.[22]

He received First Marine Amphibious Corps Order No. 1 on 16 October 1943. His brigade was directed to "seize and hold Treasury Islands, capture or destroy enemy forces in the area; establish long range radars, Adv Naval Base, incl of facilities for Motor Torpedo Boats, and a staging refuge for ldg craft."[23]

Analyzing the terrain, Row opted for what was in effect a frontal assault. Row stated:

> It was clear at the outset that the main assault landing should, if possible, be made in the vicinity of FALAMAI, because that was the only beach which was suitable for an LST landing and which provided sufficient dispersal areas for the large quantities of stores and equipment being carried. Provided that the enemy could be subdued by sp [support] fire during the approach of the ldg [landing] craft, a ldg at FALAMAI was also the best way of getting at the enemy quickly. It was, however, also necessary to effect a landing on STIRLING IS, because that Is provided the only posns [positions] from which fd [field] arty could effectively sp the inf on MONO IS, and it also provided gun areas for a proportion of AA guns to cover BLANCHE HARBOUR. Although it was considered that LST could NOT beach at STIRLING IS, it appeared that we would have no difficulty in beaching LCT.[24]

Row's plan was not subtle. He intended to land his men in the very area where the Japanese defenses on Mono would be the strongest but anticipated they would be suppressed by naval gunfire. If his calculation was incorrect, the consequences would be bloody for the assaulting forces. Row then planned to establish a beachhead and to set up artillery on Stirling Island to provide a protective curtain of steel should the Japanese launch a counter-attack. On the first night it was envisaged the soldiers would dig foxholes and would not move out of them. Anything moving in the blackness could therefore safely be presumed to be Japanese. This conceded the night to the Japanese, but in terms of defensive doctrine, it made sense.

In reality the geography of Mono dictated where Row could land his forces—and this was as obvious to Row as it was to the Japanese defenders. Fort considered that "the major assault had to be made on ORANGE BEACH at FALAMAI, it being the only suitable beach on MONO ISLAND." Fort then added a factor important from the naval point of view, "to reach FALAMAI it was necessary to proceed two miles into BLANCHE HARBOUR, which averages 1000 yards wide."[25]

Row, Radar and Shipping for Goodtime

Planning for an amphibious operation is complex at the best of times. For Row it was made harder when the Americans advanced the date of the invasion. However, even worse, the Americans insisted on a subsidiary invasion at Soanatalu on the northern coast of Mono. This caused friction because Row's shipping resources were already limited and there were considerable concerns about the safety of the forces to be landed.

The Americans insisted on a landing at Soanatalu because they wanted to install light and heavy radar units to cover the air and sea areas around Empress Augusta Bay. No priority had originally been given to this. The first hint of problems was when Row was told that General Vandegrift had commented on the absence of priority given to heavy radar. On 14 October 1943, Row met with representatives of COMAIRNORSOLS, who told him that the long range radar (Type 270) would have to be placed on the northern or northeastern side of Mono to benefit Operation Cherryblossom. Admiral Wilkinson stipulated to Row that the long range radar had to be given high priority.[26] Row was therefore obliged to plan a subsidiary landing and provide a covering force.

Based on earlier reconnaissance reports and aerial photos, it seemed likely that a small beach at Soanatalu on the northern coast of Mono could take the LCT needed to transport the radar unit. The commander of Argus Unit No. 6 considered that a Type 270 radar unit could be effectively installed there. Admiral Wilkinson agreed to provide an APD for the Soanatalu invasion. Row was concerned at the vulnerability of the radar personnel and Seabees involved in constructing and installing the radar. He therefore sought to have the whole of 30 Battalion allocated, but this was refused, no doubt due to shipping difficulties. Row had to make do with a company of infantry reinforced by a section of medium machine guns. This had to protect 60 radar personnel and 20 Seabees while they did the heavy engineering and construction work. Row was aware that heavy equipment, including a bulldozer, had to be landed and that it would take at least 12 hours to get the radar set up and another 36 to 48 hours to get it functional. This collection of New Zealanders and Americans was to be under New Zealand command once it landed. The officer in command was Major Gordon W. Logan and his command was to be dubbed "Loganforce."

The plan was for radar equipment and the engineering gear to be loaded into an LCT which would be with the main convoy. It was to proceed to Soanatalu on the night of 27–28 October once the beachhead had been secured.

Row worried about the safety of Loganforce from the Japanese, either those counterattacking from the Shortland Islands or those retreating from the southern part of Mono. At worst the radar could be destroyed before the men of Loganforce retired along the west coast and towards the safety of the beachhead of Falamai.

Row's superior, Major General Harold Barrowclough, shared his concerns:

> The question that now concerns me is the adequacy of the garrison which it is proposed to establish at SOANOTALU to protect that radar. I understand from Berkely that the garrison was to be a Company reinforced by some machine guns and possibly some mortars, and of course, it would be within range of your artillery assuming that you had adequate communications back to the gun positions. I feel very strongly that this small garrison is not adequate for the purpose in view. It was one thing to send a Company to MALSI to eliminate any Jap post there and to act as a sort of outpost to your force. Such a Company, if it were attacked in overwhelming numbers could readily retire on to your defensive line, delaying the enemy as it went and keeping you posted as to his movements, but if the radar is to be established on the North Coast of the Island, and it seems the obvious place to establish it, the task of the Infantry in that locality will not in my view be an outpost task. It should be their duty to defend the radar against attack and keep it in operation so that it can give the fullest support to operations taking place elsewhere. If that garrison is forced to retire we lose the radar irrevocably and we lose all the benefit of its warning service and its value in the Fighter Control set up. For these reasons I think the garrison should be not less than a Battalion. You have to remember that there are a large number of Japanese on Bougainville who might, before they become aware of the operation further North, come across under cover of darkness to the Treasury Islands. They would almost certainly approach the Northern or North Eastern Coast of that Island and I do not think they would come at all unless they were in strength capable of overwhelming so small a garrison as a Company. In other words, you might as well have no garrison there at all unless you make it a substantial one.[27]

He urged Row to strengthen the small detachment as soon as he got the opportunity. Barrowclough commented: "I realize that I am more concerned over your venture than I would be if I were at hand with the rest of the Division to come to your assistance. Many of my fears may prove groundless but you must forgive my not unnatural anxiety over this operation."[28]

Barrowclough's concerns were well founded. The 3NZ Division was spread across the Pacific with support units on New Caledonia and Guadalcanal and the recently combat-tested 14 Brigade on Vella Lavella. In the event of disaster he would have to depend on the Americans' sea and airpower (including the few New Zealand naval and air units under American command) to extricate the Goodtime forces. At Guadalcanal in August 1942 the U.S. Navy had withdrawn its ships in the face of threatening Japanese air and seapower, leaving the 1st Marine Division stranded. With a similar situation in the Treasury Islands history could have repeated itself.

If 8 Brigade were decimated Barrowclough would have the invidious task of explaining to a casualty-conscious prime minister of a small nation which had already suffered grievous losses how such a situation had occurred. Although Row was in command of the Brigade Group it was Barrowclough who was his commander and who bore overall responsibility.

Given the risks involved, Barrowclough did have one option. He could invoke the charter given to him by the New Zealand government and prepared by him at his behest. Under this charter Barrowclough was directed to place his forces under overall American command — but with the proviso that if he believed his forces were placed at undue risk then could he refer the situation to Wellington to refuse the Americans the use of his forces. Barrowclough's counterpart in 2NZ Division, General Bernard Freyberg, had a similar charter, the existence of which caused considerable vexation to his British superiors in the Mediterranean theatre.

So why didn't Barrowclough use this power, given the risky nature of Goodtime and threat to Loganforce in particular? The answer is that he knew that such a refusal would have immense military and political repercussions. The question of whether 3NZ Division would be used as a combat unit or simply be used to supply garrison or labor troops had hung over 3NZ Division since its inception. Given the tremendous effort his men had made to train and reach a combat-worthy status, it seemed only fair that they be given a combat role. Barrowclough had probably persuaded the Americans to give his men a chance. To refuse the use of his men for Goodtime would show bad faith and give the Americans the idea that the New Zealanders were combat-shy and not to be relied on. This in turn would diminish any chance to play any meaningful role in the peace settlement with Japan. In practical terms there was little Barrowclough could do beyond express his concerns.

Planning for Goodtime was a joint exercise between Admiral Wilkinson's staff and 8 Brigade H.Q. Staff. Arguably the preparations for the amphibious landing were as important for the success of Goodtime, if not more so, than the fighting on Mono. Some 3759 men with 1785 tons of equipment had to be transported by 31 ships of differing sizes, speeds and capabilities 350 miles to their landing areas within a specified time.[29] Furthermore, the troops had to be in condition to fight and win against an enemy noted for his determination and willingness to die. Added to the mix was that, for virtually all of the troops taking part, this was to be their first combat experience.

Planning was colored by the fact that the large American Attack Transports were not available for Goodtime. During Exercise Efate, 8 Brigade Group was embarked in three large ships and much of the staff work and tactical loading was able to be decentralized. However, Goodtime would involve 31 ships of varying sizes and capabilities. These had to be tactically loaded so that the troops, weapons, ammunition, petrol, vehicles and a large variety of equipment arrived at the correct beach at the correct time. This required a great deal of complicated logistical planning and it was found necessary to increase the size of 8 Brigade HQ staff. "The clerical staff was called on for long hours, the I Section was fully extended, the staff officers were engrossed in massive load tables and weight and measurement returns."[30]

The Kiwis were able to use manuals and guidelines provided by the U.S. Navy. These covered transport loading, shore parties, logistics, boat handling and assault waves.[31] The

Kiwis had the benefit of training exercises with the Americans and had been introduced to the complexities of loading men and equipment in an orderly and efficient manner. The American manual warned that "the failure of an amphibious operation may be brought about by improper loading. This fact is historically the rule rather than the exception."[32]

Shipping space was critical and the assaulting forces would only take what was necessary for combat. The second and subsequent echelons were to carry the things necessary to continue combat and to push inland.[33]

The New Zealanders had to learn the differences between "commercial loading" (a method that uses ship space to maximum efficiency but troops are not in an immediate condition to fight), "convoy unit loading" (troops with their equipment and supplies are loaded into transports of the same convoy, but not necessarily the same vessel), "organizational unit loading" (a particular unit's men and equipment are placed in a particular ship or part of a ship to preserve unit integrity) and "combat loading."

With combat unit loading, selected units with their essential combat equipment transportation and supplies are loaded into a single transport so that they can engage in immediate combat upon landing or, as has been said, "the troops come out fighting."[34] All three types of loading were to be used for Goodtime but for the assaulting troops, combat loading was the most relevant. Most of the vessels had to be "combat loaded" so that the first items removed from the hold would be the ones most needed in combat. This meant loading the least-essential items in the bowels of the vessel. Combat loading is a complicated, tedious business requiring the planning foresight of a master chess player. Dimensions and weights needed to be correlated to hold capacity and location. All of this was achieved without computers.

The New Zealanders had some data on the weights and measurements of their equipment derived from the move of 3NZ Division from New Zealand to New Caledonia, and the subsequent move to Guadalcanal. However, not all the equipment for the landing — such as 29 Light Anti-Aircraft Regiment, were shipped at that time, nor all of the units.

In a post-invasion analysis it was found that "in actual practice the information proved to be very accurate. It was planned to load each of the 2 LSTs and 3 LCTs to the maximum with vehs [vehicles] and rolling cargo. Every one of the ships was actually loaded so full that on none of them could put even one more jeep. It was necessary to leave behind only one vehicle of those planned to be taken fwd [forward] and that was an RD 4 [bulldozer]. By the time it was found impossible to get this veh aboard it was too late to restow vehs and substitute it for a lower priority vehicle."[35] The corollary of such tight packing of equipment was that if the vessel carrying it was sunk or damaged then the combat effectiveness of the soldiers would have been threatened.

The restriction on shipping space caused some friction with one group of Americans demanding from Row more space for their gear and being curtly dismissed by him: "You have your orders gentlemen, carry them out."[36]

There was a certain degree of inefficiency in use of shipping space. It was later discovered that much of the equipment landed on the first day was of low priority and could have been delayed to subsequent shipments or "flights." Each company was given a certain amount of space on board ship and they loaded things like bedrolls, spare boots and cooking equipment.[37]

Three: The Gamble

For 34 Battalion, planning was marked by a series of frustrations:

> First it was announced that only 600 men could be taken up in the first echelon, and companies had to be reduced in strength accordingly; of this 600 a proportion had to be set aside for unloading operations on the Treasury Beaches; the remainder were allocated into first, second and third landing waves, the number of men for each wave depending on the capacity of the landing craft that would carry them to the shore. Then only a certain tonnage of equipment could go forward. Conferences were held daily to decide what weapons, stores and other equipment might be taken by each company, and how much of this would be landed in the first echelon or retained for subsequent convoys to carry north. Once that was determined, a decision had to be made fixing what items of equipment would be needed on shore with the first assaulting troops and what could safely be left to the slower ships some hours later.[38]

One important area of planning, naval gunfire support, was left to the Americans. As the USMC history notes:

> The initial landings in Blanche Harbor were to be covered by a naval gunfire support group of two destroyers, the Pringle and Philip. Liaison officers of IMAC planned the gunfire support, as the New Zealand officers had no experience in this phase of operations. While the brigade group expected to have no trouble in seizing the islands, the naval support was scheduled to cover any unforeseen difficulties. The gunfire plan called for two destroyers to fire preparation salvos from the entrance to Blanche Harbor before moving in toward the beaches with the landing waves to take targets under direct fire. The III PhibFor, however, took a dim view of risking destroyers in such restricted waters. The desired close-in support mission was then assigned to the newly devised LCI (G)—gunboats armed with three 40mm, two 20mm, and five .50 caliber machine guns—which were making their first appearance in combat. Two of these deadly landing craft were to accompany the assault waves to the beaches.[39]

Planning occurred mainly on Guadalcanal. There were problems, however. Row recorded his frustrations in his post-action report:

> I feel compelled to mention that there were considerable difficulties during the planning stage which I think might have been foreseen and avoided. First, HQ Amphibious Force (TF 31) and also HQ FMAC were situated at least 20 miles away from the area allotted to my Bde, and the roads were, to say the least of them NOT in the nature of speedways. Secondly, there was no efficient telephone line from Corps to my HQ. For these reasons much time was lost. Information and decisions could NOT be obtained quickly, just when they were most needed. The presence of the NZLO at Corps HQ (Lt. Col. J. Brooke-White) was a great help, but it did NOT solve all the difficulties. It was NOT possible for me to move my own HQ for had I done so I would have been out of contact with my own units...
>
> I must also say that difficulties were caused by the late arrival and initial lack of knowledge on the part of Cmds of U.S. units forming part of my force. Several Cmds reported soon after 28 Sep but could NOT supply vital information regarding their units, e.g. numbers of personnel, equipment, tonnage and shipping space needed. Other Cmds did NOT report until later, and their units were still being hurriedly assembled. On the 14 Oct it was necessary to substitute Coy A 87th CB for the Coy originally allotted to me: the substitute Coy had to come from RUSSELL Is and did NOT arrive at GUADALCANAL until 18 Oct. All these officers were most anxious to help my staff and to have their own organizations prepared as rapidly as possible for embarkation; but they had obviously received very sketchy orders, at short notice, and in more than one case their personnel were a long distance away.[40]

One of the established principles of amphibious operations is that planning staff should live and work together or, at the very least, be in close proximity to each other so that communication is facilitated. The fact that Wilkinson's HQ was over 20 miles from Row's HQ, and telephone communication was "practically impossible,"[41] increased the potential for misunderstanding and for things to go awry. Two examples of subsequent difficulties were:

(a) The first army plan was based on one LST being unloaded on STIRLING ISLAND.
This plan had to be scrapped and the loading of almost all ships changed when it was found impracticable from the Navy point of view.

(b) 1 MAC laid down in O.O. [Operations Order] Maximum capacity of each ship for personnel and cargo.
The loading plans were based on these figures, but subsequently had to be changed when CTF31 would NOT agree to these figures.[42]

The planning for Goodtime was rushed. The invasion date was brought forward and variations, such as the decision to land at Soanatalu, occurred. That the planning worked satisfactorily is testament to the skillful logistical planning of the New Zealanders and their American counterparts and their willingness to work together.

There were, however, frictions between the Americans and New Zealanders. The New Zealanders had a bitter memory of unnecessary casualties suffered on Vella Lavella. In September 1943 as 14 Brigade, 3NZ Division, moved to Vella Lavella Barrowclough had offered a New Zealand battery of twelve Bofors 40mm guns to the Americans to supplement their A.A. Defenses on Vella Lavella. The offer was accepted, gun sites prepared, and officers delegated to meet each LST and arrange for the speedy off-loading and emplacement of the guns. The Bofors were set up on the decks of the LSTs.

On arrival at Vella Lavella Barrowclough found the captains of the LSTs reluctant to disembark the guns. Consequently, when Japanese bombers struck, some had to fire from the decks of the LSTs. Bombs hit LST 446 destroying a gun and killing the crew.[43] Barrowclough believed that "if my instructions had been carried out we would have suffered no casualties to that crew and it is just possible that with its better position ashore the gun might have saved the ship." He wrote to Rear Admiral Wilkinson stressing the difficulty "if arrangements which I make for the protection of these LSTs are to be overruled by relatively junior Naval Officers who are quite unfamiliar with our plans."[44] Wilkinson expressed his condolences but felt sure "from the very fact that the gun was struck that it was in the best position to defend the ship against the planes coming directly at it."[45]

Remarkably, this issue resurfaced in the planning for Goodtime. The presence of New Zealand Bofors guns on the decks of LSTs was a powerful comfort to their captains. The Commodore of the LSTs requested, and it was agreed, that nine guns would be mounted on the deck of each LST. That was fine during the approach voyage. However, the issue was broader:

> The Commodore of the LSTs explained to C.O. 29 Lt. AA. Regt how he proposed to use Bofors guns to support infantry during the landing. He was dissuaded of this when it was explained to him that he would hardly be in a position to determine the position of our own Inf and in consequence more harm than good would be done. Unfortunately no check was made on LCIs with the result that "panic firing" took place as they approached the beach, thereby causing casualties to personnel in the first wave.[46]

The most pressing issue was when the guns would be released from the control of the Commodore of the LSTs and revert to the control of New Zealand Army officers. An official New Zealand report recorded:

> A difference of opinion arose between the Commodore of the LSTs and C.O. 29 Lt A.A. Regt in regard to when guns should be released from LSTs. C.O. 29 Regt had in mind Div. Directive that wherever practicable A.A. Guns for protection of shipping be sited ashore and not on ships. Commodore of LSTs was equally insistent that greater proportion of guns remain on deck until the LST was ready to move. Fortunately it was possible to refer the matter immediately to Comd 9 Bde who ruled that guns would be released from LSTs at demand of A.A. Cmd (C.O. 29 Regt). A.A. Comd to be responsible that best protection given to LSTs. That is, if sites ashore not available, guns would be left on LSTs until available.[47]

Fort divided his transport and warships into five transport groups:

(i) The Advance Transport Group (31.1.1), Commander John D. Sweeney, ComTrans Div 12 with 8 APDs *Stringham, Talbot, Waters, Dent, Kilty, Crosby, Ward* and *McKean* screened by destroyers USS *Eaton, Pringle* and *Philip*.

(ii) The Second Transport Group (31.1.2), commanded by Captain Jack E. Hurff, ComDesRon 22, made up of 8 LCIs, LCI (L)S 222, 330, 334, 336, 24, 61, 67, 69, screened by the destroyers USS *Waller, Cony, Saufley*, with the minesweepers *Adroit, Conflict* and *Daring*.

(iii) The Third Transport Group (31.1.3), Commander James R. Pahl, ComDesDiv 44, with 2 LSTs, 339 and 485 screened by USS *Conway* and *Renshaw* and Ym minesweepers.

(iv) The Fourth Transport Group (31.1.4), commanded by Lt. (Junior Grade) Martin E. Bergstrom with APc 37, LCT (5)s 321, 325, 330 and with an escort of two PT boats from Rendova.

(v) The Fifth Transport Group (31.1.6), commanded by Lt. Locke with APc 33, 6 LCM (3)s and an aircraft rescue boat.

The screening force of destroyers was designated (31.1.5).[48]

Each of these transport groups had their own needs, capabilities and vulnerabilities. Each had to arrive at their designated time, perform their required tasks and then depart the area before concentrated Japanese airpower could maul them. Staggered departure times were intended to provide each of these groups unhindered access to their designated beaches so they could deliver their cargoes and leave before the arrival of the next group.

What was truly remarkable about the diverse armada was the way the U.S. Navy succeeded in integrating its component parts. There were 10 different types of vessels and their speeds varied from a sedate 6 knots to a faster 12 knots. Because of the distances involved and because none of the larger craft could carry an LCM, the two LSTs of the First Echelon would tow an LCM each, and 6 other LCMs would make the 85-mile journey from Vella Lavella under their own power. Since only two LSTs were available in the First Echelon important equipment such as radar, bulldozers and assorted engineering equipment would be carried in the LCTs. Radar equipment would go to Beach Emerald at Soanatalu once the landing beach was secure.[49]

Although it was not considered best practice to load the LSTs with bulk cargo and vehicles in what was essentially an assault landing, and before protective AA defenses were set up, Fort felt that, in this instance, there was no alternative because there was such a critical shortage of LSTs.[50]

The biggest danger to Goodtime and Cherryblossom was from Japanese airpower. Japanese air strength in the Solomons was estimated on 9 October 1943 to be 160 fighters, 120 medium bombers, 66 dive or light bombers and 39 floatplanes. Some 72 percent of these were thought to be based on Rabaul, 20 percent on Bougainville and 8 percent on New Ireland.[51] Lt. General George C. Kenney's Fifth Air Force was directed to use its bombers based in New Guinea against the Japanese base at Rabaul.

Once the beaches were reached offloading and unloading of stores and equipment would occur. Working parties for the unloading stage were organized, and beach masters designated. One of the basic lessons of amphibious operations, as yet unappreciated at the time of Goodtime, was that sufficient working parties needed to be allocated to move supplies and equipment off the beaches and to safe dispersal areas. In areas where Japanese airpower still survived, this ranked equal to elimination of Japanese defenders. During the Hollandia landings in New Guinea in April 1944, a single Japanese bomber had set off an inferno among tightly-packed supplies and ammunition stores.[52]

A sand table model of the Treasury Islands was prepared by 'I' Section of 8 Brigade H.Q. and this enabled familiarization of objectives and planning by participating units.[53]

In the planning for Goodtime account was taken of the duration of daylight (12 hours), the phases of the moon (during the period 26 September to 4 October the attackers could take advantage of the dark of the moon), hours of sunrise, sunset, moonrise and moonset (on 27 October sunrise over Blanche Harbour was at 0611, sunset at 1831, moonrise at 0446 and moonset at 1707).[54]

Rumors were rife among the troops as to their destination. The 34 Battalion intelligence officer, Lieutenant Speight, gave lectures on the Solomon Islands.

"Betting favored Choiseul, with Shortland and Kolombangara running it close. Talking about the future was all there was to do in the heat-laden evenings, except on those nights when films were showing at our own open-air theatre in the camp."[55]

Speculation ended on 13 October 1943, when Colonel Eyre told his company commanders that their target was to be the Treasury Islands, and that the task of 34 Battalion was to seize Stirling Island. It was believed that Stirling was ungarrisoned but this could not be guaranteed. Between 14 October and 16 October the battalion was transported on APDs to beaches on the east coast of Florida Island, off the coast of Guadalcanal, where it was put through its paces during two landing exercises.

On 15 October 1943, Row issued a memo to the men of 8 Brigade. He indicated that it had been his intention to tell all of the men of 8 Brigade together but, since the date had been advanced by 6 days, that was impracticable. He told his men that the task given to them was a good one and well within their capabilities. He anticipated light opposition to the landing, but warned that the Japanese were capable of being reinforced by barge and of counterattacking. Therefore it was prudent to dig well-sited weapons pits quickly and to protect the perimeter. New Zealand and American Air Forces would deal with Japanese planes, but he anticipated that some enemy planes might get through. The natives were "absolutely loyal" and every care had to be taken to avoid injuring them or damaging their property.

Row concluded by saying: "The enemy is a good and cunning fighter. Don't underrate him. He appears in places and at a time when he is least expected. You will have to stalk him as a hunter stalks a deer. I have every confidence that the Bde will live and fight up to its reputation and the reputation NZ soldiers held everywhere, and that our first operation will be entirely successful. Good stalking and good luck to all ranks."[56]

By 21 October Row was able to issue a detailed operations order. He divided his force into three echelons. A first echelon was to carry out the assault and two other echelons would arrive 5 and 10 days later, respectively. The assault was to be carried out by two battalion assault groups. On the right flank of the Falamai-Saveke area, soldiers from 29 Battalion with a section from the Carrier Platoon, a detachment from 54 Anti Tank Battery and a section from 23 Field Company would land on Beach Orange 1. Their task was to capture Falamai, secure the beach for subsequent landings and establish a secure perimeter. On the left flank, soldiers from 36 Battalion with a detachment from 54 Anti Tank Battery and a section from 23 Field Company were to land on Beach Orange 2 at H-Hour to secure the beach and set up a secure perimeter. A composite unit, dubbed Loganforce, consisting of a company of infantry from 34 Battalion, a section of Medium Machine Guns, a detachment from Argus 6, and a detachment from Company A, 87th C.B., were to capture Beach Emerald at Soanatalu and establish a defensive perimeter to cover the construction of long-range radar by Argus 6. The 34 Battalion, less a company and with a section from 23 Field Company, would land on Stirling Island to secure two beaches (Beach Purple 2 and 3) and set up a defensive perimeter. After perimeters were established the assault units were to maintain contact with the enemy by sending out patrols. The 38 Field Regiment was directed to establish its guns on Stirling "with all possible speed" and to be prepared to put down defensive fire on Mono, including Soantalu. The 29 Light Anti Aircraft Regiment was ordered to establish temporary gun pits on Mono to protect the ships and beach areas on both Mono and Stirling. One troop was to be ready to move to Soanatalu on 24 hours' notice. The 54 Anti Tank Battery was to take on an anti-boat role and to cover the eastern and western approaches of Blanche Harbour. The 23 Field Company, New Zealand Engineers, was to help the artillery and AA units establish their positions, to improve the landing beaches, and cut tracks so that vehicles, stores and equipment could be quickly transferred to dumps. They were to use assault boats for the laying of telephone cables between the islands.

Row issued orders for the American support units. He directed that the Detachment HQ Comairnorsols was to establish fighter command, air support control and air warning facilities as soon as possible. The Detachment Advance Naval Base No. 7 was to provide men to land in the first wave and to mark the beaches. It was to establish its headquarters on Stirling as soon as possible and to establish communications with Mono. They were then to provide naval craft for transfer of equipment and stores between the islands and then to set up an advanced naval base for PT boats and a staging area for landing craft. Row envisaged his brigade headquarters being landed on Stirling from USS *Stringham* in the second wave.[57]

The 34 Battalion's objective was to secure Stirling Island. B Company, commanded by Captain P.H. Brooks, was to land with the first wave at a beach designated as Purple 3 at the western part of Stirling. A Company, commanded by Captain A.G. Steele, was to land at a beach designated as Purple 2 to their east and to expand the beachhead. C Com-

Troops land on shore from a landing craft (War History Collection, Alexander Turnbull Library, Wellington, F-41634-1/2).

pany, commanded by Major J.C. Braithwaite, was to land 90 minutes later with the second wave, and presuming that the beachhead was secure, would pass through A Company's lines eastward toward Wilson Point to ensure the island was clear of Japanese. Battalion HQ and Carrier Patrol were also designated to land at Purple 2. The remaining administrative personnel of 34 Battalion were to be employed unloading on either Stirling or Falamai.[58]

The U.S. Navy made four APDs and LCIs available to 8 Brigade for final amphibious training 14–17 October 1943. The brigade practiced loading and unloading stores and equipment and the embarkation and disembarkation of troops at Florida Island.

Peter Basil Renshaw, a sergeant with 36 Battalion, found that his mortar platoon was assigned to A Company, the rifle company it was to support. They boarded USS *Ward*,[59] an APD, and began further amphibious training.

> Landing training took several days. We would load up our equipment and head off to Tulagi Island. At a signal with the other ships in the attack force we would climb down the nets from the ship's side and jump into barges. The barges would then circle around until after a signal they would take off at full speed to slam up on the beach designated for landing training. We learned to scramble ashore and assemble our mortars and train the guns on various bearings. It took several runs to become really good at the drill before we knew we were ready for action.[60]

Soldiers ascend a cargo net rope ladder in full combat gear (War History Collection, Alexander Turnbull Library, Wellington, F-41631-1/2).

Lighter moments were provided by some crew of the USS *Ward*, Renshaw recalled: "A massive and genial black cook served us with the best coffee I had ever tasted at meal times. In the late afternoon, our ship would pull alongside another destroyer and with the bows drawn together a movie screen would be erected to cover the bows of both ships so that we would have some entertainment."[61]

After training, Renshaw and his men returned to their camp on Guadalcanal. There, they learned that they were to be part of an attack on the Treasury Islands:

> Next morning we were called together for a preliminary briefing. Aerial maps of the enemy shore we were to attack were hung in the mess tents and we were told everything that intelligence had gathered about the sector of the beach our battalion was assigned to land on. We were told that this was reported to be heavily defended. Each mortar squad was given a bearing to train our fire on after we had got ashore. Officers were not to be addressed by rank and all insignia of rank was to be removed from uniforms.[62] We were told to cease shaving and packets of camouflage dye were issued.[63]

Renshaw and his men studied aerial photographs and were then briefed by a marine officer.

"We want prisoners," he said. "Prisoners can give us a lot of information that can be useful and we have interpreters who are trained to assess any information we get." He pointed to a Japanese American officer next to us. His Asian features looked so evil after all we had been told about the Japs that it was difficult to realize that he was actually a friendly American. "My best advice to you all is to keep those perimeters tight after you get ashore and take the first objectives and dig in for the night. It'll be a tough landing judging from the information we've been able to get, but you're all going to show those Jap bastards just how tough New Zealanders can be."[64]

Prior to World War II, New Zealand had little in the way of manufacturing industries and Kiwis developed a reputation for improvisation, "making do with a piece of 4 foot by 2 foot wood and No. 8 fencing wire." Worn out vehicles and equipment which would have been disdainfully junked by American units were repaired and refurbished by the Kiwis.

In the lead up to Goodtime the men of 37 Field Park, a vehicle maintenance unit, worked round the clock preparing D-4 bulldozers for the landing. One in particular presented a problem: "A large gasket was required in the hydraulic circuit and nothing suitable was to be found. Finally, however, an old fire extinguisher was straightened, cut, annealed and fitted with the result that the dozer did its job in the landings until knocked out by mortar fire."[65]

Major B.H. Pringle of 36 Battalion recalled that there had been much to do—absorbing plans and information, issuing camouflage suits, and daubing arms and equipment with paint.

> The day arrived for embarkation. Our boats ran their bows onto the beach opposite their respective cargos—already dumped and signposted with their ship's number. Down went the ramps and we commenced the embarkation of men, ammunition and supplies. It was a great scene of activity with the ships lined along the beach and thousands of men busy loading. On our ship we had 200 troops and 16 tons of ammunition and essential supplies. After loading in the morning we had a final practice unloading of men and cargo. This was carried out in 20 minutes and after loading again the afternoon was spent in swimming and diving off the ships. This was the last wash many of the men had for days.[66]

The invasion force had to be gathered together, and the troops, equipment and stores loaded. This was not a simple exercise. Equipment and stores weighing 1,785 tons had to be carefully stowed and 3,700 men had to be embarked.[67] One group of LSTs loaded and embarked on 23 October for the Treasury Islands via the Russell Islands and Rendova. A second group of LSTs loaded on 24 October and sailed in with LCMs on 25 October. A third group of LCIs embarked personnel and sailed on 26 October. A fourth group loaded personnel onto APDs and sailed on 25 October 1943.

The ships of the task force were divided into three movement groups or echelons, according to their speed and roles. Most were to sail from Guadalcanal, but each had to sail at a carefully regulated speed to arrive at Blanche Harbor at the precise time: 0606 on 27 October.

The experience of the men of 34 Battalion was:

> On Sunday and Monday 24 and 25 October, those men travelling on LST's and LCI's embarked. Over the previous few days all the necessary cargo and stores had been rolling down to Kukum beach [Guadalcanal] for loading. Finally on Tuesday, the remainder tramped hot and sweaty from camp down to the beaches, each man with his half pup-tent, cursing under the heavy packs, and with the uncomfortable feel of two grenades in the trouser pocket of the jungle suit. At noon we were underway, up past Savo Island, the Russells, with the other destroyers of the convoy forming a fine picture under the brilliant sunshine. At nightfall, Gatukai, Vanggunu and the outline of Rendova had come into

view. For the officers concerned there were final conferences with the ship's staff: non commissioned officers were seen glancing over maps for the last time. For many men, the hard worn pack of cards passed away the time. It was to be an early rising. Some men slept on the deck in pitch darkness for there was no moon.[68]

The experience of Bombardier Gordon Thomas of 49 Battery, 38 Field Regiment, was fairly typical. He boarded an LCI at Guadalcanal bound for Stirling Island. He noted in his diary:

> We pulled out from the beach before dark, after a practice load and unload, and anchored offshore. The boat was very crowded, and I didn't have a bunk, so I dumped my gear in a corner and slept on the deck at the rear end. I didn't have a bad night's sleep either. When I awoke on the morning of the 26th we were underway and there were about 5 LCIs in our group surrounded by about five destroyers. I don't know where the LSTs or the A.P.Ds were.
>
> The heat nearly drove me mad. There was no escape from it and with the sun's glare you couldn't read, look out to sea or anything. The holds were full of course and it was quite impossible for 40 odd men to move around with their gear on. However, we managed, but tempers sometimes became a little frayed.
>
> All hands had to be below by 1830hrs on the 26th and the smoking lamp out. Even no smoking down below. It was a bastard being shut down there. Reveille was at 0430hrs 27th. There was some "C" rations for breakfast but I couldn't eat. I would have been sick if I had eaten anything, so contented myself with a smoke.
>
> I sneaked on deck at 0420 to have a look around and it was sure a weird sight. All the craft had been launched and another two LCIs were right against us. The sea was very choppy and there was yelling between the craft. It turned out that the time of landing was put back 30 minutes and we were waiting.
>
> We loaded all our gear and stood ready for when the barge touched shore. I had on all web gear, valise and haversack, water bottle and was carrying spade, axe and rifle. At least we carried our valise in our hands too, so as they could be dumped as soon as you touched shore and they wouldn't hamper your movements. We had toilet gear and a days "A" rations.[69]

The men of A Company 7th (NZ) Field Ambulance had a similar experience. On 25 October, they went by truck from their camp on Guadalcanal to Kukum Beach, boarding an LCI bound for Purple 2 on Stirling where their job was to set up medical facilities. Sweating alongside Seabees, artillery engineers and ASC personnel the boat was loaded, unloaded and reloaded as practice for the men. "Heaven sent were the hotboxes of tea which came down from the camp."

As their LCI lay at anchor in the bay, "A little grey ship crept out from shore and from its decks came the cry 'Good luck Kiwis' and three hearty NZ cheers followed by, 'We are the boys from down under.' It gave us a thrill to know that a little part of our little navy was on the job in the Solomon waters. A neighboring LCI sent back three cheers in reply and a chorus of coo-ees and shouts followed the little ship out into the night." The ship was probably either the minesweepers HMNZS *Kiwi* or *Moa*.

> One participant recalled: Cramped and hot is a mild description of our sleeping quarters. In the infinitesimal space between the four high bunks there was room for perhaps a quarter of us to maneuver, so that while that was going on, the other three quarters just had to get on to their bunks or out on deck. Sixty of us, stacked into a space about the size of a large living room made the tropical night a good deal more tropical.

The following morning the convoy sped past the Russell Islands. As the sun rose it beat down mercilessly on to our little steel decked craft. It was too hot to put any energy into cards, reading or talking. Even a splash under a salt water hose did not attract many participants. Dusk provided some relief and the men reluctantly went below apprehensive that the following day we would wake up a in a new world, one of action, work, wounds and death. With gear ready packed we lay in our bunks, clad perhaps in just underwear, talking, singing or just waiting there in the dark for sleep to claim us.[70]

As the APDs left Guadalcanal on 26 October, a large flight of B-24 Liberators flew over the ships, returning from bombing airstrips on Bougainville.[71] This seemed a good omen.

Row and part of 8 Brigade Headquarters embarked on the *Stringham* on 26 October. The remainder had embarked on LCI No. 61 the day before.

On its departure the whole of the Goodtime force received "a farewell message of the kind to which American Commanders were addicted. It concluded 'Shoot calmly, shoot fast and shoot straight.'"[72]

The Goodtime assault force had a naval escort, Task Force 39.3, of the light cruisers USS *Denver* (CL-58), USS *Cleveland* (CL-55) and the *Fletcher* class destroyers USS *Claxton* (DD-571), USS *Dyson* (DD-572), USS *Ausburne* (DD-570), USS *Foote* (DD-511) and USS *Spence* (DD-512) to primarily protect from surface attack. It positioned itself to north and west of the transport groups. In the early hours of Monday, 27 October, the ships did a series of left and right turns at between 20 to 25 knots to make it difficult for any Japanese submarines to attack. The ships were darkened and at general quarters. At 0333 a Japanese plane dropped a flare followed 13 minutes later by another flare. The ships altered course. The Japanese "snooper" then dropped a flashing white float light about 5 miles from the ships, followed by another 4 miles away. The ships slowed to 15 knots, then went to 25 knots to shake their pursuer.

At 0359 the USS *Denver* opened fire on the Japanese plane. The "snooper," undeterred, continued dropping white flashing float lights ever closer. At 0429, USS *Foote* opened fire but without result. The ships varied their speeds and zig-zagged until 0700 when another course change occurred to avoid the LCI group. Having completed its escort mission and being too valuable to be unnecessarily exposed to Japanese air attack, the ships then set course for Port Purvis Anchorage, Florida Island, in the Solomons group, arriving safely at 1819 on 27 October.[73]

In the meantime, PT boats set up a picket line between Shortland Islands and Choiseul. At 0430 on 27 October, the USS *McKean*, carrying Loganforce, left the First Transport Group and steered for Soanatalu.

The element of surprise was critical for Goodtime's chances of success. There were about 25,000 Japanese in the Shortland-Buin area, and using the 83 barges available to them, the Japanese could quickly heavily reinforce their garrison on Mono. Radio silence was observed between the Allied ships, except for orders by high frequency radio.[74]

Although surprise was hoped for, it was not expected. A USMC official history comments:

"Practically every unit venturing West or North of Vella Lavella previous to this operation had been detected by Japanese 'snoopers' (reconnaissance floatplanes). It was therefore considered almost certain that our approach would be discovered during the night."[75]

One of the Japanese prisoners later taken by the Kiwis told his captors that the troops on Mono had received a message from Buin on 26 September that Allied ships were on their way. In any event the Japanese troops were on edge because they had seen signal lights out at sea and were aware of Allied activity.[76]

Communications, Command and Control

A good communications system was vital for the success of Goodtime, and attention and resources were devoted to this. The invaders were operating in an environment of considerable vulnerability — the Japanese had the potential to achieve air superiority, to substantially reinforce their garrison on Mono and even to initiate a naval bombardment. Allied shipping had to be rapidly withdrawn in order to avoid being ravaged by Japanese airpower. Allied air operations after the invasion were intended to switch to interdiction and suppression operations. The invaders had to be able to react quickly to Japanese threats as they eventuated. Anti aircraft guns had to be ready for Japanese aerial threats. The artillery emplaced on Stirling had to be able to lay down barrages on any Japanese troops arriving. Air and naval assets had to be communicated with, especially if a disaster threatened. The radar units set up at Soanatalu had to be able to warn of any Japanese threat to the Cherryblossom force. All of this, in an inter–Allied, inter-service environment.

The communications systems of World War II had advanced considerably since World War I, but vacuum tube radio sets were still bulky, heavy, fragile and prone to failure. They also needed generators and batteries. The more powerful radios had to be carried in vehicles. The radio equipment in the Pacific was affected by tropical dampness, atmospherics and limited range. Signals were sometimes almost too weak to read.[77]

A more reliable means of communication was to lay telephone cable between Allied positions and to set up a radio-telephone network. Although more reliable, this also had its drawbacks: lines were prone to be cut by shellfire or accidentally or deliberately cut by Japanese, islanders or even Allied personnel. A heavy vehicle driving across cable could damage it.

The limitations of communication had implications as far as command and control were concerned. This made Goodtime very much Row's operation and all Barrowclough and Halsey could do was to await developments. Row and his battalion commanders would ultimately determine the success of Goodtime.

G, J and X Sections of the New Zealand Corps of Signals undertook intensive training on Guadalcanal in preparation for Goodtime. They received training in laying submarine cables in anticipation of setting up communications links between Stirling Island and Mono. J Section was reinforced by two officers and 47 men of IMAC.[78]

Row's planning provided that the three infantry battalions would fire two colored signal flares once they had reached their perimeter lines. In the event of danger two red flares were to be fired from the threatened area.[79] Despite having the virtue of being technologically simple, this plan would prove to have its flaws.

Four

The Downed Aviators, the Treasury Islanders and the Japanese

As the date for the invasion of Bougainville approached, the tempo of Allied air operations increased. Allied planes sought to wrest air superiority from the Japanese in the Bougainville area or, at the very least, to suppress Japanese airpower. Airfields, military facilities and shipping were attacked vigorously. The quality of Japanese aircrew deteriorated as Allied air strength grew, but there were still skilled and determined Japanese pilots available. Japanese anti-aircraft gunners were also a force to be reckoned with. It was inevitable that Allied aircrew would be shot down. Given that Allied intelligence told aircrew that the Treasury Islanders were sympathetic to the Allied cause, the Treasury Islands seemed like a possible place of sanctuary. However, to get there, Allied aircrew had first to endure ordeals by fire and water.

The First Aircrew — Peck's Men

One of the more hazardous activities by Allied aircrew was the "snooper mission." Planes equipped with flares would be sent over Japanese-held territory at night and on finding a suitable target such as an airfield or shipping would fire flares to illuminate the target. On the night of 16 June, 1943, a TBF Avenger piloted by Lt. (Junior Grade) Edward M. Peck with two crew members, A.O.M. 2/C Stanley W. Tefft and Ensign Jesse Scott, Jr., was sent on such a mission. Jesse Scott recalled:

> The night of June 16 it was our turn to carry flares. After looking around New Georgia (Munda Airstrip in particular) Vella Lavella etc we proceeded to Bougainville. As pre-arranged, we climbed back of the mountains to 8,000 feet and went into a glide down the full length of Kahili Field to release our flares at 3,000 feet to light up any shipping under the protection of the airfields anti-aircraft fire and searchlights. The other TBFs were to come in to bomb any illuminated targets. Ack-Ack of every caliber opened up on us while we were in the glare of over a dozen searchlights.[1]

The Avenger's engine, hit by flak, caught fire and Peck flew out to sea. The fire was soon put out but the oil lines were ruptured and Peck knew his aircraft was doomed. He would have to attempt a very risky water landing. He crashed southeast of the Japanese-held Shortland Islands.[2] Tefft had been wounded by shrapnel in his left shin. While the plane stayed afloat for three minutes Tefft and Scott got onto the wing, pulled out the life raft, inflated it and were yelling at Peck to join them. Peck was a "by the numbers" type of aviator. He knew he had to follow procedure — destroy the plane's bombsight, dispose of the codebook held in a lead folder and follow the other drills that he had been taught for abandoning a plane. As they rowed away, Peck, who didn't normally swear, muttered "Damn, I forgot to turn off the ignition switches." It was said with such seriousness that Tefft laughed out loud.

Their problems did not end there. When their plane went down they had only a rough idea of where they were. They rowed south to get away from the Japanese-held Shortland Islands and then eastwards towards Allied-held Vella Lavella. The wind was against them and blowing so hard they made no progress, despite paddling for a day and a half. On 18 June they decided to put up sail and change course for the Treasury Islands. Tefft's shrapnel wound was causing him "great suffering." Of equal concern was that their raft was followed day and night by grey sharks which would come in uncomfortably close. One in particular unnerved the aircrew and Scott suggested that the next time it came in close Peck should whack it on the nose with an oar. Peck waited, and hit it on the head with the oar. The shark thereafter followed just out of range of the oar. It stayed with the aircrew until the second night when, apparently disappointed, it went in search of other prey.[3]

When daylight came they could make out Mono and Stirling Islands. There were coral reefs round the island and they made landfall on 19 June on a beach on the southern side of Stirling Island. They spotted a cave at the base of a 30 foot cliff and dragged their life raft to it.

Seeing smoke, they hoped there might be a friendly village and began walking in that direction. They found some coconuts to slake their thirst. Peck left Scott and Tefft opening coconuts and walked out onto a small beach. He met two islanders. Peck later recalled:

"The natives spoke only a few words of English and one of them asked me 'Man from West'? I said 'I'm American. Jap bad, no like Jap.' They must have misunderstood. I found out later that a Jap pilot had been forced down in the same spot a few days previous to our landing. The natives had taken him to a Jap camp. They apparently reached the conclusion that I too was a Jap. They ran off into the bush. I found out soon that they were heading over to inform the Japs of my arrival."[4]

The islanders reported the presence of the airman to the Japanese garrison at Falamai. Given the pro–Allied sympathies of the islanders, the question has to be asked why the two islanders reported the American airmen to the Japanese. An explanation recorded in a contemporary document is that "the Islanders at first thought they were Japanese and they immediately set out to notify other Japanese on the island." When the islanders became aware of their true nationality they provided them with shelter.[5] Arguably, to the islanders' eyes, the sunburned American may have been indistinguishable from a sunburned, olive-skinned Japanese pilot.

Having been told of the presence of an Allied airman on Stirling the garrison of seven Japanese organized a search party. The aircrew meanwhile had moved several hundred yards along the coast, keeping to the edge of the jungle. Tefft had left his hatchet behind in the jungle and went to retrieve it. He could not find it but discovered, to his horror, a Japanese search party had arrived on the beach cutting him off from his friends. Tefft heard the click of a Japanese rifle just as he was about to step out of the jungle, so he dropped behind a palm leaf before he was spotted. Six Japanese were searching the jungle and found the hatchet. Tefft squatted for some four hours in the jungle until nightfall when the tide was coming in. Timing his escape so that a cloud covered the moon, Tefft dived into the water and swam underwater as far as he could. Mercifully, his escape was not detected by the Japanese and he swam about a mile down the beach.

The other two saw the Japanese were well armed, one of them carrying a light machine gun. There was no way they could warn Tefft, so they returned to the cave. The following morning there was still no sign of Tefft, so Scott and Peck began hunting for coconuts. Peck heard a hissing sound and startled turned around to see Tefft, who walked out of the a grove of trees with "a grin on his face a mile wide!"

The aircrew moved to a new cave and rested. Their shoes were badly-worn from walking on the coral. The Japanese continued to search for them and a few days later Jesse Scott had a narrow escape. Peck recorded in his log: "June 22 Tefft and I went out to look for cocoanuts [sic]. Scott started to explore the island, was almost seen by three Japs who were searching the island (a native guide with them saw him but didn't tell the Japs) but hid behind a rock in time."

Jesse Scott told the American author Walter Lord[6] that he had gone out on a reconnaissance, but: "hadn't gone far, when to his horror he spotted three Japanese trailing him about 28 yards behind. "He dived into a large hole in the coral trying to make himself as small as possible. For the next eight hours he huddled there, his gun at the ready for a last ditch fight. The Japanese searched all around but never found him."[7]

Scott recalled that was armed with a Colt .38 special: "A gunsmith in a C.B. outfit in the New Hebrides honed the action and brought the trigger pull down to less than two pounds. I crouched with it cocked for most of the eight hours I was in the hole.[8]

"Late afternoon, they were gone. Scott now emerged from the hole and resumed his reconnaissance, including a swim across the channel for a brief look at Mono. There was no sign of the Japanese on the beach where he landed."[9]

The aircrew decided that Stirling Island was too dangerous and that they were probably safer on Mono, the larger island. Late that night they launched their raft into high and dangerous waves. At one point Tefft was swept off his feet. They worked their way clockwise around Mono looking for a good place to land. They finally picked Maloaini Bay, a secluded bay on the north coast,[10] finding a cave in which to rest for the next two nights. The Japanese were still searching for a lone Allied airman.

On 24 June, Peck and his men decided to risk making contact with the islanders. They found a path and followed it to Malsi where they encountered a group of 30 to 40 islanders on a beach. Peck told the other two to stay back while he made contact. He approached the group, with his hands held out in what he hoped would be understood as a gesture of peaceful greeting. To his surprise they greeted him with a British salute, mistaking Peck for a British "Tommy." Several of them said "good morning." One in particular, John Havea, who had been to a Methodist missionary school before the war, spoke good English. Peck thought it safe to introduce his crewmen, and they came out of hiding. Although the islanders appeared friendly, language difficulties made the situation pregnant with disaster. Jesse Scott wrote, "After getting our life raft, the natives took us to a cave about half a mile away [from Soanatalu]. They asked us if we would like some mates for sleeping, but as intelligence had told us to have nothing to do with the native women we declined. We learned later they meant 'mats,' but that night we slept on the coral."[11]

Peck appreciated the value of circumspection and was very careful not to give offence: "We were very careful with the natives. We didn't talk too much to them because we didn't want to overdo anything or make too much of a fuss. We knew how much the natives feared and hated the Japs. We knew that most of their hatred came from the way the Japs had mistreated the native women."[12]

The Japanese garrison notified Bougainville that there was at least one Allied airman on the Treasury Islands. Sixty-four Japanese were sent with orders, according to the islanders, not to leave until they had disposed of the white man. The Americans did not need to speculate on what the phrase "dispose of" entailed.

The Japanese search party was taken all over Mono by the islanders, while other islanders took the aircrew deeper into the jungle to lay up in a small but well-hidden cave. A Japanese soldier climbed a coconut tree to try to spot the Americans. He fell and broke his leg, hip and arm. The Japanese combed every foot of the island and after 14 days gave up in frustration and returned to their base. The islanders hastened to assure the Japanese officer that if the American airman showed up they would immediately notify the garrison.

To add to his misery Tefft had a sharp thorn in his right leg. The leg swelled up and became extremely painful. On 5 July fever set in and his ability to move became affected. The fugitives began staying at the houses of the islanders. The Japanese recalled all the islanders to the village in an attempt to locate the aircrew. Over succeeding weeks the aircrew was periodically moved — to Mose's father's house, Peter's house, and Ula's house. However, the chances of detection were high and the consequences for those caught offering them shelter would have been horrific. The islanders provided the aircrew with food, salt, "coconut oil for our guns" and two mosquito nets.[13]

The Americans' physical appearance underwent drastic changes. Jesse Scott remembered, "As my lightweight chambray shirt gave in to the ravages of the not always friendly jungle, I discarded it for a civilian dress shirt one of the natives offered. From my long no haircut hair down to my bare feet, I was neither the epitome of sartorial nor military resplendency."[14] The absence of uniform could, however, have provided the Japanese with the excuse, if they thought they needed one, to execute the airmen as spies.

The Americans had entered a world for which they were little prepared. Jesse Scott recalled, "The jungle has continuous sounds, especially for one who does not know that trees get old and fall for no other reason. The droppings of feeding cockatoos sound like something or someone moving nearby. Many dead and live and moving objects fluoresce at night."

The islanders were also a source of fascination: "The natives are every shade of black but do not have Negroid features ... and are not Polynesian ... really Caucasoid as to nose, lips and forehead. The women very casually wore only a loincloth — no tops. This was always a point of interest to young men who had never before been out in the world."

Language was a barrier to communication: "I did learn the native language well enough to converse with those who knew no English. I never did catch on to Pidgin English — maybe a word or two — such as 'Manawa' from 'Man O' War' for any size boat or canoe. The natives called airplanes 'Lo lo hos' but that likely was just a local thing."[15]

Pecks' men were dependent on the islanders. Walter Lord wrote:

> The local Chief Ninamo organized the village to hide and shelter the stranded Americans. This was no easy task: The Japanese were now sure the castaways were somewhere on Mono, and a search party of 24 men combed the area for them. Lieutenant Peck and his men were moved five times the first week.
>
> June 30, and life took a turn for the better. This was the day the Americans landed on Rendova and the Japanese immediately began consolidating their forces in the Central Solomons. All troops were withdrawn from Mono except a seven man observation post. The result was an informal truce, presided over by Ninamo. It was tacitly understood that the natives would leave the observation post alone, while for their part, the Japanese wouldn't look too hard for the flyers.
>
> Both sides thrived on the arrangement. The Japanese proved remarkably amiable, even alerting the natives when their radio indicated air strikes might be expected. Free from immediate danger the three Americans began to relax.[16]

Initially the Japanese garrison consisted of only seven soldiers. They had arrived in late 1942. The islanders' relationship with the Japanese was a complex one, but underpinning it was always the possibility that the Japanese could turn on the local population and slaughter them. The Japanese suspected that there were Allied aircrew on Mono, but they did not know that these men were being sheltered by the islanders. Had they done so, retribution would have been swift and terrible. On the surface the islanders appeared to be cooperating with the Japanese. Since the islanders could not speak Japanese, English was the language of communication between the two groups. All things considered the Japanese garrison's relationship with the islanders was initially quite amicable.

The Japanese medical lieutenant whom the islanders regarded as a doctor could speak a little English and was able to converse with the islanders. The islanders knew about medicines like aspirin and asked for medicines. The Japanese doctor refused but, in reality, he probably had nothing even for his own troops.

One of the Japanese soldiers had money and gave some to the islanders. The islanders gave fruit to the Japanese and got Japanese tobacco in return. The Japanese tobacco was poor and after liberation they were pleased to obtain the better quality American tobacco.[17] Some of the Japanese tried to teach the islanders basic Japanese words and numbers. Boys collecting coconuts from the trees for the Japanese would be rewarded with rice balls. The Japanese were far from home and, like troops the world over, tried to befriend the local children.

The islanders would work for the Japanese for two or three days for a can of milk or soup, a bar of soap or various other items. These would then be given to the islanders' American guests.

The Japanese lobbed grenades into the sea to stun fish, which they shared with the islanders. A couple of the Japanese would also attend the islanders' church services, leaving their weapons at their hut. They were also in the habit of moving through the jungle with minimal or no weapons, guided by the islanders.

The initial seven Japanese returned to Bougainville in 1943 and warned the islanders to be fearful of their replacements and indicating that the new Japanese garrison "sooner or later will kill you all."[18]

As their garrison swelled the Japanese would raid the islanders' gardens for food and destroy banana trees that took three years to bear fruit. The Japanese also showed an interest in the local women and harassed them. This caused friction.[19] They also showed their darker side by whipping the islanders if they were not cooperative or were perceived as not being truthful.[20]

Why were the islanders pro–Allied? The answer seems to lie with religion. They had embraced Christianity and, fortunately for the American aircrew, there were a number among them who were ardently Christian, such as Chauncey J. Estep. He recorded: "They had only one Bible on the island. John (Havea) was the only one who could read but was teaching others to read. They brought it up to us when they would visit, which was frequent, most always would ask us to read the word of God to them."[21]

He also understood, "All of the natives had biblical names.... Australian Methodist missionaries had come to the island and brought Jesus into the hearts of these dear godly souls. The tribe was descendants of headhunters from New Guinea who took Jesus into their hearts and each of them chose a biblical name for their given name. The missionaries had sent John to the Lambetty plantation on Munda for education. John spoke good English, in fact better than we, for he used no slang words."[22]

Religion provided a commonality for men from one of the most advanced 20th Century industrialized societies and the islanders from what was a rain forest hunter-gathering society.

Ben King, 339th USAAF Fighter Squadron

The next guest of the islanders was to be a young, blonde American fighter pilot. In February 1943, 24-year-old 2nd Lieutenant Benjamin Harold King, USAAF, found himself assigned to the 339th U.S. Army Air Force Fighter Squadron, soon flying a P-38 twin-engine Lightning named *Matilda* after his mother.

On the morning of July 17, King was part of a 114-strong fighter escort for a mixture of SBDs, TBFs and B-24s sent to attack Japanese ships in Kahili Harbor, Southern Bougainville. The Japanese fought back. Flying top cover at 22,000 feet the P-38s became involved in a dogfight. King shot down a Zero and then went to help Captain Johnson, who was pursued by a Zero. King destroyed this Zero but was on the receiving end of fire from two further Zeros. Their gunfire raked King's P-38, destroying his instrument panel and shooting off a piece of the left wing. More seriously, they hit his engines. He put his P-38 into a dive but his reprieve was short-lived. He was again attacked by two Zeros suffering still more damage. He found refuge in a cloud,[23] stating in his report:

> While still in the cloud, my right engine also stopped (P-38) and I decided to make a water landing rather than bail out. I continued to skid and dive to about 150 feet above the

water — then yanked the plane around to the right in a violent stalling turn. I pulled the canopy release and had just finished rolling down the windows when the plane mushed into the water — bounced, then hit again and began to sink.

The Zeros had evidently been fooled by my sudden turn, and had to pull on by to turn and come back. I jumped out on the wing and slipped out of chute. The plane was sinking quite rapidly now — I was knee deep in water before the Zeros completed their turn. And as they came in to strafe the plane settled quickly. One bullet grazed my head above the right ear, cutting off my helmet. I held on the wing and, it seemed, I went down for hours, but I guess I let go of the plane about twenty feet under water. Looking up, I could see bullets hitting all around my chute — it seemed like they made two complete passes each while I was still under water. By this time my lungs were ready to burst and I had to come to the surface. My Mae West inflated O.K. and I popped to the surface to see the two Zeros, evidently out of ammunition, flying off towards Bougainville.

To my relief, none of the bullets had hit the rubber boat, so I inflated it and climbed in bringing my jungle kit. I left the parachute floating by itself and tied all the other equipment to the boat. My position, I figured, was approximately five miles southeast of Shortland Island. I knew that the island was well populated with Japs, so decided to head for Mono, or the Treasury Islands. At that moment 2 large formations of TBFs and SBDs with fighter escort passed over fairly low. I stood up and waved everything I had but they evidently didn't see me, so I began paddling toward Mono.

Suddenly four ZEROS appeared from the direction of Kihili [sic]. I jumped over board and turned the boat over to put the blue side up — then partially deflated it to let the yellow sides sink a bit. Two of the ZEROS dove down and made several strafing runs on my chute, about 200 yards away. Luckily for me, they were firing toward the sun and evidently didn't see me. Finally they joined the other two, which had been circling, and flew off at low altitude. I climbed in the boat and paddled the rest of that day and night, seeing no friendly planes.

I continued for the next four days in the direction of Mono Island where I managed to make a landing through heavy surf. That afternoon, July 22 I met Lt. (jg) Peck and his TBF crew of two, who had been there about a month. Soon we were joined by John Heaven, a native who could speak good English and who was responsible for the following two months safety.[24]

King was helped from the sea by islanders. He was taken to Ula's house in the center of Mono where he joined Peck's men.[25] Peck had been told by excited islanders that white soldiers had landed and it was with a sense of disappointment that he discovered it was merely another downed flyer. King, however, was "plenty glad to see us."[26] He was also able to provide the cheery news that the New Georgia campaign was underway and that American forces were only some 75 miles away.

Mitchell's Men, VGS-26, U.S. Navy

The 18th of July, was to be a memorable day for the crew of a TBF Avenger piloted by Ensign Joe David Mitchell. Aviation Ordnance Man Chauncey J. Estep was the turret gunner and Aviation Radio Man 3rd Class Dale Verre Dahl operated the radio and acted as bombardier. The crew of the Avenger bomber was part of Squadron VGS-26 attached to the escort carrier USS *Sangamon* (CVE-26), involved in providing cover for resupply convoys to Guadalcanal. The carrier had docked at Efate in the New Hebrides and its aircraft detached and sent to bolster the airbase at "Cactus" on Guadalcanal.

A large strike by USN and USAF bombers was planned on Kahili for Sunday the 18th, but things had not gone well from the start for Mitchell and his crew. A pre-flight inspection revealed problems with their aircraft, so they flew in a substitute Avenger. The strike by USN aircraft consisted of 50 carrier aircraft, Avengers and Dauntlesses with a 25-plane fighter escort of F4F Grumman Wildcats. The meager fighter escort was to have been supplemented by a further 25 Wildcats, but to the dismay of the bomber crews, the additional fighter escort had taken off an hour earlier and attached itself as high cover for USAAF Flying Fortresses and Liberators. The commander of the strike force offered the aircrews the option to return to base, but indicated that he was pressing on. None of the aircrew took up the offer.

As the bombers approached Kahili at 16,000 feet to begin their glide bombing attack, they encountered a dogfight between American and Japanese fighters. A flight of Zeros corkscrewed up to attack the Navy planes. As Mitchell began his bombing run on the ships in the harbor below, disaster struck. The left landing gear dropped down and locked into place, not only slowing the plane down but also throwing it into a skid and narrowly missing the propellers of an accompanying aircraft. Mitchell dived and released his bombs on Japanese shipping.

Pulling up, Mitchell found his aircraft by itself, a vulnerable straggler. It was soon the focus of a Japanese fighter pilot intent on an easy kill. The first Mitchell knew of the attack was when hydraulic oil began spewing everywhere and he saw tracer bullets flying past his cockpit. The Japanese plane shot up the Avenger's fuselage and wings, the 20mm cannon tearing wide slits. The skilled Japanese pilot positioned himself in a blind spot so that Estep could not fire the turret gun. Mitchell took evasive action, diving, pulling up suddenly and skidding left and right. The Zero attacked again, wounding Estep in his right thigh with a 7.7mm bullet and shattering the Plexiglas of his turret and rendering the rear turret gun useless.

The Zero swung around for a third attack which Mitchell again tried to foil by throwing his aircraft around the sky. He figured that the rear gunner was probably not firing because he could not get an arc of fire, so laid the plane over and Estep managed to fire a burst. The Zero's engine coughed and its pilot broke off. In his desperation, Estep had fired almost a full canister of ammunition and the barrel of his gun was glowing cherry red.

The Zero attempted another firing run but, after a short burst, stopped firing, probably out of ammunition, and headed for home, smoking badly.

The damage had been done, however: the fuselage and wings were badly shot up but, even worse, fuel oil was leaking profusely. Mitchell knew that this plane would not make it back to base, but hoped he could coax it as far as Vella Lavella.

A squadron of Dauntlesses was sighted and a couple of these broke off and joined Mitchell's wounded plane. Dahl told Estep that he had been wounded so Estep came down from the turret with a first aid kit from the bulkhead and saw a single bullet hole in Dahl's jacket in the region of his heart and thought Dahl should be dead. When Dahl removed his jacket Estep saw one entrance hole with blood on his chambray shirt. Still puzzled, Estep asked Dahl to remove his shirt, and as Dahl raised his arms to do so Estep saw that there was an exit hole in his left armpit. Iodine was applied to the wound and as Estep later commented, 'When I put the iodine on the wound Dahl could have flown to Vella Lavella without a plane!" Estep had hardly finished tending to Dahl's wounds before the plane's engine coughed and Mitchell told the crew to prepare for an emergency landing.

Mitchell reported:

> I had removed my gun sight and locked my shoulder straps. When my engine finally cut out on me I just did have flying speed and only about 20ft altitude. I cut my switches and braced myself for the landing which was no worse than a carrier landing. As soon as the plane stopped I unfastened my safety belt and got out on the wing, with my chute on, fully fastened, to get the life raft out of the second cockpit, and the rations before the plane sank. I wanted to get the raft and rations as quickly as possible so if any of my crew members should be injured I might be able to get them out. But I hadn't much more than gotten out on the wing when I saw Dahl and Estep coming out of the escape hatch. The SBDs circled till we had the life raft inflated and were in it when they proceeded for home. We removed our shoes and secured all articles to the boat. We thought that possibly someone might come up to pick us up, so we didn't paddle that day or night.
>
> The next morning, July 19, we started to row toward what we thought was the nearest land not knowing just what islands it was but we thought that we would have wind and tide to help us because it was in a northwest direction. We cut our drinking of water down as low as we could be on. There were two of us paddling at all times. During the night of July 19 at approximately 2300 there was a PBO or a similar type plane that dropped flares near to us, but we made no attempt to signal them as we had heard some Jap planes in that area a short time before and were afraid to give our position away. About 0200 the 20th, to the northwest of us between Shortland and Treasury we saw the exchange of machine gun fire. Then one plane burst into flames and started falling. It fell into a layer of clouds and when it came out it was in two pieces both flaming. The 20th was so hot that we came close to passing out in the late afternoon. While we were resting we heard a loud whistling sound to the rear of us and looking around we saw two very large whales, about 25 to 30ft in length. We were very much surprised when they swam past our boat not seeming to pay any attention to us at all.
>
> About 2000 on the night of the 20th we reached land. There was a very high wind causing a heavy surf. Estep had seen a man killed in a high surf and he advised us against landing until we could see where we were going. So we waited till daylight and made our landing, about 0800 of the 21st, of July. The boat was over-turned but we were able to get all of our things except the chute, my gun and a few rations. We pulled our boat up on land, removed our clothes to dry them, doctored our wounds and looked around. We found some water, of which we made quick work. After our clothes had dried, we took our rations and water and started a search of the island not knowing one thing of the island except that it was land. We had walked around the coast line for about 2 hours when we found a cave which would provide a fair shelter for the night and also had good water. We spent the rest of the day and night there. Early the next morning we started to search the island further. We had walked more than an hour when I found a coconut that had been split in half leading us to believe the island was inhabited. We continued our search around the island.
>
> In another 30 or 40 minutes of walking we came to a little garden and coconut grove that had a little house in it. We walked to the beach and found that there was another island that was separated from us by a channel that was about three quarters of a mile across and straight across this channel from us we could see several houses. We decided to wait around and see who would come over from the village. In about an hour and a half

we heard some noise and some voices down on the beach. I went down to see what it was and found that it was a native. The native could speak enough English to tell us that there were 7 Japs on the island and that there were 4 Americans on the island. Of course right away we thought of a Coast Watcher and thought we would be back to Guadalcanal in 4 or 5 days, so we asked him to take us to the Americans.

He told us to hide there till night and that he was going to tell his people and would be back soon. He got in his canoe and rowed across the channel to the village and very soon five or six natives came over and stayed with us. They told us that we should stay there until after the Japs had gone to sleep, and they would then take us across the channel to their village. After dark they put us in their canoes and carried us to their village, took us to one of their houses and told us to sleep there. About 0400 on the morning of the 23rd they woke up and at about 1000 we reached the Americans and to our surprise they weren't Coast Watchers at all but Lt. Peck and crew of TBF that had been forced down a month before.

Some comical confusion stemmed from the impression given to Mitchell's men that they were being taken to a Coast Watcher. On meeting the other aircrew, Chauncey Estep asked:

"Who is Mr. Ben?" as the natives had told us he was the Coast Watcher. Not so! This young, blonde headed fellow replied "I'm Ben King." I asked "what are chances of being rescued?" He replied, "Why ask me?" I said "Aren't you the Coast Watcher?" He said "Well I guess I qualify, for I sat out in the hot sun in a one man life raft for 5 days watching the coast of the island." Lt Peck spoke up and said, "He was serious about the idea that the sun had baked his brain for he had no head covering." We then all introduced ourselves and told each other our experiences, though Ben's was a little "fuzzy." In a day or so was ok.[27]

All of the American aircrew found themselves dependent upon the islanders for their safety and well-being. The aircrew was periodically moved around the island to places of safety. Whenever the aircrew was moved, islanders following behind swept their footprints thereby removing any track for Japanese search parties. The aircrew was able to salvage various items from their aircraft, including water purification tablets, canteen water, and limited amounts of food. The islanders showed the aircrew how to obtain water from banana tree fronds, and constructed sunshades from coconut leaves. King suffered a recurrence of "strep throat" and used his sulfa tablets. The native doctor anointed him with a ritual solution brewed from leaves to produce a cure in 48 hours.[28]

On August 28 two islanders, John and Moses, came to the aircrew in a state of excitement: they had found shoe prints with markings on the heel. Although they were uncertain, the islanders thought that there were three different sets of footprints. They were found near the village, and there was evidence of "where they had hid near and laid near [the] village as if on a surveillance mission. If these were a team they did a 'sloppy job' leaving footprints, candy bar wrappers and empty ration containers. They evidently had been there since August 25th as a very young native boy had told John he saw someone. We asked John and others to search to see if they were still on the island, if so [to] bring them up to our hut. We thought if [it was] a survey party we could be rescued by plane, PT Boat or submarine."[29]

The aircrew had narrowly missed contact with the covert team landed from the *Greenling* on 22–23 August. Rescue would have to wait.

Life lapsed into monotony for the aircrew. Their health steadily improved and they began thinking of escaping from the island. They thought of signaling Allied aircraft and rigged up an elementary signaling lamp fashioned out of an old coffee can half filled with kerosene provided by the islanders and a wick made out of fiber from a pack. They planned to use this at night but had to be certain they would be signaling a friendly plane. During the day they began to practice intensively identifying Japanese and Allied planes from the sound of their engines. One airman would face away from the oncoming aircraft and another face it. The one facing away would try to identify whether it was American or Japanese, and his companion would then visually identify it. They achieved high levels of success and decided to put their signaling equipment to the test at night. To their utter frustration no Allied planes came near enough.

One of the cultural adjustments the aircrew had to make was to the islanders' diet:

> The natives brought food and water. The water was in Saki bottles and the water was needed to wash down what the natives called tapioca pudding since it was the driest food I had ever eaten. This was one of the staples of a limited diet. We also had what the natives called sweet potatoes which were not of the family of sweet potatoes we knew but a taro family root which was hard to get used to. Occasionally we have fish which the natives got when the Japanese would fish using hand grenades. The natives would bring it up and bake it in a banana leaf in the ashes of our wood fire. The natives showed us where we could gather mushrooms. Once in a great while we would have pea hen eggs which were larger than a turkey egg but they always tasted good.[30]

They also placed a heavy burden on native food supplies. Jesse Scott was thoroughly sick of sweet potatoes by the time he returned to Allied lines, but otherwise he was fit and healthy.[31] He recalled being supplied with chocolate, no doubt obtained from the Japanese. The Americans conserved their canned supplies which they would need if they tried to escape by sailing to Allied lines.

They had supplies of quinine and Atabrine, a malarial suppressant. However, they were not used because the islanders assured them that there was no 'fever' on the islands. Iodine and sulfa powder were used to treat their injuries.

Americans are, by nature, a generous people and the aircrew tried to reward their hosts by pooling their American money amounting to $87.77 and presenting it to them. This was a considerable sum of money given that the pre-war copra plantation owners had paid them the equivalent of 20 cents per day for gathering copra. The islanders were reluctant to accept the gift because they feared that when the Australians returned they would be required to explain where the money had come from. The Americans obligingly composed a letter of explanation and the islanders then accepted the gift. The money and the letter, had they been found by the Japanese, would have been a death sentence for whoever had them — a consequence neither the islanders nor the Americans seemed to have considered.

A curious equilibrium developed with seven Allied aircrew on the island and seven Japanese soldiers manning their observation post. The thought occurred to the Americans that they could surprise the Japanese, kill them and take their launch as a way of getting back to Allied lines. However, Jesse Scott and two of the Americans considered this too cold blooded even though there was no love lost for the Japanese. The Americans knew that it was standard practice for the Japanese to shoot up Allied fliers descending by parachute, to strafe them in the water and often to torture and execute them if they were unfortunate enough to fall into Japanese hands.

There was an additional complication. Western missionaries had taught the islanders that "thou shalt not kill." The islanders indicated that they were willing to overpower the small Japanese garrison and hand them over to the Americans to take away to Allied lines. The plan was that the Americans would then signal Allied aircraft to come and pick them up. However, Ninamo, the village chief, said the war was no concern of his, but peace WAS, and the present arrangement seemed fair. Everyone must keep to his place. Since native cooperation was essential to any decision taken, Ninamo's delicate balance of power prevailed.[32] Estep noted in his log for 16 August, "Plan to kill Japs is stopped by the Chief and the village school teacher." The Americans felt beholden to their hosts.

Foremost in Ninamo's mind was that the Americans could not provide a guarantee of protection and that "when reports stop being sent to Bougainville a force would come over and kill all."[33] Given that the islanders were unarmed except for Bolo knives, and that the reaction of the Japanese to the slaughter or even disappearance of seven of their men would be predictably homicidal, one cannot quibble with Ninamo's decision.

A division emerged within the Allied ranks. Jesse Scott had taken to the native way of life and believed attempts to get off the island would be futile. Dahl thought likewise. King, Peck, Mitchell, Estep and Tefft had other ideas. The Japanese had begun moving through the bush without native guides and this heightened the risk of them discovering the Allied aircrew. Peck's group thought that it was safer to try to reach Vella Lavella in a life-raft rather than stay on the island.[34] The five men drew straws for the four positions on the raft. A four-man crew would enable three men to paddle while the fourth rested. Estep lost and had to remain on the island, where he became the commander. They intended to use their rafts lashed together to paddle the 53 miles to Vella Lavella and safety. On August 20, the islanders gave the four Americans a water bottle, sugar cane, and their prayers before paddling them out two hours after dark. Rough seas and a 10-knot wind filled the raft with water. The storm defeated the Americans' efforts and they arrived back on Stirling Island and stayed at Jame's house, eventually rejoining their comrades on Mono.

The balance began to tilt against the aircrew when on August 25 more Japanese arrived from the Shortland Islands. The new arrivals alienated the islanders by stealing from their gardens and killing their pigs. Worse, they began to move through the jungle independently of the islanders and carried weapons. The Japanese became unpredictable in their movements and the risk of discovery of the aircrew ramped up hugely. It became only a matter of time before they were discovered.

The Americans tried signaling to passing American planes, but without success. Tefft's condition continued to deteriorate and on 5 September, he was given morphine. He began to get better. However, with the arrival of more Japanese on the island the feeling was that time was against the Americans. On 13 September, Peck arranged another escape attempt. They heard a "Blackcat," an American Catalina flying boat, flying southwest of Mono and hoped this could pick them up. This time Peck, Mitchell, King and Tefft were ferried out to the channel in the early hours of the morning by native canoe. They took plenty of supplies, including a lamp fashioned out of a ration can, a wick from parachute equipment and kerosene from the islanders. There, they boarded two TBF rafts lashed together and paddled for all they were worth. The wind and the current were against them and it seemed that they would be defeated.

On September 14 the seas were so rough that little progress was made. Various Allied planes were sighted and attempts were made to attract their attention. Tracer ammunition was fired on September 15 in an attempt to signal some low flying B-25s. Smoke grenades were faulty. On September 16 a dogfight between American and Japanese planes broke out directly above them, with the Americans victorious. Another attempt was made to signal to the planes but without success. They saw a low flying RNZAF Hudson PBO heading north. This time their smoke grenade worked. The Hudson made a right turn, came low over the rafts and made three circles. It then dropped supplies and headed south.[35] To the frustration of the Americans the supplies could not be found. The aircrew continued paddling towards Vella Lavella. At 1500 a PBY Catalina and four fighters were seen but did not seem to see the rafts. At 2200 a lone PBY was heard. This was a plane from the famous "Black cat" Squadron, VP-54, and was engaged in a routine night search in the area around the Shortland Islands. Tefft recalled: "We took the chance and lit the makeshift signal lamp of kerosene and a floating wick. The pilot circled us in the distance looking us over."[36]

Finally, at 2400 on September 17, the Catalina, piloted by Lieutenant Fred Gage of Squadron VP-54, came in close and attempted to signal by lamp. It circled, dropped flares to illuminate the area, and a smoke pot to reveal wind drift, then landed. Peck's group paddled over and aboard. Peck recalled, "When they got us on the plane we were all so happy we couldn't make sense. We were all talking at once and not saying anything coherent. We felt like hugging those fellows in the plane."[37] They were then en route to safety at Henderson Field, Guadalcanal, and would provide the Allies with an intelligence bonanza of their painfully-acquired local knowledge. Stirling was identified as being suitable for a fighter strip with sufficient width for dispersal areas.[38] King returned to combat flying and got his revenge on the Japanese by shooting down a Zero over Empress Augusta Bay, Bougainville, on November 1.[39]

The aircrew had been incredibly lucky. They were on the water for 96 hours and were picked up in open sea only six miles northwest of Vella Lavella. Had they continued their voyage they likely would have landed on the Japanese-held coast of Vella Lavella. American forces had landed in the south of Vella Lavella and had established a beachhead, but that would have been of little avail to the aircrew. They were doubly lucky that Gage and his men decided to pick them up. The Black Cat Squadron was a specialist unit dedicated to flying night operations and illuminating and attacking Japanese shipping. Landing in adverse visibility and sea conditions entailed significant risk and there were squadron standing orders not to do a sea landing without the prior approval of a commanding officer.

Gage had radioed his base and the duty officer could not give permission, as the commanding officer was at the movies. Gage had asked his crew if they were prepared to risk a court-martial for landing and picking up the survivors. They unanimously agreed and, since a storm was approaching, they dropped their depth charges, machine gun ammunition and other non-essential items to lighten the plane for what was going to be a hazardous landing. Visibility was worsening and the swells were five to six feet. Gage was a superb pilot and landed and taxied to 150 feet of the raft. The downed aircrew paddled to the Catalina, were taken aboard, and Gage's crew sank the raft. Gage told the survivors to take a seat and grab something tight, predicting a rough take off.

Taking off from water is a complex business; this one particularly so. Gage could not tell if he was correctly headed into the wind, nor see the swells or the horizon. He had to fly by instruments using the gyro horizon. All told, only five minutes had passed between landing and getting airborne. No sooner was the plane airborne than the message came through from the squadron's commanding officer: "You are not to land under any circumstances!" Gage simply replied, "Sorry skipper, we have already landed and have the survivors. We are on our way back to Guadalcanal."

Gage, happily, was not court-martialled. Instead he was awarded a Distinguished Flying Cross by Major General Merill Twining, who commended Gage for doing what he thought was right.

The men were told by American intelligence that they were the first aircrew that had ditched in the Bougainville–Choiseul–Shortland Islands area to make it back to Allied lines.

The four survivors were in good general health. They had multiple abrasions and cuts and healing shrapnel wounds. They were given a high intake of multiple vitamin tablets for a week, and after 10 days of rest and good food they were all able to pass the medical examination.

That left three aircrew on the island — Scott, Estep and Dahl. The departing aircrew had made arrangements with them for rescue if they got to Allied lines. A "Black Cat" would drop a parachute flare in the bay near Falamai village the night before a rescue was attempted by a PT boat, submarine or seaplane. The trio would then light a signal fire to confirm that it was safe for a pick-up.

Their spirits soared when at 2200 hours on Saturday, September 18, a "Black Cat" dropped a parachute flare. Unfortunately the flare stirred up the Japanese, particularly those who had been subjected to aerial bombardment at Rekata Bay. Rekata Bay was the home of a Japanese anti-aircraft gun nicknamed "Millimeter Mike" and Allied aircraft would be regularly shot at by this gun. Consequently Allied planes that had not dropped their bombs on their primary or secondary targets would routinely bomb Rekata Bay in the hope of nailing the infamous gun. The Japanese in the vicinity became profoundly shell-shocked. The Japanese ran for the safety of the jungle. This posed a huge threat to the aircrew and the islanders hurriedly took them to a cave and posted watchers around them to protect them. The islanders removed any evidence that the aircrew had sheltered in Ulla's hut. Despite the danger, the aircrew pleaded to be taken to Lua Point. The pleas fell on deaf ears because the islanders knew it was too dangerous. The disappointed Americans abided by their hosts' wishes.

Within two days most of the Japanese returned to Falamai village, although a few remained scattered in the bush. The islanders decided it was reasonably safe for the Americans to leave their cave and return to Ulla's house. As a precaution, a few armed with Bolo knives remained close by in case their guests were discovered. The islanders kept close tabs on the movements of the Japanese and concern was raised on September 21 when a lone Japanese soldier started up the trail to Ulla's house. For whatever reason, he turned back. Reuben decided to move the aircrew to the garden near his house. He told them that he would arrange for a hut to be built for them on the opposite side of his garden.

At 2200 hours on Monday, September 20, a "Black Cat" dropped another flare and the aircrew's hopes of rescue revived. The trio hoped that they would be rescued but the islanders seemed determined to build a hut. The Americans persisted in their pleas to be taken to Lua Point and reluctantly two of the islanders, Reuben and Isaac, agreed to take them. On Wednesday the Americans prepared a wood signal fire and waited. There was no sign of any rescuers. Forlornly, they crept back into the jungle.

On the night of Saturday, September 25, an American plane dropped another flare. This time it did not alarm the Japanese garrison, who were now used to flares being dropped. However, to the Americans' intense anguish they could not reach the rendezvous point because Japanese soldiers were busy installing telephone lines to Lua Point and Molowini. They hoped that the Japanese would not light a fire and attract the attention of an Allied rescue party. The islanders told them the reason for extending their telephone lines was that the Japanese were expecting an invasion which they thought would likely occur around October 1. This, at least, buoyed the Americans' spirits.

The Americans settled into a routine of watching dogfights overhead and keeping themselves hidden. On 28 September the islanders brought their guests an Australian flag which they thought could be used to signal Allied aircraft in daylight.

The Americans did see an aircraft on October 1 but they were suspicious. It was an American PBY5A Catalina, but what aroused their suspicion was an American flag painted on the front side near the cockpit. The Americans knew that this was against U.S. Navy policy and suspected that the aircraft was a captured Catalina flown by Japanese aircrew with the purpose of luring the Americans out of hiding. The islanders told the aircrew that the Japanese had recalled all of their outposts to their headquarters because October 1 was the anticipated invasion date. On October 2 the Americans had some visitors from Falamai village who told them that they had seen a PT boat on the western side of the island. The aircrew was skeptical of the story because the Japanese had not fired at the PT boat and Lua Point, the designated rescue site, was on the eastern side of the island.

On Sunday, October 3, the islanders brought further news that another boat load of Japanese troops—evacuees from Vella Lavella—had arrived. The Americans calculated there were now 611 Japanese soldiers on Mono.

A signal flare was again seen. They again pleaded with the islanders to take them to Lua Point, and the islanders relented. A signal fire was prepared for lighting and the aircrew and their island companions waited. Chauncey Estep dozed off, but was woken at midnight by Isaac. Isaac, who was an old man, said to Estep, "Man-a-war, Man-a-war." Estep later recalled:

> I heard nothing but I lit the signal fire for if Isaac heard an engine it was there, for the natives have eyes like radar and ears like sonar. He heard an engine but it belonged to a [Japanese] supply barge bringing supplies and another group of evacuees. Next morning a couple of native boys came, and out of breath, the first I had heard a native pant for breath, they came to warn us a Japanese patrol was on their way to capture us. If it hadn't been for a big mouth bragging we were going to be captured finally. These two natives took off, overtook and passed the patrol to warn us. The natives didn't have time to hide very far from where I was hid. I could have spit on the patrol but they never suspected us being there. As soon as the enemy passed the natives scurried us back to the hut.[40]

On October 5 the suspicious Japanese questioned the islanders when they returned to the village. They wanted to know where they had gone and what they were doing away from the village. The islanders replied that they had been fishing and, to add credence to their story, hung some fish out to dry in the sun.

On October 14 eight Corsair fighters circled above Mono protecting a Hudson PBO camera plane taking pictures of the island. To the stranded Americans, invasion seemed close. In the meantime, they went on with their routines, eating with the islanders, reading the Bible, praying and singing hymns. On the night of October 20 a supply barge arrived bringing 100 more soldiers and two anti-aircraft guns.

With the increased Japanese presence on the island and their more aggressive stance, it was only a matter of time before the Japanese discovered the fugitives. Given the small size of the island, "the men were moved deeper into the jungle, the net was drawing tighter."[41]

Unknown to Jesse Scott and his companions there was one other downed aviator on Mono. He, likewise, was unaware of the American presence.

Flight Sergeant George Ian Luoni, No. 17 Squadron, RNZAF

American fliers were not the only aviators fighting the Japanese in the South Pacific. The Royal New Zealand Air Force waged a vigorous war with a variety of American supplied fighters and bombers. It was almost a certainty that a Kiwi flier would be shot down near Mono.

The experience of the American aviators sheltering on Mono can be contrasted with that of sergeant Luoni, a fighter pilot with No. 17 Squadron, Royal New Zealand Air Force.[42] Luoni flew a P-40M Kittyhawk fighter, a well-built, sturdy aircraft but not particularly maneuverable. He took off on 23 September 1943 from an airstrip on Guadalcanal as number two in a section of four aircraft. Their mission was to act as top cover at a height of 11,000 feet for American Dauntless and Avenger aircraft attacking Japanese AA defenses southwest of Kahili. Zeros attacked the Allied airplanes, with Luoni's section attacked by three Zeros which came from underneath and in front of his plane.

The Zero was famed for being fast and nimble. It was also well armed with cannon and machine guns. Luoni's plane was hit in the oil tank and cowling and oil sprayed over the canopy and into the cockpit. It was clear to Luoni that his plane was crippled. Luoni knew that P-40s, once hit, had a tendency to "go whoof." His plane was losing height rapidly, the "oil pressure went off the clock," the engine was running roughly and smoke started to fill the cockpit. He turned the aircraft onto its back, set the tabs to fly up, undid the straps, pulled back the canopy and bailed out of the stricken aircraft at a height of 4000 feet, about two miles north of Mono. Much to Luoni's relief, the Zeros had broken off their attack. One of Luoni's comrades, Geoff Highet, followed Luoni's stricken machine and saw him bail out.

Luoni pulled the wire ripcord on his parachute and it opened. He had not parachuted before. He recalled that his burning plane "circled around following me until I hit the water."

He released his parachute before he hit the water, struck by how quiet things had become. He inflated his Mae West life jacket and then his brightly colored one-man dinghy, and using his paddle, tried to maintain the same position hoping that rescue would be under way, perhaps by seaplane, submarine or PT boat. Luoni was wearing a flying suit over his shirt and shorts and had a revolver, ammunition and jungle knife.

In mid-afternoon he saw four Japanese aircraft at about 2000 feet coming in from the north. He feared they would see his bright yellow dinghy and machine gun him in the water. He left the dinghy and swam 20 yards in front of it. The Zeros passed overhead and later turned back to Kahili. The dinghy had, meantime, drifted away and Luoni tried unsuccessfully to swim to it. The current was pulling it towards Mono Island. He jettisoned his boots and revolver, but kept the jungle knife. The water was warm and, fortunately, there were no sharks in evidence. Luoni was aware that his Mae West contained shark repellent and was confident that he would be safe.

At dusk, having been in the water for some nine hours, Luoni decided to swim to the island. He stripped off everything except his singlet and underpants, and repositioned his Mae West around his chest. He struck out for the shore, swimming and resting. The current helped him to reach the island.

He landed on the northern coastline of Mono near the Soanatalu River. Darkness fell quickly and he took shelter for the night under a tree. A violent tropical storm shook the island, but Luoni was exhausted and slept.

He woke at sun-up and ate a coconut that was lying on the beach. Surrounded by dense jungle, Luoni decided to strike out towards the west. Because he was in bare feet, he fashioned some footwear from his Mae West, wrapping his feet in the kapok and using the fabric as a binding.

A briefing from the squadron's Intelligence Officer had indicated there were Japanese on Mono, particularly in the southern area, so Luoni knew that he had to move carefully to avoid capture. It had also been said that it was likely that the natives were friendly and a possible source of help. Luoni was determined that "I wasn't going to hand myself in to the Japs." The Japanese had an evil reputation for their handling of prisoners. Sergeant Norman Vickers, another member of Luoni's section, had been shot down over Kahili on 23 September, and was beaten, starved, tortured and later died in captivity.[43]

Drinking water was plentiful on Mono, but food was a problem and for two days Luoni went without food. On the second day he saw a three-man Japanese patrol in the distance and headed for the central hills. He doubted they saw him. Natives later told him that the Japanese were aware of his presence on Mono. In all likelihood, they had neither the manpower nor inclination to mount a manhunt on the thickly-forested island. Luoni's evasion of the Japanese patrol resulted in some good luck: finding paw paw and coconuts growing where the jungle was less dense. For a period Luoni survived on a diet of these but they lacked nourishment. He supplemented his diet with the occasional land crab and fish which he ate raw. However, he got progressively weaker. From time to time he heard Japanese soldiers but evaded them by hiding in the jungle. After a few days Luoni's self-made foot wear fell apart and he suffered excruciating cuts from the coral, which made walking difficult. Luoni's situation was increasingly perilous and he was reaching the end of his tether.

He intended to try to contact hopefully friendly natives on the northern coast, but after several days of wandering he ended up at Soanatalu, where he had started. This time, he moved in a westerly direction along the coast. When he reached the area near Lua Point he chanced across a group of four native men and four native women. Luoni must have presented a fearful sight. He was virtually nude, weakened from his time in the jungle, semi-delirious and could barely stand. They carried him to their village and fed him a large boiled egg and some type of root vegetable which he found stringy and almost indigestible. They were friendly and spoke broken English. They referred to the Japanese as "Demon Men" and complained that the Japanese had stolen food from their gardens.

A lean-to shelter was made in the jungle for him and during the day Luoni would be hidden there. The Japanese regularly visited the village and the consequences of Luoni being sheltered by the natives would have been frightful for them if he had been discovered. The natives fed him roots which were not enticing, but he saw that his hosts were poor and hard up and that they gave him the best they could. They gave him a stolen Japanese loin cloth which helped to restore his dignity.

For Luoni, isolated from his countrymen, hope of rescue must have seemed remote. All he could do was take one day at a time.

Five

The Cowan Patrols

Although the Allies had reasonably detailed knowledge of the Treasury Islands the one thing that they did not know was whether the Japanese had reinforced their garrison — "War is the realm of uncertainty."[1] Row wanted a reconnaissance patrol sent to Mono Island. This carried inherent risks. If its members were captured and tortured then Goodtime's details would become known and the Japanese would take countermeasures. To minimize this risk the patrol would go in only a few days before the invasion. Row sent a memo to IMAC on 11 October seeking a patrol of an officer and six men to contact friendly natives to gather information about the Japanese defenders.[2] Row attended a conference with Wilkinson on 12 October. Wilkinson favored a Coast Watcher with a wireless being landed on the Treasury Islands by D-10 to provide information on enemy movements. The Deputy Staff Intelligence Officer, responsible for coast watching activities, vetoed sending a Coast Watcher. Vandegrift stepped in and ruled that a patrol be sent in. It would consist of four men with diverse skills and knowledge and exemplify the inter–Allied cooperation that existed in the South Pacific war.

The First Patrol to Mono: 21–23 October 1943

Command of the patrol[3] to Mono was given to a New Zealand NCO, William Albert (Bert) Cowan, a sergeant in the Intelligence Section of 8 Brigade. It may seem strange that command of such an important mission should go to an NCO rather than an officer, but there were very good reasons for this. It was a feature of 3NZ Division that sensitive and covert operations were often entrusted to NCOs. Behind the lines missions to Vella Lavella and Choiseul had previously been entrusted to sergeants. The New Zealand Army simply chose the best people for the mission. Cowan commented that during the patrol, rank was ignored and he was regarded as being "the Chief."[4] Brigadier Row offered Cowan an officer, but he declined, because Cowan believed that the officer was not suited to covert operations. (This officer was later killed while fighting with Loganforce and Cowan reflected, sadly, that if the officer had accompanied his patrol he might have survived).

Cowan was born at Tapanui, New Zealand, on 29 November 1906 and in 1943 he was age 37. He was a mature man who had a wife and children. His background in intelligence work, his maturity, common sense, ability to get the best out of people, skills in the bush, mapping abilities and mental toughness marked him as an ideal choice to lead the patrol.

Before the war he was a bushman with the Forest Service and among his skills was an ability with mapmaking and an understanding of terrain. All field officers with the Forest Service were taught how to survey and produce maps. When Cowan joined the Army after the outbreak of World War II his mapmaking skills were recognized by his commanding officer and he was posted to the Intelligence Section of 8 Brigade, consisting of a lieutenant, who would spend some time there and be posted elsewhere, a permanent sergeant, a corporal and a lance corporal. Cowan was an additional member with the rank of sergeant, albeit not permanent. Not being an officer, he laughingly explained, had its advantages: he "could get away with a helluva lot."

Sgt. W.A. Cowan, 1943 (Archives New Zealand, WAII, 1, Treasury Islands Photos, D1, #190, Official Photographer).

During maneuvers in the Kaimai ranges in 1942 Cowan mapped the difficult, dense terrain. His brigadier, Robert A. Row, was pleased with the quality of the maps and showed these to Major General Barrowclough, who was equally impressed.

On Guadalcanal, Cowan taught survival skills to potential Coast Watchers, a scheme which was the brainchild of an American colonel. The concept was to have pairs of Americans and Kiwis operating together. The idea failed, firstly, because the Japanese advance was rolled back and, secondly, the people on the courses were not up to snuff. He was then sent on various intelligence courses, including assessing the suitability of beaches for landing. Cowan was taught to assess gradient, soil compact ability and other factors. He tried teaching these to officers but, he thought, unsuccessfully.[5]

Ray Starr, a soldier with 36 Battalion, later recalled that in September 1943, while on Guadalcanal he, Cowan and five others from the Intelligence Sections of 29, 34 and 36 Battalions had been selected for a three-week training school on mapping, report writing, combat and hard physical amphibious training with the 3rd Marine Amphibious School on the Guadalcanal coast. This honed Cowan's skills in areas he would later find important.

Starr commented:

> We were taught the techniques of boarding and disembarking from both fast moving and stationary craft such as submarines, PT boats and landing craft into rubber boats, then silently paddling away from the ship on a compass bearing to a selected point on a map, all under cover of darkness.
>
> We undertook three separate exercises in the smaller Solomon Islands, sometimes landing on coastal lagoons where we had to penetrate thick coastal mangroves and later into dense jungle with rivers to ford...
>
> At a pre-set time and date each patrol locates its hidden rubber boat and survival gear, maps and reports, paddles into the darkness under a canopy of stars towards the open sea on a compass bearing. After an hour or so we are much relieved when the dark shape of the waiting ship looms up and our party scrambles aboard for a much needed shower and rest after debriefing.[6]

Cowan was given the job of training the 'I' Sections of 8 Brigade. Selected groups were put under his control. Some men he found he could use, but most he could not.

Getting off a plane on Guadalcanal, Cowan was to his embarrassment mistaken for a Coast Watcher by an American Air Force officer. The officer said he knew what the Coast Watchers did and was hugely grateful for the information they supplied and the Allied pilots rescued. Cowan would soon justify the American's praise.

When Cowan arrived with 8 Brigade at Guadalcanal his intelligence work brought him into contact with the Coast Watchers—especially "Wet Robbie" Robinson, who had been involved in a coconut business in the Solomons pre-war,[7] who needed help to handle radio signals and, for a while had two 19 or 20 year old young Royal New Zealand Navy men helping him. He had difficulty handling the machinery and signals and he then had the good fortune "to have an American chap, the equivalent of a corporal, join him."[8]

Corporal Benjamin Franklin (Frank) Nash is referred to in documents as an Australian corporal.[9] In fact, he was an American Army corporal with radio training who had somehow inveigled himself into a coast watching role which was run by the Australian Navy. While Nash was operating the communications tower on Guadalcanal, he had become intrigued by the Coast Watchers' radio transmissions. The Coast Watchers' base on Guadalcanal had no lighting or furniture so Nash requisitioned and acquired things for them. He said he wanted to join them, but was challenged for his limited jungle experience since he was from Colorado, an American state devoid of jungle. However, Nash's skills in improvisation, and resourcefulness in acquiring equipment, his evident radio skills and enthusiasm decided the issue. He simply joined them although a formal secondment did not occur for some time. In spite of his junior rank, and in defiance of U.S. Army regulations Nash, ended up working alongside Coast Watcher Reg Evans on Japanese-occupied Kolombangara as a radio operator. Nash, therefore, had some experience in behind the lines operations.

Nash's motivation to get into an extremely dangerous role outside his own army can be attributed to a burning sense of patriotism, matched by a desire to get into the thick of the action. Nash had demonstrated his bravery on 1 February 1943 when Japanese bombers attacked Henderson Field, remaining in the control tower calmly informing airborne pilots of conditions at Henderson and directing the take-off of aircraft during the most violent part of the action. He brought in a patrol aircraft which was low on fuel, receiving a commendation from Lt. General Harmon.

Sergeant David Ilala, the next member of the patrol, was in the British Solomon Islands Defense Force — a full-blooded Solomon Islander and a natural warrior keen to kill Japanese. He would prove his courage many times during Goodtime. Ilala came from a totally different world from his compatriot, Frank Wickham.[10]

Wickham is described, variously, as being a sergeant major or a warrant officer. He also was part of "that haziest of all military organizations, the British Solomon Islands Defense Force."[11] Wickham was young and good-looking, of mixed race — a blend of European and Solomon Islander.[12] Wickham's family had been traders around the islands and some features, such as Wickham Inlet, bear the family name. Wickham had been a Methodist missionary and teacher before the war and spent some years on Mono and spoke the Alu dialect fluently. He was familiar with the terrain, spoke the local language and knew the local people. Since he was the only one available who knew the island, he would be an invaluable member of the team. In theory he outranked Cowan, but Cowan was 'the Chief' and there were no problems with that.

Cowan was given 500 Australian shillings to be used to secure the cooperation of the natives.[13] This cooperation was at the core of Cowan's mission: "(a) To contact natives on MONO Is and obtain from them information re enemy strength and dispositions. (b) To evacuate intelligent natives to GUADALCANAL to be used for information and guides."[14]

Cowan's primary mission was to ascertain the strength of the Japanese force, their equipment and dispositions. He intended to get this information from the islanders. Without their willing cooperation Cowan's group could achieve little or nothing.

Where to land on Mono? The U.S. Navy wanted to land him on the north side but Cowan insisted on the northeast side. Timing was critical and Cowan thought that if they landed on the northern coast they would "have lost a whole ruddy day." Landing on the northeast side meant that the patrol would be within 100 yards of the islanders.[15] He had aerial photo-reconnaissance photos of Mono, but later commented "the photos did not show the existence of native huts."

There was the possibility of capture, torture and execution. Cowan knew the details of Goodtime in rough outline and that information could be extracted from him under torture. When asked later about this possibility, Cowan said he would not have been taken alive.[16]

The patrol members were clad in jungle gear, but wore military uniform. That, however, would have been of little moment to the Japanese, who would probably have simply tortured them for information and executed them.

Because the patrol's purpose was covert, its members were lightly-armed with short Lee Enfield rifles and knives and carried sacks of food. The group had minimal gear because it would be dropped off on the night of 22–23 October, carry out its mission and be picked up the next night.

Cowan, Wickham and Ilala left Guadalcanal on 20 October by SCAT plane and arrived at Munda later that day. They were joined by Corporal Nash with a large native canoe and taken by PT boat to Lambu Grove, Vella Lavella. There, they were briefed by Captain Pithie of 3NZ Divisional Headquarters and Commander Taylor, USN, and the next day boarded a PT boat, escorted by another PT boat, and left for Mono Island at 1830 hours. They arrived at 0100 hours on 22 October. The patrol was at least half an hour late in arriving because of difficulties in identifying the correct island.

The PT boat carried the six-man native 24 foot long canoe on its deck. Cowan described it as "essentially a large log." At least four men were needed to control it. The patrol members had long paddles but had no opportunity to practice their skills as a team. The canoe was offloaded about a mile off Mono. It was dark, and Cowan thought it got blacker and blacker. They began to paddle vigorously for the shore. To Cowan's consternation the canoe scraped the coral as they surged through the surf, making a considerable racket. The canoe landed "bang, crash" and the patrol members struggled to drag it ashore because the canoe weighed over a half a ton. After a short time Sergeant Ilala said he smelled smoke.

As daylight broke Cowan sent him to sneak around, and Ilala found that they were only a 100 yards from a village. He made contact with three island families who were worried by the noise the patrol had made. It was a surprise to Cowan because aerial reconnaissance photos of the area taken from different angles did not show signs of habitation. The bush line came down to the surf and the natives had used vegetation to thatch their roofs, making them all but invisible from the air. Cowan had serendipitously chosen the site as the place from which he intended to make contact with the islanders. Cowan recalled that "They were pleased to see us and gave us breakfast."[17] The islanders told Cowan about the downed American airmen they were hiding. Cowan had been briefed about the likely presence of Allied aircrew on Mono and been told to focus on his mission and told bluntly not to waste time on the stranded aircrew because they had not been on the Treasury Islands long enough to provide any useful information. Cowan, nonetheless, agreed to meet them.

Jesse Scott recalled that "our natives told us that two of our people had landed at what I believe is Malsi.... Not knowing if this might be a trick of the Japs, we did not go down there but instead told them to bring only one of the white men to us. As the natives brought Bert to our hut my Colt.38 Special with a trigger honed to two pounds of pull, was trained on him as he came into the small clearing. Fortunately for all of us Bert did not have small stature and slanted eyes. At the same time I was an excellent pistol shot."[18]

The aircrew were jubilant — salvation was at hand. Estep surprised himself, having been without good tobacco for some time, by asking Cowan what time it was instead of asking for a cigarette. One of the aircrew complained to Cowan of having had to live on kumara for months.

Officially, Cowan decided to imitate Lord Nelson and "turn a blind eye" to the aircrew joining his men. However, Cowan, "the Chief" was able to say "what goes and doesn't go," and he decided to take the aircrew with him.[19] On a practical level, he also recognized that the aircrew had detailed knowledge of the island. Jesse Scott said, "I was able to locate telephone lines, gun emplacements, etc., and, with the natives' help, locate these on maps the reconnaissance men brought in." Cowan knew of the existence on Mono of a New Zealand fighter pilot, but he was several miles away across Japanese held territory and it was too dangerous to pick him up. In any event, time did not permit it.

Cowan had also been instructed to bring back with him some islanders. There was limited space available on the canoe but Cowan was able to get the islanders to volunteer to come back with him.

Cowan's patrol laid low during the day to avoid contact with the Japanese. He had been instructed to rendezvous with two PT Boats a mile offshore at midnight. Having achieved their mission, the patrol with the American aircrew launched their canoe in pitch black, accompanied by islanders in their canoes, and headed for the rendezvous point. There was considerable anxiety because although their engines could be heard, the PT boats were nowhere in sight. Cowan faced the awful prospect of being caught in open waters in daylight by Japanese patrol boats or aircraft. However, his luck held good. One of the PT boats had a damaged screw and was making too much noise for the comfort of its crew. The captain of the PT boat used radar to try to locate the patrol — and multiple blips appeared on the radar screen. The blips were the friendly islanders in their canoes. In all, Sergeant Cowan and a party of 12 returned safely to Allied lines.[20]

When the American aircrew boarded the PT boat the skipper commented that they had made seven attempts to pick up the aircrew and wondered why they had not made the rendezvous. Estep asked the skipper if he had seen the lit signal fire or the Japanese barge which the aircrew had mistaken for a rescue craft. The skipper replied that he had not seen the signal fire, nor the barge. If he had seen the barge he would surely have sunk it.

Jesse Scott celebrated his return to civilization by having a tin of tongue. The damaged screw considerably diminished the speed of the PT boat, much to everyone's concern.[21] On their way back to their base on Vella Lavella, the crew of the PT boat talked about the ordeal of another boat in their squadron, PT 109, which had been sunk off Choiseul and whose crew had been rescued by Coast Watchers. The skipper was John F. Kennedy, a future president of the United States.

The three members of the aircrew arrived at Vella Lavella at dawn. They were given breakfast, dressed in marine khaki uniforms and flown to Henderson Field, Guadalcanal, where they were debriefed.

Jesse Scott on Guadalcanal after his return from Mono Island (author's collection, courtesy Jesse Scott).

Three of the seven downed aviators. From left, Chauncey Estep, Dale Dahl and Jesse Scott (author's collection, courtesy David Estep).

The reason why the rescue attempts had failed became apparent when the aircrew was taken to Naval Intelligence for debriefing. Estep later recalled: "As I was walking in the room I saw a map of the islands on the wall. To my surprise it showed Lua Point clear on the other side of the island. That cleared the puzzle of the misconnection with the PT boat. I told the officer in charge that their map was wrong. They said it was not. I told them to bring John (a Treasury Islander) in if they wanted. He could draw them a map of Mono Island from memory. They asked John in and showed him the map. He immediately told them that Lua Point was not in the right place and pointed out where it should be located. Intelligence finally agreed their map was wrong."[22]

On such a small matter as the location of a geographical feature on an obscure island in the South Pacific the lives of three American aircrew had almost been forfeited.

An indication of the depth of islanders' feeling towards the Japanese can be gauged from their willingness to let the Allies bomb their church at Falamai. It had taken them seven years to build, but the Japanese had polluted it by storing their ammunition in and under it. The islanders' attitude was that they could rebuild the church. (RNZAF Hudsons later bombed Falamai village but missed the church.)

The farewells between the aircrew and the islanders were tinged with gratitude on the part of the Americans. Estep tried to show his appreciation by "comshawing" anything he could for them. He made the quartermaster and Seabees aware of what the islanders had done. Estep recalled: "Sailors, Dogfaces, and Jarheads made my day. We collected food, calico, trinkets such as rings, watches, gold and silver chains, many other things O! What a joy it was for all these compassionate shipmates to try and repay the tribe for taking care and protecting us with their life if need be."[23]

Back at Guadalcanal, Cowan reported to Major General Barrowclough. Barrowclough was still in his tent and in his pajamas and having his first cup of tea of the day. He told Barrowclough there were 225 Japanese on Mono Island and none on Stirling. He indicated that the Japanese had two 40mm AA guns and machine guns, and set out Japanese dispositions. He confirmed that the population was solidly pro–Allied.[24] After presenting his report Cowan offered to introduce the men who had accompanied him on the patrol. Barrowclough agreed, although with some evident sense of discomfit. The men were brought into the tent and were presented in order of rank, much to Nash's irritation. Wickham, being a warrant officer, was first, followed by Ilala, who stood to attention in his bare feet, and then Nash, last. The general, sitting down to his cup of tea and in his pajamas, was clearly taken aback by all of this, but managed a few words of encouragement. Cowan was tired, having had little sleep. Nonetheless, he shaved and attended a mixed conference in the afternoon. Cowan's information was passed onto all units and the Naval Gunfire Plan was altered to hit Japanese-held areas.[25] Lieutenant Commander Pryce-Jones, of the Australian Naval Intelligence Service,[26] interrogated the natives who were brought off Mono Island.[27]

Cowan tried to convince Barrowclough and Row that he should be allowed to return to Mono. He argued that he could organize the cutting of the telephone wires linking the Japanese lookout at Laifa Point with the Japanese H.Q. near the Saveke River. The general asked why Cowan wanted to return and "was sniffy about the proposal" and critical of it, but finally agreed, albeit reluctantly. A key factor was that Cowan would radio him to advise whether the Japanese had at the last-minute reinforced their garrison.

Cowan purposely did not raise one of his major reasons for wanting to return: he wanted to warn the natives of the impending invasion and the need to take cover from the Allied naval bombardment and to get out of the way of the Allied troops as they fought their way forward. Cowan believed it would be "an absolute embarrassment" if there were casualties among the islanders who had done so much to help him and the Allied war effort. A second patrol was approved,[28] and Cowan was ordered to establish an observation post between Falamai and Malsi and to organize the natives as guides for combat units.[29]

Cowan's Second Patrol: 26 October 1943

As any gambler knows, luck averages out. Cowan's first patrol had been extremely lucky in the caliber of its people, its ability to land safely on Mono, make contact with sympathetic locals, avoid the Japanese and be successfully extracted. Cowan's luck on this second patrol would be mixed. Cowan attributed this to his "bad temper" and in point of fact he had much to be concerned about.

Cowan's first problem was that a New Zealand major was to go on the second patrol. Cowan raised with him the matter of food. The major did not know who to deal with in

Members of Cowan's second patrol, in New Zealand Army uniforms, top row: Pvt. W.M. Gillfillan, Pvt. J.B. Lempriere, Sgt. Maj. F. Wickham, Sgt. W.A. Cowan, and Pvt. C.M. Rusden, and their native guides from Mono, 3 November 1943 (Archives New Zealand, WAII, 1, Treasury Islands Photos, D1, #134, Official Photographer).

the American supply system on Guadalcanal and the patrol was therefore dispatched with insufficient rations. This caused a lot of friction. Cowan considered that the major was unsuitable because of his lack of experience with rough jungle conditions. The presence of a superior officer would also threaten Cowan's command. Cowan commented that the major did not take kindly to advice from a sergeant. Fortunately, the major was dropped from the patrol.

Frank Nash was not available, and it was decided that he would be replaced by three members of the "I" Section of 29 Battalion — Corporal William (Bill) Gilfillan, Private Carl Rusden and Private J. Lempriere. These three were inexperienced in behind-the-lines operations, which concerned Cowan. Wickham and Ilala were to return with Cowan, giving him some degree of comfort.

A radio was provided, and Cowan was instructed to radio Row to advise whether the Japanese had been reinforced. Radios were problematic for behind-the-lines operations because of their weight, fragility, and susceptibility to breaking down. Signal flares were packed so two white flares could be fired at 0520 on 27 October, "if and only if, there has been a major change in Jap dispositions." Row appreciated that this information would be too late to affect matters but "it will at least put us fully on guard."[30] Cowan was told of the details of the naval gunfire plan so that the patrol could "keep well away from the target areas."

The six members of the patrol flew from Guadalcanal and landed at Barakoma at 0815 on 25 October. The intention was that the patrol would be transported by PT boat in the same way as the first patrol. Cowan waited with mounting impatience for the two boats to arrive. Eventually a signal was received that they had run onto a reef, and eventually only one arrived. The commander of the boat for the first patrol had finished his tour of duty and Cowan had to deal with a new skipper. Cowan had problems with the new skipper right from the start, the patrol was late leaving and time was critically important. By his own admission Cowan was feeling "bad tempered."

On reaching the Treasury Islands Cowan struggled to convince the skipper to take the boat close to Mono. The skipper declared there were reefs in the area and Cowan protested that this was not the case. Cowan had to argue strenuously to get him to go inshore. Unlike the first patrol, the landing was to be in broad daylight rather than under the cover of darkness, because of the delays. Fortunately Cowan's luck held, and the patrol landed with its gear and supplies by canoe at 1150 near Havilea Village.

Cowan immediately told the locals, through Frank Wickham, that there would be a naval bombardment. Word was passed around the local population and they were able to evacuate Falamai village to avoid casualties. Cowan had expected that it would not be too much trouble for the islanders to slink away into the jungle, and so it proved. Having accomplished his primary objective of warning the islanders, Cowan focused on his other tasks.

In the early hours of 26 October, Cowan split the patrol into two groups—Gilfillan, Rusden, Ilala and two natives left for Laifa Point, via Soanatalu, to cut the telephone wires; the remaining members established an observation post where they saw two RNZAF Hudsons flying over Blanche Harbor between Mono and Stirling islands and being fired on by Japanese anti-aircraft units. In fact, there were five unescorted Hudsons which bombed and strafed the Treasury Islands. The aircrew reported dropping thirty 500 pound bombs along the south shore of Mono, "starting a large fire and demolishing huts in the FALAMAI area."[31] It is not known if the bombing caused any Japanese or Island casualties. At 1620 the Hudsons bombed Falamai and Saveke. Gilfillan's group encountered Flight Sergeant Luoni, at Soanatalu at 0900 hours but could do little for him beyond providing food and warning of the impending bombardment.

On 27 October at 0400 hours Gilfillan's group cut the Japanese telephone wire at Laifa Point. Cowan posted native scouts to watch tracks at 1115 and a party of 10 Japanese was seen moving upstream along the Kolehe River.

Cowan's radio malfunctioned, and when Cowan's radio operator finally sent a message to Barrowclough, he inadvertently reported that the Japanese had reinforced their garrison. This slip caused Barrowclough considerable anxiety and earned Cowan a chiding later.

"Sergeant Cowan had sent back ... a message which contained the sentence 'NO increase in enemy strength.' By some unfortunate accident, and to the alarm of the brigade commander this message reached the Stringham without the word NO."[32]

The confusion of war resulted in Row and Barrowclough being told by Cowan's radio operator that the Japanese had reinforced their garrison.[33] In point of fact they had, but the 50 reinforcements arrived in the dark and had not had the chance to integrate themselves into their units.

Cowan found himself with "a little army" of islanders, all keen to help. Cowan had rifles and ammunition to spare, but the islanders had no military training, let alone familiarity with modern weaponry. To have handed out .303 rifles and ammunition would be the worst thing he could do. To his embarrassment all of the islanders wanted to eat with him, but there was not enough food to go around.

The radio continued to malfunction, so Cowan had to fall back on the traditional but more reliable method of sending a runner to make contact with the Allied invaders. One of the islanders volunteered to go to the village nearby to see what was going on. Cowan gave him a letter giving Cowan's position and anticipated 29 Battalion would get it.

The islander had not gone far when he saw Japanese on the path, one lugging a machine gun. He reported back to Cowan, who decided to kill the Japanese because they were too close to their observation post. Cowan's men found the Japanese as darkness fell and blazed away. One of the Japanese was killed and the other two fled, leaving behind the machine gun and containers of ammunition. Back at his observation post on the top of a hill, Cowan discovered that three quarters of his island supporters had, on hearing the firing, "decided to go back home to see how mum was." Cowan had lost his army.

On 28 October, when Cowan was dispatching scouts to locate Japanese troops, the Japanese again came uncomfortably close to his post. At 1000 a scout reported that Japanese were "not far" from the post. Cowan told Ilala to go and see what was happening. For some reason Ilala thought Cowan was accusing him of being scared. He threw off his wrap-around, which struck Cowan as strange because Ilala had a brown skin-coloring, whereas the locals were darker, and Ilala could not pass for a local. He appeared to be angry, but set off with a local guide. Cowan expected them to come back shortly with a report about the location of the Japanese. To Cowan's surprise, Ilala returned saying simply that he had killed the two Japanese with a knife and tomahawk. Ilala appeared to have gotten rid of his bad temper, but was concerned that he had snapped the blade of the "fancy knife" he had borrowed from Gilfillan when knifing one of the Japanese.

Cowan asked Ilala what he had done with the bodies and Ilala said they had simply been left there. Cowan was annoyed because the Japanese could discover them and take reprisals against the locals. Cowan told Ilala to go and hide the bodies and to bring back any papers that were on them. Ilala and his guide brought back a rifle and bayonet, ammunition, tunic, wire cutters and a diary.

At 1145, two of Cowan's scouts returned to report about 10 Japanese had crossed the ridge at the mouth of the Kohele River. Japanese troops were clearly on the move. At 1500, Cowan sent Gilfillan, Rusden, Wickham, Ilala and two scouts to Falamai.

At 1600 two scouts returned from Soanatalu reporting that Malsi Beach had been shelled during the morning. The two scouts at Malsi had escaped unharmed.

Having survived Day Two of Goodtime, Cowan hunkered down for the night. The following day, 29 October, Cowan sent scouts out to find where the Japanese were. Two went to the ridge at the head of the river, two to Malsi and two to search the hill overlooking Falamai. At 1245, a scout returned from Malsi reporting that two Japanese soldiers were about some 200 yards south of the beach but, on being spotted, had run inland into the heavy bush.

At 1445, Scouts returned from Falamai with welcome rations and rifles and ammunition.

At 1600, Gilfillan's party rejoined Cowan's group. At 1700, things began to go wrong. One of the natives encountered a Japanese soldier. Cowan, Wickham and Ilala went to look for him. They found him an hour later and fired, possibly wounding him, as he escaped leaving behind his light machine gun, ammunition and a water bottle. Cowan worried about possible Japanese reprisal against the natives.

At 1730 Cowan and Wickham linked up with Kiwi soldiers from A Company, 29 Battalion, who were on their way to Malsi.

Cowan's role however, was not finished. He organized the local people into "Blokes Patrols" which acted as guides for the Allied troops and which were instrumental in locating Japanese survivors. One group of natives offered to help a weary Japanese soldier by carrying his rifle and equipment — guiding him into the arms of a Kiwi patrol.[34]

The 34 Battalion history recorded the appreciation of the Kiwi infantry:

> Directed by Sergeant Cowan who had now shifted his headquarters from a high point in the jungle down to the Malsi village, the "blokes" were out every day, searching the trails and gardens, and coming back at dusk to tell us where the enemy lay, what his strength was and what he was doing. They brought in prisoners. One trick they used was to invite any of the enemy they saw to be paddled over to the Shortlands. Readily assenting, the unsuspecting Jap would be persuaded to lie low in the canoe "so that the New Zealanders wouldn't see him" and to the great glee of the natives, he would then be deposited on the beach at Malsi and taken into custody.[35]

The "Blokes" worked with 8 Brigade patrols to locate Japanese soldiers by tracking them down. On 3 November, Blokes Patrols captured two Japanese, one from caves near Malsi and the other north of Malsi. A day later a combined patrol of Kiwis from A Company, 36 Battalion, and Blokes encountered two Japanese at Akea. The Japanese tried to use a log to swim out to sea. They could not be persuaded to return so one was shot and the other disappeared. On 5 November a Blokes Patrol captured two Japanese in a canoe and delivered them to New Zealand lines.

By 8 November, the Blokes had performed their role and were disbanded. Cowan rewarded them with bags of rice and food, but their motivation for helping lay with their dislike of the Japanese, who had raided their gardens and mistreated their people.

Two things are striking about the Blokes Patrols. The first is that the islanders had no military training and they were not used in a combat role. Their skills in tracking and local knowledge were used by Kiwi soldiers to locate and eliminate Japanese soldiers. The second is the islanders' willingness to take Japanese prisoners, albeit often by guile, and the willingness of Japanese soldiers to entrust their fates to the natives.

Overview

The Cowan patrols were carried out without loss to their personnel or the local people. That could easily disguise the fact that the patrols were high-risk endeavors with the odds heavily weighted against them. They were put together hurriedly. Some different personnel were used on the two patrols and there was inadequate time for the soldiers to get to know each other and to build up trust. The personnel were all relatively inexperienced in behind-the-lines operations and had not been in combat with the Japanese, let alone jungle fighting. With the exception of Wickham they were unfamiliar with the ground. Put simply, they were inadequately prepared, lacking detailed maps, and were provided with only basic equipment.

They were not clad in any special camouflage gear and were traveling light, so that if Goodtime had been postponed then they would have been in difficulties. On both occasions the patrols were landed on Mono haphazardly, once in darkness and once in daylight. They faced thick, dense jungle with only limited paths and an enemy growing in strength and moving around the jungle. The chances of discovery were high. The Japanese had established observation posts equipped with high-powered binoculars. Their defenses dotted the southern area of Mono. Reinforcements continued to arrive and the larger the number of Japanese defenders the greater the risk of the patrol encountering them. The lack of detailed knowledge of Japanese defenses and their location endangered the safe insertion and extraction of the first patrol.

The Cowan patrols were not "suicide missions" simply because provision had been for the first patrol to be picked up, and it was anticipated that invading forces would link up with the second. Nonetheless, both patrols were extremely hazardous affairs.

Each patrol had different stated objectives, which were achieved. The first was to find out whether the Japanese had been reinforced and, if possible, to find out the strength of their defenses and to bring back some local people to act as guides. The second patrol was to cut the Japanese telephone link at Laifa Point and to alert invading forces whether the Japanese had reinforced the defenders. Cowan had, of course, as his undeclared purpose to warn the local people of the impending invasion and of the potentially devastating naval bombardment.

The first patrol gleaned information from the local people. Cowan's men were not able to cover much ground — they had to hide from the Japanese and avoid contact at all cost — so he relied on the islanders to gather intelligence for which they had no training. Cowan was able to establish that the Japanese had not been significantly reinforced, but he did not know some reinforcements had arrived. Nor was Cowan able to discover the existence of a Japanese machine gun post on Stirling Island.

The second patrol was intent on cutting the Japanese telephone link between Laifa Point and the main Japanese headquarters. However, the Japanese had been alerted by their snooper planes to the invasion force, and the headquarters on Mono broadcast the news of the Allied landings at Falamai.

Cowan's warning of the impending invasion was successful. The islanders moved out of the combat zone and many found shelter in caves in the northern part of the island. He potentially saved a lot of innocent lives and kept faith with the islanders.

He and his men, with the assistance of the "Blokes," were able to monitor Japanese movements and report these to his superiors. The Blokes were especially useful in guiding Allied patrols tracking Japanese stragglers and taking prisoners.

Most importantly, Allied casualties were avoided, all the patrol members living to fight another day. This is in contrast to the Makin Raid in August 1942 where at least nine American USMC Raiders were left behind and captured by the Japanese because of command foul-ups and the difficulties of getting rubber boats through the surf. All nine were executed.[36] On Hauwei on the Admiralty Islands, on 11 March 1944, a 26-man reconnaissance patrol was ambushed and cut to pieces.[37] The Australian Army also experienced failure in April 1945, with Operation Copper when a reconnaissance patrol of eight highly-trained men, "Z Special Commandos," encountered Japanese defenders on the island of Muschu, off the New Guinea coast. Only one survivor made it back to Allied lines.[38] Overall both Cowan patrols were incredibly lucky, and the support of the Treasury islanders was integral to that luck.

There was always a risk that the patrols could have been captured and the Japanese tipped off about the impending invasion. If that had occurred it would have enhanced the diversionary effect of Goodtime, albeit at the cost of Allied casualties.

Six

Invasion: 27 October 1943

The task force arrived off the Treasury Islands in the early hours of 27 October 1943. Heavy rain and overcast skies obscured the islands. The ships moved slowly through the darkness until the flat outline of Stirling Island could be discerned. At 0540, the eight APDs of the First Transport Group hove to 1300 yards from Stirling's Cummings Point at the southern entrance to Blanche Harbor. Below decks the men of the first wave finished breakfast, began putting on their webbing, and loaded their weapons. Orders were given to disembark into the landing craft. On Frank Cooze's ship he noticed that soldiers milled about the deck with their tins of breakfast. "Each man had a tin of beans or hash with a mug of tea. There was no visible excitement but many of us threw our tins overboard with most of the contents untouched."[1]

H-hour was set for 0606 hours but was delayed by 20 minutes because the APDs were running late. This was perhaps due to inaccuracies in the charts, possibly "adverse currents,"[2] or even faulty navigation because "the radar of Admiral Fort's flagship had given a false range, probably due to a rain squall."[3]

A spotter plane sent from Munda circled Blanche Channel as the First Transport Group arrived. It had been designated to observe enemy targets and radio corrections for naval barrages.

A sweep was carried out by the minesweepers to ensure that the channel had not been mined. The invasion force then formed up. It grew lighter, and Mono Island came into view. According to one account:

> High overhead two planes wheeled and banked. They might be ours, they might be the enemy. Men of the first wave were now on deck, standing by their boat stations. The destroyers hove to. It was drizzling slightly. "Lower all boats!" and the swift landing craft slipped down their davits into the sea. In piled the troops. "Shove Off!" With a roar the craft sped away. It was getting lighter every minute. From all the destroyers the assault boats could be seen pulling away, headed for the entrance to Blanche Harbor.[4]

The USS *Eaton* took station four miles off the harbor as a Fighter Director Ship. Her companions the destroyers USS *Pringle* and *Philip*,[5] armed with 5-inch guns, commenced a bombardment of Mono Island at 0545 hours.[6] "Tons of high-explosive shells careered through the sky towards the enemy positions on Mono, the tracers weaving a weird pattern in the half-light of early morning."[7] Unfortunately, most of the shells overshot and landed

Six: Invasion: 27 October 1943

The invasion fleet stands by while destroyers shell shore positions, 27 October 1943 (Archives New Zealand, WAII, 1, Treasury Islands Photos, D1, #14A, Official Photographer).

in the sea or on Watson Island, which received "a fair plastering."[8] The naval bombardment was problematic under the best of circumstances because of close vegetation and uncertainty of precise Japanese positions.

The limited visibility compounded the problem — and the plane designated as an aerial spotter had radio failure.[9] The narrow waters and coral reefs of the Blanche Channel restricted the ability of the destroyers to get in close. They therefore had to stay to the west. Their firing was directed at pre-arranged targets and while the *Pringle* had a tendency to overshoot, it nonetheless laid down reasonably effective fire on the pre-designated target area. The gunfire from the *Philip* was considered disappointing "in accuracy, timing and quantity."[10] Fort later commented, "During the early counter battery, there appeared to be some wild shooting by PHILIP due to a fire control casualty."[11]

Frank Cooze doubted the accuracy of the bombardment: "The destroyers in the van plummeted shell after shell into the jungle but we could see no signs of damage. There was nothing to concentrate on. It was a case of firing indiscriminately into the jungle and trusting to luck that some damage would be done. If nothing else it kept the Japs quiet until we landed."[12]

For the Japanese the bombardment was the culmination of alarms and orders to go to battle stations that had begun on the night of 26 October with the sighting of signal flares and lights in Blanche Channel. Initially the flares and lights were dismissed as false alarms and the Japanese simply manned their defensive positions. The alarms began again in the early hours of 27 October when the Japanese again went to battle stations. A Japanese sailor manning an observation post noted in his war diary that at 0345 (Tokyo time), they had received shellfire but there had been no damage to his post due to the squall.

The most unfortunate Japanese were those at Falamai village who had arrived from Buin that morning. This group of 50 arrived without weapons and had not been assigned to formations. They had traveled from Japan to Rabaul to Buin and thence to Mono. They had been sent in expectation of an Allied attack. They had the misfortune to be in the area of the naval bombardment as Goodtime began.[13]

John Matehasi recalled that on the morning of 27 October he and other islanders had taken shelter in caves miles away. "We saw aircraft and ships, but never heard anything until our six men [those that had been taken off with Cowan's first patrol] returned to say be careful of retreating Japanese in the jungle."[14]

At 0623, some three minutes before the first assault was due to land, the destroyers ceased fire. The *Pringle* patrolled to the west of Blanche Harbour while the *Philip* patrolled to the south of Stirling Island. In reality, the naval gunfire was firing blind with low-caliber weaponry unlikely to do much damage to Japanese positions unless there was a direct hit. The probability is that the naval gunfire suppressed the Japanese defenders temporarily. One Japanese prisoner, Seaman First Class Gosaburo Ishiura, who had manned an observation post at Falamai, disclosed to his captors "that on the morning of 27 October positions were manned, but apparently the naval bombardment drove the troops out at least temporarily as his position was empty when he reached it."[15]

Whilst the destroyers ceased fire at H-hour minus four minutes, LCI (L) gunboats blazed away as the first wave approached the beach.

The first wave consisted of troops from the APDs at 0626 which anchored in Blanche Harbour and began disgorging their assault troops. The smaller LCIs were swung out from the decks of their mother ships and the troops clambered down the rope cargo nets draped over the side into the LCIs awaiting them. The repetitive training on rope cargo nets paid dividends because this process was accomplished in a rapid and orderly fashion. By 0800, the APDs had completed off-loading 1600 troops and 80 tons of supplies and rapidly departed for Guadalcanal, escorted by the USS *Conway* and USS *Renshaw*.

At 0600, fighter cover by 32 Allied planes took station over the Treasury Islands. Aircraft were seen by the invading troops circling over Blanche Harbour and to their immense relief the RNZAF roundels were made out on the wings.[16]

Invasion: H-Hour, M-Minute

The landing craft formed up and began to move two miles into Blanche Harbor to their designated beaches, forming into two columns, and began their race to the Falamai Village beaches. The troops crowded into the LCIs were vulnerable to the weather and enemy fire. It was intended that the assault wave and LCI gunboats should pass close to

Stirling Island on their right until they reached Watson Island. Stirling Island was thought to be free of Japanese troops and artillery. However, as the first wave passed Cummings Point, on the northern tip of Stirling, Japanese machine gun fire hit the LCIs. Five USN and eight Kiwis were wounded; one officer later died. There was little the troops in the LCIs could do other than hunker down.[17] The later waves landing on Stirling Island would find the island empty. It is thought the Japanese troops crossed by canoe to Mono Island.

During the run to the beach on Mono the landing craft were deluged with rifle, machine gun, mortar and mountain gun fire. Robert Dunlop, a private in A company, 36 Battalion, recalled: "We were under fire as we came in, and I can remember looking around and thinking it was quite interesting until I looked at the side of the LCI, and like a sewing machine, splinters started flying off the side of the LCI. I got down and was almost at the same level of the keel after that."[18]

Dunlop remembered that the LCIs were made of wood and therefore offered little protection against Japanese fire.[19]

Jeff Tunnicliffe of 36 Battalion recalled trying to keep his head down and that the coxswain on his landing craft was shot. Another crew member took over and gunners returned fire.[20]

Major B.H. Pringle of 36 Battalion observed of the first wave that "coming in, they had some narrow escapes from enemy small arms fire — the bullets (went) through these light boats and through some of the men's equipment. One of our Platoon Leaders, 2 Lt. Grant Williams, one of the best, was mortally wounded before reaching the shore. Some of the American coxswains were also wounded but gamely landed their boats, wished our boys good-luck as they jumped out, and away the boats went back to their ships."[21]

Supporting the landing craft were two LCI(G) gunboats. These hybrid landing craft were armed with a 3-inch gun on the forward deck, two 20mm guns mounted on the port and starboard sides, a 40mm gun aft, a 40mm gun on the forward deck house and two 20mm guns in the front of the control position. They were maneuverable and packed a considerable punch. One gunboat took position in the front of the first wave and the other on the flank. As one rounded Watson Island it knocked out a 40mm twin-mount gun on the landing beach between the Saveke River and Falamai Point.[22] The gunboats tried to suppress Japanese fire and is thought they destroyed several machine guns and bunkers.[23] Tracer fire streamed from the light guns and for the watching troops it made a great sight.[24] However, this was the first time that such naval craft had been used, and things did not go totally smoothly. Their fire held up 36 Battalion's advance on its left flank.[25]

Row recorded: "The close support rendered by the LCI Gunboats undoubtedly kept down casualties during the assault. These boats protected the left flank of the first wave and in addition shot at opportunity targets. One of them proceeded past Falamai Peninsula and raked that area with fire just prior to the landing (of the) 29th Battalion."[26]

The beneficial effects of the gunboats are even more remarkable when it is taken into account that their crews had not been given the opportunity to train and hone their skills. Goodtime was to be "on the job training."[27]

Private E.A. (Ashley) James, of 29 Battalion, had been offloaded into a landing craft from an APD, USS *Talbot*. The landing craft had two machine guns at the front manned by sailors. "One of the gunners appeared to be having trouble with his gun while we were heading for the beach. Our officer said to the gunner, 'Will I use my Bren?' but the gunner took not the slightest notice of the officer and went on working at his gun and had it going properly when the time came to open fire."[28]

The Padre of the 29th Battalion was Owen Baragwanath ("Bags"), a tall, well-built man. He found himself an unarmed passenger crammed in with other troops in a landing craft in the first wave. As the craft surged towards Mono he found one of his non-churchgoing companions huddling behind him using him as a shield from Japanese fire.

The landing craft carrying the assault troops from 29 and 36 Battalions beached on Orange Beach between Saveke River and Falamai at 0626 hours. The gunboats continued to supply suppressive fire after the troops had landed.

When Jeff Tunnicliffe landed machine guns opened up on the landing area and bullets zipped over his head. He was instructed to get down. He thought it was like "going over the top." He felt especially vulnerable because in addition to his Lee Enfield rifle he had 6 mortar bombs (3 high explosive and three smoke) in his webbing. A stray bullet would have had spectacularly fatal consequences. The orders were to move forward to higher ground in the expectation that the Japanese would fall back.

An opposed amphibious assault is, by its very nature, an exercise in controlled chaos. An official New Zealand history observed:

> The written word is scarcely able to convey a total picture of an opposed landing. So much is happening in so short a time in so many places. Noise predominates—an unholy orchestra made up of the crack of rifle fire and the stutter of machine guns; the crunch of exploding mortar bombs and the angrier bursts of artillery shells. Bullets hiss and spit, fragments of shell ping and whine; the regular beat of moving vehicles and machinery and the throbbing engines of the landing craft are almost lost in the confusion. Still the men in camouflaged jungle dress continue to disembark and the emptied landing craft leave the beaches to make way for those following them. Movement is swift and continuous as each man accomplishes his appointed task. No one has time to see the waves gently and regularly removing footprints hurriedly trodden in the sand.[29]

The word "beach" conjures up images of soft, golden sand and palm trees gently swaying in the breeze. If the troops from 36 Battalion assaulting Orange Beach had any such preconceptions they were rapidly disabused. The beach was gravel. This was a shock for Allan Rogers, a Kiwi infantry officer who slipped on slimy rocks as he came ashore.[30] Perversely, the gravelly nature of the beach made it attractive to the Goodtime planners because it meant that it was better able to bear the weight of the LSTs. Private Dunlop also recalls the wet rocks were slippery and boulders impeded progress.[31]

The beach was a compact strip with thick vegetation bordering it. This was an attractive feature for planners who anticipated stores and equipment could be rapidly moved off the beach by bulldozers and thereby away from aerial attack. For the assaulting troops, however, the vegetation simply hid the Japanese defenders.

Orange Beach was an obvious landing site and the Japanese had set up three machine gun positions. To take the beachhead it was vital that these be eliminated and this was done swiftly. The initial Japanese opposition was comparatively light, with light machine gun and rifle fire coming from the left flank, because they had pulled back due to the naval bombardment. Casualties in the first wave were thankfully light, and the invaders were able to get ashore in relatively good order.

A soldier with 4 RASC recalls being transferred from the swaying decks of an APD to an LCT and then making the dangerous journey to shore with the first wave: "They were having pot shots at us with mortars and artillery. Most of the Japanese stuff was short range. They had the range to the beach measured. Where we landed was a sandy beach where the Japanese had their camp. It was rocky further round. On landing we did not know where we were going to. We were led or told where to go. You need a bit of luck in life. We began unloading by hand. There were no tracks but we made our way through plenty of coconut trees."[32]

Peter Renshaw spent the night on the deck of an APD, despite the hazards of being swept overboard, and was awoken by the naval gunfire:

> We were able to snatch a quick cup of coffee before the order was sounded "away all boats." We scrambled down the nets to steady ourselves before jumping into the boats. For the first time in my life I felt fear. It was something I thought would paralyze me. Fire from the shore began to crackle around the boat as we circled around before starting our run for the shore. We could see a line of hills ahead as the boat picked up speed and began its run in to the beach. Nothing can describe the sheer terror of an attack like the landing on a hostile shore. Bullets whistled around as the boat slowed to slam up on the shore and

B Company, 36 NZ Bn., 3-inch mortar section shoot on Mono Island, 1943 (Archives New Zealand, WAII, 1, Treasury Islands Photos, D1, #138, Official Photographer).

we all flinched as the bow was lowered and we scrambled ashore. It was too late to think about anything but the job we had all been trained to do. The noise was deafening as the fire from the Jap guns and ours intermingled. My job was to get the crates of mortar bombs ashore and on site for each gun crew. "Come on for Christ's sake and get those plates in place," I heard one of the sergeants call out. Then our mortars started to fire putting up a steady barrage ahead of the rifle companies. While we were firing, the Jap artillery sited up on the hill was giving the unloading parties further along the beach a hard time.[33]

"A" Company from 36 Battalion did not establish a beach head, moving forward on the orders of their company commander and across the river. The intention was to work around the Japanese flank. Mortars under Lt. Tom Holmes were quickly set up and began pounding the Japanese positions to good effect. The assault troops moved forward. There was, however, a price to be paid and it became due very swiftly. The American destroyers were providing close in support and began firing barrages to suppress or eliminate the Japanese defenders. But they did not realize New Zealand troops had moved so far forward, and shells began landing among them. Several, including Sergeant Gregory, were killed.[34]

To compound matters, bullets seemed to be coming from all directions. Dunlop recalls: "I saw the fellow next to me — in front of me — with a whole lot of bullets run up his back. They were machine gun bullets, so it must have been Japanese firing from behind us. That night when I took my clothes out of my haversack I found a shirt with one of the sleeves in tatters."[35]

The *Pacific* records that "A and B Companies of 36 Battalion disappeared into the dense undergrowth between the Saveke River and Cutler's creek, A Company under Captain K.E. Loudon being temporarily held up by the gunboat's stream of tracer, though it went in later to rout out Japanese headquarters 500 yards west of the Saveke River."[36]

The 29 Battalion landed to the right of Falamai village where the beach was more sandy, and pushed inland. For Private James, his landing on Mono was almost anti-climatic. He recalls: "After crossing the beach and getting among the first houses and trees the pace of the advance was slow and cautious." He attributed this to

> the fact that a few days before we left Guadalcanal for Mono we were told that B Coy could expect heavy casualties and so far that had not happened. After we were ashore everything was quiet at that stage. At Guadalcanal we were shown low level aerial photos of the place where we would be landing and the village behind. A small pillbox made of stones was plainly visible; a Japanese soldier was standing beside the box looking up at the photograph. When we hit the beach the pillbox was there almost in front of us. Sergeant Strang entered it through the back entrance to check it out but there was no one there.

"B" Company cleared Falamai village and then assaulted the native cemetery which was captured "after a fierce assault upon its occupants, all of whom had been dead for many years. Not satisfied with these efforts, later parties also poured fire into the mounts and piles of stones that were NOT Japanese weapon pits."[37] Light opposition was encountered from Japanese in gun pits around the village and these were soon taken.

"C" Company pushed into the Falamai Peninsula to a point below Bryant's Brook. The Japanese defenders had fled along the Malsi trail before it arrived.

"A" Company made a flanking move on the left flank from Cutlers Creek to the Kolehe River. There was no resistance there either.

Six: Invasion: 27 October 1943

Second wave troops of 29 NZ Battalion land under fire from an LCI at Orange 1, Mono Island, 27 October 1943 (War History Collection, Alexander Turnbull Library, Wellington, F-44798-1/2).

Ironically, "D" Company, the reserve company, was to come under heavier fire than its compatriots. It landed in the rear of "B" Company, set up its headquarters at Cutlers Creek and came under mortar and mountain gun barrages as it stated to unload equipment.

The first wave of assault troops landed and headed for the treeline. Their LCIs returned to mother ships for more troops. As the second wave of LCIs approached the beach, USN crew manning the machine guns was receiving fire. They saw movement in the treeline area and began machine gunning it.[38] The Kiwi soldiers ducked for cover, but the "friendly" fire began causing casualties. A Kiwi officer on shore grabbed a rifle from one of his soldiers took aim at the U.S. crewman machine gunning his men. Before he could pull the trigger, the crewman stopped firing.

Frank Cooze recalled his introduction to Mono:

> With its guns firing into the bush our barge crept in between two islands to be met by a stream of tracer which streaked in front of us. I had visions of being cut off in my prime, but a few well directed shots silenced the Jap — much to my relief.
>
> The barge grounded on Mono Island and the ramps clanked on the sand. We streamed

off at the double to cries of "Let's go.... Come on. Let's Go!" from the barge crew who were anxious to unload and depart before the Jap bombers became too inquisitive.

The infantry made their way into the jungle while we dropped our packs and returned to the barge. We filed up one ramp, grabbed a box and scurried down the opposite beach in Unit dumps.[39]

A Japanese gun a short distance along the beach began to cause concern. A group from Les Taylor's Carriers Platoon was ordered to board an LCI and deal with it. His diary records: "As we charged in from the sea we grounded on a coral reef about 200 meters out and looking straight down the barrel of the mountain gun in its fortified position. It was our lucky day as the Japs had fled and it took us some 20 minutes before we got free and captured the gun which we dismantled and brought back to Falamai."[40]

George Hodgson, a 2nd lieutenant and commander of the Recce Platoon of 8 Brigade, recalled small waterspouts erupting around his landing craft as it nosed towards Mono. He landed in the first wave on Orange Beach with his sergeant and corporal. They landed in the 29th Battalion area with the mission of finding a suitable area to deploy the unit's

The 8 NZ Brigade group lands on one of the Treasury Islands, 27 October 1943. Note the LCI on the beach between Orange 1 and Orange 2, Mono Island, in the background. The 29 NZ Battalion prepares to attack Japanese positions ashore. A dead New Zealand soldier lies in the foreground (War History Collection, Alexander Turnbull Library, Wellington, F-41854-1/2).

six Universal Carriers (Bren gun carriers) which were due to arrive in the second wave. The group found itself under Japanese fire.

Hodgson was ordered by Brigadier Row to take his Bren gun carriers and carry out a flanking move across the Falamai Peninsula to prevent the Japanese defenders from escaping. He was dubious about this order, regarding it as a "suicide job" because his open-topped tracked vehicles got easily bogged down and were highly vulnerable to Japanese grenades and snipers—as the Australians had discovered at Buna in New Guinea.[41] Hodgson's men tried to drive the Carriers into the jungle to outflank the Japanese, but their way was barred by a mangrove swamp.[42] Far from disappointed, he suggested to Row that the carriers instead be used to haul boxes of ammunition, even though it was not a particularly efficient vehicle for hauling supplies. For the next two days this was what they did.

There were some narrow escapes: One Kiwi soldier came across a Japanese officer's Sam Browne belt and was about to pick it up when a New Zealand officer warned him it was probably booby trapped. The soldier later discovered that there was a Japanese machine gun nest behind it. If he had bent down to pick it up he would have been on the same level as the machine gun and certain death would have resulted.[43]

One of the oddest groups of invaders in the first wave of Mono was YMCA secretaries as representatives of the National Patriotic Fund Board (a voluntary organization coordinating various New Zealand philanthropic organizations). The mission of the "NAT PAT" was to provide a free cafeteria service, items of value to troops such as shaving and writing items, provide comforts to wounded soldiers and overall to attend to the welfare of troops. The beneficial morale-boosting aspects of this civilian organization secured them the permission to have YMCA secretaries take part in the invasion:

> The little band of YMCA secretaries landing with the first wave of fighting troops set to work assisting the unloading of stores and equipment and getting hot tea ready for thirsty patrols. One secretary had the unenviable experience of seeing his first brew of tea with primus stove and all blown to pieces by a Japanese mortar bomb.[44]
>
> The importance of this organization's work can be gauged from the fact that space in the assault wave was so scarce.

Bernie Harris, an infantryman in 29 Battalion, landed with the second wave. He recalled Japanese fire striking close to him and his sergeant being hit in the shoulder. He could not see where the fire was coming from. There were craters from the naval bombardment and there was a strong temptation to take shelter.

Andy Lysaght also came ashore in the second wave at Falamai Beach. He was a wireless operator temporarily attached to the 49th Battery (25 pounders) and came ashore with an officer and four others to establish a command post. To his consternation the wireless contact with the 49th Battery's forward observation post on Stirling was very poor due to Watson Island being in a direct line between the two points.[45]

The second wave of troops from the APDs were composed of mainly ASC personnel and the LCIs were loaded with supplies. As soon as the troops landed a human chain was formed and unloading began at top speed.[46] This work was difficult because the supplies and equipment had to be manhandled over the water and the rocky coral. Once bulldozers were ashore they began carving out a rough road and beach exits. Vehicles flowed along this road and ration dumps began to be established. Bulldozers also dragged steel mesh netting out of the landing craft and placed these to make unloading easier.[47]

The Japanese Headquarters on Mono sent off a final message: "Enemy landing commenced at 0540 hours. We have engaged them."[48] The initial lodgment had succeeded and the troops began to push inland.

The Arrival of the Second Transport Group

The Second Transport Group arrived at the Treasury Islands at 0630. The destroyers USS *Waller* and USS *Eaton* detached themselves from the eight LCIs they were escorting and began operating as fighter director ships. The LCIs formed two columns of four, in line astern and, preceded by the minesweepers USS *Adroit*, USS *Conflict*, USS *Daring*, approached the western end of Stirling Island. On their way into Blanche Harbor they encountered the empty landing craft from the APDs returning from the beaches. Japanese guns were firing on the escorting LCI(G) gunboats which were energetically returning fire. As the LCIs entered this cauldron they, too, began firing at Japanese positions as the right-hand column headed for Stirling Island and the beaches of Purple 2 and 3, and the left-hand column for Mono.

The After Action report from LCI-334 captures the fraught flavor of the situation:

2. This ship in the LCI formation proceeded to enter the harbor at 0641 at full speed. Heavy machine gun tracer fire from shore was observed, and was seen hitting on or near the first returning APDs, which had unloaded. The mine sweeps and LCIs 22 and 23 returned this fire with a heavy strafing of the enemy gun nests which then ceased firing.

   When the main LCI formation reached a point just north of Wilson Island, some tracer was seen coming from a nest just west of the creek at Saveke, and LCIs 222, 24, 336 and this ship all strafed the palmetto emplacement upon coming in range.

   This ship ceased firing at 0643 when opposite the creek and slowed, preparing to beach.

3. This ship beached at Orange 2 at 0646 and commenced unloading. Considerable rifle and mortar fire heard, both by our troops and the enemy, and three enemy mortar shells burst nearby, one 50 yards from our bow, on the beach, one 100 yards on the port beam, and one astern 300 yards.

   Troops completed unloading at 0719 and we retracted, with one wounded New Zealand soldier (slight head wound). At 0728 we left Blanche Harbor and formed up for the return trip, passing two incoming LSTs on the way out of the channel, came to true course 131 at 0800 and proceeded in formation as before.[49]

The other LCIs' experience was similar. Once they beached they came under small arms and artillery fire. Shells exploded uncomfortably close.

"Observers on LCI-24 spotted an active pillbox some 60 yards of her port bow, an inactive one about 20 yards from her starboard bow and a very active pillbox some 80 yards off her starboard bow. They were all well camouflaged with netting and foliage and blended into the jungle background. Two dead men lay before one pillbox and others lay at the water's edge. Soon two Japanese snipers tumbled from the tops of coconut trees near the beach."[50]

Private John Wasley with 36th Battalion HQ Company recalled his LCIs ride to Mono: "There were planes overhead and other landing craft alongside us. There was noise everywhere. Bullets were being fired towards and I remembered I wanted to have a look but couldn't so we all remained huddled in the craft."[51]

On landing, Wasley and his platoon ran ashore, only to find their advance held up by dug-in Japanese defenders.

Two reconnaissance parties of artillery men from 208 Light AA Battery found themselves carrying out the unexpected role of infantryman. A machine gun post opened fire and Gunner Michael Compton received the Military Medal for working his way to the rear of the Japanese position where he killed two soldiers and kept the entranceway blocked until other Kiwi soldiers arrived to clear it.[52]

Remarkably, the LCIs were able to complete their task of disembarking 1600 troops and 150 tons of cargo in 35 minutes and to retract without any casualties to crew and with no significant damage to the craft. By 0730, having completed their mission, the LCIs got underway for Guadalcanal escorted by the destroyers USS *Waller*, USS *Pringle* and USS *Saufley*.[53] The LCI gunboats remained.

So far, good luck had attended the men of the transport groups. That was about to change.

The Arrival of the Third Transport Group

The Third Transport Group arrived at 0700. An inquiry was made by radio as to what the tactical situation was on the beaches. For some reason the shore parties indicated that "all was satisfactory" and no mention was made of mortar fire.[54]

Preceded by two YM minesweepers, the group made up of LSTs 399 and 485 entered Blanche Harbor at 0715. There was no sign of a beachmaster and designated area for the LSTs to beach, so the commanders of the two LSTs simply chose an area and beached their vessels. LST-339 beached on Orange One and LST-485 on Orange Two at 0735.

Their landing areas should have been secured so that the unloading of precious supplies and equipment could be done safely. Instead, within five minutes of landing they were fired on by 80mm mortars, 75mm mountain guns and rifles. The Japanese scored two hits on LST-339; one started a fire which was quickly put out, and the second hit a 40mm gun killing three of its crew. LST-485 received two direct hits on its forecastle which wounded 8 men, one fatally. LST-399 was the target of a Japanese mortar crew which bracketed the vessel before scoring two direct hits.

During a momentary lull in the firing, and under pressure to get the supplies and equipment off ship and to leave the area, the captain ordered the bow ramp lowered. The first few men to leave the ship were cut down by Japanese fire and the ramp was closed. It was at this point that Aurelio Tassone earned his place in Seabee history.

Tassone's Pillbox

A large Japanese pillbox was positioned about eight yards from LST-399's port bow door. It was manned by 12 men and sited underground with a coconut log top. Well

An artist's depiction of Aurelio Tassone's exploits with a bulldozer (*The Earthmover: A Chronicle of the 87th Seabee Battalion in World War II*).

camouflaged with vegetation, it was bypassed by troops in the first wave. The men of J Section, NZ Corps of Signals, "filed past unmolested in the process of forming their forward report centre near Cutlers Creek."[55] The Japanese held their fire, seeking a lucrative target. When LST 399 carrying the 208th Battery and 29 Light Anti-aircraft units lowered her ramp, the troops in the pillbox opened fire. The anti-aircraft guns on the bow could not be depressed sufficiently to fire at the pillbox. Things were so dire that at 0815 the captain sought permission to retract, but this was refused: the pillbox had to be dealt with. Major Jim Britland was hit by Japanese bullets and unfortunately died before he reached Guadalcanal.

The unit history of the 87th NCB, *The Earthmover*, published in 1944, records the courage of Aurelio ("Ray") Tassone, a 28-year-old machinist's mate from Milford, Massachusetts:

> The landing party had no tanks, but the Seabees had landed four bulldozers to begin clearing operations. One stubborn Jap pillbox was holding up the landing. Tassone maneuvered his bulldozer to a difficult angle of fire for the Japs, then while Lieutenant Turnbull lay in the open and fired at the apertures in the pillbox, Tassone started a run for the Japs.
>
> "The big machine moved slowly toward the pillbox," Lieutenant Turnbull reported, "because Tassone insisted on running in low gear so that he would have power enough to crash the pillbox. He couldn't run in high gear and then shift to low gear, since that would mean bringing the bulldozer to a dead stop before the pillbox. He simply raised the blade and rolled ponderously forward. Jap machine gun fire rattled off the blade and it seemed that Tassone would be hit at any moment."
>
> At the proper second Tassone dropped his blade and literally buried the pillbox under a

ton of earth. After the island had been occupied men of the 87th dug into the smashed pillbox and found the bodies of twelve Japs. Tassone a slight, serious, Italian-American, was awarded the Silver Star.[56]

The Silver Star was awarded in front of assembled Seabees and Kiwis.[57] Lieutenant Charles E. Turnbull, Civil Engineering Corps, U.S.N.R., was awarded a citation for having "courageously directed the movements of a bulldozer used in the destruction of a Japanese pillbox."

A New Zealand infantryman, John Wasley, recorded: "On landing we were all held up for awhile, then a Yank Seabee [American naval construction serviceman] hopped to his bulldozer. He put the dozer's blade up so that it protected him from the bullets and he drove that machine straight at the machine gun post. When he was right on top of it, he wrenched the steering lever and he screwed that dozer around and around and that was the end of that."[58]

The American authorities were not slow to appreciate the morale-boosting and propaganda potential in the story. Tassone was sent back to the United States and on 22 June 1944 visited the Peoria Caterpillar plant: "to tell first hand the employees of Caterpillar and how Caterpillar equipment is helping to win the war.... Escorted through the plant by Bill Naumann, assistant factory manager, Seabee Tassone and Chief Moye showed keen interest in the manufacture of Caterpillar equipment. Seabee Tassone referred to Caterpillar equipment as our real secret weapon of jungle warfare.

"Seabee Tassone gave a radio interview during the evening of June 22 over WMBD and with Chief Moye spoke at the Peoria Court House Square in the evening at a War Bond rally."[59]

Tassone achieved a degree of fame. His exploits were mentioned in *Time* magazine on 20 December 1943. He was the subject of a Camel cigarettes tribute on the Abbot and Costello radio show on 23 December 1943: "In your honor, Seabee Aurelio Tassone, and in honor of all the building and fighting Seabees on their second anniversary, December 28th, the makers of Camels are sending to our Navy men in the Pacific three hundred thousand Camel cigarettes."

Tassone was even featured in True Comics No. 51, August 1946, under the rubric "Seabee's Weapon."

However, what really cemented into the public consciousness the image of the Seabee astride his bulldozer crushing the Japanese was a film starring John Wayne and Susan Hayward called *The Fighting Seabees* made in 1943 and released in 1944. It popularized the image of the Seabee, and its most dramatic scene was replication of Tassone's feat.

Tassone suffered the indignity of having his feat ascribed to a New Zealander. In his report to Nimitz on 10 November, Wilkinson commented on the "gallant and efficient conduct" of NZ 8 Brigade and then went on to describe an incident in which LST-399 came under fire from a pillbox and that "a resourceful New Zealander mounted a bulldozer, raised the blade for protection, drove it over the pillbox and buried seven Japs under the coconut logs. This I believe to be a novel use for the versatile bulldozer."[60] Unfortunately for Tassone the story of "the resourceful New Zealander" gained traction. The official USMC history *Bougainville and the Northern Solomons*[61] describes how: "a resourceful New Zealander mounted a D-8 bulldozer and with the blade raised high to protect him from fire he rolled heavily down the ramp, several New Zealanders covering him with Bren guns as he came out. Working to the blind side of the pillbox, he lowered the blade and plowed the pillbox and its occupants under the earth, tamping it down well all around, effectively silencing its fire."

The "resourceful New Zealander" also features in the Royal Navy history dealing with the war with Japan. The description, however, is similar to that of the official USMC history.[62]

Many New Zealanders would have been familiar with the operation of a D-8 bulldozer because of their farming backgrounds. However, no New Zealander has ever claimed to have carried out this act of heroism and there is nothing in the New Zealand archival material to suggest that the driver was other than Aurelio Tassone. George Hodgson, a New Zealand officer, commented with pride that he had been present, along with other Kiwi officers, when Tassone was awarded his medal.[63]

There is, however, another dimension to the story. New Zealand sources record that as 29 Battalion advanced towards Falamai, they eliminated Japanese soldiers firing from gun pits. When the next wave of troops landed, a Japanese pillbox which had remained hidden opened fire. Two privates approached the pillbox under cover of light machine gun fire and silenced the Japanese by throwing grenades into it. An American bulldozer was then called in to cave in the top of the emplacement, killing the defenders.[64]

The New Zealand Freelance, a contemporary newspaper, with the heading "Okay Boys! Let's Go. How Kiwis Fought Their Way Ashore Against Japanese Forces," provides some corroboration: "Courage of a high order was needed and shown by two intelligence men, Privates Ted Owens and Cedric Banks of Tauranga, who rolled grenades into a strongly fortified Japanese pillbox. But the highlight of that particular operation was the action of the driver of the bulldozer who lifting the blade to protect himself from gunfire drove over the top of the pillbox. The yells of the terrified Japs were matched only the vociferous and strong language of the driver."[65]

Owens and Banks are credited in the New Zealand official history, *The Pacific*, with demolishing a Japanese post using hand grenades. It then refers to "another enemy strongpoint 20 yards from the shore coming to life" and causing considerable damage until

> it was silenced by a resourceful American carpenter's mate 1st Class Aurillo [*sic*] Tassone, of the CBs, who, using a bulldozer as a tank and its shining blade as a shield, crushed the garrison and buried the 24 Japanese occupants in one operation. He was awarded the Silver Star. A party of anti-aircraft gunners landing with the second wave, attempted to liquidate this strong-point, and Gunner M.J. Compton disposed of some of the occupants before the bulldozer arrived. Captain H.H. Grey, also a gunner, collected a party and played an infantry role by seeking enemy outposts.[66]

The unofficial history of 29 Light AA Regiment provides further details on the actions of Gunner Compton:

> The first wave of infantry left a few isolated enemy strong-points near Falamai and one of these caused some trouble to the reconnaissance parties of E & H troops of the 208th Battery when they landed from LCIs. The two troop commanders, Lieutenants H.W. Milne and J Lendrum, promptly organized a bayonet charge and Gunner M.J. Compton, showing great initiative, shot at least three of the Japs and earned for himself the Military Medal — the only decoration for bravery won by the regiment. Even after the charge some of the

enemy held out and Gunner Compton tried again to get at them with grenades. They were very sheltered, however, and it took a bulldozer to crush the nest and put it out of action.[67]

The 29 Battalion history records that the first wave landing went smoothly. However, a Japanese weapon pit some 20 yards from the beach went undetected until Japanese sniper fire began inflicting casualties:

> A section of carriers guided by Privates E.V. Owen and E.C. Banks of the I Section reached the scene and grenades were thrown into the pit. Silence followed and the section continued to search through the village. Perhaps 40 minutes later, further fire came from the enemy position, and this time no mistake was made. An American bulldozer turned into a simple on piece job. For this coolness and leadership in the reduction of this post Private Owen was awarded the Military Medal; the only decoration won by a battalion member in this section, and one well earned by a man of 46 who had a son serving in the RNZAF.[68]

An unofficial history of 38th Field Regiment notes that "Captain F.J. Mitchell assisted in the destruction of a pill-box by engaging the occupants with his tommy gun while a bulldozer was run over the emplacement."[69]

Perhaps the answer is that all of these accounts have elements of truth. It would be strange that the New Zealanders being fired on should remain passive. Independent of Tassone and Turnbull, other soldiers would have been returning fire and trying to destroy the pillbox. On balance, it seems likely that the destruction of the pillbox was a combined Allied effort. That takes nothing away from Tassone's heroism.

A New Zealand artillery officer witnessed Tassone's actions. John Foote was designated as a reserve officer with 50 Battery HQ. He landed from an LCI with 200 troops. The din of gunfire was terrific and Foote found himself with six others taking cover in the flanges of a mahogany tree. The commander of 49 Battery was wounded and Foote escorted him to a first aid post, then made his way to Falamai Beach to find the commander of 38 Field Regiment. He reported to the colonel, who had just returned from Stirling Island looking for suitable positions for his guns, and who told Foote to take over command of 49 Battery. Foote saw a Japanese machine gun nest open fire on an LST which had opened its cargo doors. He saw that the Bofors guns on the LST's deck could not depress far enough to fire at the Japanese. A lone bulldozer then came out of the LST and buried the Japanese machine gun nest.[70] Foote also recalled that the onlookers were all cheering as Tassone went about his work.

The landing on Mono was Foote's baptism of fire, and he recalled feelings of trepidation facing Japanese fire. He was also in the unenviable position of taking command of a unit whose men he did not know, and who did not know him.[71]

Seabee activity continued simply because there was pressure to get the job done. The LSTs had to be unloaded. Gear and equipment poured out and space on the beach had to be carved out. One Seabee bulldozer began ripping a road through the thick undergrowth so that cargo could be taken from the beach. Other bulldozers began creating areas for unloading and one created a trench 90 feet long, 9 feet deep and 4 feet wide out of the hard coral so that a direction finder unit could be installed. The drivers rode their bulldozers unprotected from Japanese fire.[72]

The Signals men went about the job of getting their equipment ashore and operable.

Japanese artillery fire wounded Signalman F.E. Fry of J Section and he had to be evacuated, and Signalman T.M. Horan received a slight arm wound.

Even without the effects of Japanese fire the Sigs had a difficult job. Their vehicles were routinely overloaded:

> Typical of the load carried by most signal vehicles was that of G Section's jeep which went ashore at Falamai beach. With the rear seat removed it was laden with four heavy wet batteries, a battery charger, a container of white spirit, oil, tent, shovel, pick, three cans of water, three telephones, and three and a half miles of Don 3 Cable. Its chassis springs had ceased to function as such.[73]

Sigs personnel proceeded to create an intricate web of communications linking various headquarters, artillery and anti-aircraft units, and infantry units. This was done by means of wireless, radio-telephone and field cable. Within a short period of time a communications network existed from the front line infantry back to Brigade headquarters. Potentially Blanche Channel separated units on Mono from those on Stirling, but this problem was resolved by way of wireless.

The delicate communications equipment needed to be sheltered from the elements and enemy fire. Initially camouflaged tents were used but priority was given to excavating shelters to protect the wireless equipment, telephone exchanges, and cipher clerks.

The Japanese gave impetus to the digging of protective bunkers. A lone Japanese float plane appeared as darkness fell and in an incredibly flukey piece of bomb aiming, dropped its only bomb near J Section's underground wireless station. The station was a key communications point and although its personnel were unharmed the bomb shredded all of the lines coming in to the station. It was imperative that communications be restored so the linesmen of J & X Sections were immediately set to work to repair the damage. This was done with some trepidation because the Japanese were renowned for their skill in infiltration tactics.[74]

The Push Inland

As planned, 29 Battalion pushed inland and fanned out to establish a deep defensive perimeter with its eastern flank anchored on the Kolehe River and its western flank abutting the positions of 36 Battalion.

For its part, 36 Battalion, which had landed to the left of Falamai, thrust towards the Saveke River, forcing the Japanese to retreat. The Japanese headquarters was surrounded and eliminated.

The Japanese were still capable of surprising the Kiwis. Robert Dunlop recalled:

> We had to dig a perimeter around what was the Japanese headquarters, which was pretty empty by that time except for the ones that had been killed. There was a big marquee — a big tent. After I dug my foxhole, I thought I would have a look around inside for a few souvenirs, because the Americans were good at buying souvenirs, and they always had more money than what we did. I ended up with a big clock, a Japanese flag, a Japanese rifle, a bottle of sake, and a Japanese water bottle with Japanese writing on it.
>
> When I came out through the tent flap, a Japanese ran outside beside me. He fired a shot into the air, all our fellows dropped to the ground and the Jap ran straight through them and into the jungle. I would like to think he is alive today.
>
> I was grateful to him, really. He must have had a bead on me [in the tent], and he could

have shot me so easily, but if he had he would have alerted all the rest of the men — the rest of our company — and he wouldn't have got away.⁷⁵

The fact that his life had been spared in this way was a source of wonderment to Dunlop for the rest of his days.⁷⁶

Although the Kiwis were pushing forward, deadly fire from two 75mm mountain guns and a 90mm mortar located in the heights above the beachhead continued to rain down on the increasingly crowded beachhead. The 29 Battalion history describes the scene:

> All sense of time was lost that morning, but unloading operations were scarcely under way when the beach and village came under steady and accurate mortar fire. At first it was believed that this fire came from Watson Island, but later deductions were more accurate for the mortars were sited upon what is now known as Artillery Hill, overlooking the Saveke. Their field of fire was an extensive one; their ranging reasonably accurate. A number of casualties were in consequence suffered by the battalion. Warrant Officer E. Stephenson, Sergeant W.J. Pearson and Private C.J. Sargent were killed. Members of battalion headquarters had a narrow escape in that less than ten minutes after they had shifted to a less vulnerable position a bomb landed in the centre of their hastily vacated area. The

The walking wounded head toward LST 485 on Purple 2 Beach, Stirling Island, 27 October 1943 (Archives New Zealand, WAII, 1, Treasury Island Photos, D1, #29, Official Photographer).

enemy mortar fire was even more dangerous than the moving of battalion headquarters might suggest.[77]

Two New Zealand soldiers were badly wounded within minutes of setting foot on Mono. They received help from an unexpected quarter — three war correspondents: "Stretcher bearers gently lifted the badly wounded men into a barge.... Pat Robinson of International News Service, a veteran of the last war, bandaged the leg of one boy, John Fairfax of the *Sydney Morning Herald* injected morphia into the other lad, easing his agony from three severe wounds, and Archer Thomas of the *Sydney Telegraph* read him instructions from the morphia packet."[78]

Frank Cooze saw and felt the effects of the mountain gun and mortar fire:

> The LSTs were disgorging their cargo when the Japs opened up with mountain guns and mortar fire, scoring a direct hit on one of our guns in action on the deck of the barge. They then pounded our positions on the beach making them untenable.
> I saw a lump of red hot metal fly past too close for comfort. It had already disappeared when my reflexes came to life and I dived into the nearest hole. Unfortunately the hole contained two crouching figures. A muffled voice cried "For -- sake, get off my -- neck!"
> "Are you hurt?" I asked anxiously as we sorted ourselves out. "Something flew past me."
> "Well, why didn't you jump on it, then" replied our cook, spitting out a mouthful of sand. "I'm no -- ostrich!"[79]

In quick succession, about 0735, two LSTs were hit and small fires broke out. Casualties were suffered and the unloading process was held up. Troops disembarking came under fire not only from artillery but also from concealed Japanese machine gun positions.

At 0740, Fort, on the USS *Eaton*, saw the LSTs being fired on, although the source of the fire was unclear. He asked the commander of LST Group 15 where the fire was coming from. The commander replied that it appeared to be coming from astern and that there had been near misses on both sides. Fort ordered the LCI gunboats to go to the aid of the LSTs and they engaged machine gun positions on Mono.

At 0830, the *Philip*, located to the south of Stirling and acting in a fire support role, was given a target by a shore fire control party. *Philip* requested permission to open fire and this was granted by Fort. The target was 1200 yards north of the entrance of the Saveke River. The *Philip* fired five salvos and the mortar fire ceased.[80]

Cooze found that the Japanese were not the only problem on Mono: "We moved into the edge of the jungle, keeping a wary eye open for snipers. Next moment our gear and rifles were flung on the ground as we fought off hundreds of red ants, half an inch long. They were fighting mad. So were we!"[81]

His unit unloaded their anti-aircraft guns onto temporary positions on the beach, then one was positioned in the deserted village in a clearing close to the beach and the crew began digging in.

For Cooze's unit, the resumption of Japanese fire was especially dangerous:

> Trenches were half completed when the mountain guns and mortars opened up again and plastered the area. The heat was terrific and when several huts and vehicles burst into flames it was almost unbearable. A Jap ammunition dump in one of the huts blew up and filled the air with sound and shrapnel. The gun crew lost most of their gear by fire.
> During a lull the troop commander and I took a bulldozer to the other side of the clear-

ing to clear a site for another gun. Mortars followed us and we had a jolly little game of hide and seek. The driver, the officer and I all tried to dive underneath the bulldozer. A native hut a few feet away collected a direct hit and burst into flames. We had our fingers crossed![82]

John Foote's artillery unit could not dig in its guns because the beach where it landed was made of stones and rocks. The guns were shifted into secure positions and fields of fire cleared. They would receive a lot of work over succeeding days.

The Fifth Transport Group arrived at the western entrance to Blanche Harbor about 0830, followed by the Fourth Transport Group some 20 minutes later.

At 0853 planes over Mono caused consternation. Anti-aircraft fire erupted, but did not result in any hits. This was just as well because the planes were RNZAF P-40s!

At about 0900 hours, mortar and artillery fire crashed down on the beach area. It seemed to come from the hilly area to the northwest of the Saveke River. The dense jungle made it hard to pinpoint where the Japanese were.

At 1000 hours, two platoons of 36 Battalion were ordered to locate and destroy the Japanese artillery raking the beach. One 90mm AA gun had been destroyed, one 25 pounder gun damaged, and a Bofors gun, ammunition and medical stores destroyed. An Army Service Corps truck from 4MT Company, loaded with ammunition, received a direct hit with spectacular results. The driver of ASC truck loaded with ammunition had fortunately taken cover from the mortar fire after he had driven his vehicle out of the LST. The bemused driver tried to find his vehicle only to discover that it had received a direct hit and been obliterated. The following day the vehicle's bumper was nearby and other parts were found in a palm tree forty feet from the ground. The vehicle's destruction proved to be a quartermaster's dream. As the ASC history relates: "By a remarkable coincidence nearly all of the quartermaster's subsequent shortages also seem to have been loaded on that truck, the capacity of which must have been tremendous."[83]

A platoon of 36 Battalion forced the 90mm mortar to cease fire and withdraw, but much to the dismay of the Allies, the Japanese resumed firing.[84]

Falamai village had provided cover for Japanese snipers, but they were eliminated.

Kiwi soldiers from 36 Battalion approached the village and had just passed through it when Japanese artillery fire rained down on it. Bernie Harris was particularly fortunate. He and another soldier had been ordered by Lieutenant Reid to clear the church. The door to the church was ajar and Harris's companion, Private 'Slim' Ellis, had a look while Harris covered him. They saw nothing and moved on.[85] A shell went in and took the roof off the church, which was incentive for Ellis and Harris to move on. They had gotten 20 to 30 meters when the next shell struck. Shortly after, at 1140, there was a huge explosion and the church erupted in flames. The Japanese had stored their ammunition there and, whether deliberately or accidentally, a Japanese round set off the explosion which flattened the church and set fire to the surrounding reed and bark huts. Harris and Ellis were thrown some distance by the blast and were stunned, but otherwise unhurt.

The blast from the explosion destroyed supplies and equipment nearby. Valises, stationery and records for 23 Field Company were destroyed in the explosion and subsequent fire.[86]

The Union Jack flies over a devastated Falamai village, Mono Island, 1943 (Archives New Zealand, WAII, 1, Treasury Islands Photos, D1, #19, Official Photographer).

The liberation of Falamai was marked by the raising of the Union Jack by New Zealand troops. The fire ravaged the village and the destruction was completed by the Seabees, who leveled the remaining rickety shacks to clear exits from the beach.[87]

Reports began reaching Admiral Fort on the destroyer USS *Eaton* that two LSTs had been hit and that unloading operations had been disrupted. Fort decided to intervene and the *Eaton* approached the invasion beaches. Warned, however, that an air raid was imminent, *Eaton* reversed course to obtain sea room so that it could maneuver. When it transpired that the air raid warning was false, *Eaton* returned to Blanche Harbor and, along with the LCI(G) gunboats, began shelling likely Japanese positions.[88]

The solution to the Japanese harassing fire came from the Kiwi troops. At 1000 hours a platoon from 36 Battalion, led by 2nd Lieutenant LTG Booth, pushed through the dense undergrowth and up a steep slope to where he believed the Japanese guns were. They stormed the Japanese positions to find that, although the mountain gun barrels were still hot, the defenders had escaped. Booth on hearing the sound of a mortar led a section 500 yards further up this hill, capturing a 90mm mortar. Ten Japanese were killed and the rest fled into the jungle. The destruction of the Japanese artillery effectively ended the Japanese ability to dispute the beachhead.

Private Jackson Whaitiri from the Chatham Islands was a participant in destroying

Six: Invasion: 27 October 1943

Soldiers with a Japanese anti-tank or mountain gun, captured by 36 Battalion, halfway between Avon and Saveke Rivers (War History Collection, Alexander Turnbull Library, Wellington, WH-0295).

the Japanese guns. As his platoon moved up the Saveke River in search of the guns they found themselves the target of mortar fire.

> All of a sudden the Jap started to pile a lot of small mortar fire right on us. It was pretty exciting for a time, and we moved on a bit to what had been a hut with a Jap wireless set in it before our own mortars had burnt it out. A big wireless set it was too, about four feet by three. Up on a hill just behind, about a hundred yards further on were the Jap mortar positions. They were on a flat spot and had a grand outlook over the beach where all the unloading was going on. One gun seemed to be forward and one set back.
>
> We scrambled up the hill as fast as we could lick, but the Jap was too fast for us and cleared out. He didn't want to wait. We found all sorts of empty ammunition boxes strewn all round the place. There wasn't any live ammo there, and the Japs must have bustled along to shoot it all off before they tried a get-away. The guns were red hot when we got there, so we weren't far behind the crews.

Leaving six men behind, eighteen soldiers then set off through dense jungle to find the Japanese observation post. Whaitiri found the going hard with his Thompson sub-machine gun getting caught repeatedly by jungle vines and undergrowth. Japanese voices were heard in the distance and the men pushed on. The bush thinned out and the Japanese were seen. The Kiwis crept up on them.

> Then we let them have it with tommy guns, and went over the top and at them. When our officer fired the first shot everything went loose. I hopped it to a ditch and got about

fifteen yards from a machine gun post before I saw it. A Jap was peppering away as hard as he could lick, and I could see the splutter from his gun. Then a yellow hand came round a tree, and a head followed it. I didn't make any mistake. The old tommy gun got him clean.

The Japs were spreading all around us. They were big blokes about six feet, and there must have been more than twenty of them. They had a hut about ten yards from their "O Pip" (Observations Post) and quite a lot of them were in there. We could see them packing up a few things. Funny thing to do at that time of the fight, but that's what they were doing, all the same. A lot of pistol flares were lying on the floor. One Jap came out of the door, but he didn't get far. Someone shot him, and then our officer rolled a nice juicy grenade in, and the boys let go with the Bren. The Japs were squealing and running all round the place.

We didn't have it all our own way. The Japs had plenty of grenades and they were shooting them off from nowhere. Two machine guns opened up on us too. They had dug a big mortar pit, but there wasn't anything in it right then. The fight was a really hot go for about twenty minutes, when the Jap quit and ran for it...

The Jap had a wonderful view from his "O Pip." We could see the whole harbor and the beach where all our boys were working on the ships. We could even see the destroyer off the coast about four hundred feet below us. No wonder the Japs were hitting us. They had a huge pair of binoculars, about three feet long, as heavy as lead, mounted on an enormous set of legs. They could have seen miles out to sea with them. But they were ours now, just like the mountain guns and the mortars the Jap had left behind.[89]

The Pacific records: "All enemy resistance in the immediate vicinity of the landing was overcome soon after midday and battalions dug in along their perimeters from 400 to 600 yards in the jungle, which was much thicker than information had led them to believe."[90]

It is a military commonplace that the boundary line between two units is a weak and dangerous place. The men of the 8 Brigade Headquarters' Forward Reporting Center found themselves in such a place; the boundary between 36 and 29 Battalions. They were too far forward and, to their dismay, found themselves in combat rather than simply reporting it to Row. Meantime, the Brigade Headquarters had set itself up on the much quieter area of Purple 3 on Stirling.[91]

Engineering support was provided by 23 Field Company, New Zealand Engineers. Stores and equipment were unloaded on Mono under shell fire and some items were damaged. Number One Platoon was attached to 36 Battalion and its men began bulldozing tracks and roads for dumps. Sapper Jack Keith Duncan was awarded the Military Medal for his work in coolly operating a D-4 bulldozer under heavy artillery fire while bullets ricocheted off it. As an unofficial history notes, "His fine example was a very steadying influence on unloading and carrying parties."[92] Number Two Platoon also created tracks and laid down beach matting. Their D-4 bulldozer was hit by shrapnel and, by 1030 hours, was so badly damaged it became inoperable. The Number Three Platoon had by far the easiest time because it landed on an uncontested beach on Stirling Island.[93]

There were casualties. However, medical treatment for the wounded was soon on hand. "A" Company, 7th (NZ) Field Ambulance, landed on Mono. It traveled on two LC. Is with the intention that one group commanded by Captain Rogers would set up a beach dressing station on landing and the other, under Captain Giesen, would deal with the equipment, provide stretcher bearers and, in due course, set up an advanced dressing station.

Twenty-five minutes after the first wave of infantry landed, "A" Company landed in two groups about 300 yards apart on the beach to the west of Falamai.

Lieutenant G.L. Lynds of "A" Company, 7th (NZ) Field Ambulance recorded:

As we poured up onto the deck with full equipment adjusted, we stepped into a world at war. The Infantry were still clearing up small pockets of resistance along the beaches and the noise of rifles, machine guns and bursting grenades filled the air. Machine-guns aboard our L.C.I.s added to the din. Not a single Jap was to be seen, but that was not surprising, for dense jungle seemed to form an impenetrable barrier along the entire beach.

The next few hours were our busiest. Even before disembarkation, we saw our first casualties laying on the beach, awaiting the medical attention we were bringing. Several were already beyond our help, having paid at highest cost. A number of men were dispatched to attend to the more serious cases, but before we could proceed to our casualties as a Company, there were our ships to be unloaded, and this task, with the combatant troops so fully occupied, largely fell to us. There were some uncomfortable moments as facing the fire from the jungle, we went about the unloading. Several (not medical though) were marked with streams of blood where small pieces of flying shrapnel had found their mark.

The main thing seemed to be that the rush of activity had relieved the tension of long waiting, and with something for our hands to do we were happier. We found all we wanted in the way of work, and having completed the unloading and hacked small clearings in the dense undergrowth for the gear, we put our surgical haversacks into full operation. We were too busy to give much thought to the fighting going on within a hundred yards of us. The Infantry could well handle that, and were even then proving the fact. Meanwhile casualties came in thick and fast, most of them walking cases with slight injuries. We found that the men once patched up, were as keen as mustard to get back to their cobbers in the front lines. Of course, most of them had to be detained for rest, and some of them forcibly restrained.

Shrapnel wounds seemed to be the most common, for by this time the Japs were making the larger L.S.T.s their targets for mortar bomb and machine gun fire. Beach parties were exposed to much of this, and our beach dressing station at Cutler's Creek was in the centre of it. It was pretty "thick" there for awhile and the shelter afforded by the over-hanging rocks of the small creek bed saved many of the patients from further serious injury. Compound fractures of the femur, chest wounds and head injuries required special care and attention. Stretchers were at a premium and in several cases plasma sets were sustaining life.

By this time the Advanced Dressing Station on the eastern bank of the Saveke River was being set up, and the "dug-out" theatre being constructed. This party was quite near the Jap H.Q., much nearer than we imagined at the time, but in the jungle it is not easy to be kept informed of the situation forward.

The fire of the Jap mountain guns passed directly over our heads and several shells bursting with terrific concussion in the trees directly above us, cost us several wounded. Among these, were Norm McInnes with deep shrapnel wounds in the thigh and hand, Bill Smith — who had done such a splendid job — with a wound in the thigh and Clem Paterson, who owes his life to his tin hat, with a scalp wound. We withdrew the party back towards the beach for awhile till the Jap gun positions had been silenced.

By midday the more serious cases were being carried aboard the L.S.T.s for immediate evacuation, a job that had to be done with speed or they were to pull out as soon as their discharging was completed. It was heavy shrapnel. These evacuations greatly relieved the situation at the beach dressing station, which was working under pressure. Both Capts. Giesen and Rogers were there now doing a great job under difficult conditions with careful improvisation, the patients were held in comparative safety and comfort. Morphia helped many of them through hours of pain.

Our cooks soon made themselves popular, both to patients and personnel. "Snow" Evans had the tea billy boiling within an hour and a half of our landing, and we have since often wondered just how we'd have managed without those stimulating hot drinks. They really saved us throughout the whole of the first few days, for it was difficult to feel hungry when looking a K ration in the face! C ration, for most of us, was very little more appetizing.

At mid-morning, when most of the gear had been handled, liaison scouts were sent out to contact the several unit R.A.P.s and to ascertain the number of casualties being held by them for evacuation. Soon, squads were organized and stretcher-bearers bringing in their heavy carries. This was a tiring, heavy job, toiling through mud and thick undergrowth and along slippery native tracks.

By mid-afternoon, our H.Q. Company had established their M.D.S. on Stirling Island, and the patients held at the beach dressing station were evacuated.[94]

One of the defensive measures was the deployment of four six-pounder anti-tank guns of G Troop, 54 Anti-tank Battery. These guns were intended to cover "the seaward approach to the Falamai village area."[95] G Troop was in two groups, two guns each accompanying 36th and 29th Battalions. The guns were loaded onto LST 399 and disembarked in the second wave. At first sight the deployment of six-pounder anti-tank guns seems curious because they were facing seaward. They would have been outranged and outgunned by even a Japanese destroyer. However, their real purpose would have been to engage and sink any Japanese Daihatsu landing craft, trawlers or other craft.

By the end of the day all the LSTs were on their way back to the relative safety of Guadalcanal. LCI 330 had disgorged 299 men and 15 tons of cargo in a mere 14 minutes.[96] One LST still had 34 tons of unloaded supplies on board, but the rest had successfully disgorged their cargoes.[97] The isolated instance where an LST had not been fully unloaded was

> because of some misunderstanding of the respective functions of the crew of the craft and the New Zealand unloading parties. After the trucks and jeeps on LST 399 were driven ashore, work on this craft almost ceased and the American commander reported that unloading became "inexcusably slow." The commander of the LST could not convince the troops that unloading was a troop responsibility, and there was some disorganization of beach parties because of casualties. Otherwise all arrangements, despite the temporary hold-up because of exploding ammunition, went according to Row's well conceived plan, and by nightfall most of the landing craft were on their way back to Guadalcanal, there to load the second flight.[98]

This points to inadequacies in the planning of Goodtime due to inexperience and a lack of appreciation of how important it was to allocate sufficient men to working parties to not only swiftly unload the amphibious craft but also to safely disperse their contents. There was confusion as to the role of Kiwi troops, and to those involved in combat it seemed inconceivable that they would be called on to undertake the heavy and difficult work of unloading and dispersing supplies. Had Japanese air attacks on the beachhead been heavier, these operations could have been imperiled.

Shortly after 1943 hours three bombs were dropped on Orange Beach. Two air raids killed two and wounded nine Kiwis of 36 Battalion. As the Third Transport Group, escorted by *Philip* and the two minesweepers, withdrew at 2024, they had the uncomfortable experience of being illuminated by flares and float lights, but no bombs were dropped. *Saufley* joined the group. At 2257, a float light and two bombs were dropped near LST 399 resulting in minor damage to radio equipment. The rest of the trip to

Guadalcanal was uneventful.[99] On arrival, repair work began. LST-485 had been hit by two 80mm mortar rounds on its main deck but was not seriously damaged. LST-399 had, as well as being subjected to machine gun fire, been hit three times on its left side probably by the troublesome 40mm mountain gun. Repairs were made and the craft were able to join the Third Echelon.[100]

For some of the Japanese the shock of battle led to dislocation and uncertainty as to what they were to do. One soldier, Superior Seaman Kohei Mizuno, later told his captors that on 27 October he had been with his knee mortar squad midway between Falamai and Kolehe River. Ten men left for the hills but lost two of their wounded on the march. They then linked up with the men from the 3rd Observation Post, a machine gun squad and a trench mortar squad. This group of some forty men set off for the hill behind the Japanese headquarters. By the time they arrived the headquarters staff had left so the group struck out for Soanatalu, eventually linking up some days later with a sizeable Japanese force under Ensign Nakaseko.[101]

First Night on Mono

By 1800 hours darkness was falling and a defensive perimeter had been established. The weather had cleared up during the afternoon but "a dismal rain" now began.[102] The troops were instructed to dig foxholes for cover and not to move from them. The engineers of 23 Field company prepared booby traps and placed them around the perimeter. The booby traps consisted of trip wires and hand grenades with instantaneous fuses. The only recorded casualties were some land crabs, although booby traps around Falamai may have caused Japanese casualties.[103] The Japanese tended to drag away their dead and wounded.

Japanese activity was focused around the Saveke River and the site of the Japanese headquarters. The Japanese may have been trying to regain supplies or command cohesion. Several attacks were repulsed. Row later reported that the Japanese were active on the left and right flanks of the perimeter and that the beach area was subjected to mortars, rifle and machine gun fire, but that the Japanese appeared to be trying to ascertain the invaders' dispositions.[104]

The ASC history records:

> That first night on Mono Island was an unenviable experience. Very soon the expected enemy planes arrived, flying quite low over the trees with a drone which seemed continuous, and left no question of sleep. The first bomb dropped in the edge of the sea close to the ASC bivouac area, and the men crouching in their shelters were sprayed with water, dirt and leaves. One of the worst features of the raids was that there could be no retaliation at that stage. Japanese knee mortars were also lobbing shells into the area inside the perimeter, and it seemed as though the enemy were trying to set fire to the dumps to provide a mark for low flying aircraft. At about midnight he did succeed in setting the dump of rations and unit equipment at beach Orange on fire, and when the blaze spread to ammunition, fragments fell in the 4th MT Company's area.[105]

By nightfall all of the guns of 208th Battery, 20 Light AA were sited in provisional positions along the beach at Falamai and 214th Battery had set up three guns on Wilson

Island with eight more on Stirling and one left behind on Mono.[106] Although many feet were itching to get to the firing pedals when the bombers came in low, the targets were invisible and the engagement of unseen targets was prohibited.[107]

Priority had to be given to unloading the LSTs and there was little time for the troops engaged in this to dig foxholes. David Williams recalled that "when darkness falls it falls with a clang in the tropics." His men were given a defensive position but found it difficult digging in the heavy bush because of tree roots.[108]

George Hodgson recalled that there was limited time to scrape a two man foxhole and that the rain created an unpleasant muddy slush at the bottom. It wasn't cold, and his men did two hour watches. Japanese bombers struck in the middle of the night and Hodgson heard yells and curses coming from his corporal. In the morning Hodgson crawled over to the corporal's foxhole to find him calmly cleaning his rifle. Hodgson remarked, "thought they had got you." The corporal replied, "So did I, but look at that bastard," pointing to a coconut beside his foxhole which had been loosened by the shelling the previous day and fallen on him during the night. "I thought that the whole bloody Jap army had moved in on me!"[109]

Les Taylor laconically summed up the end of his first day on Mono in his diary: "Dug in for the night in fox holes. Bombed from the air and strafed mortars from the ridge, sniped and machine gunned, grenades and mountain guns. Hell of a night."[110]

Frank Cooze captured the experience of his first night on Mono:

> Four-man foxholes were hastily dug in the jungle and roofed with palms for protection against air attacks. We dozed in those holes, fully clothed, for many nights with our hands on our weapons and knives.
>
> The velvet blackness of the night was relieved only by fireflies flitting in and out of the trees. Birds called with a sound like clacking sticks. Toads croaked as lizards and land-crabs scuffled through the undergrowth. We spoke in hushed whispers while sand and gravel trickled down on us from the walls and mingled with insect repellant smeared on our hands and faces. A sudden crash as coconut or damaged palm struck the ground would startle us into straining wakefulness.[111]

Although the Kiwis had experienced tropical conditions in Fiji and Guadalcanal, their first night on Mono was something else. Peter Renshaw, a sergeant from 36 Battalion, expressed it this way: "Sometimes you could hear things. Your imagination would run away with you. Sometimes fellows would think they heard something and they'd cut loose with a shot you know, and in the morning we'd talk about it. You wouldn't sleep, you'd be tensed up all the time. You might doze off. Land crabs, huge crabs, would come out of the coral and scratch around. They were horrible things."[112]

The land crabs had one other feature that unnerved the Kiwis. They clicked their large claws together and made a sound reminiscent of a rifle bolt being drawn back. A Kiwi noted in his diary: "Of insects they are very much the same as Guadalcanal, but there are huge land crabs. Annoying things to get in the foxhole in the dark and you can't get a light to get at the bloody things. You can just stand and curse."[113]

Later, having endured nights in a foxhole, he commented: "This living under the ground is a bastard. I hate the bloody crabs and rats in the hole at night. They walk around and when you are going down they knock dirt down onto you. There's trickle, trickle, trickle all night. It is pitch black and you daren't make a move to get them."[114]

The pitch blackness, the incessant rain, eerie noises from the jungle animals, and the dramatic stories they had heard of Japanese night-fighting abilities caused nerves to be stretched taut. The hard coral and the tangle of tree roots and vegetation made digging foxholes difficult in the extreme. This all contributed to a feeling of vulnerability for troops experiencing combat for the first time.

For David Williams, night-time provided challenges:

> You had to get used to distinguishing the noises of the jungle to the noises of the Japs and you didn't need a lively imagination to imagine that they were all Japs creeping up on you, especially at night. Night in the tropics is particularly black especially while you expect to see stars and so on. In the case where you're in deep jungle you don't see stars. So it was black as the inside of a cow.
>
> A lot of people got trigger happy especially on the first couple of nights and they either let go with their automatic weapons or rifles or threw grenades. Grenades were better if there was a genuine problem, because it didn't give away where you were. On the other hand it was important that you threw the grenade and it didn't bounce back into your weapon pit which wasn't a good idea.[115]

For the Kiwis, the jungle was an alien place and, used to the wide open spaces of their homeland, the confined environment of the Treasury Islands bordered on the claustrophobic. A Kiwi noted in his diary: "The jungle is very thick and you can only see the sky in places. The blackness of the night is terrific. You honestly can't see your hand in front of your face and have to feel every inch you move. When we change shifts you have to feel the other chap to see where he is."[116]

For Robert Dunlop, the defense of A Company's perimeter was fraught with tension:

> Our foxholes were pretty close together but it didn't seem to make any difference to the Japanese. They penetrated our lines, and several of our fellows were killed at night. And the nights were the most frightening for me, and I think a lot of our fellows were trigger-happy. There would be grenades going off all the time. They would hear a noise and throw a grenade at it. A couple of our fellows actually got killed doing that. They dug a fairly deep foxhole and put coconut logs across the top. They went to throw a grenade, and their hand hit the log. The grenade fell back into the foxhole and they were both killed.[117]

Dunlop could not wait for the morning to come: "The natives owned a rooster which each morning heralded the coming day. Nothing was more pleasing to hear in the early morning [than] the crowing rooster and realize the long night was soon ending."[118]

There was one feature of Mono's insect life that Dunlop found particularly unnerving: "There were these fireflies that would fly around at night, and they seemed to circle your head. They seemed like they were illuminating your head to give a good shot for the Japs."[119]

One night about midnight Jeff Tunnicliffe of 36 Battalion noticed a strong smell of apple blossom. Thinking that this came from a Japanese infiltrator, one of Tunnicliffe's comrades primed a grenade and threw it. It landed in tropical mud and exploded. Tunnicliffe's lieutenant was furious. The grenade had landed near his foxhole and he had been showered with mud.[120]

For "A" Company 7th (NZ) Field Ambulance, "there was that eternal job of digging holes to be done" in preparation for the night. Foxholes were no easy job with coral and tree roots. Lieutenant G.L. Lynds recalled:

> We were expecting enemy planes after dark. Darkness, as it always does in the tropics, came upon us all of a sudden, but some managed a refreshing dip in the tide before bed. Yes, most of us had ideas of bed and of sleeping comfortably on top of the ground, with a foxhole nearby for an emergency. We were soon disillusioned, for after dark the enemy bombers, directed by Jap ground troops, drove us underground, where we remained in the slush and mud till daybreak. It was our first experience of being bombed, and it continued sporadically all night. We were intensely relieved when dawn broke — just as suddenly as darkness had fallen the previous night. Several had heard the stealthy tread of supposed Jap infiltrators during the night, and reports from the Battalions told of their deadly work. At least one man had been killed by knife wounds. There were a number of bomb injuries to treat.[121]

Frank Cooze also had experience of Japanese infiltrators: "One night a party of Japs infiltrated into our area. Our ears were assailed with the sound of padding feet. High pitched voices chanted, 'Are you there, Joe? ... George! ... Jack! ... Come on, let's go....' The voices ceased as suddenly as they had begun and our ears ached in the heavy, suffocating silence. Someone ran past my foxhole and machine guns spattered the shadows with their messengers of death."[122]

The Japanese had a reputation as formidable jungle fighters who excelled at infiltration and night warfare. In reality few of the Japanese soldiers had experienced combat, let alone been trained in tropical warfare. The perception by the Kiwi soldiers was, however, that the Japanese were at home in the jungle. The Kiwis nonetheless found their behavior bizarre:

> The Japs indulged in a lot of night work on Mono. It was impossible to stop their infiltration completely, as our perimeter was a wide one, and at times a score or more Japs prowled among our lines and foxholes, chattering among themselves, singing sometimes, and conducting themselves with a strangely carefree abandon that suggested a queer twist of psychology, or, what might well have been possible, an overindulgence in their alcoholic Saki, of which many bottles were found in abandoned camp sites.
> They sat on fallen trees, felt gingerly for men's heads in foxholes, threw coconuts and pieces of coral here and there, clicked signals to each other with wooden sticks. Four sat for two hours within a yard of a wounded New Zealander. They never saw him. One poked a skinny hand under the log roof of a big foxhole. He was riddled with a tommy-gun burst.[123]

Hunkered down in their foxholes, the one particular fear that the soldiers had was having their throats cut:

> A South Island corporal now knows what it feels like to have his steel helmet lifted slowly back while he slept in his foxhole. He woke to semi-consciousness one night as his hat was being pulled gently upwards. Not realizing what was happening he drowsily pulled it back on his head. The next moment a hand jerked it up again, and the truth dawned upon the corporal. Someone was trying to lift his chin up to expose his throat. The corporal did not doze anymore. He lashed out with his fists and a dark form slid off in a hurry. Rumor has it that the corporal slept no more that night, nor the night after.[124]

Major Pringle recorded that 36 Battalion had secured its beachhead objective and the men dug in for what was to be a disturbed night: "B.H.Q. [Battalion Headquarters] was about 200 yards off the beach and we were heavily bombed and shelled through the night. The shells were bursting all around us and on the beach below, a dump burnt all night with some of our equipment amongst it. With ammunition, both S.A. [Small Arms] and shell exploding in the fires, the blaze and the Jap planes flying just above the trees, it was a trying night for us all. On looking at the effect of the strafing in the morning we realized how fortunate we were."[125]

Japanese bombing on the first night was particularly unpleasant. David Williams recalled:

> And during that first night also the Japanese bombed us from an airstrip in Bougainville called Kahili which was only about 30 miles away and they came at hourly intervals and you'd hear them shut off [their engines] and the swish of the bombs. And the bombs mostly in that case hit the trees above us and you got some people wounded in a slightly ungallant position across their buttocks because they were in their weapon pit head down and the shrapnel from the bomb would come down that way. One of my friends who got wounded in that way didn't feel very proud when he was asked where his wound was that it was on his backside. However, he was no coward.[126]

Several air raids occurred and 36 Battalion suffered 2 killed and 9 wounded. An ammunition dump was set on fire and 29 LAA Regiment lost ammunition and equipment.[127]

Stirling Island

The task of taking Stirling Island was given to 34 Battalion and, of all of the attacking troops, they had by far the easiest job. There was no opposition. The first wave landed on Beaches Purple 2 and Purple 3 at 0625 hours. On Purple 3 an officer in B Company, 34 Battalion, with "pistol raised high and with an encouraging shout to the men in his barge[128] leapt from the boat into the water, which turned out to be shoulder deep. This made a spirited charge up the beach not half so impressive as it might have been."[129] The YMCA secretary, Pat Parker, came ashore with the assaulting troops of B Company and was soon brewing up tea for the soldiers.[130] Gordon Thomas found his arrival anticlimatic. He noted in his diary: "Our barge hit ground at 0650hrs, 27 October 1943 on a beach named PURPLE 2, on Treasury Island. We filed out to be amazed to find no opposition. The barge wouldn't get very close to the shore, and we waded in water up to our guts. All hands in and we unloaded the boat smartly, up one side and down the other, while a party cut tracks into the jungle."[131]

The men of Company A of 7 (NZ) Field Ambulance were also destined for Purple 2.

> Ready long before the appointed time, we at last heard the dull boom of the destroyer barrage which told us that the infantry was on its way to shore. The ship lights went on, we lost way, then at last came the welcome bump as we hit the beach. Within half a minute we heard the thump of running feet on the deck overhead and soon it was our turn. Up the companionway, past two or three officers, a flashing glimpse of green jungle, sunlight filtering through coconut trees, down the gangway at the double, then a jump over the yard wide beach into the damp clean bush of Stirling Island. There was little time to look around. Everyone had a job, packs were dumped, lines of men streamed up one gangway to stagger down the other carrying boxes and bundles. The clearing gang were hacking a track into the bush. The L.C.I.s backed away and then we began to notice a few bangs, booms, and rat-tat-tats from the other side.[132]

To indicate a successful landing, the troops were given a special rocket device which was intended to throw a white flare into the sky. It did not work, despite the efforts of a number of officers and specialists.[133]

New Zealand and American forces unload ammunition at Purple 2 Beach, Stirling Island, in October 1943 (Archives New Zealand).

The first LCIs landed about a half hour after the initial landing on Stirling. They were hove to, awaiting confirmation the beaches were secure. C Company landed from an LCI and passed through the area occupied by A Company and headed to the south coast. Patrols were sent to the area east of Purple 2 and reached Soala Lake and Wilson Point. A small party of U.S. Marines landed at Wilson Point on Purple 3. These were unarmed signals personnel.[134]

At about 1000 hours, 34 Battalion was ordered to send a platoon to Watson Island because it was thought that mortar fire on the Falamai area was coming from the Island. Lt. Black, from A Company, had his men search the island before reporting it clear of Japanese. As a consequence, two sections of 34 Battalion's mortar platoon were ordered onto Watson to set up positions to provide fire support for the troops on Mono. They moved onto Watson Island that afternoon without being told that Lt. Black's platoon was still on the island. In a situation pregnant with potential for tragedy, the mortar crews stalked Black's platoon for about three hours before realizing that Watson was occupied by friendlies.[135]

Patrols by the Carrier Platoon from Purple 2 made contact with B Company and explored the southern coast. B Company probed the western area and reached Cummings Point where Japanese machine gun fire had been received by the invasion force earlier. There was no sign of Japanese. According to Trevor Whaley, a signaler attached to 29 Light Anti Aircraft Regiment, the Japanese machine gun had not yet left Stirling. He recalled:

Six: Invasion: 27 October 1943

New Zealand and U.S. forces unload cargo from LST 485, Purple 2 Beach, Stirling Island (Archives New Zealand, WAII, 1, Treasury Island Photos, D1, #26, Official Photographer).

At 0700 hrs on 27 October 1943 (officially 0656 hrs), I landed from LCI 67 on beach Purple 2, Stirling Island. With no opposition, we (a group consisting of a major and five other ranks) set off inland — the Sigs personnel leaving their rifles at the beach as we were laden down with telephones, a ten line telephone exchange and reels of cable. Total armament consisted of 3 pistols — the gallant major, the Sigs officer and the Intelligence Officer plus his two men with rifles. This time, however, we passed through not only the 34 Battalion perimeters but beyond their advanced patrols as well. That oft mentioned machine gun brought our party to an abrupt halt. We could not see the Japs, and I'm sure they could not see us. While halted by their activity, we also came under fire from the 34 Battalion mortar platoon who assumed we were Japs, I guess. At post-war 34 Battalion reunions I have several times accused them of trying to kill us and failing to do the job properly. The story ended with our somewhat hasty return to Purple 2, but what happened to the Jap gun and crew nobody appears to know, although it has been suggested that they returned to Mono Island at some time during the hours of darkness.[136]

Because 36 Battalion was having trouble manning its perimeter on Mono, a platoon was detached from C Company, 34 Battalion, and sent as reinforcements.

The mundane, but heavy, work of unloading stores and setting up supply dumps occupied the men on Stirling. The battalion's second in command, Major J.M. Reidy, was in command of beach operations and the work proceeded apace. Artillery had been ferried across from Mono during the day and efforts made to emplace the guns.

So the first day came to an end. The sound of firing from Mono had died down, to be renewed only at intervals throughout the night. Anti-aircraft gunners had a quiet day, with only one enemy plane running the gauntlet of the air cover and breaking through. The artillery had ferried their guns across from Mono to Stirling and were digging them in. Night drew on, with men listening to the curious noises of the jungle and to the sound of Japanese bombers cruising in low overhead. There was tenseness a bomb might fall near; a Jap might lurk behind a tree, within reach of the foxhole; at dawn we might be fighting hard to repel the expected enemy counter-attack from the Shortlands. Pup tents kept out some of the rain.[137]

Foxholes were dug to provide cover for personnel but also to protect the vital guns:

We have our foxholes in a perimeter round the gun positions. They are dug in the shape of a Y and one man is on watch all night in each hole. If any trouble occurs he just has to kick the feet of the other two to awaken them. A sig wire surrounds the lot which you fix onto your wrist and three sharp tugs given by anyone who senses danger is passed around and brings the bty to their guard. Fortunately so far nothing has happened, although the three tugs frequently get passed around. The jungle noises are amazing, birds, crickets and every goddam insect under the sun sets too, and what a noise![138]

The positioning of artillery units on Stirling was an integral part of the Goodtime plan. In the event of a Japanese counterattack, the 25 pounders on Stirling would be crucial. Efforts were made to get the guns off the vessels and emplaced rapidly. Bombardier Thomas noted in his diary: "We recced positions for the guns which came over shortly after the landing and were in action by midday. A plane came along our beach strafing in the afternoon and made us bite the dust, but fortunately hit nobody."[139]

The headquarters of 8 Brigade, artillery units and 34 Battalion were landed successfully on Stirling Island.

The humidity of the Treasury Islands sapped the energy of the troops. One on Stirling recorded: "I nearly died of thirst the first day or two. I wanted to swig, swig at my bottle every five minutes. My tongue hung out for a cup of tea, even to wash the dry rations down if nothing else."[140]

Soanatalu — Beach Emerald

Of all the Goodtime landings, the one by Loganforce at Soanatalu River was the riskiest. The invaders' numbers were limited and they were separated from the main invading force. Located on the northern coast of Mono, the invaders were vulnerable to a Japanese invading force from the Shortland Islands and from air and sea attack.

However, fortune smiled on the invaders. The troops were transported by an APD, the USS *McKean*. The landing at Beach Emerald, at the mouth of the Soanatalu River, was unopposed. The men went over the side of the destroyer and crawled down cargo nets into the waiting LCMs which had been launched from the destroyer. The Americans and the New Zealanders had been kept separate and communication was initially only through their officers. That situation would soon change as both groups would find themselves fighting for their lives.

The combined force of Seabees and Kiwis was landed at 0630 on 27 October and established a defensive perimeter to the beach. The beach itself was relatively small and hemmed in by cliffs and ridges. A Seabee recalled, "The beach was only about 10 feet wide and about 30 feet long. Beyond this was jungle so dark you could barely see your hand in front of your face."[141] The site for the radar installation was inspected and Emerald was confirmed as able to take an LCT. Arrangements were made to have the radar units and a bulldozer delivered that night.

Loganforce was commanded by Major Gordon White Logan, the commander of 8 Brigade Machine Gun Company. He had previously been in 34 Battalion and the majority of the troops that made up Loganforce were from his old battalion. Logan exemplified many of the characteristics of the officers and men of the citizen soldiers of 3NZ Division. Born in Blenheim, in the South Island of New Zealand, in February 1900, Logan missed being sent overseas during the First World War. While at school he was involved in the Cadets Corps and received training in basic military skills. The military life must have appealed to him because he joined a Territorial unit, the 1st New Zealand Mounted Rifles (Canterbury Yeomanry Cavalry), in June 1918, progressing from trooper to sergeant in four years. He took exams and became a 2nd lieutenant in 1923, a lieutenant in 1927 and a captain in 1932. The Territorials were only part-time soldiers and periodically practiced drill and held annual camps. His unit was literally a cavalry unit, albeit without the social trappings the title might suggest, and many of the men in it found their way into 8 Brigade. The military was not popular in the inter-war period and Logan's application to his military career demonstrates a degree of single-mindedness. In his civilian life Logan practiced the family trade of a cabinet maker, employed in the family business.

When World War II broke out in Europe in September 1939, the New Zealand Army was chronically short of trained officers to command its growing ranks. In August, 1940, Logan was granted the temporary rank of major in the Canterbury Yeomanry Cavalry, and it seemed likely he would receive a commission in the regular army. Logan had received an Efficiency Decoration "for long and efficient service in the Auxiliary Forces" in October 1941. Although he had not seen combat, let alone commanded troops under fire, Logan clearly thought he was due a command and he sold the family business.[142]

The cream of New Zealand's men was sent to 2NZ Division in the Mediterranean. Logan, however, was gazetted as a captain in October 1941, and found himself in 34 Battalion and part of the force known as 8 Brigade Group sent to garrison Fiji. On 2 June 1943, he was appointed to command the Machine Gun Company with the rank of major.

Row must have considered Logan a safe pair of hands, even though Logan lacked combat experience. Essentially, Loganforce was an independent command and the task of establishing a defensive perimeter and guarding American radar specialists and their equipment was a delicate and important one.

Logan's small force consisted of a small headquarters, a section of machine guns from 8 Brigade Machine Gun Company, D Company of 34 Battalion, a field ambulance detachment from 7(NZ) Field Ambulance and an artillery observation unit from 38 Field Regiment. A wireless crew from J Section, New Zealand Corps of Signals, had the job of relaying fire orders from the forward observer to the artillery on Stirling, eight miles away.[143] As well as these New Zealand troops, Logan also had under his command a detachment of 20 Seabees from 87NCB and 60 radar specialists. Logan's orders were to ensure the safety of the Americans and to expedite the construction of the radar installation.

Shortly after landing, D Company's troops advanced, probing for signs of any Japanese. A perimeter of 150 yards' radius was established and patrols sent out to 400 yards. Having established that there was no imminent enemy threat, the Seabees used their bulldozer to create a road up the steep slope from the beach. The radar equipment was delivered and the Seabees set about using the bulldozer to construct platforms for the radars. The radar site was on "a high precipice" and the Seabees had to "cut a road through jungle on a sharp 45 degree slope."[144]

"Three gun emplacements for guarding the position were established on the beach, NZ on the right and left and U.S. in the center. It was hot and wet with knee-deep mud (approximately 18"). Some troops advanced up and over the cliff and dug in fox holes (which they lined with the leaves of banana trees and where they slept every night during the mission) to spend the night."[145]

The first sign of Japanese soldiers was at 1100 hours when a lone Japanese soldier with his rifle slung blundered into the area occupied by 14 Platoon, D Company. He was promptly shot and killed. At dusk about six Japanese soldiers were seen and shots were exchanged. As darkness fell the troops occupied their foxholes and settled in for the night.[146] Given the high state of tension, it was almost inevitable that friendly fire casualties would result. All of the Allied troops had been ordered to stay in foxholes during the night. Unfortunately, a Seabee, Seaman Second Class Edwin Ostman, for reasons unclear, disobeyed these orders. A fellow Seabee recalled, "He ran off into the jungle. Shortly thereafter shots were heard and Ostman was missing in action. A year or so later a bulldozer digging a new road uncovered his body. It was determined that he had been buried next to the New Zealand Aid location. We figured that as he ran toward the New Zealand area in the dark they probably shot him thinking he was a Jap. Nonetheless, there was no ill-feeling towards New Zealanders and we were impressed with their courage and very friendly personalities."[147]

In his memory the Seabees named their camp on Stirling Island "Camp Ostman."

One of the beneficiaries of Loganforce was George Luoni. Bert Cowan, on his first patrol, had learned of the existence of George Luoni. However, Luoni had been several miles away, there were too many Japanese soldiers between them, and Cowan's time was limited. Regretfully, he had decided he could not rescue Luoni; that would have to wait.[148]

On the night of 25 October, during Cowan's second patrol, Privates Carl Rusden and Bill Gilfillan and Sergeant David Ilala were brought by a native to the village where Luoni was sheltering. As they halted outside a native hut, Luoni stumbled out "with a fervent, surprised, 'Good God. You are New Zealanders.'"[149] They told him that the invasion was imminent; they gave him some chocolate and cigarettes and told him to get out of harm's way, as there would be a naval bombardment. Cowan knew of Luoni's situation and had instructed his men to pass the message to Luoni. They had a job to do and "could not stop to muck around."[150] That night the natives strapped him across an outrigger canoe and he was rowed to the northeastern tip of the island. He took shelter, with the natives, in one of the caves till the bombardment ceased. He commented, "We knew where the Army was going to land, which was the opposite end to where we were."

With four natives, he traveled back to the village which sheltered him, being greeted by American Seabees from Loganforce busy putting bulldozers through the natives' garden and demolishing two huts. The village chief was clearly appalled by the destruction. Luoni had made the safety of the Allied perimeter but he was weak and, for most of his journey, he had been carried by his native companions. Medical attention was provided by Lt. Foote of the New Zealand Medical Corps. The next day he was put aboard an LCI and sent to the field hospital on Stirling Island, where he remained for six days, recovering.

Brigadier Row arranged for him to be evacuated to Guadalcanal. The ship that took him back to Guadalcanal was a PT boat tender. The captain gave up his cabin so that Luoni could make the journey in more comfort.

The New Zealand government had dispatched a telegram to his mother advising her that her son was missing in action and believed to be dead. The family was devout Catholic, and his mother offered considerable prayer for her son's safe return. Religion was a factor in his survival: prayer and a determination not to give in propelled him forward. He would begin each day on the island determined to take 20 paces. If he could do those 20 paces then he knew he could keep going.[151]

The Ordeal of the USS *Cony*

The USS *Cony* was to be one of the significant Allied casualties suffered in Goodtime. Like so many of its sister destroyers, such as the USS *Philip* and USS *Pringle*, the USS *Cony* (DD508) was a Fletcher Class destroyer built after the attack on Pearl Harbor. Constructed in Bath, Maine, by the Bath Iron Works Company, *Cony* was commissioned on 30 October, 1942, and by Goodtime it was an experienced ship that had seen considerable action in the Solomon Islands. It was designated as an escort and Fighter Director Ship for both Goodtime and Cherryblossom. *Cony* would not keep its second appointment.

Cony left Kukum, Guadalcanal, to escort Transport Group Two. The voyage was without incident. At 0557 on 27 October, it took station four miles west of Mono's Laifa Point, patrolling at 20 to 25 knots. By 0950 the first two Transport Groups had departed and it continued patrolling and functioning as a fighter director ship and using its radar. The morning was relatively uneventful.

One of the ship's gunners, Stanley Baranowski, recorded in his journal:

October 27, 1943

> We got up at 3.30 A.M. and at 5.00 A.M. we went into GQ [General Quarters]. We were laying off from island "Treasury" because we were fighting director for our planes. Nothing happened all morning. Everything was going good, then at 3.00 P.M. got contact with a lot of planes—enemy. Then at 3.15 P.M. they came at us. So many of them. We started to fire everything we had. Bombs dropping all around us. 17 of them missed us. Then at 3.25 P.M. we got 2 direct hits on port and starboard. Shrapnel flew everywhere. Lots of men were hit. 3–5 guns went out. Fire broke out on engines, they went out of order. We started to leave Treasury at 4.00 P.M. Worked on fires. Was up all night taking care of wounded.[152]

This gives a hint of the drama and the terrible injuries inflicted on her by Japanese bombers. The action report "Seizure of Treasury Island" October 27, 1943, provides further detail.[153]

> At 1508 radar detected aircraft approaching from 47 miles away. By 1511 the aircraft had closed to 40 miles and it was clear that a raid was imminent. [USS] Philip retreated from Blanche Harbor and positioned herself about three miles to the west of Stirling. [USS] Cony increased her speed to 30 knots.
>
> At 1525 a large formation of Japanese horizontal bombers came in from the west towards the shipping in Blanche Harbor. Allied fighters attacked the bombers, and four or five were shot down. Seventeen bombers dropped their bombs into the waters of Blanche Harbor with no damage to Allied shipping: the Allied fighters had foiled the attack.

Seven minutes later Japanese Val dive-bombers attacked Cony and Philip, coming from the southwest. The Vals were deadly. The aircraft looked obsolescent with its fixed undercarriage, but it was a highly effective dive-bomber, particularly in the hands of skilled aircrew. The Allied fighters, having inflicted serious losses on the horizontal bombers, were caught out of position and were not able to intercept the Vals. Cony began a series of "radical turns" to evade Japanese bombs. About a dozen came in three or four waves from different directions in carefully orchestrated attacks. Cony fired desperately, even engaging the planes with its 5 inch guns. Several bombs fell about 100 yards from Cony before her luck ran out: at 1634 two bombs hit her main deck near the Number Four 5 inch gun, and on the ship's port side.

Allied fighters began attacking the Vals. Lt. Samuel Howie, of 339 Fighter Squadron, USAAF, flying a P-38, saw them about to dive on their prey. As he approached the destroyers they warned him away because he was in their anti-aircraft defense zone. Murray figured that since the USN gunners had not been able to shoot any down he would be safe. So, undeterred, he shot down two and latched onto the tail of a third. The Val's rear gunner fired at Howie but Howie's aim was better, killing the gunner and sending the Val crashing into the sea.[154]

By 1547 the Japanese retreated towards Bougainville. *Philip* had also been attacked by six Vals but was more fortunate, bombs exploded on its starboard side with no significant damage or casualties. A Japanese plane hit by *Philip*'s guns left the area trailing smoke. One of the LCI gunboats, LCI(G)22, in the western part of Blanche Harbor, was attacked by two dive bombers and one bomb landed 50 yards from it. One of the attackers was hit by anti-aircraft fire and left the area trailing smoke. Miraculously, none of the beached LSTs, which were truly sitting ducks, were attacked.[155]

The Japanese planes left *Cony* with grievous damage. The explosions had been felt all over the *Cony*. Fires broke out in the aft engine room and scalding steam was escaping from ruptured pipes. The fire, steam and rising water forced abandonment of the aft engine room. The starboard engine was still functioning and it continued to make an impressive 24 knots and to twist and turn. Flooding was also occurring. Fires had also broken out in the aft living spaces and in the No. 4 handling room. This posed a significant threat of an explosion, so the aft magazines had to be flooded. The No. 5 gun had a live shell stuck in its barrel and hoses were used to drench both the inside and the outside of the barrel. Some crew members had been killed outright. Others were badly burned, scalded or seriously wounded. Damage control teams desperately fought the fires which raged in the interior of the ship. Barney Benard was badly burned while manning his gun. He reported to the after repair party and helped fight fires until he was ordered to report to the forward battle dressing station for medical treatment. He later died as a result of his burns.

Cony's ability to defend itself was severely diminished. Number 3, 4 and 5 five-inch guns were inoperable. Three of the 40mm guns were without electrical power and the 20mm gun on the fantail had been knocked out. Its ability to maneuver and fight was severely compromised. The aft engine room was still flooding and wreathed in steam. The fires in the aft living areas were still raging. The captain had little option but to hand over its role to *Philip* and to retreat at 1610. On only one engine, it could do only 20 knots, which later dropped to 15 knots. At 2000 it rendezvoused with the USS *Waller*.

An hour before *Cony* had managed to bring the fires in the aft compartment under control, but they continued to smolder and would periodically break out again. Attempts

This photograph of the USS *Cony* shows bomb damage, 1943 (U.S. Navy).

were made to pump out the engine room which was flooded to a depth of 12 feet. John E. La Moure, a crewman, recalled that "they spent a nervous evening, dead in the water, listening for Japanese patrol boats looking to finish them off." At midnight the ships were joined by the tug USS *Apache*. By 0630 on 28 October, the fires in the aft living space were out. At 1049 the remaining engine froze and was shut down and the *Apache* took *Cony* in tow. She safely arrived at Purvis Anchorage, Florida Island, at 2127.

The *Cony* was a mess. Fires and flooding had caused extensive damage: bulkheads were buckled or ruptured, the engines damaged and a hydraulic ammunition hoist disabled. It had come close to being lost and only the determination of its damage control teams and crew had saved it.

Cony is thought to have shot down at least five Japanese planes. One was claimed by the 5 inch guns and the others by the 40mm and 20mm gun crews.

It had lost four men killed in action. Another four were seriously injured, of whom two later died. The three seriously wounded were transferred to the U.S. Base Hospital on Tulagi and seven slightly wounded or burned were treated and remained on board.

Cony was given emergency repairs at Port Purvis and then sent to Mare Island Naval Shipyard near San Francisco for a complete overhaul. By March 1944, it had returned to the Solomons, where it took part in anti-submarine and escort work including the invasion of Saipan and the battle for the Philippines. It survived the war and was decommissioned in June 1946.[156]

The air battles over the *Cony* almost claimed another victim. On returning to his airfield on Munda, Lt. Samuel Howie proceeded to do three victory rolls. By the third victory roll it seemed to onlookers that he was so low that it was a certainty his P-38 would crash. Howie completed the roll with only inches to spare.[157]

The First 24 Hours on the Treasury Islands

Goodtime was a success. The Allies had landed in good order on the two islands, and the radar units at Soanatalu would soon be operational. Artillery positions had been established on Stirling and, best of all, the casualties had been relatively light. Twenty-one New Zealanders were killed and 70 were wounded, and nine Americans were killed and 15 wounded.[158] Casualty evacuation had occurred smoothly. No shipping had been sunk and the landing craft were free for further operations.

Although the Japanese units had fought tenaciously, their efforts to prevent an Allied landing had failed. Short of a counter-invasion from the Shortland Islands, the Japanese on Mono Island were doomed. A "Condition Black" was declared on the night of 27 October—a warning that counter invasion was imminent. However, this was a false alarm.

A patrol line of PT boats guarded Mono. Nothing would have gladdened the American sailors more than a chance to machine gun Japanese soldiers packed in landing craft.

For Barrowclough based on Vella Lavella, the wait for news had been particularly trying. Elaborate arrangements had been made to intercept any news about Goodtime. American air crews informed him that the preliminary naval bombardment had been very effective but that the area was obscured by smoke. He received a signal from Row late in the day telling him that a successful lodgment had been made and that casualties were light. Further reports arrived but Barrowclough still had concerns about the second echelon of troops and their vulnerability to air attack.[159]

Logistical Support

Getting the soldiers ashore was only the first part of successfully seizing the Treasury Islands. Those troops had to be kept supplied with food, ammunition and the thousand and one things necessary to maintain combat efficiency. Logistics may be unglamorous but it is also essential. Logistics troops also braved Japanese fire and air raids.

Ray Otto, a driver with 4 ASC Company, remembered:

> "[We] came ashore off the LST's with our GMC trucks 6 x 4s loaded with provisions after the landing of the infantry battalions. We stayed with the trucks after landing and I just can't recall for how long. I think it wasn't until next day we started unloading. I don't know how long we were there before we were able to establish our start of the ration dump over on Stirling Island. The provisions were on the LSTs and I can remember making a number of trips driving up the ramp loading, them along the track to our dump.... I was kept quite busy delivering rations to the various camps and at one time I had the job of

bread from the American camp to our own troops. They did have better stoves, ovens etc. than the Kiwis had."[160]

4MT Company set about creating supply dumps on the coast of Mono so that the troops would have access to petrol, ammunition and rations. At Falamai and on Stirling Island larger dumps were established. The emphasis was on getting supplies unloaded and out of sight of Japanese aircraft. As heavy trucks and machinery traveled to and from the dumps the thin layer of humus on top of the coral was rapidly dissipated. In some areas the troops had to contend with deep, glutinous mud. This combined with heavy rain made the movement of vehicles difficult.[161]

The Japanese Response

The purpose of Goodtime was primarily a diversion — to confuse the Japanese and draw their attention away from Empress Augusta Bay. A similar diversion was occurring on nearby Choiseul. Both operations confused the Japanese High Command in Rabaul.[162]

A Japanese patrol plane detected the Allied invasion force at 0420 hours on 27 October, reporting that the convoy of 15 transports and 3 cruisers was 10 nautical miles southeast of the Treasury Islands. The Japanese response was sluggish and uncertain. The commander of the 8th Fleet put his units on alert but was uncertain where the blow would fall. The garrison on Mono reported enemy landings and that they were engaging the enemy. Communications ceased shortly thereafter.

For the Japanese, the question was whether this was simply a diversion and that the real blow would fall in the New Guinea area. Fighting was taking place on Lae, Salamua and Finschafen and this was going badly for the Japanese. Was the Treasury Island attack simply a diversion, or a precursor to something more serious? On learning of the landings on Mono, the Japanese commander of the South East Asia Fleet ordered his forces to concentrate on the Solomon Islands rather than New Guinea and ordered Japanese planes to attack vessels off Mono. He also ordered the Japanese submarine RU-105 to move to Mono at top speed and began putting together a naval force made up of the light cruiser *Nagara*[163] and 10 destroyers in the Rabaul area. He intended to use this force to launch a night-time attack on the Allied vessels. Although American advances in naval radar technology had, to a large extent, negated the Japanese advantage in night fighting, the superior Japanese Long Lance torpedo would have made the Japanese attackers extremely potent. At this stage of the war the Japanese Navy was a formidable opponent, particularly in a night action. The Japanese cancelled the attack when aerial reconnaissance in the early hours of 28 October reported no sign of Allied activity. The Japanese commander refocused his forces on the defense of the New Guinea area.[164]

The principal Japanese response to Goodtime was to be by way of airpower. At 1130 hours on 27 October, 39 Zero fighters and 10 carrier bombers were dispatched to the Treasury Islands, and at about 1330 hours they unloaded their bombs. The pilots reported sinking two transports and two cruisers.

The 1st Air Squadron and 11th Air Fleet were in the process of concentrating when American forces invaded Bougainville on 1 November 1943. Japanese airpower was thereafter involved in air battles over Bougainville.

Wounded

The New Zealand medical units for Goodtime were 7 Field Ambulance (244 men) and 2 Field Surgical Unit (11 men). Both units had not experienced combat. Limitations on shipping space meant only 128 men from 7 Field Ambulance and 10 from 2 Field Surgical Unit were in the first echelon. There was also a severe limitation on their equipment and gear, let alone vehicles.[165]

The plan envisaged setting up a field hospital on Stirling Island, close to the beach, and an advanced dressing station and beach evacuation station on Mono. An officer and four other ranks would accompany Loganforce. (The small number reflected the belief that there would be little opposition.) Casualties would be moved from the beach dressing station to the field hospital on Stirling by small craft and, once stabilized, the wounded would travel by LST back to Vella Lavella, where there was an American hospital.[166]

The LSTs were 2000-ton vessels capable of accommodating 100 prone and 200 sitting patients.[167] One, LST 485, had an improvised operating theatre and two experienced American surgeons reinforced by a doctor and two corpsmen from LST 399. The commander of 7 Field Ambulance, Lieutenant S. Hunter, arranged for casualties from the initial landing to be dealt with by LST 485. Forty-seven casualties were dealt with by this LST, which sailed directly back to Guadalcanal. During the thirty hour trip the medical staff worked without breaks and performed 15 major operations.[168] These casualties went to 2NZ Casualty Clearing Station.[169]

Evacuating the wounded from Purple 2 Beach, Stirling Island, October 1943 (Archives New Zealand, WAII, 1, Treasury Islands Photos, D1, #28, Official Photographer).

Once the first wave had landed, a rudimentary beach dressing station was to be set up in a small creek bed on Mono close to the beach and in the center of the perimeter. A more elaborate dressing station would be set up on the left flank. However, the heaviest casualties were occurring on the beach, and an Advanced dressing station was not established until the late afternoon. Stretcher bearers were used to move the wounded. Casualties were received by the LSTs until late afternoon when casualties began to be sent to the MDS on Stirling to avoid overloading the craft. By 1630 all casualties had been evacuated from the beachhead and the beach dressing station was set up on the planned site.

The medical staff set to digging foxholes with some degree of urgency as darkness was rapidly falling. Mortar and aerial bombing occurred during the night but without casualties to the medical personnel.

Casualties once again began flowing into the Advanced Dressing Station the next day from 0800 to dusk. That night Japanese infiltrated the area around the station, gunfire and grenades exploding periodically. There were no casualties but the ADS personnel were withdrawn to Stirling the following night. A small beach dressing station was set up on Mono the following morning. Each night its personnel were evacuated to Stirling, returning the next morning.

The Field Surgical Unit landed on Stirling with the invasion at 0645. There was no opposition, which was fortunate because the infantry had been landed in a different area and no secure perimeter had been established for it. The main obstacle came from the

Medics working on a wounded soldier (War History Collection, Alexander Turnbull Library, Wellington, F-41597-1/2).

terrain: a track had to be hacked through heavy jungle and an area cleared. Equipment was then hauled from the beach. Despite these problems, a rudimentary dressing station had been set up by noon and by 1300 it was receiving casualties. Surgical theatres were set up, and fully occupied until 2200.

The facilities treated a steady flow of patients over the following days. When the Second Echelon arrived five days after the initial landings, the outgoing LSTs evacuated 51 patients. Likewise, the Third Echelon LSTs removed a further 37 patients. Stirling provided a relatively safe haven for medical treatment in the initial stages of Goodtime.

Due to shipping limitations, only a minimum of tents were brought in by LCI. More tents and heavy equipment were intended to be shipped across to Stirling within 48 hours. This did not occur. Unloading difficulties proved more formidable than expected. Some equipment was unloaded in the wrong place and some was destroyed by Japanese artillery fire and aerial bombardment. When fires broke out equipment was pulled to the outskirts of the beach to save it and was lost for several days until order was established. The result was overcrowding of patients and, even worse, a breakdown of sanitation. Dysentery patients were received at an early stage, and many of the nursing staff contracted the disease.[170]

Allan Rogers of 36 Battalion was wounded and found himself on Stirling. He was greeted by a familiar face in the form of Major Geissen, the doctor. "Good morning Rogers, the boy next door!"[171]

One of the features of jungle warfare for a defender is that movement ceases at night and soldiers remain in their foxholes. Anyone or thing that moves in the dark is a legitimate target. Explicit instructions were given that anyone who moved at night would be regarded as enemy. Consequently no casualties were received at advanced dressing stations or regimental aid posts once dark fell.[172] Wounded were simply kept in a foxhole until daylight.

Most of the wounded on Mono suffered multiple wounds, generally flesh wounds. These were usually from rifle, grenade, machine gun or mortar fire. There was a low proportion of abdominal wounds compared to those suffered by New Zealand soldiers fighting in the Mediterranean. The reason for this is thought to be that Mono involved close combat jungle fighting in which abdominal wounds are more likely to be fatal.[173] There was, in fact, a relatively high proportion of fatal wounds.[174]

Overall, surgical and medical treatment for those wounded on Mono worked well. Operations were generally carried out within 12 hours of the soldier being wounded and there was a relatively speedy evacuation. The New Zealand casualties went to 2 CCS on Guadalcanal. Some 61 percent had to be further evacuated to 4 General Hospital on New Caledonia. The remaining 29 percent returned to their units.[175]

The treatment and evacuation of Allied wounded was an example of smooth interallied and inter-service cooperation. Officially, the USN was responsible for not only providing the Kiwis with transport shipping (and by implication protection), but also with the evacuation of casualties. American inter-service rivalry meant that the American Army, Navy and Marine forces maintained their own separate hospitals and medial facilities, providing potential for things to go awry. However, things worked well, in no small measure due to the goodwill and close liaison of Allied medical personnel. Patient records accompanied wounded soldiers and the Americans were generous with medical supplies.[176]

Seven

Goodtime — The Air Aspects

One of the riskiest elements of Goodtime was that it was to take place in Japanese-dominated airspace. The dangers of operating in such an environment had been hammered home to Allied commanders in Malaya, the Philippines and the Dutch East Indies. Substantial Allied forces had crumbled before the Japanese onslaught as their airpower was eviscerated by the Japanese and their armies and navies hamstrung by accurate Japanese air attack.

Although attritional air battles had taken place in the Solomon Islands, both the Imperial Japanese Naval Air Force and Imperial Japanese Army Air Force were forces to be reckoned with.

The overall aim of the Allies was neutralize Rabaul, the main Japanese base in the South Pacific which had plentiful airfields. In addition to Rabaul there were airfields on Bougainville, so the Japanese were capable of mounting quite devastating aerial attacks on Task Force 31 and the Goodtime troops. The question for Allied planners was how to deal with this risk. They could put a Combat Air Patrol over Goodtime to protect shipping and troops. Alternatively, airpower could be applied to attacking Japanese airfields and suppressing Japanese air activity.

The planners opted for both. In the initial stages of Goodtime a Combat Air Patrol over the beachheads provided basic cover to Allied shipping. However, the emphasis was on raids on the airfields on Bougainville. After the first day, with Allied shipping dispersed, the combat air patrol was decreased and the Kiwis and Seabees were left largely reliant on their own anti-aircraft guns. Allied airpower was switched to cover the ships and landing craft off Empress Augusta Bay.

The closest Allied airbases were in the New Georgia Group. Allied fighters faced a restricted loiter time over the Treasury Islands. There were limited fighters available and some, like the P-40 Kittyhawk, were obsolete.

The air cover was provided by the 13th Air Force, commanded by General Nathan Twining, USAAF. He had 16 American P-38s of the 339th Fighter Squadron flying top cover with P-40 Kittyhawks from No. 18(F) Squadron Royal New Zealand Air Force and P-39s from the U.S. Army Air Force 347th Fighter Group below.[1]

Effective fighter cover was the key to protecting the Goodtime shipping and the troops once ashore. Japanese planes, if left unmolested, could bomb and strafe and threaten the success of the invasion and ongoing operations. To be effective, Allied fighters needed to be warned of approaching Japanese planes, particularly their height and direction of approach. One of the lessons of the Battle of Britain was the importance of integrating radar units with fighter control. Priority was therefore given to getting trained radar personnel and Fighter Direction Officers into place on shore and getting their equipment operational quickly. Five Fighter Direction Officers and 4 enlisted men landed on Stirling on the morning of 27 October and, assisted by Seabees, found a suitable site for setting up a radar unit. A communications truck was unloaded from an LCT at 1100 and by 1300 was operating. By monitoring Allied frequencies the truck's crew and other radar posts were able to sound two Condition Red alerts, enabling troops to take cover before Japanese planes attacked. Two officers began plotting radar reports on a small board and another kept a check on friendly aircraft in the vicinity. A telephone line was laid during the day and connected to a switchboard to provide warning of air raids and information to the anti-aircraft crews.

Great hopes had been held for the radar station, code named "Orion," at Soanatalu, but attempts by the men on Stirling to contact it by radio failed until 30 October. Fierce fighting around Emerald further restricted its effectiveness, and much of the fighter direction relied on reports from radar units "Jupiter" and "Eskimo" in the first few days.

On Stirling the 75th NCB dug

a ditch 40 feet long by 15 feet wide and 8 feet deep, finishing it by noon on October 28. Officers and men of Argus 6 Fighter Direction Group, Comm 8 and 1st Marine Air Wing Comm Group all pitched in and put up sandbag walls in the centre of the dugout making a room 20 feet long. The C.B.'s using a crane covered it with a double layer of logs. At each end of the room a blackout tent has been placed, one housing the radar equipment and the other as a standby tent to house FDO, Fighter Command and Operations Officers as well as an equipment table.[2]

A complex communication set up linked "Terrier Base" and the Fighter Direction Centre, COM AIR NOR SOLS with Bomber support, Air Support Command, Radar Reporting, AA Batteries and the Navy Headquarters.

Some radar units did get established on Mono. A Type 602 radar was in operation by noon on 27 October. Located on a rock ledge some 100 yards east of Soanatalu, it was soon picking up targets at a range of up to 47 miles. IF[identification friend or foe] interrogation of targets proved problematic. A further Type 270 radar was installed half a mile inland at an elevation of 135 feet. The Seabees built a road and the unit was moved into position on 29 October. A second Type 270 unit was placed 100 yards inland east of Soanatalu. In theory the effective radar reach was 107 miles but the range was in practice more like 70 miles.[3]

A fighter control team was set up on Rear Admiral Fort's flagship, the USS *Eaton*. However, being a *Fletcher* Class destroyer with limited space and given the fact that Fort was in charge of the operational naval aspects, the amount of space allocated to the fighter control team would have been limited.

A detachment headquarters, Commander Aircraft Northern Solomons under Major V. Leary, landed in the first echelon on Stirling Island and established a fighter command and early warning system. However, it was not fully operational until the Type 270 radar installation was set up at Soanatalu.[4]

One of the interesting aspects of Goodtime is that it featured combat operations not only by the New Zealand Army but also by the RNZAF. However, the co-operation was indirect and controlled by the Americans. The RNZAF in the Solomons was organized as No. 1 Islands Group. This in turn was controlled by Commander Northern Solomons Air.

Air operations in the Northern Solomons were carried out by the U.S. Navy, the USAAF, the Marines, and the RNZAF. Each had their own organizational doctrine and colorful personalities but subordinated their differences in pursuit of defeating Japanese airpower. One analyst observed that the Solomons air war saw "the emergence of a truly joint air operations organization. In many respects the Solomon's Campaign of 1942–1944 was to be the high-water mark of joint and unity of air operations until the Persian Gulf War in 1991."[5]

It helped that the U.S. Navy had set up the organizational structure, and that its aircraft carriers had been moved out of the Solomons. This meant that no one service dominated air operations. There was certainly plenty of scope for all the services: "The multifaceted nature of the air battle for the Solomons required the unique capabilities that each service brought to the fight. There was a place for long range Air Force bombers, the sea services dive bombers and fighters from all the services. Even the substandard equipment of the services contributed mightily to the outcome whether it was Air Force P-39s and P-400s, Marine SBDs or Navy PBYs. In effect there was scope for really full play for the mission doctrine and equipment of all the services."[6]

The RNZAF was equipped with the obsolete P-40 Kittyhawk, a fighter which was, as George Luoni discovered, no match for the nimble Japanese fighters in a dogfight. Nonetheless, it was a sturdy, well-built aircraft and filled a variety of roles including bomber escort and ground attack.

For the American air commanders, Goodtime was a small part of the overall air campaign focused on obtaining air superiority over Empress Augusta Bay. The official RNZAF history records:

> Throughout the day the fighter patrols were maintained over the Treasurys to give protection to the landing forces and shipping. The RNZAF wing flew 10 patrols on this day. The first operations of the day were a patrol by eight aircraft with No. 18 Squadron over the islands from 5.40 in the morning until 8.40 and one by four aircraft from 5.40 until ten past eight covering the task force immediately before and during its landings. Four other patrols of four aircraft each flew over the landing operations at two hour intervals. No. 15 Squadron flew four patrols during the day, two of 4 aircraft and two of eight.
>
> No contact was made with enemy aircraft until the afternoon when 30 to 40 Val dive bombers and 50–60 Zeke and Hamp fighters[7] attacked the landing craft unloading at the beaches. At the time both American and New Zealand fighters were patrolling to the northwest and northeast of the islands. In all, three groups of enemy planes were successfully intercepted by the Allied fighter screen but a fourth group got through and damaged the fighter director ship, the USS Cony, with two direct bomb hits. Flights from both New Zealand Squadrons intercepted enemy formations and between them shot down four Japanese fighters with no loss to themselves.[8]

On 27 October, four of RNZAF No. 18 Squadron P-40 Kittyhawk fighters flew over the Treasury Islands between 1530 and 1600 hours. They were vectored by the fighter director ship towards incoming Japanese aircraft. The aircraft were at 20,000 feet and the incoming Japanese aircraft were at 2000 feet. Near Toko, southwest of Bougainville, the RNZAF, using their height advantage, dived on 4 Japanese Zero fighters and shot one Zero down.

Unlike operations on land, where it is possible to seize a geographic feature and use it to dominate the surrounding area, air cover is transitory. The Allied aircraft were not able to provide total air cover even when they were able to obtain local air supremacy, so the Japanese were able to penetrate the initial Combat Air Patrol (CAP) and to hit the USS *Cony* and LSTs.

Only a limited number of Allied aircraft were in the vicinity of the Treasury Islands at one time. Continuous cover was not maintained — the aircraft involved had to be rearmed and refueled and their crews rested. Nonetheless, Row said that "Fighter cover was excellent. Ground tps were NOT attacked at all by enemy aircraft. Naval forces were NOT so fortunate in that the destroyer was attacked at 1530 hrs by high altitude and dive bombers and suffered two hits."[9]

The main purpose of the CAP was to protect shipping. Once that shipping had retreated from the Treasury Islands air resources were allocated elsewhere. The operations logs for No. 15 and No. 18 Squadrons record that they provided air cover over the Treasury Islands on 27 October, but in the following days their main effort went into providing cover for American bombers striking Koro and Choiseul and conducting local patrols.[10]

The perception of Gordon Thomas was that the Allied air units were effective: "Our RNZAF protected the convoy and I believe if it wasn't for them intercepting enemy planes we would have had some nasty smacks. The Yank Air Force was to bomb Kahili for 4 hours from the time of our landing and we were dug in that time, so dig in we did. Kahili is only 40 miles away and the nearest point of Bougainville 36 miles. We are the most Northern Allied troops."[11]

Once Empress Augusta Bay had been secured, an airstrip was established at Torokina and fighter cover in turn secured the Treasury Islands.

The fighter cover provided during daytime had been relatively effective, but no cover was provided at night, and that is when the Japanese attacked. Mono was small and the Falamai area easy to find. Anti-aircraft guns, lacking any radar guidance systems and without early warning, were ineffective against Japanese area bombing. The radar at Soanatalu was unreliable in distinguishing enemy planes from friendly ones. It also had a limited arc of 180 degrees. The dead ground should have been covered by other radars on Vella Lavella but this did not occur, so Japanese planes were allowed to achieve surprise.[12]

Compounding the difficulties of the air defense gunners was the unwillingness of some Allied pilots to identify themselves. There were few daylight targets for the gunners and orders specifically prohibited firing at night unless the target was illuminated by searchlight. "They were never able to do more than 'flick' an enemy plane during a raid, much to the disgust of the gunners, who were anxious to spray any bombers which sounded within range."[13]

Thom Sen, a gunner with 208 Battery, 29th Light AA, recalled that his anti-aircraft gun was ordered not to fire at Japanese planes unless they had specific orders. When a Japanese aircraft dropped a bomb near the brigadier, those restrictions were lifted.

Between 27 October and 10 November, there were of 54 "Condition Red" alerts. Most of these were triggered by Japanese floatplanes searching the eastern and western approaches of Blanche Harbor looking for Allied shipping.

Communication difficulties continued to hamper air defense efforts. Communication frequencies with Munda and Vella Lavella were often ineffective in the early morning.[14]

The problems of Allied air defense are illustrated by the lack of reaction to an RNZAF plane on the afternoon of 28 October. Flight Lieutenant St. John Spicer, the pilot of a Ventura, was given the task of dropping a document to a colonel on Mono Island. He recorded:

> The New Zealanders took Treasury last night. It was 290' high there and we came in low and saw two fighters over the island. It is only four feet across between the islands. The fighters (who) made passes on us were American, so they did not shoot. We expected AA from the Japs or the New Zealanders as we came in from no-where without being announced.
>
> Anyway we found the point between Mono Island and Stirling Island where the New Zealand artillery was—flew low down on the point and dropped the package. There were New Zealanders on the point and three large barges. Flew over the island and saw a bit of fighting in the centre. We were lucky, as an hour earlier there were 70 Zeros (Zekes) over the island. The NZ fighter squadron shot down four. We saw none, thank goodness![15]

The usual reaction of edgy ground troops to low-flying planes is to let rip with all possible ordnance. The best explanation for the absence of ground fire is that the defenders were caught by surprise.

One aspect of aerial operations did not feature in Goodtime. In July 1943, the 1st Marine Air Wing began training air liaison parties to support air-to-ground operations during Goodtime. But the nature of the terrain, the closeness of Allied troops to Japanese lines and the presumed effectiveness of naval bombardment meant it was not needed.

The outstanding feature of air operations during Goodtime was that the Allies did not suffer any aerial losses. On the other hand, the Japanese suffered significant losses as they tried to bomb Allied shipping and the beachhead.

Eight

Loganforce at Soanatalu Desperate Defense: 29 October to 3 November 1943

Loganforce at Soanatalu was the scene of feverish activity as the invaders began establishing themselves. In the morning of 29 October, a bulldozer was used to dig the foundations for a field hospital. Trees were felled using axes and crosscut saws and logs used to create a stout bunker. Next, the bulldozer returned to the beach to dig a bunker for heavy gun emplacements, walled with coconut and mahogany logs. Although the Kiwis were there to provide protection for the Yanks, both groups built the bunker. The Kiwis provided the food and introduced the Yanks to brewing tea 4 or 5 times a day.

The Seabees rapidly set to work preparing the radar site and hauled the radar into position. By 31 October the radar was fully operational with a range of 124 miles.

Convinced that the Japanese were withdrawing to the north of Mono, Row sent a company and two platoons from 34 Battalion to Soanatalu. His estimate of Japanese intentions was essentially correct. The Japanese had been devastated by the fighting on 27–28 October and fell back to the observation post on Hill 1165, where their headquarters was. A group of about 80 from the headquarters and neighboring units found themselves under the command of Ensign Nakaseko of 7 Kure SNLF with a mountain artillery warrant officer as second in command. Thinking Malsi was likely to have been seized by the Allies, the group decided to strike out for Soanatalu. The plan was for the warrant officer and about 60 men to attack along the beach from the west and seize a Japanese landing barge. They would then signal Nakaseko to attack with the remaining 20 men down the Soanatalu Valley. It was a desperate plan and, if unsuccessful, the group vowed that they would commit suicide. A captured Japanese diary records an intention "to enter into a decisive battle."[1]

The plan began to unravel as the group retreated northwards. The wounded started to drop out and the group had only limited supplies of food. Signal flares were fired on 28, 29 and 30 October to alert Japanese planes to their presence, but no supplies were dropped.[2] By 30 October their rations had gone and the men were eating the roots of trees and weeds. A few fish were caught. They continued northwards towards Loganforce.[3] They planned a decisive penetration on the anniversary of Emperor Meiji's birthday but, given the condition of the soldiers, they decided to advance the attack[4] — the longer the delay, the weaker they would be physically.

The Allied soldiers had, meantime, pushed their defensive perimeter out to about 1000 yards. There had been no sign of Japanese, but this changed late on 29 October. About 1630 hours, a group of about 20 Japanese attacked part of the western perimeter defended by 14 Platoon, 34 Battalion, under the command of Lieutenant R.M. Martin. Two sections from another platoon arrived as reinforcements and the defenders had the benefit of a barrage laid down by 3-inch mortars. The fighting lasted till dusk, when the Japanese retreated. They had suffered at least five dead. The Allies had no casualties. That night was quiet except for defensive shelling of the western perimeter by New Zealand artillery.[5] Gilfillan and Rusden from Bert Cowan's second patrol had found their way to Loganforce's perimeter after having contacted Flight Sergeant George Luoni.[6] The Japanese attack merely succeeded in ruining yet another night's sleep for Gilfillan and Rusden. "In the morning these two searched the enemy dead before consigning them to the deep."

It was erroneously thought that the Japanese were retreating across Mono bound for Ulapu, west of Soanatalu, and that they would try to seize native canoes there and escape. Row therefore drew units from 34 Battalion on Stirling, where there was no threat, and sent them to reinforce Loganforce. A Carrier Platoon, C Company Headquarters, and one platoon from C Company arrived at Soanatalu at first light on 30 October. Almost as welcome as their presence were their resupplies of mortar ammunition. The Carrier Platoon was deployed eastwards towards Malsi to patrol that area. Meanwhile, patrols were dispatched to cautiously probe the area outside the southern perimeter. These made no contact. In contrast, the western perimeter was quite active and the Japanese seemed to be trying to ascertain Allied positions.

The following day the Carriers returned to the perimeter from Malsi. It seemed that the Japanese were massing on the western flank with the intention of attacking Soanatalu. Patrols had cautiously probed the Japanese lines and it was thought that there were about two hundred Japanese preparing to attack. It seemed all hell was about to be unleashed. Logan requested reinforcements but these were not available.

Logan and his men had been on alert since the first Japanese probes and sleep deprivation was beginning to tell. He knew that his men were outnumbered and that the Japanese were desperate. Logan also knew that he had the support of batteries of 25 pounder artillery and that if his force was hard-pressed he could expect reinforcements either from Allied forces in southern Mono or by sea. His troops were also reasonably well dug in.

A Seabee recalls:

> The site for the radar had been scouted and the plan was to cross a small river in order to access the mountain. However, the river had overflowed its 6-foot banks and created impassable mud beyond its banks. At one point, the bulldozer was so stuck in the mud that it could move neither backward nor forward. Through some Seabee ingenuity, they got the bulldozer out of the mud and returned to the Cliffside, about 90–100 feet above the water, cleared the area and installed the radar unit at this position. Mission accomplished — radar unit up and working. From this vantage point the men observed the beginning of the naval and aerial assault on Bougainville.[7]

On the morning of 1 November, Logan sent out a reconnaissance patrol, commanded by Lieutenant J.A.H. Dowell, towards Ulapu. It encountered brisk resistance only 1500 yards from Soanatalu. A firefight lasting about half an hour ended when the outnumbered patrol withdrew to the safety of the Soanatalu perimeter. It suffered one fatal casualty, Corporal R.H. Haresnape of D Company, 34 Battalion. It had, however, confirmed the strength of Japanese forces in the Ulapu–Soanatalu area.

In light of this, Logan's men dug in deeper and booby trapped the perimeter. A blockhouse had already been created on the beach near a beached Japanese barge and the men of C Company, commanded by Major J.C. Braithwaite, with the Carrier Platoon, held a perimeter further inland.

On the afternoon of 1 November, a bizarre incident occurred. A Seabee, Clair Charles, recalled:

> A NZ (soldier) was standing in the road, shaving with a mirror, and saw in the mirror a Jap walking into camp with his rifle over his shoulder. After the Jap had walked about 10 paces past the NZ (soldier), the NZ soldier took his rifle, shouted "halt," the Jap wheeled and kneeled and both soldiers fired simultaneously. The Jap bullet hit the sight on the NZ gun, ricocheted across his forehead drawing blood but causing only a superficial wound. The NZ bullet entered the muzzle of the Jap's gun splitting the barrel. The Jap jumped down over the bank of the roadside, where a New Zealander shot him. The Jap was wearing green GI coveralls and apparently thought he could just walk through the camp to the beach.[8]

Another explanation is that the Japanese soldier was unaware that Soanatalu was in American hands and thought the camp was full of Japanese reinforcements. He might have been dehydrated and starved, and after being in combat in the south of the island, was most likely intensely fatigued. He was wearing a Japanese uniform similar to "green GI coveralls."

On the night of 1–2 November, the Japanese gathered a force of about 80 and made a concerted effort to overrun Loganforce's perimeter and seize a Japanese barge on the beach. They approached over the hills from the south and down the Soanatalu river valley, striking soon after dark. On the western perimeter, Lieutenant Martin rang D Company headquarters and told them there were large numbers of Japanese in his area. Ominously the phone went dead a short time after. The Japanese used mortars, grenades and machine gun fire. Fighting would flare up in intensity, subside and then flare up again throughout the night, reaching a crescendo shortly after midnight.

On the eastern perimeter and in the headquarters area the Japanese infiltrated the Allied lines. By 01.30 hours on the morning of 2 November they had moved a significant force through the perimeter and were able to range through the defenses and intermingle with the defenders. This, the terrain and the darkness negated Logan's advantage of artillery. At this point things began to fall apart for the Japanese. Most of their force had concentrated on the steep slopes of the western perimeter, about 50 yards to the west of the beach. It seems the Japanese plan was to break into this area, and use the infiltration as a diversion. Action now centered on the blockhouse on the beach. The Japanese landing barge acted as a beacon for the desperate Japanese, offering them the best chance of their getting from Mono to the Shortland Islands. The blockhouse stood in the way.

A series of vicious firefights now raged around the blockhouse to daybreak. It was defended by six New Zealanders and three Seabees commanded by a New Zealander, Captain Les J. Kirk, second in command of D Company. Kirk's men were armed with an interesting assortment of Allied and Japanese weapons—two Japanese machine guns taken from the barge, a Thompson submachine gun, rifles and grenades. The first Japanese attack was at about 01.30 hours. They killed Staff Sergeant D.O. Hannafin and, shortly thereafter, Captain Les Kirk was momentarily knocked unconscious by a bullet which grazed his head. Japanese grenades knocked out the machine guns. Both sides began throwing grenades at each other at 10 to 15 yards. The Allies did have an advantage, however; they had rigged a screen to deflect grenades. When the Japanese were heard approaching, the screen would be lowered so that grenades could be thrown at them.

Given the intensity of the Japanese attack the defenders debated whether they should withdraw to the main defense perimeter up the hill. Kirk and another soldier proposed drawing Japanese fire so that the others could escape, but finally the defenders decided to try to hold out. The Japanese fire continued and Kirk's luck ran out: he was hit again and became unconscious. He died the next day.

Command of the defense passed to Private C.H. Sherson. He was wounded and command then passed to Private Joe Smith, the cook. Smith led his combined force against sustained Japanese attacks with rifle fire and grenades. It was a desperate defense against soldiers who were equally desperate—kill or be killed!

Just when the Japanese seemed on the verge of success their attack faded away. By 0430 the battle was over, apart from Japanese snipers on the beach firing sporadically. At daybreak a patrol was sent from Company Headquarters to relieve the men in the blockhouse. It was greeted by the sight of 26 Japanese bodies strewn around the blockhouse. Perhaps even more extraordinary was the sight of Joe Smith calmly preparing breakfast.

On the western perimeter, No. 14 and No. 16 Platoons had been hard pressed but had steadfastly held their positions with only one casualty, a wounded private, G.D. Clarke. In contrast, the inland perimeter had been comparatively peaceful with the Japanese blundering into and setting off booby traps.

In the light of day the Allied soldiers were able to survey the carnage. The Japanese had suffered more than 50 percent casualties, including their commander.[9] About 50 Japanese corpses were discovered—the 26 around the blockhouse, 15 on the western perimeter and 9 around the eastern perimeter and Logan's headquarters. There were two Japanese bodies near the Japanese landing barge, proof that success had been tantalizingly close for the Japanese.

Curiously, there were no Japanese wounded. It was thought they had either killed themselves or been helped out of the area by their comrades.

The Japanese were well equipped, as evidenced by the haul of weaponry and equipment recovered: 4 Nambu machine guns, 5 "knee mortars," about 36 rifles, 2 pairs of binoculars and, most prized by souvenir-hunters, a Japanese officer's sword.

The defenders had one piece of good fortune. Superior Seaman Kohei Mizuno had been part of a grenade discharger squad. He later disclosed to his captors that during the battle his "knee mortar only fired one grenade which did not explode, while the second attempt resulted in a misfire. The other 4 knee mortars did not function properly either, due to mechanical difficulties, rust caused by dampness, or faulty grenades."[10]

Although the Japanese had been hurt, Logan did not know how much of a threat they still posed. He prudently redeployed his men to give the two hard-pressed platoons on the western perimeter some relief. He moved Lieutenant W.M. Maxwell's platoon from

C Company, 34 Battalion, from the inland perimeter to the western perimeter and did likewise with the Carrier Platoon. These comparatively fresh platoons waited.

For his leadership of the defense of the blockhouse, Private Joe Smith was awarded the Military Medal, a high award for an enlisted man, for taking command, "and by his resolute actions and calmness, kept the defense intact, finally, after five hours fighting completely annihilating that portion of the enemy force which had penetrated to the beach."

That afternoon, 2 November, Kiwi soldiers located Japanese positions slightly to the right of their perimeter. Artillery support was called for from the artillery units emplaced with 25 pounder guns on Stirling Island. The barrage lasted about an hour and a half. When the dust settled 5 Seabees, armed with Browning Automatic Rifles, and Kiwi soldiers swept the mountain to ensure that there were no survivors. They came under Japanese fire and some of the Seabees and Kiwis were injured by shrapnel from Japanese grenades.

The following night, 2–3 November, the Japanese again attacked the western perimeter. The attack began shortly after dark and continued through to dawn. It did not have the intensity of the previous night's attacks but there were casualties nonetheless. Private G.W. (Joe) Hanson of the C Company and Corporal R.S. Dimery of the Carrier Platoon were killed and Signalman T.R. Tolley, of G Section, was slightly wounded when a bullet penetrated above his left eye.[11]

On the following two nights there were only minor skirmishes. It was evident that organized Japanese resistance had been crushed. Follow-up patrols encountered small groups of Japanese; otherwise there was no further action in the Soanatalu area.[12] On 5 November, Kiwi linesmen linked J Section's reporting center at Falamai with Malsi and then extended the line to Soanatalu.[13]

One of the key factors in breaking up the Japanese attacks was the harassing artillery fire delivered by artillery batteries about 60 miles away. Night firing allowed the gunners of 49 Battery, 38 Field Regiment, little rest.[14]

A prisoner, Komino, captured by 34 Battalion on 30 January 1944, had been stationed at an observation post at Falamai when the landings began. He retreated to Soanatalu where he was part of the attack on Loganforce. He lost his rifle and was isolated from his comrades. The situation appeared hopeless to him so he "went off into the hills somewhere off the headwaters of the Malsi river. Here he stayed living on roots and drinking rain water. He stated that his clothing stank so much that he threw them away and decided to come down to the camp for new clothes and food."[15] When captured by the Kiwis he was wearing a New Zealand jungle suit and boots and was armed with a New Zealand bayonet and a Japanese grenade.

Logan recorded a radio broadcast in late November. Even allowing for the bombast and positive spin for the benefit of the home front, the stress still shines through:

> We spent our first ten days after the landing living in our clothes—wet and muddy, with eyes peering through the heavy rain into pitch darkness, ears straining to distinguish between the hundred jungle noises from those made by the stealthy enemy. It was a terrific strain as the Jap, fighting mostly by night, attacked and attempted to infiltrate our positions, using all his well known tricks night after night. Some would get through only to bump into our inner defenses, but wherever they went our boys were too good for them.... After fighting day and night for over a week things began to ease and everyone was able to

take a breather. There was one occasion when we were at it without sleep for over eighty four hours.... Mere words cannot describe this nerve wracking business of night fighting — one cannot relax even for a moment. Any movement by night and our answer (was) a grenade with devastating results to Tojo, as evidenced by our checkup of enemy killed after daybreak. They simply could not take it and were beaten off night after night, even after penetrating our outer defenses."[16]

The fight for Soanatalu from 29 October to 3 November proved costly for 34 Battalion, with five killed and nine wounded.[17] The fight broke Japanese forces and ended their organized resistance.

Isolated groups of Japanese did what they could to evade capture and get themselves off the island. Superior Seaman Mizuno joined two other survivors in constructing a raft. They lashed the raft together using pilfered telephone lines and set off for the Shortland Islands on the night of 6 November 1943. The winds and currents defeated them and the raft drifted back to Lua Point. The dispirited Japanese hid in the jungle occasionally encountering Allied patrols and other Japanese. The Japanese split into small groups to evade capture but whichever way they turned they seemed to encounter Allied troops. They grew weaker and more disheveled as time went by. Paradoxically, their best source of survival came from raiding their enemies' camps for supplies.

Loganforce needed to be supplied, particularly as food and ammunition were expended. Supply was accomplished by sending barges around the coast.

Overview of Loganforce

Loganforce's performance is notable for being an American–New Zealand effort. The Seabees should, in theory, have been non-combatants — there simply to do construction work. However, they lived up to the Seabee motto "We Build, We Fight." They were integrated into the defense at a time when every rifle counted. This endeared them to the Kiwis. There can be no more powerful image of inter-allied harmony than two nationalities fighting shoulder to shoulder. Both groups were warriors in the truest sense. They faced combat with equal or superior numbers of desperate Japanese, and won. This is all the more astonishing because it was the first combat for the Kiwis and Seabees.

The efforts of the Japanese should not be denigrated. Night attacks are hard military maneuvers to pull off because of difficulties of retaining command and control. Over broken terrain with thick jungle against an entrenched enemy the chances of success diminish hugely. The Japanese attacks were planned and organized and infiltration of the Allied defense perimeter was successful, at least in part. It is likely that the Japanese leaders were at the forefront of inspiring their men and became casualties early in the battle. For most of the Japanese, too, it would have been their first battle and their inexperience was reflected in an inability to mask and destroy the Allied blockhouse on the beach. This would also be a factor in the high ratio of their casualties. No one can doubt the determination and courage of the Japanese attackers, nor the Allied defenders.

Nine

Consolidation and Elimination of Japanese Defenders

For Frank Cooze's anti-aircraft unit the night of 27–28 October had been a disturbed one. The stress began to tell:

> The morning found us tired and weary. We picked at our too-rich rations and wondered what the day would bring forth. On the Shortlands thirty miles away there were 15,000 Japs. Fifteen miles further on, Bougainville was garrisoned with 45,000 Japs. A heavy counter-attack was expected, but the Japs didn't nibble at the bait.
> We sat in groups in the steaming heat and cleaned our rifles. Our jungle suits were greasy and stiff with sweat and dirt. They were beginning to smell! Lonely figures wandered about looking for lost gear or replacements. One or two were trying to shave with a trickle of water grudgingly squeezed from their water bottles.
> A burst of shots spattered in the tree-tops. For a fraction of time all motion ceased. Then the clearing was alive with running figures as everyone dived for cover. Hundreds of bullets seemed to be striking through the trees but no one was hit.
> "What the hell's going on?" said a gunner as he flung himself down beside me.
> "Don't know," I replied. "Might be the start of a raid. Their shooting is pretty lousy, isn't it?"
> "The raid didn't materialize. We learned later that the Japs had been firing explosive bullets at the tree-tops for a lark."[1]

Goodtime had been launched with grey, overcast, drizzly conditions. These continued the next day. Lieutenant Lynds noted that the onset of daylight "brought the heaviest rain we had yet seen. It saturated us and everything." For 7th (NZ) Field Ambulance on Mono there was work to be done: a surgical theatre had to be set up.

> By midday, the theatre was finished and it seemed that at least we had something of a "home." With shelter tarpaulins too, for patients and our kitchen, we felt that things were settling down. The Japs were retreating to the hills and the roar of our artillery fire began to replace the cracks of rifles. It was a fairly quiet day, but a busy one for handling of equipment, and in the late afternoon the first wounded Jap was brought in. It was a severe stomach wound, over twenty-four hours old. This, together with his wet sodden clothing, made him no "sweet smelling bundle." He was later evacuated to our M.D.S. where he died."[2]

It was essential for medical facilities to be operational quickly. The invasion shipping had left the area, redeploying for Cherryblossom, leaving the invaders on the Treasury Islands largely on their own.

The 28th of October was marked by torrential drizzle and the troops were fatigued, unshaven and dirty. Their foxholes were often filled with water and nerves were stretched taut by a low level strafing attack. Morale was raised by having the billy boiled and the issue of tea boosted morale greatly, the ASC troops distributed C rations to the weary troops.[3]

The laying of telephone lines from Mono to Stirling was given priority and both J and X Sections were involved.[4] Effective communications between Allied units on the two islands was critical to the successful defense of the islands in the event of a Japanese attack. Although the Japanese defenders on Mono had been pushed back, a few Japanese on high ground still sniped at small craft crossing between the islands. There were no safe zones on the Treasury Islands, even for those behind the front line. The laying of the telephone lines was far from simple, and made even more difficult by the lack of motor-powered small boats. Instead, assault craft, which had to be paddled, were employed for the line-laying. Care had to be taken that the sharp coral did not snag or cut the cables. Considerable ingenuity was shown by the Sigs. Old cable drums were used as weights to anchor the cables and tethered coconuts were used to float sections of the cable over areas of shallow water to avoid damage from coral. The little islets in Blanche Channel, Wilson and Watson, were used as stepping stones.

Unfortunately for the Sigs personnel, the W130 assault cable was not particularly robust when faced with the beaching of landing craft and the effects of tides and currents. The chafing of the lines eventually ruined them, requiring ongoing repair. Eventually, it was replaced by the heavier W110 cable.[5]

On Mono fresh drinking water was vital and the engineers established roads to Keogh's and Bryant's creeks and by 1600 hours had water purification underway. Stands and turnaround areas for the water carts were started. On Stirling a track was bulldozed towards Soala Lake. Wells were dug and water filter kits were used to produce 40 gallons of water an hour.

The engineers completed the demolition of two Japanese mountain guns located above the Saveke River to ensure that their former owners did not use them again. Another group of engineers was kept busy blasting the coral reef near the PT boat base to enable the Americans easier access to their dock.[6]

On 28 October, the Allies consolidated their beachhead and sent patrols out to locate the Japanese. No significant contacts occurred that day. During the afternoon a company of 29 Battalion set out for Malsi. Japanese tracks were discovered in the high country around the Kohele River and Saveke River and artillery barrages were planned for that night.[7]

For Peter Renshaw, 28 October spelled the end of his combat career, felled not by a Japanese soldier but by microbes. His mortar unit had moved inland and dug in. He recalled:

> Then I began to feel deadly sick. I wanted to vomit but I couldn't. I knew I had to report to the Regimental Aid Post. I had to wait my turn to see a doctor. Wounded were being treated. "I think you've got a dose of hepatitis, Sergeant," said the doctor.

> I went down to the beach after letting one of the other sergeants know that he was in charge. Lieutenant Holmes had been badly wounded.
>
> I joined a party of other sick and wounded and we went down to the beach to be loaded onto a barge. The beach was a shambles. Rows of bodies wrapped in blankets and awaiting burial lay in neat lines.[8]

Renshaw was evacuated to the New Zealand base hospital on New Caledonia and later returned to civilian life in New Zealand.

Les Taylor discovered on 28 October that the Japanese were not the only danger. He noted in his diary:

> Started patrols up the ridge to get the mountain guns and mortars which had been giving us hell. Carrier platoon followed a platoon of A. Coy up the ridge over the "Squiki River" where A. Coy had attacked the ridge the previous day. Dead Japanese, guns and mortars 75mm and equipment were passed as we climbed the ridge and evidence of yesterday's battle for the ridge. Was too cautious to touch any equipment because of booby traps. We felt the Japanese were only ahead of us as we reached the summit, but we suddenly came under heavy gunfire. Some of the shells passed over the ridge and others burst in the trees around us. We had been caught in our own gunfire from 25lbers which had opened up to clear the Japanese off the ridge. A. Coy had 2 men killed so it did not take long to decide it was no place for us, so we took off like a gang of school boys going on a picnic down the ridge to the safety of the beach.[9]

Given the close quarter nature of jungle warfare such "friendly fire" fratricidal incidents were almost inevitable. This, of course, was of little consolation to the families of those involved. Eric Bergerud has estimated that 16 percent of Americans killed during the Bougainville campaign were from friendly fire.[10]

On the night of 28–29 October the Japanese tried to recover their supplies located near the Saveke River. This supply dump had been discovered by the Kiwis previously, but since it was outside the beachhead perimeter all that could be done was to place booby traps and establish the range for mortars. The Japanese, under cover of darkness, infiltrated and sniped at troops. The 36 Battalion claimed it killed seven Japanese. Les Taylor's diary entry reads:

> Another hell of a night. Japs came right through our lines throwing grenades and sniping. Crouched in fox hole all night, grenade in one hand, tommy gun in the other.
>
> Nearby, someone copped a grenade in their fox hole and the screaming was terrible and unbelievable in the dark. Nobody would go to his aid and plain suicide to leave the fox hole. Screaming and moaning went on for hours it seemed and it was when he started crying for his mother I thought the night would never end. Had a grenade land about a yard from my fox hole and blew dirt down the hole. We left after putting logs over the top for safety. Have felt trapped with the log roof and have decided to remove it for safety. Have not slept yet since we landed and feel really awful.[11]

Nor were conditions pleasant for Lt. Lynd's comrades:

> Tired and weary, not having slept the previous night, and with a special infantry guard set, we were all early to bed anticipating a restful sleep. It was not to be. This time not planes but infiltrating Japs. They began shortly after dark, and whether it was by means of some "walkie-talkie" machine or vocal chords, some fellow made the night hideous with his singing and screeching cries. It seemed evident that it was one of the Japs, and among his renderings, at least the Yank expression "Come on boys, lets go" and "Isa Lei" were recognizable. The racket seemed to last for several hours, to what purpose we could not tell, unless it were just part of a war of nerves. The night became very noisy with bursts of rifle

and tommy-gun fire and the din of bursting grenades. The infantry guards and our own A.S.C. were certainly not sleeping and at morning the holes found in water, petrol tins and odd articles of clothing bore ample evidence of the amount of lead that had been flying about. Whether any Japs were actually killed was never clearly substantiated, but there were no Jap corpses in the area when daylight came. Of course, it is possible that the Jap dead and wounded were carried off by their own mates, for this is known to be their practice. It seemed that some of the enemy were directing their bombers in by flare. The nearest "egg," fortunately a small one, landed no more than a dozen yards away from our kitchen. No one got above ground that night. It would have been suicide to do so. In the morning almost every man had his own tale to tell of the night's experiences. Some of them were pretty hair-raising, for many of our men were unarmed except for sheath knifes. A patient lying prostrate on a stretcher in the theatre tells of three Japs seeking shelter from the grenades and tommy-gun fire, coming in and squatting in line beside his stretcher and then sneaking out again. It seems remarkable that during the night not one of us suffered injury. The Japs had been around all right, they had left one or two odds and ends (which were promptly souvineered) and a few of their footprints were to be found in the mud.[12]

The Japanese undertook one low level strafing raid and several quick bombing raids and bombed Mono with 30–40 bombs. These did no damage but one Japanese plane was claimed as shot down by 208 Light AA Battery. The 29 Battalion history comments: "There was silent rejoicing in every heart on the second night when the raiders came again and were met with the fire of newly established anti-aircraft defenses. The sense of helplessness disappeared and morale rose."[13]

It was the practice of the Japanese to send a lone plane over Allied lines at night to disturb sleep and attack targets of opportunity. The sound of Japanese engines was distinctive — whether because of poor quality fuel or because they deliberately desynchronized their engines. Troops on Guadalcanal during the battles there had nicknamed their nocturnal intruder "Washing Machine Charlie" and this nickname was also given to intruders over the Treasury Islands. For Doctor Arthur N. Talbot, on Stirling Island, this posed a question of priorities: "During the night we were often disturbed by one Jap [airplane] who came around with engines desynchronized kicking up a lot of noise. We called him 'Washing Machine Charlie.' One night I was lying in my little coral foxhole, and another doctor was lying about twenty feet away. I was lying there with my tin hat over my face and when I looked over at him he was lying there with his hands over his face and his tin hat over his crown jewels. He had his priorities right."[14]

Field artillery on Stirling fired at suspected concentrations of Japanese troops to the north of the defense perimeter. However, a patrol sent out to investigate the following day returned without contacting the enemy.

Soldiers from 36 Battalion encountered a 37mm anti-tank gun west of the Saveke River. As night fell on 28 October, the wet and uncomfortable soldiers concentrated on improving their foxholes and hunkering down for another sleepless night. The Japanese were an unpredictable foe.

29 October

Snipers can have an impact out of all proportion to their numbers. They strike unseen, deter movement and sap morale. The Kiwis inside the perimeter on Mono were being relentlessly sniped. Counter-measures by 36 Battalion killed seven snipers. Row later commented that "there were fewer snipers than were imagined by the troops and that in fact, there was probably more sniping done by the JAP from the high country outside the perimeter, than from inside the perimeter."[15]

Bernie Harris, of 36 Battalion, remembered that in the morning and afternoon his unit took rifle fire from the trees but they could not tell from where. His friend Lefty gave them a burst with his Bren.[16]

A New Zealand war correspondent, Lt D.W. Bain, recorded that Japanese sniper fire came from trees and that nine snipers were eliminated by spraying the treetops with bullets. The story is told of "The Corpse that Walked": "Late one afternoon shots from the green top of a coconut palm whizzed close to a private's head. He turned his automatic rifle into the palm and was rewarded by the falling of a sniper's rifle and the slumping of a barely discernable body amongst the greenery. The Jap had been tied to a tree and his body stayed where it was. Dusk was falling, so the body was left alone. In the morning it was gone."[17]

The Japanese on Mono were Special Navy Landing Force troops who were trained riflemen. However, they were not specialist snipers. That was of little moment to their targets.

For the men of 7th (NZ) Field Ambulance, 29 October was

> quite a trying day, for although our medical work decreased, we were feeling the strain of the two days' strenuous work and the two sleepless nights. From well back in the jungle odd Japs sporadically fired into the area with a type of explosive bullet, and the explosions of these were for a long time interpreted by us as being the cracks from the rifles of snipers cleverly hidden in the tree tops. Many volleys of rifle fire were sent into the leafy branches of likely trees. All day long, patrols searched out these stragglers, but with little success, only a couple of snipers being accounted for. Their fire was sufficiently disturbing, though, to keep us on our toes all day, and to inspire us to take what cover we could find whenever the bursts were heard. No doubt, it was telling on our nerves a bit.[18]

Because of the risk and strain on the medical staff the decision was made on the mid-afternoon of 29 October to relocate the medical facilities across Blanche Channel to Stirling Island where a medical dressing station had been set up. According to Lt. Lynds:

> It was no easy job, for our tired bodies, and the loading of peeps and the unloading of them again onto the barges seemed more than twice the job it actually was. Darkness was rapidly falling when the last barge was loaded, there being two peeps, equipment and remainder of the personnel on board. Of course the barge had to stick on a coral rock and all the racing of the engine could not budge it. The noise of the roaring motor apparently attracted the attention of the Japs in the hills above us, for the cracks of explosive bullets again burst from palm tops in front of us. We decided to run the peeps off again and leave them ashore for the night. There followed a great deal more roaring, and eventually we slowly backed off the offending coral. It was a relief to see that stretch of friendly sea between us and the enemy for we were badly in need of rest and sleep.[19]

However, for A Company, rest and sleep were not to be. The corrosive and potentially lethal effects of stress and sleep deprivation explain what happened next:

> Being properly dark when we reached the other island and it was not easy to get our bearings and find a "hole" to sleep in. We were not very particularly [sic] though, and we knew

that we could sleep anywhere. We would have done so too, but we did not know that one of our junior officers, who had arrived there after dark and did not just know the disposition of the Company, was going to wake up and think himself and his batman surrounded by Japs! Seeking to enlist the help of the guard, he soon had us all more or less believing that there were Japs about. Actually, the noise of movement was that coming from the various foxholes round about, where fellows relentlessly crouched with senses alert. The net result was another almost sleepless night. Was that officer popular, when the true facts became known in the morning! It was unfortunate that the night's excitement resulted in Ernie Roper receiving an accidental knife wound.[20]

Because the Advanced Dressing Stations were withdrawn to Stirling it was thought necessary to have a small medical party on the beach on Mono each night to accept any casualties. It was not a desirable duty, because nerves were stretched taut by the fear of Japanese infiltration: "Staff Sergeant Steptoe, attending a seriously injured man overnight, heard a rustling sound outside the tent, a noise that came steadily closer. Then the tent flap was cautiously lifted and in the darkness something groped its way forward. The only weapon to hand was a sheath knife and in the morning pinned neatly to the ground for all to see was a large land crab."[21]

For the Kiwi engineers work continued on creating and improving roads, preparing sites for Bofors anti-aircraft guns and radar. Mud predominated. The weather continued to be wet, and to add to their misery, they had to sleep in wet clothing. For 20 of the engineers their situation was even worse because their valises had been destroyed in the explosion at Falamai and they had only what they stood up in.[22]

Patrols were sent out from the perimeter to find the snipers, but without result. Units strengthened their defenses and cleared the perimeter of snipers. Under cover of darkness the Japanese tried to infiltrate through the infantry to reach their abandoned food and supply dumps near the Saveke River.[23] To Row's frustration the Japanese removed their dead and wounded so no estimate could be made of their losses.

On the night of 29–30 October an LCI gunboat three miles northeast of Mono rammed, machine-gunned and sank a small craft carrying an unknown number of Japanese.[24]

30 October

By the third day, the enemy retired to the high country in the middle of the island.[25] There was, therefore, little, if any, contact with Japanese forces and the opportunity was taken by 36 Battalion to shorten its line to a better defense line nearer the Saveke River.[26]

A company of 29 Battalion reached Malsi without incident and occupied it. A patrol from 36 Battalion heading towards Laifa Point found a hurriedly abandoned Japanese 37mm anti-tank gun with plentiful ammunition.

Persistent rain and the movement of heavy vehicles reduced the roads to a terrible state. The engineers responded by creating new tracks and reinforcing the roads near the vital water points. Timber was cut and laid lengthwise creating wooden or "corduroy" roads.

There was concern about Japanese nocturnal activity in the Saveke River area. The

Kiwi engineers laid booby traps in this area. Six of these were sprung and bloodstains were found but no bodies. The supposition was that the Japanese had carried their dead or wounded away.[27]

Japanese aerial attacks slackened but one determined Japanese pilot dropped bombs and strafed the Falamai area three times. No casualties or damage were suffered.[28]

31 October

By 31 October, the Allied defensive perimeter at Falamai had stabilized, Malsi had been taken, and good defensive positions had been set up at Soanatalu. Row now began to think in terms of clearing the Japanese from the high country around the heads of the Saveke and Kolehe Rivers. The improved situation was not however evident to the troops.

Les Taylor's diary entry for 31 October 1943 records: "Another bad night with Japs about and all the strange jungle noises playing havoc with one's nerves. Planes still come back at night, fly around for awhile and eventually come in on a bombing run and one has to sit waiting for it. Think I slept for about an hour, not sure of anything really. Went on patrol along coast, saw nothing but got covered in mud again, waded out into the sea when we got back to clean up before crawling into fox hole for the night. We are wet all the time so it didn't really matter."[29]

That was the last Japanese activity in the Falamai area. Row felt more confident when a second echelon of his troops arrived on 1 November. With the additional men Row ordered patrols up to company size sent out to locate the enemy.[30]

Japanese organized resistance had effectively been broken within the first two days of Goodtime. Thereafter, small groups of Japanese were encountered, most intent on both filching food and supplies or escaping off the island.

The Kiwis rapidly learned hard lessons in jungle fighting from their Japanese opponents. Nonetheless, they were still not seasoned professionals and their fire discipline at night was weak. Units of 29 Battalion had moved to the Malsi area and, as the battalion history notes:

> The perimeter developed its night life in astonishing fashion. There was no doubt that enemy stragglers did enter the battalion lines at night, notably in the D Company Sector, where Private I.M. Thompson was killed, but indiscriminate firing, although perhaps understandable, did little to relieve matters. Out of the fog of fact and fantasy came tales of fox hole grappling, of Japanese hurling insults in good English, of shrieks in the darkness, to all of which credence may be given without fear or doubt. On the other hand, tales of swords and gold scabbards, of enemy officers enjoying a leisurely midnight meal on the very edge of a New Zealand weapons pit, of Japanese hauling boxes of ammunition to the coconut tops around battalion headquarters, may be equally set at a discount — unless of course, you were there![31]

For Frank Cooze the night was full of terrors — some real, some imagined, as he and his comrades tried to get some much needed sleep:

> I wakened from a fitful doze to find someone shaking my feet. "What's wrong?" I cried. "Shish-h-h," whispered the man on watch. I dropped my voice to a sibilant whisper.

"What's wrong?" I repeated as I grabbed my rifle and pulled the cocking piece from half to full cock. "Shish-h-h," was the only reply.

I crouched on my knees and strained to see through the darkness. The jungle was still — not a shadow moved!

"Tell a — — — man what's going on," I exclaimed irritably. "Sh-h-h ... listen!"

Listening intently I heard a rustle — then quivering silence. The rustle came again and stopped. A piece of wire twanged a few feet away. There was stealthy movement on top of the logs roofing our foxhole. A few grains of falling sand shattered the silence. "Sh-h-h," someone quavered.

"They're fixing a booby trap," I whispered.

I couldn't stand the suspense any longer. "I'm not going to be caught in here like a rat," I whispered. "I'm going outside."

I got to my feet an inch at a time and stared into the gloom while my spine tingled and my flesh crept. A hand tried to pull me back but I shook it off. There was absolutely nothing to be seen. Not a leaf stirred. The jungle was still as death.

In the morning we found a four-foot snake in the logs of our foxhole and cursed ourselves for a sleepless night.[32]

1 November

Although organized Japanese resistance had been smashed on Mono, Japanese air activity continued, and Allied nerves were on edge: "Some excitement was caused on 1 November, when just as dawn was breaking, the lookouts of several guns reported white ghostly shapes floating in the air over the western entrance of the harbor. Inspired no doubt by memories of the damage done on other fronts by parachutists, gun operations ordered fire from all guns within range and several guns got away a few rounds each before the shapes resolved themselves into barrage balloons flying above some LSTs just entering the harbor."[33]

The cause for the excitement was the arrival of the Second Echelon, made up of two LSTs, four LCI(L)s, two fresh LCI gunboats and an APc escorted by *Waller*, *Saufley*, *Pringle* and *Philip*. This collection of ships had departed from Guadalcanal on 30 October and beached on Orange Beaches at 0600 on 1 November. The LSTs deployed large, tethered, white barrage balloons as protection against aerial attack. The balloons were streamed on the night of 31 October–1 November as the formation approached the Treasury Islands. The balloons were sighted first by the Allied forces ashore while the LSTs were obscured by Stirling Island. This led the units ashore to believe that the balloons were some type of enemy airship and that an attack was imminent. AA units ashore began firing at the balloons and it took 20 minutes before they could be stopped. No hits were recorded. On arrival at their beaches the LSTs hauled down the balloons.[34]

The two LCI gunboats relieved their predecessors from the First Echelon. Once the four LCI(L)s had completed unloading at 0830 they left for Guadalcanal, accompanied by the First Echelon gunboats and with *Philip* and *Pringle*. By 1650 the LSTs also had unloaded and left for Guadalcanal with *Waller* and *Saufley*. Both groups arrived at Guadalcanal without any problems.

On 1 November, the American invasion of Bougainville at Empress Augusta Bay occurred. This triggered a clash between American and Japanese fleets, the outcome of which would determine the success or otherwise of both Goodtime and Cherryblossom.

Tactical Communications

During Goodtime one of the most arduous, unpleasant and dangerous jobs was to maintain tactical communications between units. Signals platoons were required to lay telephone wires between units and even behind jungle patrols. Given the tropical conditions, the terrain and the limitations of contemporary valve radios, the laying of telephone wires linking units together was critical for the combat effectiveness of 8 Brigade.

The "Sigs" had the frustrating job of not only laying the telephone wire but also of maintaining it. The wire was vulnerable to destruction by heavy vehicles going over it and to tropical weather such as electrical storms. The other source of destruction was the Japanese, who cut the wires. This led to Sigs personnel going out in all weather to establish the cause of problems, under constant threat of Japanese snipers, or an ambush.

One Japanese soldier did his utmost to cut telephone wires laid between Malsi and Soanatalu. His efforts caused some hilarity among the Sigs personnel because the line was disused.[35]

Stirling Island: Consolidation, 28 October 1943–3 November 1943

Welcome reinforcements arrived on 28 October in the form of Lt. Commander Robert B. Kelly, USN, and the PT boats of Motor Torpedo Boat Squadron 9. They set up a base on Stirling and began patrolling that evening.[36] There was plenty of work for the PT boats as they set up a blockade of Southern Bougainville, the Shortland Islands and Choiseul, ranging far and wide shooting up Japanese barges.

The Sigs section began hacking through the dense undergrowth and laying a communication line between the headquarters of 38 Field Regiment and 8 Brigade headquarters. As more units arrived on Stirling the communications web became more intricate.[37]

Patrols were sent out by 34 Battalion, and Stirling was thoroughly combed. By 29 October, Stirling was clear of Japanese troops. C Company set up an observation post at Wilson Point. Frustratingly for Lieutenant H.C. Wynyard and his two sections of C Company, there was little to observe. In the succeeding days he sent a series of plaintive messages to Battalion Headquarters begging to be relieved and for his men to be given something to do. One message read:

"No sign of Japs. Attacked by a strong mosquito force. Took immediate repellant action. Please get us out of here — Wynyard."[38]

For the soldiers on Stirling, the nights were uncomfortable. An outer perimeter of foxholes protected the vital communication centers. Sentries were assigned and did their best to stay awake and alert. As on Mono, movement was prohibited and a rope was strung between foxholes with tugs on it to convey messages. The Sigs personnel had a special problem — their personnel needed light to do their work, especially those tasks involving ciphers. However, a complete blackout had to prevail:

> It was not particularly comfortable for the operators cooped up in the covered foxholes where the condensation immediately spelt trouble for wireless sets and also exchanges. The mobile proved of little assistance owing to the humid conditions within their enclosed operating cabin when the blackout shutters were drawn into position. Signalman D.E. Plummer, of G Section, had a long and busy day operating a ZCI radio station on Stirling Island from which he retransmitted messages from brigade headquarters to Loganforce at Soanatalu and also to a spotter plane in the skies above the islands.[39]

An additional cause for concern was the belief that the Japanese were homing in on the wireless stations. These were strafed on three consecutive nights despite the fact that they had moved their location some distance. A decoy remote controlled station was set up and was duly bombed by the Japanese.

For the troops on Purple 1 and 2 there was no lack of work or danger. Stores, ammunition and equipment had to be unloaded and placed in dumps. Crates had to be sorted. Japanese planes attacked Stirling nightly, although their bombing was haphazard. About 20 bombs were dropped in the Purple 2 area, but caused no casualties or damage.

The danger was not exclusively from the Japanese. Four Kiwis, sheltering near Laita Cove from a stick of bombs, were horrified when the gun crew of a nearby 40mm Bofors, attempting to knock down a low-flying intruder, depressed the barrel so low that tracer began hitting the bushes over their foxholes.[40]

Nerves were still on edge. Sergeant Trevor Whaley, a signaler attached to 29 Lt. AA Regiment, recalled that on 31 October, he and Sergeants Cooper and Robinson were sent to the RHQ site on Stirling with an IP tent and a UC10 exchange to maintain contact with the guns, the new radar at Soanatalu and the searchlights:

> At some very late hour we received a "Condition Black"— invasion imminent — the only one I had or have ever received. Shortly after, there was an ungodly scream from an American outfit some 300 or 400 yards away. With the "Condition Black," the bait bit[41] and now this we were sure an attack was about to happen. Robinson and I with one up the spout and safety catches off had our rifles across our knees while Cooper opted for a hand grenade, the pin of which he instantly pulled and instantly dropped. There we were awaiting attack, way out on our own, in a completely blacked out tent, with a hand grenade in the sweaty hand of Cooper, while he scrabbled about amid the plant life on the floor of the tent, seeking the pin to replace it on the grenade. Robbie and I had two major problems— would Cooper's sweaty hand lose its grip and blow us all to bits or would the Japs get us first? The pin was found and replaced and no Japs appeared but it was a very strained quarter of an hour. For whatever reason, we did not get condition Green, nor any other indication that the "invasion" was a false alarm, and we discovered the next morning that the scream was of rage because the American concerned had had his hat taken.[42]

Because Stirling had been secured, the forces there became a source of replenishment for their more embattled comrades on Mono. The dismemberment of 34 battalion became almost complete when at 8 A.M. on the 31st word was received that B Company was to move to Saveke to relieve a very tired company of the 36th Battalion, which had been having a hard time every night. B Company transferred that day and, in exchange, Captain K.E. Louden's Company of the 36th came under the command of the 34th. The men were thankful to move into Captain Brooke's positions down at Purple 3, where they hoped to recover much lost sleep.[43]

When it became clear that the Japanese on Mono were retreating and that the threat from the Shortland Islands had not materialized, 34 Battalion H.Q. was moved to Malsi on the northeast coast of Mono. They took with them the refreshed company from 36 Battalion. Aware that the Japanese had attacked Soanatalu in strength, and also conscious of the possibility that Malsi might be next, the Kiwis began digging in and siting Vickers machine guns. Luckily for the troops, the Japanese were focused on Loganforce.

A tragedy occurred on 3 November. Writing on 4 November, Bombardier Thomas noted:

> At 2 o'clock yesterday morning Keith L__ got out of his hole to have a leak and for some unknown reason walked in front of Doug R__'s hole. Goodness [knows] why he did it, and no one will ever know because Doug did the natural thing and pumped four holes in him in about two seconds. The fire was so rapid it is hard to believe it was done with a rifle. When Doug found out who he had shot he nearly went mad and has been having a hell of a time just sitting around in a stupor. The greatest agony of the lot. He is very shaky on his legs, and can't walk by himself and can never sleep. I will never forget him sitting there just looking into space. If you Goodday to him he says Goodday back, but that's all. He has forgotten about his wife and home and when we had another opportunity of getting a letter away, he didn't seem to understand at all.[44]

The Caves, Mono Island, November 1943

Since organized Japanese resistance seemed to have evaporated, 8 Brigade Headquarters directed that patrols be sent out to comb the island to locate and destroy any Japanese remnants. This was highly dangerous work because the Japanese were well-hidden in dense jungle and desperate. Their strength and weaponry was not known. There was always the danger of patrols being isolated and ambushed and significant casualties being suffered. This was not the type of work for the rash or the fainthearted. Nor was it a job for the physically unfit, for the terrain was very hard going.

Two infantry companies under the command of Major J.M. Reidy cleared the area between Falamai and Malsi and Captain H.W. Williams led a patrol which searched the area around Laifa Point without contact. Then the Kiwis encountered Japanese soldiers who had taken shelter in the rocky caves on the northern coast of Mono. They showed little inclination to surrender. A series of small scale, no-quarter clashes occurred around these caves.

The official history of the Solomon Islanders' participation in the war records that after the main battles were over it became a matter of hunting down Japanese stragglers:

> Much of this work was done by Bentley's Solomon Islanders under Sergeant Ilala. One New Zealand patrol, to which the sergeant was attached, came upon a band of Japanese who had taken refuge inside a cave and had fortified the entrance with two machine guns. A frontal attack would have been suicidal. But Ilala, clambering among the rocks above the

cave, came upon a narrow crevice which he thought might turn out to be a back door. His guess was right. He wriggled down the crevice and took the Japanese cavemen in the rear. With his carbine he shot six of them and finished the rest off with grenades.[45]

Corporal F.A. Armstrong, of 36 Battalion, was awarded the Military Medal. On 5 November, Armstrong was the point scout with Sergeant Ilala for a large fighting patrol from D Company, 36 Battalion, commanded by Major I.G. O'Neill. The patrol had set off from Falamai across the island and had discovered a raft and paddles near a cave on the northern coast. They decided to investigate the cave. A Japanese soldier fired at Ilala and Ilala's rifle jammed. Armstrong ran towards the Japanese and fired at him at close range. The soldier fell down a cliff. The pursuing patrol then stumbled on 11 Japanese armed with a light machine gun, rifles and grenades in caves on the shoreline. One of the Japanese fired at and killed Sergeant Ron Baird. The patrol threw grenades at him but the Japanese soldier scooped them up and threw them back out of the cave entrance. Armstrong, seeing the problem, crawled down to a ledge above the cave. He pulled the pin from a grenade, waited for three seconds and threw it into the cave. He repeated this with a second grenade. Neither grenade was returned by the Japanese. Ten were killed and one was wounded and taken prisoner.[46] The patrol reached Soanatalu that night, and the following day traveled back to Falamai by barge.

On 6 November a clash occurred between Japanese soldiers and soldiers from 34 Battalion. A Company of 34 Battalion was ordered to move from Soanatalu to Malsi. It was moving along the coastline when it encountered 12 Japanese in a cave some 800 yards east of Soanatalu. A firefight lasted for nearly two hours. Although the 12 were killed, four Kiwi soldiers were wounded. One of them, Corporal D.J. Flynn, received a Mention in Dispatches for his actions in directing fire into the cave while he lay wounded at the mouth of it.[47] A New Zealand soldier was also killed in this action.[48]

As the New Zealanders secured their grip on Mono they sent out patrols to mop up any Japanese survivors. On 8 November, a platoon of soldiers from Company A, 29 Battalion, under the command of Lieutenant E.C. Chandler was given the task of searching the area around Soanatalu. Chandler divided his men into two groups—one group searching the top of the cliffs and the second, below, searching the coral shoreline. The latter group discovered a deserted machine gun post in the Ulapu area. Alerted to the possible presence of Japanese, the troops proceeded with all due caution. Suddenly they came under fire from a lone soldier. Chandler fired his revolver. The soldier darted into one of the caves in the cliff face. Chandler ordered the troops on the top of the cliff to close in while his group threw grenades into the mouth of the cave where the soldier had last been seen.

Private A.H. Norris, in the cliff party, arrived quickly on the scene and entered the nearest cave, an action which should have cost him his life. His eyes took a second or two to adjust to the gloom and, to his amazement, he saw several Japanese soldiers crouched down facing in the direction of the other cave entrance. Norris called out "hands up" and, then, the suicidal absurdity of this demand occurred to him. As the startled Japanese turned to face him, Norris fired two bursts from his Thompson submachine gun and took cover behind a rock. He then threw a grenade. The explosion rocked the cave and most of the Japanese were killed. A seemingly unconscious Japanese soldier was dispatched by another burst by Norris.

If this seems unchivalrous, it should be borne in mind that the Japanese had earned a reputation for feigning surrender or death and then trying to kill those trying to take them prisoner. This tendency to "play surrenders" made Allied troops wary of accepting Japanese surrenders. A total of 10 dead Japanese were found within the cave. The following day another body was found on a ledge above the floor of the cave. This one had been hit in the shoulder by Chandler's revolver bullets and, although he had tried to bandage his wounds, death overcame him.

The dead Japanese provided souvenirs to Chandler's soldiers in the form of two swords, binoculars, watches, weapons and equipment.

This would almost have fatal consequences two days later for a New Zealand soldier called Fitzgerald, who decided to visit the caves to see if there were any further souvenirs to be had. Unfortunately for Fitzgerald a Japanese not involved in the fighting on 8 November had returned. A grenade was tossed at Fitzgerald and he suffered cuts to his scalp. Fitzgerald then fired at this attacker, killing him.[49]

In another incident involving the Treasury Islanders:

> Two of them were paddling a canoe across a small bay when they spotted two of the enemy who excitedly waved them in. The islanders approached with a proper display of reluctance. The two fugitives, promising various rewards, begged to be paddled to the Japanese-occupied Shortland Islands. After a show of misgiving, the natives finally agreed, and the Japanese got into the canoe. They were warned by the natives that New Zealand patrols were about and that in order not to be seen they would have to lie face down in the bottom of the canoe. This the Japanese did, thus assuming a position from which it was impossible for them see where they were going. They were paddled to the nearest New Zealand outpost and handed over as prisoners of war.[50]

On 9 November a further sweep of the cave area by a small patrol from A Company, 29 Battalion, found a Japanese soldier who approached the New Zealanders with his hands in the air yelling, "Don't shoot." They held their fire but as soon as he got close to them he threw a grenade which wounded one of the patrol members. The Japanese soldier was not given a second chance — he was promptly shot.[51] This incident made the New Zealanders' wary of taking Japanese prisoners.

Thereafter, Allied patrols were sent out, and minor actions occurred. By then, most of the Japanese had been killed or captured. One Japanese soldier attempted to swim to the Shortland Islands but became disorientated in the dark and swam in a semi-circle. He was picked up by a patrol of the island "blokes" and handed over to the New Zealanders.[52]

The captured Japanese were an enigma to their captors. The 34th Battalion history recorded:

> Perhaps the only feeling these unemotional little yellow men displayed was one of surprise, for had they not always been told of the way they would be tortured if they fell into the hands of the enemy? They accepted food and cigarettes without change of expression. The intelligence section perhaps still recalls the prisoner who was invited to draw a sketch where the rest of his friends were hiding. Nothing loath, he took possession of a cane knife, drew a rough map of Mono on the ground, and proceeded to point to all parts of the island, accompanied by dangerous slashes of the cane knife through the air. It was surprising how many people were not so anxious to continue watching the demonstration.[53]

An account records that one badly-wounded soldier on Mono elected suicide rather than surrender.[54] He was not alone, and it seems that a number of wounded Japanese on the Treasury Islands were likely killed by their comrades or, alternatively, committed suicide. Brigadier Robert Row commented: "It is difficult to ascribe a reason for his attitude towards surrender even when his situation is quite hopeless: perhaps he really believes that he will be tortured and killed if taken alive."[55]

Because of their powerful taboo against surrender, the Japanese were utterly unprepared when they were captured. They did not know how to act. Some provided their captors with detailed information about their units and defensive positions.[56]

Despite the death before surrender rule, 11 Japanese were taken prisoner on Mono, two of whom died of wounds. Most had become isolated from their comrades and were often wounded, sick and starving. One prisoner of war report recorded: "He seemed to be quite happy to be a prisoner and was very satisfied with his treatment in the hospital where he was taken for treatment of his infected ear the second day after his capture. The fact that he would probably have to be operated on and consequently lose his hearing in one ear did not seem to dampen his cheerfulness."[57] His world shattered, and bereft of support, one P.O.W. even indicated a desire to go to America.[58]

By the end of November 1943, 223 Japanese had been confirmed as killed. There were, however, still Japanese survivors. For the Allies the casualties had been mercifully light, with 40 New Zealand dead and one hundred and forty-five wounded, and twelve American dead and 29 wounded.[59]

The Third Echelon Arrives, 6 November 1943

The Third Echelon, made up of 2 LSTs, 4 LCI(L)s, an APc, and *Conway*, *Pringle*, *Conflict*, *Adroit*, and *Daring*, left Guadalcanal on the evening of 4 November, and arrived off the Treasury Islands at dawn on 6 November. The LCI(L)s rapidly completed their unloading and departed escorted by *Pringle* and *Conflict*. *Pringle* had picked up two Japanese soldiers some 4 miles southeast of the Treasury Islands. They had forlornly been trying to swim to the Shortland Islands.[60]

To secure their hold on the Treasury Islands, the Allies had not only to land a sizeable contingent of men but also supplies necessary to sustain them at full combat capacity. During the 11 days following the amphibious assault, Wilkinson's force landed 6,315 men, 367 tons of rations, 422 tons of petrol drums, 1,152 tons of ammunition, 1,157 tons of vehicles and 722 tons of general cargo.[61]

The 4th Motor Transport Company had the responsibility for the dumps of stores and supplies. As consolidation commenced it began to sort out the supply dumps and get the precious supplies stacked above the wet ground. It received reinforcements of 70 more men with the Second Echelon. By 6 November the company was at full strength. As more ships arrived the supply dumps grew in size.[62]

Equipped with these supplies, the Allies could now begin developing air and naval bases.

Defensive Stance

By 12 November, Row considered the Treasury Islands secured and, accordingly, devised a plan of defense.[63] Japanese land units on Mono no longer presented a threat, but the threat from air attack remained.[64] Row deployed his troops to cover the Falamai and the Soanatalu perimeters and Stirling Island from land, sea or air attack. The 29 and 34 Battalions, supported by artillery and AA units, held Mono, and 36 Battalion, less one company on Mono, held Stirling with artillery and anti-aircraft units. The engineering units were directed to construct access roads off the beach areas and from Falamai to Malsi and Soanatalu with all speed.[65] The 4 Motor Transport Company had the huge task of building up and maintaining reserves of ammunition, petrol, oil and lubricants and general supplies.

The Kiwi engineers undertook the herculean task of constructing a road up the mountain near the site of the Japanese headquarters at Saveke. The road was essential so that field and anti-aircraft guns could be positioned with the best possible fields of fire. The road ran for about two miles through heavy bush and rose to a height of 500 feet. A coastal road and a maze of access roads were built on the Falamai Penninsula.[66]

Another manifestation of the Allied victory over Japanese land forces was that the men began sleeping above ground. During the combat phase the men had taken to sleeping in cruciform foxholes with canvas held on timber frames above them in an attempt to keep out at least some of the torrential rain. It was a considerable relief to be above ground once more, although Japanese air raids still made the foxholes necessary. Tents were now erected and mosquito netting deployed. Over time the men learned to use ivory nut leaves for building the walls and roofs of huts in the native style. These were cooler and more comfortable in contrast to the army issue tents which suffered terribly from mildew and were anything but waterproof.[67]

Another manifestation, of perhaps a less welcome nature, was the reassertion of army bureaucracy. Routine orders began to be generated and calls were made from higher headquarters for the usual military minutiae of reports, lists of equipment and ordnance, supply requests, etc.[68]

The other sign that things had changed significantly was the arrival of the Governor-General of New Zealand, Sir Cyril Newall. He inspected New Zealand and American units and "a couple of diminutive Jap prisoners who were temporarily released from the job of washing the Provost Sergeant's jungle suit." There was the problem of providing the eminent visitor with suitable food. Embarrassment was avoided when the 'Q' Section of 8 Brigade headquarters obtained fresh New Zealand butter and mutton from an American naval unit.[69]

A welcome addition to the Treasury Islands garrison was the arrival of a detachment of 20 men of the New Zealand 1st Field Bakery unit. They arrived on 17 November, and were greeted by Japanese dive bombers which proceeded to attack the LSTs they were on. Fortunately no casualties were suffered. The unit set up camp on Stirling near Purple 1, built ovens and began supplying much appreciated fresh bread.[70] On 9 December, torrential rain flooded their camp and inundated the ovens with two feet of mud and water. Baking ceased and the field bakery was relocated to Lakemba Cove on Christmas Eve.

Active patrolling took place along the coastline of Mono. Four six pounder anti-tank guns were emplaced to deal with any seaborne invaders. Observation posts were set up at Soanatalu, Malsi and Luana to keep an eye on the Japanese, an enemy renowned for his unpredictability. In a scene reminiscent of the Cold War, troops on Mono kept watch on an enemy watchtower on the Shortland Islands with powerful binoculars in the sure knowledge the Japanese were looking back.[71]

Air raids continued but generally caused little damage. One in particular caused consternation: On the morning of 27 November, a Japanese plane attacked an LST in broad daylight. Rations were running short and "supplies were down to a few tins of the M & V [meat and vegetables] hash portion of the C ration," and the LST contained the next week's rations. "Nobody breathed again until it was certain that the ship was unharmed."[72] There were almost nightly air raids and there was a belief among the gunners that the planes were seeking to pinpoint their gun positions. Planes were overhead sometimes four or five times a night: "These raids were voted good shows, resembling a glorified Fifth of November. [Guy Fawkes night in New Zealand, celebrated with fireworks]. The heavy concentration of anti-aircraft of all calibers in the area, glowing lines of tracer, tremendous reverberation of sound, an occasional glimpse of a plane twisting and turning in the searchlights, provided a first class spectacle which was shown with pride to reinforcements by the old hands."[73]

The sounding of a Condition Red was the signal to move into the bombproof shelters, but over time, some troops stayed above ground to witness the spectacle in the night sky.

This sang-froid disappeared when bombs began to drop too close for comfort and the gunners of the 49th Battery deepened their foxholes, added splinter proof tops and went to earth with increasing speed on every raid. "It was too hot at this time even to sleep in pajamas let alone blankets, and it was not unusual to see a heavy sleeper who had awakened late, ignoring the mosquito menace and scurrying to his foxhole clad only in a tin helmet. Extreme discomfiture fell also to an officer who spent several minutes of one Condition Red bawling 'put that light out' with lusty and picturesque variations only to find he had been addressing his remarks to an unsuspecting and distinctly uncooperative firefly."[74]

The newly-completed airfield on Stirling attracted Japanese bombers. The 12th of January 1944 saw a massive response to Japanese aerial raiders. The Japanese aircraft struck at night, being too vulnerable during daylight. That night they struck in a series of four waves, the first three consisting of six aircraft and a final wave of three. The defenders let loose with everything at their disposal—"61, 692 rounds of ammunition were used up that night: 90mm, 4628 rounds; 37mm, 7818 rounds; 50 in., 46,421 rounds; 40mm, 3096 rounds. The claims were four aircraft destroyed and one possible by the anti-aircraft guns and one shot down by night fighters."[75] The 34 Battalion history recorded that "tens of thousands of rounds were flung into the air that night, making a fantastic picture."[76]

An eyewitness to the "million-dollar barrage" was Gordon Thomas:

> We had a terrific A.A. Barrage last night. The Jap planes tried to get in to an hour the first time at 9 o'clock and for 40 minutes the second time at 12 o'clock but didn't succeed. A few bombs were dropped on Stirling and 6 Yanks killed and about 30 wounded. The airstrip wasn't damaged at all. The A.A. Fire was terrific. The 90mm put up 200 odd each, and the Bofors 250 odd each. The din was deafening. The noise surges all the time, sometimes off, then comes on heavy again and gets heavier and heavier until you think the place is going to go up with it, then it eases off again. I was damned glad when it was all over. When a

bomb dropped it made the A.A. fire seem like child's play. The sight was marvelous to see, strings and strings of tracer tearing up into the sky...

The second raid was more quieter, at least the A.A. fire was just as heavy only I don't think there were any bombs dropped.[77]

The intensity of the barrage can be gauged by the fact that a nearby anti-aircraft gun ran out of ammunition after firing 150 rounds, and requested a jeep from Thomas's unit to bring more from another nearby unit. Thomas thought that it was "terrible mismanagement" of the anti-aircraft gun to run out of ammunition after only an hour's firing and commented "one of these days there will be a proper raid and they will wonder what's struck them."[78]

The islanders found the Japanese bombing difficult. They sheltered in caves. For those in caves south of Malsi the sanitary conditions were bad. All the islanders could do was to pray and endure.[79]

An unofficial history notes: "Neighboring units, no doubt dazzled by the flow of tracer, entered into the spirit of the thing and N troop crews on Watson Island got useful assistance from members of the 36th Battalion and from U.S. Naval personnel, who helped to carry and clip ammunition. Headquarters staff also had a busy night getting the ammunition to their guns. Most of the bombs went into the sea."[80] In another example of inter-allied cooperation, some of the artillery personnel from 50th Battery, 38 Field Regiment, who were visiting American friends at a nearby AA unit found themselves roped into carrying ammunition for the AA guns through virtually the whole night."[81]

American ships in Blanche Harbor joined in the AA defense. The problem was that sometimes the sailors set their fuses to explode far too loudly. One night Forbes Greenfield, a Kiwi AA gunner, recalled that American shrapnel rained all around his gun position, but fortunately no one was hurt.[82]

Units on Mono counted themselves fortunate that most of the Japanese bombs fell on Stirling Island. But not all, as one Kiwi gunner found:

> We soon learnt to listen to the whistle of the bombs and immediately decide how close they would fall. If it was a close one there was a rush for the slit trench. One night this happened, the bomb landed close in the bush, absolute silence, then a voice in the trench said "get your bare arse out of my face." That was life in the jungle. Another hazard was the shrapnel from American ack-ack, their fuse setting was bit slap-happy and shells would explode at 500 feet, which was right in our faces. Then the guns down the foot of our hill would fire up the face of the hill and we would have the shells zipping past our tents, oombang, oombang, oombang. Sure learned to keep your head down.[83]

A raid about a week later came in under the defenders radar, and no alert was sounded. Several bombs fell on Stirling, wounding several soldiers and killing Gunner T. Crannitch.[84] Fortunately, the air raids decreased in intensity as Allied airpower tore away at Japanese airbases, aircrew and planes.

Although the airstrip on Stirling was the prime target for Japanese bombers, shipping was also a priority target. Stirling had become a base for not only Allied bombers but also a naval base for PT boats and destroyers. Destroyers would arrive at dusk, refuel and be away by dawn. Fuel, ammunition and supplies began to arrive at Stirling. The Seabees created a steel pontoon, and on 30 January, it accommodated its first Liberty ship, the USS *Robert C. Grier*. Thereafter supplies of material flowed into Stirling. By that time the Japanese did not launch any heavy air attacks.[85]

Japanese Hold Outs

Although organized Japanese resistance on Mono was crushed by 12 November, Japanese soldiers were periodically encountered. These soldiers, lacking support, tried to steal food and equipment from Allied encampments. A report from 34 Battalion recorded that "at least one or more Japs entered the tent lines of A. Coy and 88 American C.B. Unit–Malsi area. Numerous items were taken from two NZ tents and two groundsheets (American) from the back of a truck in the C.B. lines approx 30 yds from the NZ tents concerned." Items taken included knives, shirts, boots, socks, cigarettes and biscuits.[86] The dense bush and gullies of Mono made Japanese soldiers difficult to find and it was only when they tried to raid native gardens or Allied camps that they became vulnerable. Time was not on their side. Despite its lushness the jungle was, in fact, a desert. A veteran Coast Watcher concluded that "no-one can live hidden in the jungle without outside aid." He also concluded "at its best the food that the jungle can supply is enough only to sustain life, and under a prolonged diet of it, mental and physical vigor decline until there is no ability left to do more than support life itself."[87] Deprived of their own supplies, the combat-effectiveness of the Japanese withered as illness and hunger took over. Their choices were stark. In very small numbers and reliant on themselves, they could either lie low and hope for a Japanese invasion, attack the Allies and hope to die gloriously, or they could try and get off the island.

Kiwi troops understood that they had to approach Japanese soldiers cautiously and that accepting surrenders entailed a degree of risk. D Company of 34 Battalion was faced one day with the problem of whether it should immediately shoot, or attempt to take prisoner, an armed Japanese who was fast asleep. "War in the jungle had to be ruthless, for the Jap was a treacherous prisoner and never tamely to capture."[88] Caution prevailed.

Patrols by Kiwi troops were faced with the risk of ambush by desperate Japanese soldiers. The Japanese proved unpredictable. On one occasion Bob Dunlop's patrol from 36 Battalion encountered a group of Japanese soldiers. They threw away their weapons and dashed into the sea. Their chances of reaching Japanese held-territory across the shark infested waters were minimal. The last Bob Dunlop saw of the Japanese was as black dots bobbing in the water.[89]

On 14 November a patrol from 34 Battalion found a Japanese soldier cutting down a coconut tree north of Malsi. His surrender was demanded but he tried to escape and was shot. The patrol found the body of a Japanese who had hung himself in a cave nearby.[90]

Signs of Japanese survivors continued to be found and Allied intelligence officers could never be sure how many remained. Two Japanese were killed by a patrol from 34 Battalion west of Lake Akea on 23 November. They were armed only with a bayonet between them but, nonetheless, refused to surrender. On the same day a Japanese sniper wounded a Kiwi soldier from B Company, 36 Battalion. A search by New Zealand soldiers found only two-day-old footprints.[91] A few days later the body of a Japanese soldier who had used a grenade to kill himself was discovered near Lake Akea. Another Japanese described as "very thin and starved in appearance and armed only with a grenade was found in a cave east of Lake Akea and killed around the same time."[92]

It seemed clear that the Japanese had fragmented into isolated groups or often by themselves. Such men, starving and lacking any sense of direction, were prone to desperate acts, even surrender to the enemy.

The last two Japanese prisoners captured by Cowan and the Blokes were docile. Although the prisoners could not speak English they appeared to Cowan as "smart boys from a good school." Cowan thought that they were "a cut above the others" and were "high school kids." They appeared relieved to be captured because they had no further obligations. He gave them a smoke of good American tobacco. The prisoners were so cooperative that Cowan did not tie them with ropes. An unarmed Kiwi padre led the prisoners into captivity, much to the amusement of the Kiwis.[93] Cowan also had the chance to see Sergeant Harry Shinto at work, talking to Japanese prisoners. Cowan thought that it appeared to be hard work and the prisoners were not likely to have had any useful information in any event.

In what must be one of the most bizarre encounters on the Treasury Islands, unarmed Kiwi soldiers blundered into Japanese stragglers during a cross-country running race. An athletic carnival was organized on Boxing Day and lasted four days. As part of it, a cross-country race using the native track between Soanatalu and Malsi began on 28 December 1943. Lieutenant I.G. Turbott, an intelligence officer and an outstanding athlete in pre-war Auckland, was in the lead when he encountered a Japanese soldier at the side of the track. Although Turbott was unarmed, he gave chase but the soldier eluded him. Turbott then returned to the race and won.

The next group of runners coming in reported seeing another Japanese soldier in the same area. Private Keith saw a Japanese soldier in a kneeling position apparently taking aim at the runners. He threw a piece of coral and the Japanese soldier took off: "It would have been interesting to learn the reactions of the Japanese at the sight of the New Zealanders, straining every nerve, running, scrambling, slipping and sliding through the jungle for no apparent reason, in the middle of a hot day. They probably thought it was a manifestation of the perpetual drunkenness attributed to New Zealanders by Tokyo radio."[94]

One night in December 1943 two Japanese soldiers took a native canoe from south of Malsi and began paddling vigorously in an attempt to reach the Shortland Islands. Unfortunately for them, they were noticed and within half an hour a PT boat was dispatched and "a stream of tracer was fired at the canoe and its occupants killed."[95]

About the same time, two Japanese came across an islander in the jungle and asked for food. The islander agreed, but on returning to his village he gathered men who returned and, after a struggle, captured one of the Japanese. The other tried to use a grenade, but received a black eye for his efforts.[96]

A Japanese SNLF soldier, detailed to an observation post in the hills behind Falamai, had retreated to Soanatalu when the New Zealanders landed. "He was in action there and when [his] position appeared hopeless went off into the hills somewhere off the head waters of the MALSI R. Here he stayed living on roots and drinking rain water. He then stated that his clothing stank so much that he threw them away and decided to come down to the camp for new clothes and food. The first night he obtained clothes and last night 30 January, 1944, attempted to obtain food. His rifle was lost some time ago."[97] The theft of food, clothing and weapons from A Company, 34 Battalion, gave rise to the joking allegation that they had a Japanese soldier on their ration strength.[98]

The legend of the Japanese in the chow line was a staple among Allied troops in the Pacific. As a Seabee veteran later wrote, the story "ran from Guadalcanal to Okinawa. Almost everyone I met who served in the South Pacific thinks it happened on his island. Between you and me I think it probably happened on a lot of them!"[99] On the Treasury Islands there was at least a grain of truth in the legend.

At Malsi in the early hours of 30 January 1944, a Seabee mess cook, Herbert Wagner, set out for the mess hall carrying a flashlight and an unlit lantern. "Hearing a noise he turned the flashlight in the direction of the sound and saw a Japanese soldier armed with a bayonet, crouched in the bushes. Wagner swung the lantern, striking the Jap's arm and wrist with it, tackled the Jap, overcoming him in physical combat and turned his prisoner of war over to the 88th Battalion guard that arrived at the scene in response to Wagner's call. Wagner sustained bayonet lacerations on his hand, ear and scalp."[100]

The unofficial history of 34 Battalion records that "The Jap's hideout was later discovered very close to our open air picture theatre, so it is a fair assumption that he enjoyed some of our films from a strategic position in the very back stalls."[101]

The emaciated Japanese soldier, clad in a stolen New Zealand uniform, was eventually led off to a barge and captivity by two burley New Zealand soldiers, Sergeant McNeill and Vic Hodge. Curious New Zealand soldiers on the beach frightened the Japanese soldier and he grasped the sergeant's little finger as he was led away.[102]

The 34 Battalion's new chaplain, Padre A.H. Lowden, had a close encounter with a Japanese. He struck up a conversation with a soldier 50 yards away who made a few remarks in good English. It was only later it dawned on him that the soldier was, in fact, Japanese.[103]

Attempts were made to convince the Japanese to give themselves up. Notices written in Japanese were pinned to trees in the jungle saying that they should surrender and would be fed and well-treated. Five or six of these notices were also tacked to trees in the areas around the native gardens. "The only response was that one notice was carefully removed from its tack, turned upside down, and re-hung. This was probably the Japanese equivalent of saying 'Nuts!'"[104]

Things became progressively more difficult for the Japanese survivors as more frequent Allied patrols were sent out with native trackers and even dogs from American units. The Carrier Platoon of 34 Battalion was searching an area near Lake Akea, between Malsi and Soanatalu. Two Japanese broke cover up ahead and Private "Jungle" Holmes fired a .455 Webley revolver that he had recently bought, at one of the Japanese, hitting him in the head at a range of 63 yards. As the history of 34 Battalion noted, "Not even gunmen on the silver screen would normally dare to hit their target at this distance."[105]

The Japanese used Coast Watchers and it seemed that there was one on Mono in April 1944, despite manhunts by each of the infantry battalions. Patrols combed the island finding traces of Japanese survivors, but no radio was found. An American radio direction-finding unit was dispatched from Guadalcanal, setting up at Malsi and Soanatalu to fix the location of the Japanese radio operator by triangulation. It picked up a signal in the

Soanatalu area and patrols were dispatched, to find no sign of Japanese. On 16 May the Americans fixed on a position near the coastline south of Liana. Patrols searched without success. Further fixes put the position of the Japanese transmitter offshore. It transpired that a Japanese submarine had been the source of the signals. Later this submarine was sighted and sunk.[106]

The Seabees Get to Work

The Treasury Islands are inert lumps of volcanic and coral rock. To be strategically useful they needed to be developed into an advanced base. This required one of Admiral Chester Nimitz's most important weapons, the Seabees.

Company A and 25 men of the headquarters company of the 87th Naval Construction Battalion under Lieutenant Charles E Turnbull[107] landed on 27 October, but the rest of the battalion did not arrive until 28 November. The first Seabees improved the beaches for landing craft, built gun emplacements and even constructed a wharf for the PT boats on Stirling.

The seizure of the Treasury Islands was simply the start of their work. Although the islands seemed unsuitable for the construction of airfields it soon became evident that Stirling Island with its flatness, good landing beaches capable of taking LSTs, excellent coral and good water supplies held great possibilities. An assessment on 5 November by specialists proposed a fighter strip on Stirling, and after further surveys it was decided to move the bomber strip 'W' designated for Bougainville to Stirling.

Construction of an airstrip began at 0800 hours on 29 November 1943, and crews faced formidable obstacles. Bulldozers cleared away a heavily-timbered area and Seabees then used hand saws and axes. These were in short supply, and progress was slow. Frustrated, Lt. (J.G.) W.E. Mannix, the battalion supply officer, and chief storekeeper John T. Ahaesy hitched a ride on a PT boat. Mannix headed for Munda and Ahaesy for Guadalcanal to find the needed equipment. Ahaesy "convinced a grizzled supply sergeant that his hoarded axes and saws would be doing more for the war effort in the hands of the 87th building a vital airfield on Stirling than rusting in a warehouse."[108] The sergeant provided 200 axes, 25 cross-cut saws, 500 pairs of shoes and 2000 coveralls. But how were they to be delivered? An LST would take two weeks. The unarmed SCAT planes would not venture near the Japanese-held Shortland Islands and Bougainville. Again Ahesy's powers of persuasion worked on the officer in charge of a group of transport planes of a Marine Parachute Service Command Unit. Four days after the start of airfield construction the supplies were dropped by 90 multi-colored parachutes on the unfinished strip.[109]

After the trees were cleared the Seabees had to strip away at least a foot of dark humus from decayed vegetation before the work on the coral substrate could begin. The coral was relatively easy to manage and rough grading proceeded rapidly.[110] Salt water was sprinkled on the surface to create a type of concrete. Work proceeded round the clock after floodlights were erected and only dimmed for air raid warnings. Light towers were built on skids and a system of flares and telephone communications warned of

Seabees work on an airfield on Stirling Island in 1943 (author's collection, courtesy George Hodgson).

approaching Japanese aircraft.¹¹¹ "The only discouraging aspect of this operation was the fate of the multitude of telephone lines then extending between the exchanges and subscribers on the island. These became open game for the bulldozers and falling trees and provided plenty of scope for airing the extensive vocabulary of the [Kiwi] linesmen who were constantly employed repairing them."¹¹²

The pay-off was when a USAAF a B-25 Mitchell "Ficklefinger" landed on 17 December 1943. Pilot Lt. Schwartzwalder and the six man crew had been bombing Bougainville. The aircraft had flak damage and began leaking gasoline. Fearing an explosion, Schwartzwalder headed for home and tensely watched his fuel gauge descend. He hoped to reach friendly territory before he and his crew had to either bail out or crash land. Then the landing strip on Stirling came into sight. He began his approach, but overshot the short section of finished runway, pulled up and came in from the opposite direction to execute a good landing by jamming on all brakes. The crew rapidly left their leaking plane. It was later repaired and made operational.¹¹³

It was not only forlorn bombers that availed themselves of Stirling's airstrip. On the 19th day of construction the pilot of a carrier-based F4U Corsair fighter, returning from striking Rabaul, had become disorientated and was low on fuel. He spotted the airstrip and landed spectacularly in an unfinished area, hit a boulder, and the plane flipped over. The Seabees extracted the pilot from his cockpit, dazed and only slightly injured.¹¹⁴

Within a month an airfield 5600 feet long and 200 feet wide had been built. The 87th then began constructing taxiing areas and hardstands. They were reinforced in December by the 82nd Battalion and the 88th Battalion in January 1944. These men helped with taxiway construction and built five 1000 barrel aviation gas tanks.[115] Stirling would become home for B-24 Liberator and B-25 Mitchell medium bombers and be regularly visited by heavy B-17 Flying Fortresses. Twin engined P-38 Lightnings and other Allied fighters regularly touched down. In February, Bombardier Thomas noted in his diary: "The Mitchells leave here pretty well every day for Rabaul. It's great to hear them taking off. They circle till all the planes are off the ground then head north. They have been losing quite a few over Rabaul too. It's a pretty well defended place that and the Jap Ack Ack fire is very accurate."[116]

The Seabees also built medical huts, mess halls, fresh water facilities and roads. A New Zealander on Stirling Island watched a Seabee at work: "A Yank bulldozer has been working by the orderly room today making a new road. You could watch and marvel at it for hours pushing the jungle aside as if there were nothing there. Trees up to 18 inches are no trouble. They run up to them and give them a smack, wait for the top to rebound then smack again. Sometimes if they won't go they root the blade into the ground on one side and tear half the roots away."[117]

In January 1944 the airstrip was extended by 300 feet to 7000 feet, although the "airstrip ended with a drop over a 70ft cliff."[118] Prefabricated steel buildings were used to construct a hospital. The 87th Battalion concentrated on building docks for large cargo vessels: "Four 6 by 18 pontoon, pre-assembled hinge-connected barges with an overall dimension of 43 feet by 428 feet, were secured to four 16-by-16 foot timber cribs set on the shore line, by four 16-by-16 foot ramps consisting of three standard ramp girder covered with heavy planking. On January 20, 1944 the dock was first used by a cargo vessel."[119]

What few clumps of jungle remained after the airfield was completed concealed food and supply depots and the huts and tents of the island's busy inhabitants.[120]

The PT boat base was also developed, with a wharf, fuel facilities, three pontoon dry-docks and two piers. Camps were created for the naval base HQ, two bomber squadron crews and the men of Acorn 12.

A detachment from the 6th (Special) Battalion that arrived in late January was a special "combat stevedoring" outfit trained to work under enemy fire, and its men were rapidly put to use loading and unloading supplies and equipment. More personnel arrived in March.

By July, the Seabees had completed the major construction work and the base was turned over to CBMUs 569 and 587. By late 1944 the war had moved north and steps began to move units to more effective locations. The last Seabee unit, CBMU 569, left in June 1945.

Most Seabees found their time on Stirling Island unpleasant:

The 87th's "Devil's Island." To one and all "The Rock" represented an 11 month interlude spent like degraded castaways on a 1 × 3 coral landspeck in the lonely Pacific. Why Stirling's operational codename was GOODTIME was never learned. From the first days of the mud-drenched bivouac in October and November 1943 until the day of departure in September 1944, the men lived in the crudest and most primitive manner imaginable. Propriety and customs were soon all but discarded.

Sleep was virtually impossible in the bivouac area. It was in fact a hellish nightmare of jagged coral, swarms of persistent insects and hordes of such monsters as giant iguanas, scorpions, land-crabs, centipedes and the deadly coral snake.

Pup-tents were small protection against the incessant rains. Throughout the long restless nights, the eerie wailing of air-raid sirens and the deep barking of AA guns were interspersed with weird jungle noises. Attacks of dysentery added to the general misery. It was invariably a hollow-eyed, water soaked crew reporting for early duty...

As the vast island development program expanded chigger bites caused the most lost man hours. Other prevalent afflictions were jungle rot, fungus, ulcers and heat rash. Lacerations became infected overnight. The men gulped daily doses of atabrine, salt tablets and vitamin pills to stay on their feet.[121]

The Seabees had been issued lightweight pith helmets to shade their heads. However, they could also be cumbersome, and a Seabee noted: "The use of our pith helmets varied considerably. They were helpful working on a coral airstrip and, along with our ponchos important to have on in tropical downpours, but otherwise most of us seem to have preferred going bare headed or wearing the traditional sailor's cap."[122]

For the Seabees of the 87th NCB, Operation Goodtime was not the end of their war. The first of three echelons left from Stirling Island on 5 September 1944, and after a brief sojourn on New Caledonia, arrived on Saipan from 27 January 1945. On 20 April 1945, the Seabees arrived on Okinawa. They would not leave until 7 November 1945, after the war ended.

The Kiwis Go into Garrison

The completion of Goodtime was the end of combat for most 8 Brigade soldiers. That, however, did not mean that they were away from mortal danger. The Japanese still made air raids, mainly on Stirling Island's air strip, but with few casualties. Between 17 November and 7 December 1943, there were 96 air raid warnings and the anti-aircraft guns fired 26 times. Between invasion day and the end of February 1944, 34 Battalion experienced 268 air raid alerts.[123] In early December, Gordon Thomas recorded in his diary:

I had the wind up last night, really for the first time, from the Jap bombers. A plane was buggering about but everything had got quiet, when all of a sudden we heard him coming down in a dive right at our position. I thought if he were to drop one then it would collect us nicely, a thought flashed through my mind whether I would have time to reach the hole, or whether I would just flop to the ground. Anyway I made a dash for the hole. I didn't wait to put any boots on either. I was completely nude and crowded in the hole against the dirt sides and for all that it mattered the hole may have been covered in velvet.[124]

The air raids had a wearing effect on the nerves of the defenders. Thomas dryly noted: "Poor old J B is a real fox hole king. As soon as the siren goes he's into the hole and stays there until the all clear goes, whether its daylight or dark. He must be in misery all the time."[125]

Now and then the Japanese attackers would score hits. On 4 February 1944, Japanese bombers struck the airfield on Stirling, destroying three B-25 Mitchell bombers. Five bombs struck the camp of 38th Field Regiment, wounding one New Zealander and ripping tents with shrapnel.[126]

Air raids were no respecters of units which could be considered non-combatants.

J. Allen of 8 Brigade handling mail on Mono Island, 1943 (War History Collection, Alexander Turnbull Library, Wellington, PAColl-5547-025).

The Kiwi Post Office Unit on Stirling Island was hit by a bomb which struck the coconut trees above it, sending deadly pieces of metal into the unit's tent and sorting cases. Letters were ripped to shreds. Fortunately there were no casualties because the men had dived into a nearby foxhole. After a couple of days the unit was again operational.[127]

Air raids were not the only deadly threat: so were falling coconuts and trees. The Kiwi soldiers learned not to sit under coconut trees. Falling trees killed several soldiers.[128] Crocodiles were also something to be wary of.[129] *Spam*, the newspaper of 34 Battalion, reported the shooting of a nine-foot crocodile[130] by a New Zealander, Lieutenant Butler, and three Americans armed with rifles. It was proposed that a Boys anti-tank rifle be used, but this was considered "Not a fair go." One crocodile came down the river, shots were fired at it and it was chased away to sea. "As usual the Yanks went about it in a big way and permitted the use of machine guns but it still isn't known if the croc got away. He is listed as 'probably sunk.'"[131]

Crocodiles were not the only sea creatures that seemed to be on the side of the Japanese. *Spam* also reported that Captain Graham, of D Company, was taking an early morning swim when "he was torpedoed in the lower right leg by something particularly vicious in the way of marine monsters—probably a stingray." *Spam* noted that Graham was in "extreme agony" and immobilized for several days.[132]

The Kiwis, like the Americans, had a fairly grim time. The wet season meant daily rainfall and a humid, oppressive atmosphere. Electrical storms were frequent, with lightning bolts playing havoc with signal cable.[133] One storm in particular impressed Gordon Thomas:

> Am having a hell of a wet spell. It has been raining and overcast for a week or so now and last night and today the downpour hasn't ceased.
>
> We had a big thunderstorm last night and I don't mind admitting that I had the breeze properly up for a few minutes. The storm was right among us and two claps of thunder right on us were deafening. They appeared no more than 50ft up. The lightning of course was what put the wind up me and it seemed as if it might wipe the place off the map. I can hardly believe that nobody was struck, not even a tree.[134]

For Sigs personnel the weather posed particular threats:

> Synonymous with the tropical heat of the islands which caused rivulets of sweat continually to run down the men's bodies as they worked, was the torrential rain, deafening thunder and vivid lightning that even succeeded in penetrating the protective and distributing (P & D) frames of the exchanges and bowling operators from their seats. Blown light globes on the exchanges and shorted rectifiers in the wireless sets, were common victims. Typical of the fortunate escapes experienced by most, at some time or another, was the evening when occupants of a tent at J Section avoided injury when a lofty coconut palm crashed across the top of their shelter.[135]

On a more mundane level it was hard for the soldiers to keep dry. Soaked clothes had a tendency to develop mildew overnight. The author of the unofficial Kiwi history, *The Gunners*, noted: "The humidity also caused rust so violent that rifles had to be cleaned twice a day; mildew which rapidly ruined leatherwear; failure of insulation in wireless sets and other signal equipment; and fungus growth on binocular and dial sights. The weather indeed, always had something new up its sleeve. Violent thunderstorms which burned telephone cables for miles and set fire to thatched roofs, cloudbursts when several inches of rain fell in an hour, gusts of wind which felled 100 foot trees across the tents, all added to the spice of life."[136]

Although the Treasury Islands were thought to be non-malarial the troops were nonetheless issued Atabrine, a malarial suppressant. The sources of quinine had been seized by the Japanese early in the Pacific War and the Americans had been obliged to fall back on manufacturing the artificial Atabrine. No one was too sure how effective Atabrine would be or what was to be considered an effective dose. In North Africa, Atabrine was thought to have produced vomiting and uncontrollable diarrhea to the point where "many would have preferred malaria."[137] The reaction of troops in the Solomons was not so dramatic, but they did not like the way the bitter tasting Atabrine turned their bodies a yellowish color. It was rumored that continued use of Atabrine produced sterility or even worse still, impotence. Consumer resistance resulted in orders that the consumption of Atabrine was to be monitored by officers.

Despite the incessant rainfall a supply of clean drinking water was problematic. The seemingly plentiful supply of water from local streams was treated with caution because it was thought that there had been outbreaks of dysentery among the islanders and the Japanese garrison and the steams were polluted. The engineers of 23 Field Company set up a system of 44 gallon drums which were filled with stream water and purified with alum and chloride of lime.[138]

Diseases were an ever-present threat. Gordon Thomas was hit by a bout of dysentery:

> Last Monday and Tuesday 1st and 2nd [November 1943], I was stricken with dysentery, and bowled over like a pack of cards. Up till Sunday night I was as fit as a fiddle and working hard, when all of a sudden on Sunday night away I went, and had to use the edge of the foxhole for a lavatory, not to mention the trousers. On Monday morning Alf Heskith gave me about half a cup of castor oil and man was I crook. I hardly had the energy to stand up, let alone make the latrine. At teatime on Monday he gave me some pills to steady things up, but I went all Monday night just the same. Even a cup of tea set things going. I had another 6 pills on Tuesday morning and another 4 that night and was ready for a biscuit diet on Wednesday. Two days without any tucker and hardly a drink and I was ready to eat. Today I am like a young horse, eating well and ready to go.
>
> Our water supply is still poor only having drinking water and that still has to be brought over from Mono by barge. Its not very good water either.
>
> All the Battery has dysentery by the way and I think most of the Brigade. I'm buggered if I can imagine what causes it. Perhaps the change of water, even though it is purified.[139]

Along with others in his battery, Thomas complained of being afflicted by ringworm and septic sores. He found the sores hard to deal with: "I generally have three or four on

A line shoot by the 54th anti-tank battery guns at Wilson Point, Stirling Island (War History Collection, Alexander Turnbull Library, Wellington, F-44768-1/2).

my legs at a time. It takes a few days to clear one up but no sooner is one better then another one starts to fester. They start off as an itch. You just have to rub it for a few minutes and a little pimple can be felt and before an hour has gone, even if you don't touch it again there is a sore about as big as a sixpence."[140]

For the men of the 49th Battery, 38 Field Regiment, ringworm was rife and, for some, the effects of septic sores and weeping eczema were so chronic that they had to be evacuated.[141] In the tropical heat simple cuts rapidly became sores that seemed to take forever to heal.

Even the simple pleasure of swimming in the sea had a catch to it—coral cuts rapidly turned septic. "Rubber soled jungle boots were the approved bathing costume."[142]

By late November 1943, the rigors of hard work and the tropical environment were taking their toll on the ASC personnel of 4MT Company. Some 50 percent were reporting sick on a daily basis. The main ailments were heat rashes and skin problems caused by perspiration resulting from the tropical heat and the labor of moving heavy stores of petrol, ammunition and supplies. It is indicative of the problem that four of the company's officers left the Treasury Islands in the first weeks of Goodtime due to sickness.[143] The most effective way of dealing with skin problems was to allow the troops to wear minimal clothing, but this in turn exposed them to sunburn and insect attack.

For the gunners there was also the sheer hard labor of moving artillery pieces and ammunition in a tropical climate. In early January 1944, the 49th Battery was moved to Mono and took up a position on a hill overlooking Blanche Harbor. As one veteran noted:

> Shifting to Mono was very, very hard work. The Battery was sighted [sic] 500 feet up a hill so a road had to be cut through the jungle and mud to a more or less flat spot which immediately turned into knee deep mud. 25 pounder guns are heavy enough without having to drag them through that stinking muck. And the heat, just no let up. Eventually finished it all then on to training with shoots lasting hours. That is why I am deaf and the Government pays for my hearing aids.
>
> One shoot I was standing between guns 2 and 3 when the gun to my right made a very weird sound. No mighty bang, just a half hearted groan. Then the shell came out of the barrel and dropped nose down. I thought "this is it" but nothing happened. The safety shield in the nose cone had not been flicked aside as in normal firing. So no explosion.[144]

The occupiers of the Treasury Islands could not afford to relax and were vigilant. Japanese forces were still close at hand. In March 1944, intelligence predicted that the Japanese would launch an offensive against the American perimeter on Bougainville and that they might also try to retake the Treasuries. The predicted Japanese attack on Bougainville did, indeed, eventuate, but the attack on the Treasuries did not.[145]

For the soldiers conditions were uncomfortable. "The weapons pits were not conducive to sleep. It was necessary to choose between a soft bed in inches of mud, or a dry bed on sharp flinty coral. In the former one shared the place with land crabs, in the latter with centipedes. For all that, those holes represented home and after a few hours spent on patrol it was good to return to them."[146]

As well, there was sense of isolation, even though Mono was relatively small: "Units and sub-units (Companies, etc.) were very isolated on Mono where their only link was often by native tracks which inhibited the usual flow of news and gossip. More roading was put on Stirling where the airstrip, port facility, PT Base and Island (Brigade) H.Q. were all located."[147]

Sometimes the weather contributed to this sense of isolation. A machine gun company of 34 Battalion was positioned at Malsi. A sandspit usually made it relatively easy to get access to this unit on the southern side of the Malaoini River. Fierce storms and torrential rain would, from time to time, turn the river into a raging torrent, and the sandspit would disappear, cutting off all contact except by landing craft.[148]

One of the things that lessened the sense of isolation for the men of 34 Battalion was a landing craft crewed by Americans and captained by a larger-than-life personality known as "Hank." The Americans were so popular they were adopted as members of 34 Battalion. Access to Malsi was either by a difficult native track and the sandspit or by Hank's landing craft. Virtually "every working party, all foods and stores, every man going out of camp on duty, travelled on Hank's barge. He was no mean coxswain, and we had many an occasion to admire his skill as he negotiated the difficult landing at Soanatalu or Luana in a heavy sea. Prior to the war, Hank had never been off the land."[149]

The size of the force on the Treasury Islands grew significantly from the initial invasion troops on 27 October to peak of 16,000 in March 1944. Administration work grew as records were kept of the food, ammunition, petrol and all the other necessities of war flowing onto the islands. The American air and naval units had to be kept supplied as they battered the Japanese.[150] Unloading and storing supplies were a constant feature of life as the Treasury Islands developed into a significant air and naval base and supplies had to be unloaded and secured. The demand of American forces for aviation gas was voracious. The PT boats engaged in slashing Japanese supply lines used 250 drums of petrol each night.[151] As supplies arrived, working parties were needed.

Unloading heavy 44 gallon oil drums presented challenges: "Many days were spent at this grueling task, which was not without its danger as the drums came hurtling out of the open bows of an LST, down the ramp and on to shore. As fast as the men on the ship could roll the drums out and send them leaping crazily down the ramp, so the waiting men on shore grabbed them and rolled them into the stacks. There were a number of injuries, fortunately none serious. In handling bombs, explosives, or other ammunition there was no extra pay."[152]

Wilson and Watson Islands, the small islands in Blanche Channel, were found to be ideal locations for the storage of petrol. The landing craft were able to run up to the beaches on these islands to deliver or pick up petrol drums as they were needed.[153]

The drums had to be safely stored. For Doug Eaton, on one occasion, the problem became potentially lethal:

> About 30 of us were dispatched with necessary tools to clear the undergrowth of the many small islands dotting the harbor between Mono and Stirling in preparation to store 44 gallon drums of aviation spirit being unloaded off a Liberty ship.
>
> Either the American Navy coxswain was a new chum on the barge or was trying to show us how clever he was because he approached the island going about twice the normal speed he should have been doing. Consequently, he hit a very tall coconut palm growing right on the water's edge with a hell of a bump. Naturally we looked up to see how many coconuts were going to fall on our heads. No coconuts luckily, but a four foot bright green coconut snake came wafting down and landed right in the middle of the barge.
>
> Pandemonium — everyone trying to climb up the walls of the barge at once. One brave

man however, by the name of Ital Elbourn grabbed a spade, jumped down into the barge and promptly chopped the snake into little bits.[154]

Films were shown at least once a week. The 29th Battalion created the St. James Theatre, an open-air theater at Falamai. Seating consisting of rough hewn logs arranged in rows capable of seating six hundred was hacked out of the jungle at Malsi. Similar, albeit smaller, theatres were created at Soanatalu. The Seabees created "The Seabee Bijou" on Stirling. There were two visits from the Kiwi Concert Party, and various USO performers were also featured.[155]

For Doug Eaton, the chance to go to the movies brought its own dangers and pleasures. B Company's camp site on Mono seemed to be located as far away as possible from the rest of the battalion on Stirling, where they had a theatre:

> However, out of the blue came the American Navy to save us, in the shape of a large concrete oil tanker towed all the way from the States by tug and moored in deep water not too far from our camp. It was attached to the shore and within easy walking distance towards Falamai from our camp.
>
> The tanker's job was to refuel the American fleet in the area, mostly at night time and it was manned at all times with a permanent crew who lived on board. It also supplied provisions to the fleet but most important of all it was the film exchange for the area. As each ship came in for fuel it swapped its supply of movies before leaving again and as quite a lot of ships had come direct from the States or Hawaii their films were new ones we hadn't seen before.
>
> It didn't take long to get to know the very friendly crew and officers and we were given an open invitation to come on board every evening to watch the movies as soon as it got dark.... With up to three destroyers moored alongside at once, all with their extractor fans going flat out, the pumps on the tanker going flat out, and the pungent smell of diesel in the air it was a bit noisy and smelly at times but the film carried on and it was a most interesting night out. To provide some excitement at times the Nips would arrive overhead now and then which of course meant blackout — no film, shut down the pumps and sit still on the tanker which of course was full of diesel. Luckily most of the bombing seemed to be directed at Stirling, so we had a wonderful view of it all especially the Ack Ack, a lot of which burst over our heads raining down shrapnel on our tin hats, destroyers and the tanker.[156]

The Treasury Islands became less frontline and more of a backwater. The Brigade Group moved from the operational command of IMAC to the more administrative command known as "forward area." Later the islands became part of the Sixth Island Command (New Georgia).

In an effort to entertain the troops the 3NZ Division Band arrived on Mono on Christmas Eve 1943 with the purpose of providing a program of Christmas carols. Having waded ashore from their barges in waist deep water and being doused by a tropical downpour, the bandsmen attempted to complete their assignment. They were due to entertain the troops in "The St. James Theatre" at Falamai. The theater was essentially an open air stage with log seating. The band's plans were wrecked by a Japanese air raid. The band and audience scattered to foxholes and lights were doused. Fortunately no damage or casualties were suffered, and after the all-clear the band resumed where it had left off.[157]

As the fighting ceased military bureaucracy reasserted itself. A New Zealand history commented: "The administrative side of headquarters had therefore to become familiar with the returns required by the U.S. Army authorities which, contrary to popular belief, are no less tedious and lengthy than our own."[158]

Brigadier Goss, being the "Comgen" of not only New Zealand but American forces, presented American awards and decorations to American personnel under his command.[159]

In another instance of inter-allied cooperation, the Kiwi linesmen were supplemented by American "wiremen." As the number of personnel grew so did the demands on communication facilities. Poled telephone lines were set up on Stirling replacing the more haphazard method of tying signal lines to trees. The formidable task of transferring over 200 miles of signal cable onto the insulators on the cross arms of the poles was duly completed.[160] Another manifestation of Allied consolidation was the replacement of the submarine cable linking Stirling and Mono with a special heavy duty rubber coated cable. However, it had a short life — a Liberty ship anchoring in Blanche Harbor dragged its anchor, cutting the cable. The only option was to lay a new one.[161]

The Kiwis undertook various engineering works. The 23rd Field Company spanned the Saveke River with a sturdy bridge made from coconut palms.[162] With the islands secure, the soldiers were assigned tedious garrison duty. Patrols made no enemy contact. Commanders struggled to keep boredom at bay. "The only alternative to looking at a wall of verdant jungle, interesting enough until familiarity bred violent objection by all except ardent naturalists, was to turn about face and look at the sea. A more attractive prospect because the outlines of the islands, far and near, gave it variety."[163]

Some sailed boats, swam, played cards and thought of home. Canoeing and yachting in particular were popular and the men created boats from the plentiful supply of local timber. The Treasury Yacht club was the ultimate manifestation of this passion.[164] One group of Kiwis sailing a boat encountered an anchored American ship. An American sailor learned over the side rail and sourly commented, 'You guys don't want the war to end, do you?' and then spat into the water.[165] The reality, however, was that the Treasury Islands were no holiday camp.

At first there seemed to be the prospect of further action and joining with 14 Brigade in an attack on Emirau. However, that came to nothing because the New Zealand government demobilized some of 3NZ Division to provide men for manufacturing and farming back home. Troop numbers were run down, and on 15 May 1944, the Treasury Islands were handed over to an American garrison and the last men of 8 Brigade were shipped to New Caledonia. Most were glad to be heading home.

The Kiwis' sojourn on New Caledonia was marked by a sense of lack of purpose. There was little training, work was light and officers tried to divert the men with recreational activities such as cricket, football and badminton.

Brigade headquarters closed on New Caledonia in August 1944. As stores were cleared in Mangere, New Zealand, 3NZ Division was dismantled. On arrival back in New Zealand the identity of all units was lost:

> A soldier was simply infantry, or artillery or medical. Men were sorted in their respective districts and sent away to the camp nearest their own homes. A small staff from each unit was assembled at Mangere Camp, near Auckland, for the purpose of returning the last of

Engineers of 8 Brigade stand on Saveke Bridge, which they built (War History Collection, Alexander Turnbull Library, Wellington, WH-0602).

the unit equipment to ordnance. On the afternoon of 20 October 1944 at 5 P.M. headquarters of the Third Division ceased to function.

That moment also marked the end of the life of the 34th Battalion. There was no ceremony to accompany its passing, no handing in of colors or of keys. It simply passed into history[166]

News of Goodtime

One of the facets of the war in the South Pacific that really irked 3NZ Division's commander, Major General Harold Barrowclough, was that his soldiers received little publicity in comparison to the men in their sister division, 2NZ Division, in the Mediterranean. Few journalists made it to the frontlines in the South Pacific due to the difficulties of getting there, the unpleasant tropical conditions and the lack of glamour and newsworthiness associated with what were sometimes slow, attritional grinding infantry operations. There were no Ernie Pyles in the South Pacific.

On top of this the Americans controlled the flow of news and censored it. New

Zealand journalists complained about the delay and obstruction they encountered from American authorities when they tried to send off copy. The Americans argued that there was a need to preserve operational security and that Japanese should be kept from learning that there were New Zealand troops in the Allied order of battle. This was particularly galling for Kiwi soldiers, who received newspapers from home with liberal accounts of 2NZ Division's operations in North Africa and Italy, but little or nothing of what 3NZ Division had achieved in the South Pacific.

Layered over all of this were the tensions between MacArthur and Nimitz. The rivalry between the American Army and Navy had profound effects on American strategy in the Pacific War, resulting in a dual advance undertaken by MacArthur up the coast of New Guinea, and the Central Pacific Drive commanded by Nimitz. In theory, MacArthur commanded the Cartwheel forces but, in reality, IMAC was a U.S. Navy formation and Goodtime was planned and carried out by the U.S. Navy. It was, therefore, of considerable embarrassment and discomfort to Halsey and Nimitz that the news of Goodtime came not from Nimitz's headquarters but rather from their egotistical rival, MacArthur.[167]

Significantly, the news of Goodtime appeared in the Wellington newspaper, the *Evening Post*, on 2 November 1943, from a *Sydney Sun*, correspondent who erroneously declared that it was a "purely NZ operation."[168]

News of the major combat operation that 3NZ Division undertook in World War II was effectively squashed. It was little wonder that an ill-informed New Zealand public had the view that the "Coconut Bombers" of 3NZ Division were having a comfortable war in the South Pacific.

The American servicemen likewise received little publicity. John M. Rentz concedes: "The story of Bougainville and the Northern Solomons is perhaps not so arresting nor so stark as those of Tarawa or Iwo Jima, and received comparatively scant attention at the time, being forced to inner pages of the press by more dramatic contemporaneous events in the Gilberts [The invasion of Tarawa] and in Africa [the clearance of North Africa, invasion of Sicily and invasion of Italy]."[169]

In comparison to Guadalcanal, Iwo Jima and Okinawa, few Americans have heard of Bougainville. An American historian, Harry M. Gailey, entitled his book on the Bougainville Campaign, *Bougainville: The Forgotten Campaign 1943–1945*.[170]

Row's Reward

A successful commander can expect some promotion or acknowledgement for a job well done. If Brigadier Robert "Digger" Row, the commander of 8 Brigade, harbored such thoughts, he was rapidly disillusioned. Row was relieved of his command and returned to New Zealand.

Barrowclough, whilst acknowledging that Row and his brigade had performed satisfactorily, was concerned about Row's age[171] and relieved him so that a younger officer could gain the experience of command. Barrowclough appointed Brigadier Goss to take over. Row was returned to New Zealand on 9 December 1943 once the Treasury Islands were secure. Row received a bar to his Distinguished Service Order. He was placed on the retired list on 5 July 1944.

Row's removal resulted in some strained inter-allied relations. The Americans were the dominant military force in the New Zealand–American partnership, and if they were entrusting American soldiers to New Zealand commanders they wanted to be sure of their competence and personalities.

Halsey had met Row and seems to have been impressed by him. Halsey became aware of Row's removal indirectly and it appears to have upset him. A conversation took place between Halsey's Chief of Staff Admiral 'Mick' Carney and Colonel C.W. Salmon, the New Zealand representative at Halsey's Southern Pacific headquarters. Salmon relayed Halsey's concerns to Lt. Gen Edward Puttick at NZ Army H.Q. in Wellington:

> The Admiral (Halsey) and Admiral Carney would like to be informed of any changes of command personnel before such changes are made. The request has come because of a recent change made by 3NZ Division of Brigade (Brigadier Row to Brigadier Goss). Admiral Carney put it that he had learned this accidentally from one of his officers, and although in no sense questioning the change of appointment or the reasons for it (he looks upon this as NZ's own domestic matter) that he would have like to have heard of it officially before it was made just in case they had any viewpoints to express; and he would appreciate it if the New Zealand Chiefs of Staff would advise COMSOPAC in the future.[172]

This touched a nationalist nerve in New Zealand. Puttick responded on 8 December 1943, upholding Barrowclough's right to appoint and change his brigade and other commanders at will.

An extensive purge of older officers took place throughout the whole of 3NZ Division. Many of the senior officers had served in World War I and no longer had the vigor to command satisfactorily in a tropical environment. Younger men were therefore promoted. As the 34 Battalion history politely describes it, the reshuffle "was designed to give younger men the opportunity of exercising command in the forward area, and also to have experienced men take back their knowledge to those left behind at the base."[173] Even after the disbandment of 3NZ Division there was the possibility of the New Zealanders being involved in the invasion of Japan, so the restructuring to give younger men experience of command did make sense.

Row was not the only one to have his career terminated abruptly. Gordon Logan, the commander of Loganforce, although awarded the Order of the British Empire and mentioned in dispatches, relinquished command of 8 NZ Infantry Brigade Machine Gun Company on 1 December 1943 and was "placed on the New Zealand Roll on account of age." He was transferred to New Zealand and plaintively wrote to the Army on 12 January 1944 that he was "desirous of remaining under employment with the Military Forces if that is at all possible," because he had sold his business before going overseas and would find a return to civilian life difficult. He was accordingly re-posted to the Canterbury Yeomanry Cavalry with the temporary rank of major. This unit became the 3rd Armored Regiment, Royal New Zealand Armored Corps, and in October 1949 Logan retired with the rank of major.[174]

The battalion commanders McKenzie-Muirson and Eyre were returned to New Zealand. Their careers ended and they merged back into civilian society.

Kiwi-Yank Relationships

The relationships between the Kiwis and the Yanks of Goodtime varied hugely. Members of the two groups came into contact with one another in the course of training and preparation for Goodtime, particularly the amphibious exercises. Generally, the two nationalities were kept segregated in their units and their unit areas, but operating closely to one another with the common threat of danger, friendships were forged that spanned decades for some Kiwis and Yanks. On the other hand, prejudices and stereotypes sometimes got in the way of constructive relationships. Kiwis of that generation were often reserved, valuing understatement and lack of display. This contrasted with Yanks, who were often confident and outgoing and who could not understand the Kiwis reserve. The Yanks often saw the Kiwis as another form of "Limey," or Briton. For their part, the Kiwis tended to regard the Yanks as a monolithic group and did not understand the huge differences that existed even within units, and that the term "Yank" was deeply offensive to those Americans from the Southern states.

On a command level the relationship was generally an excellent one with Barrowclough and Row, in particular, getting on well with Halsey and Wilkinson. Despite problems with language and everyday expressions, communication was generally good. One of the unrecognized triumphs of Goodtime is the way the two nationalities were able to work together, share the dangers and make Goodtime a success.

The Kiwis and Yanks diverged mightily on food, or what the Kiwis called "tucker." The Yanks generally loathed the mutton that Kiwis were brought up on, and the Kiwis did not appreciate Yank delicacies such as chili con carne and Spam. The men of 8 Brigade were in an American supply area and had to eat American food whether they liked it or not.

Gordon Thomas noted: "The tucker is dynamite, I have a lot of trouble forcing the Yank hash down and we get it for breakfast, dinner and tea. Yesterday morning is the first morning in my life that I have had dry bread only for breakfast. There was some hash too but I couldn't face it."[175] "Tea" for Kiwis meant either drinking cups of tea in the mid-morning or mid-afternoon, or referred to a substantial meal in the early evening.

An 8 Brigade veteran recalled that "it was a source of annoyance that when on garrison duty our troops were used to unload smaller refrigerated ships bringing fresh fruit and vegetables and meat from home to feed Americans while we existed on their dry rations."[176]

The author of the Kiwi unofficial history, *The Gunners*, commented:

"American food, a novelty for perhaps a week, was a rapidly acquired distaste to most people. Fruit and tomato juices and tinned fruit did not pall, but dehydrated eggs, Spam and Vienna sausage soon became equivalent to terms of abuse."[177]

Not all American food was viewed with disdain. Ice cream was regarded by the New Zealand Army as a luxury while the Americans, in contrast, saw it as a necessity. Kiwi Army Service Corps personnel who had the job of distributing the ice cream to soldiers on the Treasury Islands resolved the problem by obtaining the cooperation of American units which had ice cream–making equipment. As a result both Kiwis and Yanks were provided with ice cream.[178]

Americans were paid more than their New Zealand counterparts. This sometimes rankled the Kiwis, who were exposed to the same risks of being killed or injured. However, that paled into insignificance in comparison to the subject of women back home.

The men of 8 Brigade were only too conscious of the effect of American soldiers, sailors and airmen on the women of New Zealand. The Americans were generally more glamorous, better paid, and had better tailored uniforms than the New Zealanders. With their knowledge of the latest dance crazes and their more outgoing manner than the naturally reserved New Zealand men, the New Zealanders usually were a poor second. This naturally produced a degree of resentment that even the common danger did not displace.

Some Kiwi soldiers believed, "the Yanks don't want us and we are a nuisance to them. The Yanks never did want us here."[179] A small minority of Americans, particularly when drunk, proclaimed the superiority of the United States and reminded the Kiwis that they were fighting to defend New Zealand. Fights and ill-feeling were rare on the front line, but in places like New Caledonia fights broke out between alcohol and testosterone charged young men.

There was a considerable divergence between the resources available to the Yanks and the Kiwis. The Kiwis were amazed at the amount and variety of equipment and material available to their ally. It seemed that much of this was not being actively utilized, or could be easily replaced. An ethos arose among otherwise law-abiding New Zealanders of borrowing or acquiring, by fair means or foul, needed items. This left the Kiwis with an unsavory reputation as pilferers, which they gloried in. A standing joke among the Americans was that once the New Zealanders reached the frontline it would take them two days to end the war—one day to find the Japanese equipment and one day to steal it.[180] In fairness, other units, including the Seabees, involved in the war in the South Pacific also acquired a similar reputation.[181] Barrowclough's "Forty Thousand Thieves" were matched by the "Lynd's Forty Thousand Thieves" of the 87th NCB.

Frontline soldiers often have a different perspective of their entitlement to items from those in the rear. The Kiwis believed American items were written off once they left the continental United States. Goods and equipment such as bulldozers were sometimes simply abandoned by American units. In contrast the New Zealanders' supply system was so basic or deficient that worn out or damaged items had to be repaired and reused. Shoes and jungle boots were in short supply and Kiwis "went about with makeshift repairs, soles flapping at every step. The simultaneous marked increase in American apparel among the troops at this stage might have been a mystery to anyone unacquainted with the Third Division."[182]

On the other hand, Kiwis were often amazed at the extent of American generosity. Jeff Tunnicliffe recalled that there was no friction or resentment in the front line and that "the Yanks were very generous, especially with food."[183]

Some Kiwi troops who had been in combat were assigned to loading and unloading of supplies, ordnance and equipment. Being "wharfies for the Yanks" caused disquiet. The work was dangerous, arduous, boringly repetitive and something for which they had not been trained. However, the logistical situation in the South Pacific, where port infrastructures were non-existent, made such use of Kiwi soldiers unavoidable.

Generally the relationship between Yanks and Kiwis at "the sharp end" was amicable, if only because of the shared dangers. There was natural bond between the young men of the two nationalities. Both groups had been sent from their homes to fight the Japanese and both had to contend with boredom and homesickness. For George E. Tschudi, a 19 year old Seabee truck driver, there was a curiosity about the New Zealanders. He and his co-driver had to make daily trips to a fuel dump on Stirling and they passed AA emplacements manned by New Zealanders. "Each of these gun crews ate and slept in the immediate area of their gun locations. My partner and I often commented on how friendly these fellows were, always waving and shouting greetings to us as we drove by. One day we decided to stop and chat with some. From that day on and for many months to follow, tea with that particular gun crew became a matter of routine. They would share their baked goods from home with us and we in turn would sometimes provide a tin of pineapple slices or pears that we managed to procure in our travels."[184]

David Williams, an officer with 36th Battalion recalled: "3 NZ Division put the divisional sign of a Kiwi on all our crates and cases and then unit identification. After every move items went astray and I used to put a list of missing or found items at the foot of divisional orders which went to all units on the island. One day I got a phone call from an American unit saying 'We've got a box here with a short arsed duck on it.' I enjoyed that description of our national emblem."[185]

Sometimes inter-allied relations took strange forms. Forbes Greenfield and another bombardier were ordered to carry out survey work for the AA guns:

> During the morning of Christmas Day (1943) I and my surveying mate were in a dinghy in Blanche Harbor when I heard planes. After a very nervous look I decided they were Dakotas so all was well. They came in fairly low over the airstrip works then proceeded to drop parachutes of many colors. Was quite spectacular. On arrival back at camp at dinner time discovered what all the hooha was about. It was our Christmas dinner — roast turkey, roast potatoes, Xmas plum pud and even a spoonful of ice-cream. The Yanks had sent enough for all New Zealanders too.[186]

The Americans were fascinated by Japanese weapons and equipment. An American soldier wanted a captured Japanese machine gun, and Cowan said he could have it. Cowan marveled that the American could have moved this heavy, bulky item back to Guadalcanal but was sure he would have sold it to souvenir hunters there and made a fortune. Cowan conceded that he did not have an entrepreneurial streak.[187] The islanders also catered to the American desire for souvenirs and even five-year-olds produced grass skirts for sale to the Americans.

Overall, the essence of Allied relations is of Kiwis and Yanks on the beach at Falamai and the blockhouse at Soanatalu standing shoulder-to-shoulder fighting against a common enemy. Kiwis and Yanks would fight alongside each other again in the post war world — Korea, Vietnam and Afghanistan. The foundation of the American–New Zealand relationship was in many ways built in the battles for the Solomons, even though there is a historical amnesia of this.

Ten

Aftermath and Legacies

On 28 October 1943, one day after Goodtime, Lieutenant Colonel "Brute" Krulak's 2nd USMC Parachute Battalion landed by boat on Choiseul Island in another diversion code named "Operation Blissful." The 650 Para-Marines ranged along the coast of Choiseul for the next nine days striking hard against the Japanese. The Japanese commander, Lieutenant General Haruyoshi Hyakutake, ordered reinforcements from Bougainville, even after the landing at Empress Augusta Bay. He was so rattled by the diversionary operations that he delayed ordering counterattacks on Bougainville.[1] Less than 300 Japanese soldiers resisted the American landing at Empress Augusta Bay. This was probably just as well given the surf conditions which swamped eighty-six landing craft.[2]

The diversionary actions were successful. They aided the American objective of seizing part of Bougainville. The taking of the Treasury Islands allowed landing strips on Stirling and PT boat bases to be created. Aircraft from Stirling could pummel Rabaul. PT boats from the Treasury Islands could play havoc with Japanese barges and shipping. Radar posts provided early warning of Japanese raids.

Reaction to Cherryblossom

The Japanese reaction to the landing at Cape Torokina at Empress Augusta Bay on 1 November 1943 indicates how the Japanese could have reacted to Goodtime. A strong Japanese response to the Empress Augusta Bay landing was anticipated and the Japanese did not disappoint. The landing beaches were strafed by Japanese aircraft. The IJN dispatched the heavy cruisers *Myoko* and *Haguro*, the light cruisers *Agano* and *Sendai* and six destroyers with orders to destroy the American transports. The Japanese had a number of advantages: their superior Long Lance torpedoes, the high quality of their optical equipment coupled with their well developed night-fighting doctrine, air support (including airplane—dropped flares) and the range of their eight-inch guns.

The Japanese were facing Rear Admiral Merrill's Task Force 39 of four light cruisers and eight destroyers. The key advantage that the Americans had was radar, and in the night-fighting that began at 0250 on 2 November 1943, radar was a battle winner. Led by one of the most aggressive destroyer men the U.S. Navy produced in World War II, Captain Arleigh Burke, the American destroyers closed with the Japanese and fired 25 of their torpedoes. The Japanese fleet was reduced to disarray as ships maneuvered to avoid the torpedoes. Ships collided; the *Sendai* and *Hatsukaze* were sunk and the cruisers *Haguro* and *Myoko* severely damaged. The Americans received only relatively light damage. The assault effectively ended the naval threat to the beachhead.

The Japanese launched a counter-invasion. At dawn on 7 November, Japanese destroyers off-loaded 475 soldiers into 21 landing craft. These soldiers landed, fought off American counterattacks, and dug in. An artillery barrage and air strikes annihilated them by 9 November.

Within 12 days of the Americans' invasion they had landed 23,000 tons of cargo and 34,000 men, 155mm heavy guns were emplaced and the perimeter extended. By the end of 1943 the 3rd Marine Division was withdrawn and the defense was undertaken by the 37th Infantry Division and the Americal Division.

The Japanese were still not quiescent. A series of desperate Japanese attacks in March 1944 were repulsed.[3]

The beachhead on Bougainville was well-established and the Americans carved out an airfield on Torokina. The Royal New Zealand Air Force provided fighter and bomber squadrons which flew from Torokina to regularly pummel the Japanese defenders.

Barrowclough's men from 14 Brigade took the Green Islands (Operation Squarepeg) in February 1944, adding yet another link to the steel perimeter isolating the Japanese at Rabaul. In the evocative words of the historian Stephen R. Taafe, the completion of Operation Cartwheel neutralized "Rabaul and the surrounding area, leaving its isolated garrison to spend the rest of the war scratching at the top of its American-designed and built coffin."[4]

The Kiwi soldiers were not privy to the grand strategy behind Goodtime, but they rapidly realized their role was diversionary, particularly when American newspapers published news of its success. Trevor Whaley noted in his diary of 18 November 1943 that he "read the front page of a couple of American newspapers showing that New Zealanders had landed on Treasury Islands with 20,000 Japanese on Shortland Island and 60,000 at the southern end of Bougainville, the former two hours away by barge. Their praise of this operation was high." A further note in the diary records that the "I" bloke said we were just "bait."[5] For some veterans, their high-risk endeavor added an extra degree of bitterness to the lack of recognition of their efforts.

After almost seven decades, and putting to one side the fact that the Treasury Islands/Bougainville Campaign was successful, there are some questions. What was the degree of risk that the New Zealanders were exposed to? Were New Zealanders simply used as cannon fodder by a seemingly uncaring ally? To what extent were New Zealand commanders and politicians aware of the risk and agreeable to it?

The Degree of Risk

The invading force far outnumbered the Japanese defenders and, given the weight of numbers, it was realistic to expect that no matter how hard the defenders fought they would be overwhelmed. It would simply be a matter of time. The real risk to the Goodtime forces lay in the Japanese response. If the Japanese had challenged the invasion by fully committing air, naval and land forces, the result could have been bloody.

The Japanese forces in the Northern Solomons in October 1943 were still potent and American-Australian forces could not clear them from Bougainville. The Japanese forces on the Shortlands did not surrender until the general Japanese surrender in August, 1945. Japanese airpower underwent a process of attrition in 1943 and the quality of aircrew, serviceability and aircraft performance declined markedly in late 1943–44. Japanese naval craft in late 1943 still retained some degree of potency, as shown by the rough handling American destroyers received at the Battle of Vella Gulf in September 1943. Japanese soldiers continued to resist even when faced by overwhelming odds and with no chance of survival.

The Japanese could have transferred reinforcements from the Shortland Islands. They had the capacity to do this at night, and a landing on the northern coast of Mono was feasible. All it required was the resolution to do so.

Certainly, American forces would have tried to intervene. PT boats patrolled the area, but in limited numbers. Japanese Daihatsu barges were often armed with potent weaponry and they would have fought determinedly. If accompanied by Japanese destroyers or cruisers, and airpower the Japanese could have fought their way through.

At base if Operation Goodtime had been fully successful, then the Japanese main effort would have been concentrated on the Treasury Islands. The Japanese had a window of opportunity between 27 October and 1 November to take the bait. As Barrowclough reported to his prime minister, "Once the U.S. troops landed at Empress Augusta Bay that was likely to draw Japanese attention from the Treasury Islands, but that new threat would not be apparent till at least five days later and much might happen in those five days."[6] The aim, as a diversion, was to focus Japanese attention and efforts away from Empress Augusta Bay. American strategy by comparison was focused on Bougainville, and it would likely have taken a major disaster for the Americans to have refocused their efforts on saving the Goodtime force.

The risk facing the Goodtime force was significant and the potential for disaster was ever-present. The first few days of Goodtime were critical because there were limited numbers of troops ashore, and it took time for artillery and AA batteries to be emplaced.

Cannon Fodder?

War is an inherently risky activity—more so with allies. Winston Churchill once exclaimed in frustration that the only thing worse than fighting without allies was fighting with them. It is natural for commanders of one nationality to lack sensitivity to the casualties incurred by an ally. This was the case in Italy in 1944 when the American commander of the Fifth Army, General Mark Clark, complained bitterly about General Bernard Freyberg, the commander of 2NZ Division, closing down the offensive to take Monte Cassino when New Zealand casualties reached a certain level.

So were New Zealanders in Goodtime simply used as cannon fodder by uncaring

American commanders? Arguably, the answer is no. Halsey was an aggressive, sometimes almost rash commander but, unlike Clark, he had a sensitivity to casualties, and the island-hopping campaign across the Pacific shows this. Likewise, Wilkinson and Vandegrift did not have reputations as butchers, but rather as skilled exponents of amphibious operations.

It seems clear that New Zealanders were used in Goodtime because Barrowclough wanted a combat role for his troops and because American forces were in such short supply in the South Pacific. Arguably, if the New Zealanders had not undertaken the job then it would have been given to some of the units burned out from the New Georgia Campaign (with all the consequent risks that this entailed) or troops taken from the Cherryblossom force.

Anyway, it was not only New Zealanders whose lives were on the line: if a disaster had occurred, casualty rates among American Seabees would also have been high.

The New Zealand troops were well-trained, they were well-led, and well-equipped. There was a well-founded basis for the belief that they could do the job.

Awareness of Risk

The two most immediate New Zealand military commanders, Row and Barrowclough, were concerned about risk. Barrowclough even wrote to his superior, Lt. Gen. Edward Puttick, in Wellington, about his concerns. Everyone recognized, however, the Americans would provide the necessary backing. That faith was, as it turned out, well placed, and Goodtime worked out satisfactorily.

It is unlikely that Puttick shared Barrowclough's concerns with his political master, Prime Minister Peter Fraser. Fraser, as a life-long socialist, was inherently suspicious of the military and, moreover, was appalled by the high casualties New Zealand troops suffered in the ill-fated Greek campaign. So, Fraser, while wanting to make sufficient military effort to secure New Zealand a place at the peace table, had an acute sensitivity to casualties. When 3NZ Division deployed to a combat role, Fraser was far from enthusiastic. He had even gone so far as to warn Halsey that the division could not expect reinforcements or further New Zealand personnel to build up to a three brigade division. It is likely that if Fraser had been aware of the full extent of the risk to New Zealand troops, he would have ordered 8 Brigade withheld.

Fraser's lack of enthusiasm for 3NZ Division's combat role is evidenced by the decision to withdraw it from combat in 1944 and begin its disbandment.

The Double Effort

Both Australia and New Zealand in the period 1939–42 focused their efforts in the war against Germany. Both nations sent the cream of their manpower to fight in the Mediterranean. With the threat from Japan growing in late 1941 the needs of Australasian defense grew. After the start of the Pacific War the Australians pressed for and achieved the return of their divisions to Australia. Those troops were to be prominent in Australian–American efforts to wrest Papua–New Guinea from Japanese control.

New Zealand, on the other hand, allowed its 2NZ Division to remain in the Mediterranean, where it distinguished itself in the Desert War, the battle for Tunisia and the Italian Campaign. Political pressure in New Zealand to follow the Australian example was stoutly resisted by Winston Churchill, arguing that shipping difficulties prevented the return of New Zealand troops.

With the withdrawal of the Australian troops from the Mediterranean, the British Commonwealth needed the New Zealanders to remain. A deal was struck between the British, Americans and New Zealanders and, in return for 2NZ Division remaining in place, American Marines were sent to New Zealand.

2NZ Division remained in the Mediterranean until the end of the European War, and the need for reinforcements and replacements ultimately led to the disbandment of 3NZ Division.

Some of the troops from 3NZ Division, on their return to New Zealand, were sent on to 2NZ Division. They reinvigorated 2NZ Division and played a key role in its success in northern Italy. A significant number of soldiers from 8 Brigade therefore ended up doing "double duty," serving not only in the Pacific but also in the Mediterranean.

Amphibious Warfare Legacy

Goodtime saw the first use of two Landing Craft, Infantry (Large) gunboats. They were maneuverable, flexible and packed quite a punch and performed impressively, delivering a weight of fire on the Japanese defenses after the naval gunfire had ceased. They destroyed some Japanese defenses and suppressed others and shepherded the vulnerable assault craft to their beach heads. Undoubtedly many Allied lives were saved by these craft.

Gunboats became a regular feature of amphibious operations in the Pacific[7] because Goodtime validated Captain Roy T. Cowdrey's decision to modify LCIs for this role. Forty-eight LCI(L)s were converted to this role before the introduction in 1944 of the purpose-built LCS (Large) Mark 3.

Effects and Consequences

A small section commanded by Sergeant A.G. Hill was attached to 8 Brigade on Guadalcanal. It was a Graves Registration Unit and was tasked with creating a cemetery at Falamai. It would eventually contain 40 New Zealand and 20 American graves.[8] A pen drawing of the cemetery was photographed and copies sent to units to send on to the families of those killed.

The remains of the New Zealanders were later disinterred and reburied at Bourail Cemetery on New Caledonia. The American dead were reburied in American cemeteries.

John Dower recorded the dehumanizing effect of the war in the Pacific on its participants. To deal with war's horrors soldiers saw their enemy as animals or lesser beings. Desecration of enemy corpses was a common feature of the Pacific war on both sides. Particularly gruesome was the extraction of gold teeth. A soldier with 4 RASC recalled with revulsion seeing Americans on Mono taking the heads of Japanese and washing them to see whether they had gold teeth to be plundered. He commented, "We couldn't hack that."[9] Neither could Major General Barrowclough, who gave orders that Japanese corpses were to be interred.[10] However, it was not that simple. In the tropical heat bodies rapidly decomposed and became difficult to handle. The RASC soldier also recalled some 10 days after the landing seeing a dragline used to disinter Japanese corpses from a trench they had occupied. The bodies were in terrible condition. "In that heat there was no simple way of dealing with bodies." They were placed on a landing craft and then taken out into Blanche Harbor for disposal.[11]

The Japanese prisoners were held in a barbed wire cage (where they were the subject of curiosity by Kiwis and Seabees), interrogated and processed, then sent to POW Camps.

Allied casualties, although light, were significant. There were roughly 250 Japanese defenders on the Treasury Islands. They were all either captured or killed. In turn, they inflicted, by November 1943, 40 New Zealand and 12 U.S. killed, 145 New Zealand and 29 U.S. wounded.[12]

The ratio of Allied casualties to Japanese casualties in most battles of the Pacific War was heavily weighted against the Japanese. This was largely due to the weight of firepower the Americans were able to deploy. The firepower available during Goodtime, however, was limited and fighting involved mainly infantry combat.

The Americans were well-pleased with the results. In his inimitable style, Bull Halsey congratulated the units of Task Force 31 using superlatives such as "expert," "thorough" and "aggressive" and urged his men to keep the Japanese on the run.[13] American commanders were impressed by the combat performance of 8 Brigade and were consequently willing to use New Zealand troops in further Cartwheel operations.

New Zealand's participation in Operation Cartwheel and its naval and air contributions to the Pacific War ensured that New Zealand had a place on the deck of the USS *Missouri* in August 1945 when the Japanese surrendered. By that stage 3NZ Division had been disbanded and New Zealand's representative at the surrender ceremony was an airman, Air Vice Marshall Leonard Isitt. New Zealand had shown itself to be a capable and trustworthy ally, and this assisted the New Zealand–United States relationship as British influence diminished east of Suez and American power became predominant in the Pacific.

The Treasury Islanders

The seizure of the Treasury Islands also had the dividend that it went some way to restoring British prestige. The islands were the first in the Solomon Islands retaken by a Commonwealth force. The Union Jack floated over Falamai and the District Officer asserted his authority. At the conclusion of the military phase of Goodtime, the British

Civil Administration had been restored by a Coast Watcher, Major David C. Trench, representing the British Resident Commissioner at Guadalcanal.[14] Trench landed with the First Echelon.[15] Those Solomon islanders wavering in their loyalty to the British Crown and influenced by Japanese propaganda could see that the British Empire was on its way back. The loyalty of the Treasury Islanders to the British Crown was considered to be steadfast: "During the Japanese occupation the chief of the island died and the people took the unusual course of not electing a successor, although it was obvious upon whom the choice must fall. When Bentley landed with the New Zealanders he expressed surprise that the people were without a chief but they explained, 'We wanted to postpone the election until the return of the British government, so that we could have the district officer's advice, as we have always done in the past.'"[16]

For the Treasury Islanders the results of Goodtime were mixed. They had been liberated but many of their gardens and food sources were destroyed. The number of island casualties is not known. There would undoubtedly have been more but for Sgt. Cowan's timely warning of the naval bombardment.

Thomas noted the effects of the invasion on the local people:

> The Sunday before last I went up to some native villages and was amazed at the terrible conditions under which they are living. It's a wonder something hasn't been done to help them. I should think it's the resident commissioner's job but apparently he isn't worrying. The natives are living in caves between Luana Cove and Malsi on the coast. There are natives most of the way and it's a very interesting walk indeed. The Soanatalu barge pulls in at Luana Cove at 1130 and you pick it up at Malsi on its way back from Soanatalu at 1330 so there is just ample time. The natives didn't seem to want to talk much, apparently the novelty has worn off. I gave several packets of cigarettes but they just said thanks and turned away. They have no possessions; don't seem to have beds, blankets or anything. Their caves are as bare as can be, just bare rock and there's a little bit of a thatched lean to, to them. They have mongrel dogs and they are very mongrel indeed. There's kids galore and they all seem to be healthy and happy. The kids go naked, the men and older women have a wrap around their hips, and the younger women have petticoats of some description. The men and women look very much alike and at any distance at all the only way I could distinguish the women was by their breasts. They have their hair cut the same and are all jet black. They can mostly talk English after a fashion, having been taught by the missionaries. They have their own native minister. A select number of natives are schooled and trained at schools up here in the Islands and occasionally they reach schools in Fiji and I believe in New Zealand.[17]

The church at Falamai had been demolished by Japanese fire. The men of 8 Brigade rebuilt it in appreciation of the islanders' help and as a way to commemorate their Kiwi and Yank comrades who had been killed. It was intended that "a Church of Remembrance" be non-denominational as long as the Allies were on the island, then it would be handed over to the islanders. The site was occupied by an ammunition dump covered by two Kiwi Bofors guns until early 1944, when plans were drawn up by 23 Field Company, New Zealand Engineers, and timber was cut under the supervision of the islanders. Sawn timber was difficult to obtain and construction progressed slowly. The islanders thatched the roof, and concrete steps were laid. Pews and church furniture were installed. A dedication service was held on 26 April, attended by islanders, New Zealanders and Americans "Peace — and the dignity of peace — dwelt over Falamai again."[18]

Mono Islanders thatching roofing sections for the Memorial Church at Falamai. Note the U.S. Navy hats on two men (Archives New Zealand, WAII, 1, Treasury Island Photos, D1, Photo #193).

In the postwar years the church was in dire need of restoration, and by 1958 an appeal was launched among the New Zealand veterans. This led to the formation of the Mono Trust, which not only saw to the repairs to the church but also the provision of four oil lamps for lighting. Cash grants were made to the island primary school. From 1964 to 1985 funds were raised to enable island children to attend Goldie College on Munda and the Honiara Technical Institute on Guadalcanal. A kerosene refrigerator was provided for the medical clinic, a battery-powered radio, two typewriters and also building materials which enabled extensions to be made to the primary school and a new kindergarten. Between 1976 and 1979 the Mono Trust was involved, along with the Solomon Islands Wartime Comrades Association in Honiara and the New Zealand Ministry of Foreign Affairs, in providing clean water for Falamai village. The aid was often of a practical nature—books, sports equipment and musical instruments. The trust was dependent for its funding on the veterans of 3NZ Division. Sadly, as their ranks began to deplete, the Mono Trust also began to fade and was wound up in the 1990s.

There are still physical reminders of Goodtime on the Treasury Islands. On Mono old PT boat parts have been put to use as water tanks. An old gas cylinder is used as a community and church bell. The concrete foundations of an old food cooler can still be discerned. A road built by the Allies is still used. The baseball area is now just an empty grassy area. The paramount chief's grave is decorated with New Zealand beer bottles which have dates of their manufacture ranging from 1939 to 1944 on the bottoms. On Stirling Island the airfield built by the Seabees at such cost is still operable. There are a lot of wrecked Allied planes corroding in the tropical conditions. The concrete foundations of warehouses and gun emplacements can still be seen. Also, an old fuel dump and various Allied roads can still be seen. The piles driven into the coral and used for securing vessels still exist. There are thousands of old Coca-Cola bottles in the jungle, a residue from thirsty American personnel.

The Treasury Islands are difficult to get to and generally a seaplane or boat is used. The airstrip at Stirling is somewhat, overgrown. Visits by New Zealand politicians are guaranteed a hospitable welcome and the islanders fondly recall their liberation from the Japanese.[19] In 1993, on the 50th anniversary of the invasion, 16 Kiwi veterans—accompanied by their children and grandchildren, went to Mono. While the rest of the Solomon Islands commemorates 7 July as Independence Day from British rule, the visitors found that the Falamai villagers celebrate Independence Day on 27 October — the day they were liberated from Japanese occupation.

The islanders sang a special anthem of their thanks to the New Zealanders. The visitors were feted and villagers provided them with "New Zealand House," a specially built building for their accommodation. Families contributed scarce linen, bedding and crockery for their guests. A choir of up to 30 islanders sang for their visitors each evening meal. They provided their guests with one of the village's few freshwater taps for their shower. A thatched wall was built around most of the shower but the local children were fascinated by their visitors and peeked through it.[20] The Solomon Islands are New Zealand's strategic northern ramparts. Goodwill earned during World War II still has resonance in the modern world.

The Solomon Islands have been what is euphemistically called "a failed state." In 1998 regional factionalism broke out in open war. The islands succumbed to financial collapse, corruption and associated breakdown of law and order. War lords like Harold Keke came to the fore. To restore order, RAMSI (the Regional Assistance Mission to the Solomon Islands) was formed. Consisting of its Pacific neighbors ranging from Kiribati to Vanuatu, the coalition was led by Australia and New Zealand, the two major contributors. RAMSI deployed on 24 July 2003, at the request of the Solomon Islands National Parliament to restore order and to get the economy working once more. RAMSI was described as being "a partnership with the Solomon Islands people and the participating nations." The reality was that military personnel and police provided a foundation for restoration of effective government.

Veterans

The return to New Zealand from the Treasury Islands of the Kiwi soldiers of 3NZ Division was not that of conquering heroes. On arrival there were no victory parades. The numbers of returning troops were deliberately kept small to avoid pressure on shipping and trains. Most men of 3NZ Division took up employment in war industries and simply merged back into the civil society from which they came.

For some their experiences during Goodtime would stay with them for the rest of their lives. Veterans were haunted by seeing comrades fall dead or wounded in the landing craft on their way to Falamai. An officer was haunted by his actions in lobbing grenades into Japanese-occupied caves. One can only imagine the private hell of the New Zealander who mistakenly shot and killed his comrade. Post traumatic stress disorder would not become a recognizable medical condition until the 1970s. Many of the veterans of World War II who had seen and experienced things of utmost horror would become, in Alison Parr's words, "silent casualties" in their post-war lives.[21]

Others came home with grievous medical conditions. Malaria was not a huge problem, but for those individuals who caught the disease it meant many years of sweats and disruption to life. Most New Zealand doctors were not familiar with it and some veterans simply had to endure. Malaria was not the only problem — hepatitis, dengue fever, scrub typhus and a myriad of other diseases afflicted soldiers in the Solomons. The medical services' ability to stave off large-scale casualties is one of the true success stories of 3NZ Division in the South Pacific.

For the New Zealand, American and Japanese families who lost loved ones during Goodtime, the pain has spanned generations. Having family members killed in a small and almost forgotten battle is no less painful than their being killed in one of the epic battles.

The New Zealand public was deliberately kept in the dark about what the Kiwis were doing in the South Pacific. For some ignorant people the soldiers were "coconut bombers," "pineapple fusiliers," or "banana pickers," as though they had a comfortable war in the South Pacific while the real war was fought in Europe. That attitude and ignorance is commonly borne by the Australian, Canadian and, to a certain extent, the American troops who fought against the Japanese.

Aftermath — Personalities

Major General Harold Barrowclough commanded a further invasion by 14 NZ Brigade, called Operation Squarepeg, to retake the Green Islands in February 1944. This operation was also successful and added one more link in the steel fence around the main Japanese base at Rabaul. Barrowclough hoped for further operations with the Americans but when 3NZ Division was disbanded he found himself a divisional commander without a division to command. He was posted to Freyberg's headquarters and there, hoped he might replace Freyberg. Instead he was sent onto Montgomery's headquarters in Europe as an observer. He maintained a life-long interest in military affairs, particularly compulsory military training.

After the war he returned as a senior partner in a prestigious law firm in Auckland. He became a judge in the High Court and later Chief Justice, and was instrumental in setting up the Court of Appeal. He died in 1972.

Bert Cowan was awarded a Distinguished Conduct Medal[22] for his efforts, and when

3NZ Division was disbanded returned to New Zealand.[23] He was one of New Zealand's quiet heroes. After the war he rejoined the Forest Service. He lived out his life quietly and, even at his funeral, there were few neighbors and friends who had any inkling of his heroism. Cowan was a soldier and, while recognizing that the Japanese had to be fought to defend his homeland, he derived no pleasure from killing them. He deplored the waste of life and it is noteworthy how many Japanese were taken prisoner by the Blokes patrols under his supervision.

Frank Nash received the Legion of Merit from the Americans and the Military Medal from the Australians after Goodtime for his efforts with the Coast Watchers.[24] He was then involved in coast watching on Bougainville, spending some 26 months behind Japanese lines. He survived the war and returned to Colorado to resume ranching. He died in 2005. He never participated in veteran's parades nor made people aware of his wartime exploits.

In an example of art imitating life, Lt. Joe Cable, the main hero of Roger & Hammerstein's hit musical *South Pacific*, is an American Coast Watcher, albeit a marine. The author, James Michener, might have been inspired by Nash.

Frank Wickham continued his missionary activities in the post-war period. The Wickham family remains influential in the Solomons.

David Ilala returned to civilian life and had a family. He received recognition from the British government for his heroism.

After being rescued by Bert Cowan, Jesse Scott was sent back to Whidbey Island Naval Air Station, Washington State. He had scars on his feet and ankles from coral cuts for the rest of his life. Post-war he was an auctioneer in Colorado. He kept in touch with Frank Nash and died in 2007.

The other American aviators—Peck, Mitchell, Teft and King—stayed in the military and achieved high rank. Ben King returned to flying operations and scored seven victories in air battles in the Pacific and Europe. In Europe, he flew a P-51 Mustang, called *Matilda II*, downing four German fighters. He flew combat operations in the Korean War, was involved in the covert air war in Vietnam and reached the rank of brigadier general, USAF. He died on 7 October 2004.

George Luoni became a successful stud farmer in the North Island of New Zealand and died in 2009.

Fractured Legacy: Goodtime and *South Pacific*

In an odd, unintended, fractured, distorted fashion Goodtime continues to resonate in modern culture. During the Pacific War a U.S. Navy lieutenant named James Michener was stationed on Espirtu Santo. Michener, a gifted storyteller, after the war penned a series of short stories in a book called *Tales of the South Pacific*.[25] This won him a Pulitzer prize and the attention of legendary songwriters Richard Rodgers and Oscar Hammerstein. Inspired by two of Michener's stories, they produced a smash hit 1949 Broadway musical simply entitled *South Pacific*. This, in turn, was used as the basis for the 1958 Academy Award–winning movie *South Pacific*.[26]

The movie depicted two love stories set against the backdrop of the fictional island paradise of Bali Hai and featured in its ensemble of characters, an American Marine Coast Watcher, American Navy nurses, Seabees, exotic women and a French plantation owner. With a backdrop of brilliant blue skies, tropical sunsets, lush green foliage, coconut palms and golden sands, the South Pacific seemed like an earthly paradise where the living was easy.

The musical and the film contributed to a misleading image of the war in the South Pacific. Few who had fought in the Solomons would have described the Solomons as "enchanted" or of life there as easy or idyllic. The sad consequence of the movie was to reinforce the popular perception that the war in the South Pacific had somehow been pleasant and the personnel sent there had an easier time of it than their compatriots in Europe.

In his autobiography, Michener wrote that the inspiration for Bali Hai was "a tiny, miserable village on Mono Island."[27] The resemblance between the names of "Falamai" and "Bali Hai" is obvious.

Michener's books continue to sell, the play continues to be performed and the movie is now even more widely available on multimedia. The Rodgers and Hammerstein view of the war in the South Pacific remains an indirect legacy of Goodtime.

Analysis of Goodtime

As the American historian Samuel Eliot Morison succinctly put it, "The Japanese were caught flatfooted at the Treasuries."[28] Surprise was achieved, the islands were seized, the Japanese defenders wiped out and the islands secured. Importantly, naval and air bases were rapidly constructed and operations started against neighboring islands and Rabaul.

Especially important for future operations, there was no loss of the vital amphibious shipping. Some damage was done to LSTs, but this was minor and did not prevent their participation in Cherryblossom. The *Cony* needed repairs, but its place was taken by other vessels.

Operation Goodtime was a success, but not a perfect one. Things did go awry and misunderstandings occurred, some of them fatal. Given that Goodtime was put together hurriedly and required different services and nationalities to work together, it is a wonder that Goodtime worked as well as it did.

Planning was dogged by poor coordination. Row's headquarters was too far from Wilkinson's. Some units arrived only shortly before the start of Goodtime. All units were inexperienced in large scale amphibious operations. The invasion convoy was late arriving off the beachheads. The delay was minimal but could have led to ships becoming targets while waiting.

The preliminary naval bombardment was in some ways ineffective. The destroyers were largely shooting blind due to vegetation and weather. It is also arguable that the destroyers failed to close the range and thereby limited their effectiveness. The artillery-spotting plane that should have been directing fire suffered a malfunction. These deficiencies were, however, overcome by the novel use of gunboats.

The Japanese did reinforce their garrison, but by only 50 men, and they were swept up in the battle. Interdiction of the channel between the Shortland Islands and Mono had not occurred effectively prior to Goodtime, but the establishment of a PT boat base, an airfield on Stirling and radar soon remedied that.

The confusion of the landing and friendly fire from U.S. Navy personnel resulted in at least two New Zealand dead and others wounded. It was argued that this was due to boat crews not being properly briefed.[29] A simpler explanation is that this was due to the stress from exposure to combat for the first time and resultant trigger happiness.

Aerial protection over the Treasury Islands was porous. Allied troops continued to suffer some casualties from air attack even after ground combat had ended. The Japanese may have owned the night skies, at least temporarily, but achieved little beyond nuisance attacks on the Allied land units.

Rapid unloading of ships' cargoes was crucial, firstly, for the safety of shipping, and secondly, so stores could be accumulated and available should supply ships have to leave the area hurriedly, as occurred at Guadalcanal in August 1942. Some New Zealand troops ordered to unload an LST were reluctant to do so because they "were not easily convinced that unloading by hand was necessary."[30]

However, these things pale into insignificance when compared with Operation Galvanic which took place a month later on 21 November. A disregard of tidal effects had disastrous results for 2nd USMC Division. The comparison is strained because of the differing numbers of Japanese troops and their level of preparedness. Tarawa was a fortress and the blood price to seize it was higher. Nonetheless, Galvanic shows how easily an amphibious operation can go awry. Goodtime worked. It was extremely risky, but the risk paid off and the Allies were able to island-hop and isolate or wrong-foot some 24,000 Japanese troops in the south of Bougainville, the Shortland Islands and Ballale.

Barrowclough dispatched a lengthy report to Prime Minister Peter Fraser saying that the Treasury Islands had been wrested from the Japanese and by late 1943 had ceased to be a scene of active operations. He noted: "It is a significant indication of the Japanese impotence in this area that 8 Brigade were able to stage an elaborate aquatic sports meeting only 17 miles distant from Japanese held Shortland Island and only 25 miles distant from his airfields at Kahili and Kara."

Barrowclough was careful not to overblow the importance of Goodtime and went on to say: "They were relatively minor actions so far as this Division is concerned and indeed a proportion of the Divisional troops were not engaged at all."[31]

For Barrowclough, the significance of Goodtime lay in the successful completion of operations in cooperation with the Americans. He believed: "that throughout the whole operation the greatest friendship and cordiality existed between the American troops and ourselves. The spirit of willing and complete cooperation was everywhere in evidence."[32]

Barrowclough contemplated the continued use of his troops in the South Pacific and hoped that the next operation would involve the full 3NZ Division. The men of 8 Brigade acquitted themselves well and had learned important lessons not only in amphibious operations but also in jungle warfare. These lessons had to be absorbed and the men of not only 8 Brigade but also those of 3NZ Division had some seasoning yet to take place. Fire discipline at night, for example, was still too lax. Nonetheless, given the complexities of Operation Goodtime and that it had been the brigade's first combat operation, things had gone remarkably well. However, for the men of 8 Brigade, Goodtime was their last Pacific combat. Had 3NZ Division been committed to further amphibious operations in the South Pacific, it seems likely that it would have gained a reputation as a well-run, proficient combat unit.

The contribution of the Seabees cannot be minimized. They were a vital part of the landing operations and their sweat and skills built the radar, naval bases and airfields that allowed the Treasury Islands to be a significant asset in the Bougainville Campaign.

For the Treasury Islanders war brought with it the destruction of their houses, gardens and possessions and inflicted suffering on the people. Once free of the Japanese occupiers, the islanders had to contend with the presence of Allied troops, albeit a benign group of occupiers.

The strategic significance of Goodtime needs to be seen as part of the overall Bougainville campaign. This campaign successfully anchored MacArthur's flank and enabled American and Australian troops to push northward up the coast of New Guinea. It also contributed to the encirclement of the main Japanese base at Rabaul and ultimately led to the Japanese garrison there being neutralized.

From the Japanese perspective, the defenders of the Treasury Islands fought resolutely and exacted a price in Allied blood. Their best chance of defeating the invasion was in the landing phase. Once the Allies had landed and consolidated their beachhead the outcome was no longer in doubt. As time went by, the Allies strengthened their position by establishing artillery and AA guns and landing more reinforcements. The Japanese command structure on Mono was fractured early in the battle and organized resistance became more difficult. The attacks on Loganforce were the last desperate gasps of Japanese resistance. The remaining Japanese faced only the dismal prospects of becoming prisoners, committing suicide or dying while attacking the enemy. None of the Treasury Islands garrison managed to escape.

John Rentz's verdict on Goodtime is: "Viewed from the tactical level, seizure of the Treasury Islands was sound. These islands if held by the Japanese, would be a thorn in our side, requiring a long line of supply between the Southern and Northern Solomons. Conquest of these islands denied this opportunity to the Japanese and, moreover placed our forces in a position to cover the flank of our own supply and communication lines."[33]

Goodtime and, for that matter, the American phase of the Bougainville campaign, can only be considered a high stakes gamble. That gamble succeeded brilliantly with the result that by early 1944 Rabaul was neutralized and Allied forces were able to move into the Philippines and the Central Pacific unhindered by the remaining Japanese forces in the Solomons. The strategic and operational acuity of Halsey, Wilkinson and Row and the tactical abilities of the Kiwi and American soldiers, sailors and airmen made it all happen.

Appendices

A: Composition of 8 Brigade, 3 NZ Division

Headquarters 8 Brigade	77 men
8 Brigade HQ Defense Platoon	39 men
"J" Section Signals	61 men
5 Provost Section	18 men
64 Light Aid Detachment (Engineers)	24 men
No 1. Reconnaissance Section	52 men
Malarial Control Section	8 men
Brigade Machine Gun Company	141 men
2 Field Surgery	11 men
7 Field Ambulance	244 men
29 Battalion	729 men
34 Battalion	729 men
36 Battalion	729 men
38 Field Regiment	716 men
54 Anti-Tank Battery	131 men
208 Light Anti-Aircraft Battery	251 men
HQ 29 Light Anti-Aircraft Regiment	114 men
214 Light Anti-Aircraft Battery	251 men
23 Field Company	249 men
4 Motor Transport Company	234 men
Total all ranks	4808

(Archives New Zealand, Wellington Office, WAII, 1, DAZ 151/1/23)

B: United States Forces: The Land Component

198 Coastal Artillery (AA)	973 men
Boat Pool 10	324 men
Communications Unit 6	119 men
Commander Air Northern Solomons	125 men
Company A 87 Naval Construction Battalion	250 men
2 Platoon A Company Signals	49 men
Advanced Naval Base	104 men
Naval Fire Control	7 men
Total all ranks	1966

(Archives NZ, Wellington Office, WAII, 1, DAZ 151/1/23)

Gordon Rottman's Order of Battle

2 Operations Platoon, Co. A 1st Corps Signal Battalion
Air Liaison Parties No. 4 & 5 Com Air Nor Sols
Det. HQ Co., 87 Naval Construction Battalion
Company A, 87 Naval Construction Battalion
Detachment, Naval Advance Base Unit No. 7
Air Warning Unit No. 2 (USN)
Argus 6 (USN)
Communications Unit No. 8 (USN)
Boat Pool No. 10 (USN)
198 Coast Artillery Regiment (Anti-Aircraft)
3 Battalion (USA) (90mm and 37mm guns)

(Gordon L. Rottman, *U.S. Marine Corps World War II Order of Battle, Ground and Air Units in the Pacific War 1939–1945*, London: Greenwood Books, 2001, pp. 291–2)

Further Reinforcements

These units were later reinforced by the remainder of 87 NCB on 28 November 1943, the 82 NCB and 88 NCB in January 1944, a detachment from 6 (special) NCB in 1944, and CBMUs 569 and 587 in July 1944. Acorn 12 also provided support.

C: The Allied Naval Component

From the naval forces under the control of Commander South Pacific, from the Naval Forces under the control of Commander Third Amphibious Force, and from the landing craft under the control of Commander Landing Craft Flotillas, Third Amphibious Force, the following were designated by Commander Task Force Thirty-One to participate in the initial landing on Treasury Islands and the Second and Third Echelons.

Destroyers—*Pringle, Waller, Saufley, Philip, Renshaw, Conway, Cony, Eaton*
APDs—*Stringham, Waters, Dent, Talbot, Kilty, Crosby, Ward, McKean*
LSTs—399, 485, 71, 460
LCI(L)s—222, 330, 334, 336, 24, 61, 67, 69, 328, 331, 332, 335, 333, 63, 64, 65
LCI gunboats—21, 22, 23, 70
LCTs—321, 325, 330
APCs—33, 37
ATS—*Apache, Sioux*
Ams—*Conflict, Adroit, Daring*
YMs—197, 260
22 MTBs from Lambu Lambu and Lever Harbor[1]

D: The Japanese Order of Battle and Weaponry

The Japanese Garrison on the Treasury Islands

7 Combined SNLF (7 men)
Kure 7 SNLF (112 men)
17 Air Defense Unit (55 men)
16 Air Defense Unit (11 men)
Total: 189 men (all navy)

Senshi Sosho—Minami Taiheiyo Rikugun Sakusen <4>, Boeicho Boeikenshujo Senshishitsu (this is inaccurate; at least 222 Japanese were killed and some 11 prisoners taken).

John M. Rentz's Order of Battle

1st Japanese Base Force
(a) 7 Combined SNLF
(b) Kure # 7 SNLF
(c) 16 AAA Tai (Company)
(d) Sasebo # 6 SNLF

(Rentz estimated that "about 250 Japanese troops defended the Treasures." John M. Rentz, *Bougainville and the Northern Solomons*, p. 119, Footnote 14).

Japanese Weaponry

1 25mm AA gun without ammunition
1 heavy machine gun—Type 92, 7.7mm
5–6 light machine guns

Grenade dischargers (mistakenly called "knee mortars" by the Allies due to a mistranslation)
1 trench mortar
2 mountain guns (40 men in 2 squads)
1 two-wheeled anti-tank gun
Various rifle squads armed with rifles and grenades

(Derived from prisoner of war interrogation reports)

E: Distances to the Treasury Islands in Nautical Miles

Enemy Bases		Allied Bases	
Faisi, Western Province, SI	26	Barakoma, Vella Lavella, SI	73
Ballale, Shortland Islands, SI	30	Segi (or Seghe), Western Province, SI	155
Kahili, Bougainville Island, PNG	39	Munda, New Georgie, SI	115
Tenekau Bay, Bougainville, PNG	93	Russell Islands, Central Province, SI	238
Buka-Bonis, Bougainville, PNG	130	Henderson Field, Guadalcanal, SI	290
Rabaul, East New Britain, PNG	280	Woodlark Island, Milne Bay, PNG	200
Kavieng, New Ireland, PNG	405	Milne Bay, SI	360
Gasmata, West New Britain, PNG	325		
Nauru, Republic of	800		
Truk, Micronesia	930		

(Estimate of the Situation)(SI = Solomon Islands; PNG = Papua New Guinea)

F: Beaching Times

Ship or Landing Craft		Time of Beaching
APDs	(first wave)	0606 hrs.
	(second wave)	0700 hrs.
LCIs		0630 hrs.
LSTs		0715 hrs. (approx.)
LCTs		0830 hrs. (approx.)
LCMs		0900 hrs. (approx.)
APC 37		0830 hrs. (approx.)

(Row Report)

G: Weapons of 8 Brigade, 3 NZ Division

The 3 NZ Division was largely armed with British-designed and supplied weapons or weapons manufactured in New Zealand. This resulted in a logistics nightmare for U.S. quartermasters, as U.S. designed weapons were often of a different caliber, requiring different ammunition.

A. Infantry Weapons

1. Grenade: Type 36 Mills bomb — a round pineapple-shaped grenade, 3.75 inches in length, weighing 1 pound, 11½ ounces, designed to be thrown or fired from a special rifle attachment. Its effectiveness derived from its shrapnel rather than its blast. New Zealand troops were trained in grenade-throwing. An effective weapon in jungle warfare because a grenade thrown by hand did not usually disclose the location of the thrower. Grenades were in short supply in the initial stages of the war.

2. Short Magazine Lee Enfeld rifle: No. 1. Mk III (SMLE) — A bolt action rifle of .303 inch caliber, reliable and accurate with an effective range of 600 yards. It carried a 10-round detachable magazine. The standard New Zealand rifle.

3. Bayonet: Although armies throughout the world gave their troops bayonet training and sought to instill in them "the spirit of the bayonet," more often than not the bayonets were used as a utility knife for entrenching or opening tins.

4. Machine Guns:

   (a) Lewis gun: An American-designed light machine gun. Used extensively in World War II in aircraft and on the ground in all theatres. Relatively portable with a cylindrical magazine and able to be fired by one man. Lewis guns became less common once Bren guns became available.

   (b) The Vicker's machine gun — Mk I: A medium machine gun of British manufacture. used extensively in both World War I and II. A belt-fed machine gun which required a two-man crew. Fired .303 inch bullets. Weighed 40 pounds. Fired 450 rpm. The heavy version fired .5 caliber ammunition, which was far too heavy for use on the battlefield.

   (c) Thompson sub-machine gun M1928: The famous "Tommy gun" favored by Chicago gangsters of the Prohibition Era. Firing .45 inch caliber bullets, it had tremendous stopping power and was effective in close-quarter jungle warfare. Fired 800 rpm. Weight 10 pounds, 2 ounces.

   (d) Bren machine gun: A light machine gun firing .303 inch rounds. Of Czech design, but manufactured by Britain, it was claimed by some to be the finest light machine gun of World War II.

5. Mortars:
Ordnance, ML (Muzzle Loading) 2 inch mortar

   (1) Smooth bore, muzzle loading, 2 inch mortar — of British design, essential for jungle warfare. The basic support weapon for infantry for delivery of smoke, illumination or high explosive rounds. Aimed by lining up a white line painted on the barrel. Elevation was over to the firer. Maximum range 500 yards. Fired a projectile with an impact fuse in

the nose. Weighed approximately 10½ pounds, including small base plate. Standard weapon in an infantry platoon.

Ordnance, ML mortar 3 inch

(2) Smooth bore, muzzle-loading 3 inch mortar. Maximum range 1600 to 2800 yards. Weight 112 pounds. Close support weapon. A standard infantry support weapon which was robust, reliable but of limited range relative to its contemporaries.

6. The Boys Anti-tank Rifle Mk I: Literally a heavy rifle firing an armor-piercing .55 inch round. Developed prior to the start of World War II by the British as a means of dealing with tanks. The increase in the thickness of tank armor rendered it obsolete in Europe. It ceased production in 1943. Because of the lack of development of Japanese tanks, the Boys anti-tank rifle retained some utility against light Japanese tanks. Used in Europe and Asia, but rarely with success. Although present on Mono, it was unpopular because of its bulk and weight.

7. Pistols: Pistols were issued to officers, the crew of crew-served weapons and vehicle crews. Considered a status symbol but, in combat, pistols were often discarded in favor of rifles, as they marked out the owner as being a worthwhile target to Japanese snipers.

(1) Webley .38 inch Mk IV — 6 chambered revolver. .352 caliber. Standard issue in the British Army.

(2) A variety of American pistols were traded or acquired unofficially.

B. Artillery[1]

(a) 25 pounder gun — a versatile British-made field gun capable of firing high explosive or armor-piercing rounds. Although successful, it was not compatible with U.S. ordnance. Its use was limited by jungle conditions — although portable, thick jungle made firing these weapons difficult — shells were deflected by foliage and it was difficult to see the enemy. Capable of firing HE 25 pound shell to 13,400 yards.

(b) Oerlikon anti-aircraft gun — also known as the "Pom Pom" gun because of the sound made when firing. A 4-barrelled anti-aircraft gun effective against low flying aircraft.

(c) 2 Pounder gun — anti-tank gun. British anti-tank weapon which was obsolete by 1941. Effective against lightly-armored Japanese tanks. Fired 2 pound AP shot out to 8000 yards.

(d) 40 Millimeter Bofors AA Gun — Standard anti-aircraft gun. Single barreled, high rate of fire, used by U.S. forces.

C. Armored Fighting Vehicles

(a) Universal Carrier, or "Bren gun carrier" — an open-topped tracked vehicle with a driver and passenger capable of mounting a Bren gun through a slit in front. Able to transport supplies and men in the rear compartment. Of limited use in a jungle setting.

D. Transport

(a) Jeeps or in the language of the time, "Peeps," general purpose vehicle made by the U.S., 4-wheel drive, very versatile.

(b) Ford one-ton trucks.

H: Uniforms and Personal Equipment of 3 NZ Division

1. Head gear: Troops wore the standard World War II pattern British steel helmet in combat. It protected the wearer's head from shrapnel. However, because of its heaviness some troops fighting in thick jungle (particularly 14 Brigade on Vella Lavella) preferred bush-style caps with a firm front brim to protect the face from the sun. In non-combat situations a variety of head gear appears to have been used, including the New Zealand "Lemon Squeezer" hat, forage caps and cork solar topees.

2. Clothing: New Zealand Army supplied woolen clothing. Jungle suits made out of cotton twill were either acquired from the U.S. or made in New Zealand factories.

3. Boots: Boots were the standard leather variety used by the New Zealand Army. Leather had a propensity to rot and boot repair and replacement was a problem.

4. Pack and webbing: Standard New Zealand Army pack. British pattern webbing.

I: Amphibious Operations Vessels

Type	Nationality	Armament	Typical Load	Speed	Nos. Built
Daihatsu	Japanese	2 MGs or 2–3 × 25mm guns	1 × 7 ton tank or 70 men	8 knots	3229
LST	U.S.	7 × 40mm	20 × 25 ton tanks	10 knots	982
LCVP	U.S.	2 MGs	36 men or 2.5 ton vehicle	8 knots	22,492
LCT	U.S.	2 × 20mm	3 × 50 ton tanks or 150 tons of cargo	8 knots	965
LCI(L)	U.S.	4 × 20mm	188 men or 75 ton cargo	15 knots	1000

(Gardiner, Robert, ed., *The Eclipse of the Big Gun: The Warship, 1906–1945*, London: Conway Maritime Press, 1992, pp. 149–50).

J: Order of Battle: Goodtime Assault Landings

1. Mono Island

(1) Beach Orange One — Falamai to Saveke

The 29 Battalion with one section Carrier Platoon; one detachment 54 anti-tank battery; one section 23 Field Company. Task: Capture Falamai, secure beach for further landings and establish a defensive perimeter.

(2) Beach Orange Two — Falamai to Saveke

Left flank — 36 Battalion with one detachment, 54 Anti-tank Battery; one section 23 Field Company. Task: Secure beach for further landings and establish a defensive perimeter.

(3) Beach Emerald — Soanotalu

One Company 34 Battalion, one section MMGs, Detachment Argus No. 6, Detachment Company A, 87th CB. Task: Capture Beach Emerald, establish a defensive perimeter to protect the installation of a long range radar by Argus 6.

2. Stirling Island — Beaches Purple Two and Three

34 Battalion less one company with one section, 23 Field Company. Task: Secure Beaches Purple Two and Three and establish a defensive perimeter.

(Archives NZ, Wellington Office, WAII, Series 1, DAZ151/1/22, 8 NZ Brigade Group Operational Order No. 1, 21 October 1943)

Chronology

1941

7–8 December, Japanese forces attack Pearl Harbor, Hawaii and Malaya. The Great Pacific War begins

1942

23 January, Japanese forces land on Bougainville and Rabaul and destroy Larkforce, the Australian garrison

15 February, Singapore falls to Japanese forces

7 August, 1st U.S. Marine Division lands on Guadalcanal

1943

16 June, TBF Avenger piloted by Lt. Edward Peck shot down

17 July, 2nd Lt. Benjamin King's P-38 shot down

18 July, TBF Avenger piloted by Ensign Joe Mitchell shot down

15 August, American forces invade Vella Lavella, New Georgia Group

22–23 August, USS *Greenling* lands reconnaissance parties on the Shortland and Treasury Islands

25 August, the Japanese reinforce their garrison on Mono

14 September, 8 Brigade Group arrives at Guadalcanal from New Caledonia. Row is advised by Barrowclough that 8 Brigade will be used to seize the Treasury Islands

22 September, Admiral Halsey issues plans involving the seizure of the Treasury Islands

23 September, Flight Sergeant George Luoni is shot down in the vicinity of Mono

27 September, Major General Barrett completes operations plan and issues orders to 3 USMC Division

28 September, Row meets Major General Charles D. Barrett and learns the details of Goodtime

29 September, Row receives corps commander's letter of instructions and begins detailed planning

12 October, Halsey sets 1 November as D-Day for the invasion of Bougainville and instructs Admiral Wilkinson to take the Treasury Islands

14–17 October, APDs and 8 LCIs available — landing exercises Nggela Florida Island Group

15 October, Admiral Wilkinson appoints Rear Admiral George H. Fort as Commander Southern Force

16 October, 8 Brigade receives IMAC Operation Order No. 1 and begins preparations

21 October, Row holds conference and issues verbal orders

21–22 October, Sgt. Cowan's first patrol on Mono

22–23 October, Cowan's party is evacuated

22 October, IMAC issues Operations Order No. 2 directing 2nd USMC Parachute Battalion to conduct Operation Blissful

23 October, LSTs loaded and stage through Russell Island and Rendova

24 October, LSTs loaded and sail from Guadalcanal on 25 October

25 October, LCIs loaded and sail 26 October

25–26 October, Cowan's second patrol on Mono

26 October, APDs loaded and sail

27 October, H-Hour 0626

28 October, Operation Blissful, U.S. Marines conduct diversionary raid on Choiseul. The Marines are withdrawn on 4 November

29 October, Japanese snipers active on Mono

30 October, Japanese units begin retiring to the middle of Mono

31 October, U.S. radar begins operating at Soanotalu

1–2 November, Japanese attempt to over-run Loganforce; Battle of Empress Augusta Bay: U.S. Navy defeats IJN attack

1 November, Operation Cherryblossom — U.S. forces invade Bougainville at Empress Augusta Bay. Row receives reinforcements.

5 November, Corporal Armstrong's patrol encounters Japanese defenders

6 November, the Third Echelon arrives at the Treasury Islands

8 November, Lt. Chandler's patrol encounters Japanese defenders at the caves at Ulapu

11 November, Admiral Halsey, Major General Mitchell and Lt. Colonel Adams arrive and dine with Brigadier Row at his HQ on Mono

12 November, 8 Brigade goes into defensive mode

21 November, Operation Galvanic — 2nd USMC Division assaults Tarawa

29 November, Seabees begin construction of airfield on Stirling Island

17 December, B-25 *Ficklefinger*; does an emergency landing on Stirling Island

1944

12 January, "The Million Dollar Barrage": Japanese planes receive a vigorous response from anti-aircraft on Treasury Islands

30 January, the Liberty ship *Robert C. Grier* ties up at the steel pontoon on Stirling Island

26 April, the first draft of New Zealand soldiers departs for New Caledonia on USS *President Monroe*

15 May, Treasury Islands are handed over to an American garrison and the final troops of 8 Brigade are shipped to New Caledonia on USS *Tyron*

5 September, the first of three echelons from 87 NCB leaves Stirling Island

20 October — 3 NZ Division is disbanded

1945

15 August, Imperial Japan surrenders to Allied forces on the quarterdeck of USS *Missouri*

Glossary

AA — Anti-aircraft, also "Ack Ack."

AA & QMG — Assistant Adjutant and Quartermaster General, i.e., Senior Administrative Military Officer (also "A & Q").

AAA — Anti-Aircraft Artillery.

Acorn — United States Navy code name for a CB unit tasked with constructing, operating and maintaining advanced plane and sea-plane bases.

ADC — Aide de Camp — A military assistant to an officer of high rank.

Adjt. — Adjutant.

Adm. — Admiral.

ADMS — Assistant Director Medical Services.

ADOS — Assistant Director of Ordnance Services.

ADS — Advanced Dressing Station, a medical facility located farther back from regimental aid posts.

AHQ — Army Headquarters (Wellington, NZ).

AK — United States Navy acronym meaning cargo ship.

AKA — United States Navy acronym meaning Auxiliary Cargo Transport, Attack. "K" stands for transport, a common U.S. Navy abbreviation.

ALP — Air Liaison Parties. Dedicated air-ground support units. In July 1943, 1st Marine Air Wing trained ALPs to support USMC and 8 Bde. in Operation Goodtime.

Amb — ambulance.

AMCU — Anti-Malarial Control Unit.

Americal Division — U.S. Army division formed on New Caledonia in January 1942 out of two National Guard regiments and a regiment put together.

Amphibious Operation — an attack launched from the sea by air, naval and landing forces, with the aim of landing on a hostile shore.

Amtracs — USMC term for amphibious tractors or vehicles designed to carry troops or personnel from ships to inshore areas.

ANZAC — Acronym for "Australia and New Zealand Army Corps" from World War I, but also used in reference in World War II to refer to the Australia–New Zealand defense area. During World War II Australia and New Zealand, despite being part of the British Empire, did not have a unified command organization.

AP — Armor Piercing ammunition; also ammunition point — a place where ammunition is collected for operations; also U.S. Navy acronym for a transport ship (Auxiliary, Personnel).

APA — United States Navy acronym meaning auxiliary ship cargo attack (Auxiliary, Personnel, Attack), large U.S. transports used to transport troops, including troops of 3 NZ Division (see also "Unholy Four").

APc — U.S. Navy acronym meaning small coastal transport ship (Auxiliary, Personnel, coastal).

APD — United States Navy acronym for Auxiliary, Personnel, Destroyer. A "four stacker" obsolete American destroyer modified by the removal of funnels to provide accommodation area for troops. Originally designed to provide fast transport for USMC raiding parties in line with the raiding philosophy developed by the USMC in the interwar years. APDs were used in World

War II for the transport of elements of 8 NZ Brigade and 14 NZ Brigade to Japanese-held areas in the Solomons.

AR—All Ranks, i.e., officers and enlisted personnel.

Arcadia—Allied code name for a conference held in Washington, D.C., 22 December 1941 to 14 January 1942. The meeting between Winston Churchill and Franklin D. Roosevelt confirmed "The Germany First" policy. At this stage of the war the British tended to dominate their American counterparts.

Argus—U.S. codeword for radar units involved in fighter control, e.g., Argus Unit Seven deployed on Green Island in 1944. This involved New Zealand radar sets and operators as well as specialist U.S. personnel. The U.S. Navy purpose for Argus units was "to provide during the development stage of a United States naval base a comprehensive air warning, surface warning and fighter direction organization which will co-ordinate all radar operations under the area commander." Typically, an Argus unit was made up of 20 officers and 178 men (source: ONS Combat Narrative, Solomon Islands Campaign).

Arisaka—Japanese .25 caliber rifle.

ASC—Army Service Corps.

A/T—Anti-Tank.

Atk By—Anti-Tank Battery.

Avgas—Aviation fuel.

Avenger TBF—U.S. single-engine aircraft (a Torpedo Bomber) made by Grumman. Used by U.S. Navy and RNZAF.

B-17—Flying Fortress, USAAF strategic heavy bomber produced by Boeing. A state of the art weapon before American entry into World War II. Proponents of air power saw this as a means of coastal defense for the United States and a means of defending the Philippines from Japanese attack. Although tough, the bulk of B-17s in the Philippines and Hawaii were destroyed in the initial Japanese aerial onslaught in December 1941 and the promise of early air power remained unfulfilled. Used extensively in the European Theater.

B-24 Liberator—USAAF strategic heavy bomber produced by Consolidated. One of the most successful American bombers of World War II because of its long range and good payload.

B-25 Mitchell—USAAF twin-engine medium bomber produced by North American, used extensively for bombing. A variant was used for strafing to good effect against naval vessels.

Backhandler—Allied code name for the United States amphibious invasion of the western part of New Britain on 15 December 1943 in conjunction with a similar invasion of Cape Gloucester on the other end of the island. Part of Operation Cartwheel.

Bandit—Enemy aircraft.

BAR—Browning Automatic Rifle, a U.S. machine gun.

Barrowclough's Charter—The instructions given by the New Zealand government to Major General H.E. Barrowclough for the committal of New Zealand forces to combat. Barrowclough had the power to decline to commit New Zealand forces to high-risk military operations. A certificate was required from Barrowclough to the New Zealand government confirming that the risks were reasonable before 3 NZ Division was to be committed to combat.

Bde—Brigade. A unit of roughly 7,000 to 8,000 troops of various types usually made up of three infantry battalions or three tank battalions.

Beachhead—A designated area on a hostile shore which is the objective of an amphibious operation. When seized it allows the attacker to land troops and equipment with the aim of further operations inland.

Beachmaster—An officer (generally naval) tasked with controlling the beaching of landing craft and amphibious vehicles.

Beach Red—A particular area of the beachhead. It was common for the beach areas to be given a color designation for planning purposes, e.g., Beach Red, Beach Green, Beach Yellow, etc.

Beaches—Orange One and Orange Two: landing beaches on Mono Island located between the mouth of the Saveke River and Falamai Point. Purple One, Purple Two and Purple Three: landing beaches on the north of Stirling Island. Emerald One: landing beach at Soanotalu on the northern side of Mono Island.

Betty—Allied code name for Mitsubishi G4M medium bomber.

B-Force — The designation given to New Zealand soldiers deployed to Fiji in 1940. This unit was later designated 8 Brigade Group and was the core of what would become 3 NZ Division.

BGS — Brigadier, General Staff, chief staff officer at corps or army level.

Binary Division — 2 Brigade Division, c.f., the usual three brigades.

Blissful — Allied code name for a diversionary landing by 2 Parachute Bn., USMC, on Choiseul Island designed to divert Japanese attention away from the main U.S. landing at Empress Augusta Bay, Bougainville, on 1 November 1943.

BLO — Bombardment Liaison Officer.

Bloke — Person (NZ).

Blower — radio telephone (NZ).

Blue — color used in U.S. planning to designate U.S. forces.

Bn./Btn./Batt. — Battalion, a unit of roughly 700 to 900 troops, predominantly infantry, commanded by a lieutenant colonel. Contains three to four rifle companies and a company of supporting weapons, or three squadrons of tanks plus HQ.

Boat pool — Boats used for assault landing from mother ships.

Bofors — A 40mm multi-barreled light antiaircraft gun of Swedish design.

Bogey — Unidentified aircraft.

BRA — Brigadier Royal Artillery.

Bren Gun — A light machine gun used by Commonwealth forces.

Bren Gun Carrier — A light open-topped tracked vehicle designed to carry a Bren Gun but also used for reconnaissance and general transport and haulage work (see Universal Carrier).

Brigade — A formation usually consisting of three battalions plus command and supporting elements.

Brigade group — A flexible formation. Generally these were brigades supplemented by additional support elements.

B.T.O. — Big Time Operator. A term of derision used by troops in PTO to describe individuals with an inflated view of their own importance.

Bty. — Battery, a tactical and administrative unit of artillery roughly corresponding to a company in other branches of the army.

Butai — Japanese unit or detachment.

CA — Heavy cruiser, also Coastal Artillery.

Cactus — Allied code name for Guadalcanal.

Call sign — Code identification of a sender or receiver of a wireless telegraphy or radio telephony message.

The Canal — Guadalcanal.

CAP — Combat Air Patrol; a protective aerial umbrella usually provided over a specified area by fighter aircraft.

Capt. — Captain.

Carrier — Bren Gun Carrier.

Carrier Platoon — Platoon normally equipped with Universal or Bren gun carriers. On the Treasury Islands the carrier platoons quite often acted as infantry.

Cartwheel — The Allied code name for the two-pronged drive up the coast of New Guinea (by MacArthur's forces) and the Solomon Islands (by Nimitz's forces) designed to isolate and neutralize the main Japanese base in the South Pacific at Rabaul. Operations began on 31 June 1943 and were completed by 1 March 1944, leaving the 98,000 garrison bypassed and ineffective.

CAS — Chief of the Air Staff (NZ). Also close air support; a term used to describe air power dedicated to the needs of army units.

Casualty Clearing Station — A medical unit sited between a Medical Dressing Station and a Field Hospital.

Catalina — PBY5A U.S. twin-engine flying boat manufactured by Consolidated, extensively used by U.S. in patrol, air-sea rescue and anti-submarine work. Also referred to affectionately as "Dumbo" after Walt Disney's flying elephant.

CB — Construction Battalion. Also "Seabee," a U.S. Navy term for naval construction units which performed prodigious feats of engineering, particularly airfield and base construction. These units were integrated into 3 NZ Division operations. Alternatively, confined to barracks.

CBMU — Construction Battalion Maintenance Unit.

CCS — Anglo-American Combined Chiefs of Staff, also casualty cleaning station — a medical unit sighted between a medical dressing station and a field hospital.

Cdr.—Commander.

CE—Chief Engineer.

CG—Commanding General.

CGS—Chief of the General Staff.

CinC—Commander in Chief.

CINCPAC—U.S. Commander in Chief U.S. Pacific Fleet (Admiral Nimitz).

CL—Cruiser, Light.

Cleanslate—Allied code name for the invasion of Russell Islands, 21 February to 20 March 1943. Mounted from Cape Esperance, Guadalcanal, it was a stepping stone operation in the drive to retake the Solomons.

CNO—Chief of Naval Operations.

Coast Watcher—Allied personnel deployed on various Pacific islands with the purpose of covertly observing and reporting on Japanese aerial and naval movement. The Japanese also deployed Coast Watchers.

"Coconut Bombers"—A term used to describe New Zealand soldiers who served in the South Pacific. The term is probably derived from the shortage of weaponry in the early stages of World War II. Instead of grenades all the soldiers could do in training was to lob wooden imitations. Some soldiers viewed the term self-deprecatingly whilst others regarded it as a form of abuse. The term "pineapple pickers" was also used by members of the New Zealand public.

COMAIRNORSOLS—Commander Aircraft Northern Solomons (November 1943–January 1944).

COMAIRSOLS—Commander Aircraft Solomons (TF33). Established on Guadalcanal on 15 February 1943 to control all USMC, USN, USAAF, RNZAF and RAAF units based in the Solomon Islands. The main combat command for ComAirSopac controlling air activities in the Solomons in New Britain areas.

COMAIRSOPAC—Commander Aircraft South Pacific, commander of all land based aircraft in the South Pacific command area. Responsible to Admiral Halsey and SOPAC.

COMAMPHIBFORSOPAC—Commander, Amphibious Force, South Pacific Force.

Combat Loading—The loading of transport and cargo ships in such a way that items needed for combat could be easily accessed and unloaded first. Not as efficient as "commercial loading" but essential for the success of an amphibious operation.

Combined Operations—The British expression for amphibious operations. The term correctly emphasizes the necessity of inter-service cooperation.

COMGENFMAC—Commanding General First Marine Amphibious Corps.

COMGENSOPAC—Commanding General South Pacific.

COMINCH—Commander in Chief (U.S.: Admiral Ernest King).

COMSOPAC—Commander South Pacific Area, initially Ghormley and then Halsey.

Condition Black—Invasion imminent.

Condition Green—All clear.

Condition Red—Air raid warning status, air raid imminent.

Condition Yellow—Air raid probable.

Conv. Depot—Convalescent depot.

Corps—Military unit composed of two or more divisions.

COS—Chiefs of Staff. Term used to describe either British or New Zealand heads of service of the Army, Air Force and Navy.

C.O.—Commanding Officer.

Coy./Co.—Company, three platoons of infantry.

C.P.—Command Post.

Cpl.—Corporal.

CRA—Commander Royal Artillery (NZ) (of division).

CRE—Commander Royal Engineers (NZ) (of division).

CREME—Commander Royal Electrical and Mechanical Engineers.

Crook—New Zealand slang word meaning very ill.

CTF—Commander, Task Force.

CTF31—Combined Task Force 31. A U.S. naval force active in the Solomon Islands commanded by Admiral Theodore Wilkinson. This force provided transport and naval gunfire support to 3 NZ Division.

CTG—Commander, Task Group.

CTU —Commander, Task Unit.

Cumshaw —American expression meaning to scrounge or obtain by begging or pleading.

CW —Coast Watcher, Allied personnel deployed in the Pacific Islands to observe and report on Japanese aerial and naval movement.

DADME —Deputy Assistant Director Mechanical Engineers.

DADOS —Deputy Assistant Director Ordnance Services.

DCGS —Deputy Chief of General Staff (NZ).

DCM —Distinguished Conduct Medal (NZ).

DD —U.S. Navy acronym meaning Destroyer; Ordinary destroyers are referred to as "DD," to distinguish them from other destroyer-like vessels, such as Destroyer Escorts (DE).

D-Day —Designated day on which an operation is to commence. When a plus symbol is used it signifies days after D-Day, when a minus symbol is used it signifies days before D-Day, e.g., D+5 refers to 5 days after the invasion, D-5 refers to 5 days prior to invasion.

DDMS —Deputy Director Medical Services.

DE —U.S. Navy acronym meaning Destroyer Escort.

DEME —Director of Electrical and Mechanical Engineering.

Dipper —Allied code name for the invasion of Bougainville by U.S. 3rd Marine Division, 1 November 1943, and consolidation of Northern Solomons 27 October 1943 to 15 June 1944.

Div. —Division, a unit of 12,000 to 14,000 soldiers.

Div. A & QMG —Divisional Adjutant and Quarter Master General.

Div. Arty. —Divisional Artillery.

Div. G —Divisional General Staff Branch.

Div. HQ —Divisional Headquarters.

Div. Tps. —Divisional Troops.

Div. Workshops —Ordnance unit responsible for the maintenance of weapons and equipment.

DOD —Died of Disease. Alternatively, Department of Defense.

Dog Day —D-Day or Invasion Day. "Dog" refers to "D" in the U.S. phonetic alphabet, e.g., "Plan Dog."

Dovetail —Code name for USMC four-day amphibious exercise at Koro, Fiji, in July 1942, immediately prior to the Guadalcanal landing.

DSO —Distinguished Service Order, a British medal.

Ech. —Echelon: a movement of troops in a group. Implies a portion of a unit separated from a parent unit. In terms of the reinforcements to 2 NZ Division, 1st, 2nd and 3rd Echelons refers to the main contingents dispatched from New Zealand.

Elkton III —Code name for U.S. plan for seizing Eastern New Guinea and the northern and central Solomons with a view to capturing Rabaul.

Engr. —Engineer.

ETO —European Theater of Operations.

Exec —Executive officer (U.S. Navy).

Exercise Cyclops —Code name for amphibious landing practice by 8 Bde. and parts of Division Headquarters in New Caledonia.

Exercise Efate —Code name for amphibious training practice by 8 Bde. at Efate, New Hebrides, in 1943.

FD —Fighter Director.

Fd. —Field.

Fd. Arty. —Field Artillery.

Fd. Am. —Field Ambulance.

Fd. Coy. —Field Company of Engineers.

Fd. Hyg. Sc. —Field Hygiene Section.

FDO —Fighter Director Officer.

Fd. Regt. —Field Regiment of Artillery.

Fifth Air Force —The USAAF air unit operating in the South West Pacific. In June 1944, it combined with the 13th USAAF to become the Far Eastern Air Force.

Flight —An army expression meaning a movement of troops from one area to another, usually by sea.

FM —Fleet Marine Force, Pacific. Also, field manual (U.S.).

FMAC —First Marine Amphibious Corps, also "1 IMAC."

FMC —Field Maintenance Center (NZ).

FMF-Pac —Fleet Marine Force, Pacific (U.S.).

FO—Forward Observer, an artillery spotter usually deployed close to the front to observe the fall of artillery shells and report suitable targets for artillery.

Forearm—Allied code name for the invasion of Kavieng.

FSR—Field Service Regulations, British Army manual setting out tactical doctrine.

FSS—Field Security Section/Service.

Fwd. Base—Forward Base, main supply and maintenance area.

G1—Personnel (U.S. Staff).

G2—Intelligence (U.S. Staff).

G3—Operations (U.S. Staff).

G4—Logistics (U.S. Staff).

Galvanic—Allied code name for the invasion of the Gilbert Islands, 13 November–8 December 1943, which included the assault on Tarawa Atoll, 20 November–4 December 1943.

G Branch—Staff of division involved with operational matters.

Gen—General.

General Quarters—The quarters or positions manned at action (naval term).

GHQ—General Headquarters.

Gnr.—Gunner.

GOC—General Officer Commanding.

Goodtime—Allied code name for the invasion of the Treasury Islands, 27 October 1943 to 6 November 1943. A diversionary operation involving the invasion of the Treasury Islands by 8 Bde. 3 NZ Division with U.S. Marine, U.S. Navy and U.S. Army attachments. 1st Marine Air Wing provided air support, as did the Royal New Zealand Air Force. Initial landing numbered 3,795 due to limitations in sealift capabilities.

GQ—General Quarters.

HE—High Explosive.

H-Hour—Designated time for commencement of an operation.

Higgins Boat—Landing craft for infantry and light vehicles (LCVP).

HMG—Heavy Machine Gun.

HMNZS—His Majesty's New Zealand Ship.

HMS—His Majesty's Ship.

HQ—Headquarters.

Hrs.—Hours.

Hudson/Ventura—U.S. twin-engine plane made by Lockheed. Frequently used for patrol reconnaissance and anti-submarine work. Used by the U.S. and RNZAF. The Ventura was a development model of the Hudson.

I/C—In Command.

IFF or IF—Identification, Friend or Foe.

IGHQ—Imperial General Headquarters (Japanese).

IJA—Imperial Japanese Army (Kogun).

IJAAF—Imperial Japanese Army Air Force.

IJN—Imperial Japanese Navy (Tikoku Kaigun).

IJNAF—Imperial Japanese Naval Air Force (Koku Butai).

Ind. Bty.—Independent Battery.

Inf.—Infantry.

"I" Section—Intelligence Section.

JCS—Joint Chiefs of Staff. A committee consisting of U.S. Service Heads, Admiral Ernest King, General George C. Marshall and General Hap Arnold tasked with the coordination of U.S. military strategy.

Kaigun—Imperial Japanese Navy.

KDOR—Khaki Drill Other Ranks, uniform worn by New Zealand soldiers.

KIA—Killed in Action.

Kido Buitai—Japanese carrier striking force.

Km.—Kilometer.

Kogun—Imperial Japanese Army.

Koku Butai—Imperial Japanese Naval Air Force.

Kokutai—Japanese land-based naval air group.

LAA—Light Anti-Aircraft.

LAD—Light Aid Detachment (NZ). An engineering unit attached to a battalion to assist in repair and maintenance of vehicles and equipment.

LCA—Landing Craft, Assault.

LCC — Landing Craft, Control.

LCG (M) — Landing Craft, Gun (medium).

LCI — Landing Craft, Infantry, large landing craft capable of holding 200 men. Of shallow draught, but with seagoing ability. The work horse of the Pacific War.

LCM — Landing Craft, Mechanized.

LCP — Landing Craft, Personnel.

LCP (R) — Landing Craft Personnel, Ramp.

LCS — Landing Craft, Support.

LCT — Landing Craft, Tank.

LCVP — Landing Craft, Vehicle Personnel.

Lewis Gun — A light machine gun used by Allied forces.

LFASCU — Landing Force Air Support Control Units, ground air support units.

Liberty Ship — Name given to mass produced, prefabricated merchant vessels built in American ship yards.

LMG — Light Machine Gun.

LO — Liaison Officer.

L of C — Lines of Communication.

Loganforce — An ad hoc unit which landed on the northern area of Mono Island to establish a radar station, consisting of men drawn from 34 Bn., 87 NCB and Argus 6. The unit encountered brisk combat with Japanese units intent on escaping Mono.

LSF — Landing Ship, Fighter direction.

LSI — Landing Ship, Infantry.

LSM — Landing Ship, Medium.

LST — Landing Ship, Tank — a large seago-ing landing craft capable of carrying tanks and large numbers of men and supplies. An essential part of amphibious operations in the Pacific.

LT — Landing Team (Battalion).

Lt., Lieut. — Lieutenant.

LtA/A — Light Anti-Aircraft.

Lt. Col. — Lieutenant Colonel.

Lt. Gen. — Lieutenant General.

LZ — Landing Zone.

M & V — Meat and Vegetables.

M1 — Garand semi-automatic rifle, the standard U.S. rifle in World War II.

1 MAC — 1st Marine Amphibious Corps.

Mae West — An inflatable lifejacket worn by Allied aircrew. The item was named after the well-endowed Hollywood actress.

MAG — Marine Air Group.

Maj. — Major.

Maj. Gen. — Major General.

MARDIV — Marine Division.

MAW — Marine Air Wing.

MC — Military Cross.

MDS — Medical Dressing Station.

MG — Machine Gun.

MIA — Missing in Action.

mm — Millimeter.

MM — Military Medal (British).

MMG — Medium Machine Gun.

MO — Medical Officer.

MP — Military Police.

MT — Motor Transport.

Nambu — Japanese 7.7mm light machine gun.

NAS — Naval Air Station (U.S.).

NATS — Naval Air Transport South Pacific. Air transport system operated by U.S. Navy, considered safer than SCATS. Operated by U.S. Navy in rear areas and flew administrative passenger missions.

NCB — Naval Construction Battalion, i.e., Seabees.

NCO — Non-Commissioned Officer.

N Force — New Zealand troops dispatched as a garrison to Norfolk Island in 1943: 36 Infantry Battalion, 215 Composite AA Battery, the 152nd Heavy Battery and 9 Mobile Field Troop (1488 men).

NLF — Northern Landing Force.

No. 1 Islands Group — The main administrative and command organization of the RNZAF in the South Pacific.

NZA — New Zealand Artillery.

NZASC — New Zealand Army Service Corps, Army unit used for supply and support.

NZE — New Zealand Engineers.

NZEF — New Zealand Expeditionary Force.

NZEF(IP) — New Zealand Expeditionary Force in the Pacific.

NZLO — New Zealand Liaison Officer.

NZOC — New Zealand Ordnance Corps.

OC — Officer Commanding.

One Day's Supply — The quantity of supplies used in estimating the daily expenditure by a unit.

One Mac (1 MAC) — First Marine Amphibious Corps.

OP — Observation Post or "O Pip."

Operation Kiwi — NZ Code name for deployment of 3 NZ Division to New Caledonia and the Solomon Islands.

Orange — Color used in U.S. planning to designate Japanese forces.

Orders Group Conference — NZ Army expression meaning military planning meeting between commanding officers at which orders are given and received.

Ordnance — A military term referring to artillery, but also in a wider sense encompassing military stores such as ammunition, rations, etc.

ORs — Other Ranks (i.e., not officers).

Pacific Star or Clasp — A New Zealand medal awarded to military personnel who served in an operational theatre of the Pacific. Operational areas were defined to include Guadalcanal, New Georgia, Treasury Islands, Green Island, the Gilbert and Ellis Islands but not the garrison areas of Fiji, Tonga, New Caledonia, the New Hebrides, Norfolk Island or Fanning Island.

Para-Marines — Marines who have received specialist parachute training.

PBO — Lockheed PBO-1 (Hudson), a twin-engine maritime patrol aircraft that served with the U.S. Navy. Range 2200 miles; speed 255 miles per hour.

PBY5A — Catalina, a twin-engine U.S. Navy flying boat.

Peep — An early word for the American four-wheeled utility vehicle now commonly known as a jeep.

POL — Petrol, Oil and Lubricants.

POW — Prisoner of War, also PW.

Prov — Provisional, a unit formed from assets taken from other units on a temporary basis.

PT Boat — Patrol Torpedo Boat (U.S. Navy), i.e., motor torpedo boat.

PTO — Pacific Theatre of Operations.

Q — Quartermaster.

Quad — Lorry for towing British field guns.

RA — Royal Artillery.

RAMC — Royal Army Medical Corps.

RAMSI — Regional Assistance Mission to the Solomon Islands.

RAP — Regimental Aid Post.

RASC — Royal Army Service Corps.

RCT — Regimental Combat Team.

Recce — Reconnaissance, also recn.

Regt. — Regiment.

Res. — Reserve.

Ret. or Retd. — Retired.

Rikusentai — Japanese Naval Infantry.

RNZA — Royal New Zealand Artillery.

RNZAF — Royal New Zealand Air Force.

RNZASC — Royal New Zealand Army Service Corps, the organization responsible for the supply of stores to the New Zealand Army and transport services. Stores could range from rations to petrol and ammunition. Under the Director of Ordnance Stores (DOS). There are Deputy Directors of Ordnance Stores (DDOS), Assistant Directors of Ordnance Stores (ADOS) and at divisional level the Deputy Assistant Director of Ordnance Stores (DADOS).

RNZN — Royal New Zealand Navy.

rpm — rounds per minute (i.e., rate of fire of weapons).

RSM — Regimental Sergeant Major.

RT — Radio Telephony, wireless transmission.

SBD — Dauntless, a U.S. Navy single-engine torpedo bomber, nicknamed "Slow but Deadly," obsolete by 1942.

SCAT—South Pacific Combat Air Transport Command.

Sec.—Section. In aviation terms, a unit of between 2 and 4 planes, in artillery terms, 2 to 3 guns, in infantry terms a third of an infantry platoon.

Sgt.—Sergeant.

Sigs or Sigg—Signals, i.e., communications personnel, radio operators, etc.

SMLE—Short Magazine Lee Enfield rifle, standard rifle of Commonwealth forces in World War II.

SNLF—Special Naval Landing Force (Japanese).

SOPAC—South Pacific Area Command. A U.S. area of command that encompassed the Solomon Islands. From October 1942 to late 1944 Admiral Halsey commanded this area. He was, in turn, responsible to the Commander, Pacific Fleet, Admiral Nimitz.

Sqdn.—Squadron, in aviation terms, a unit of 18 to 36 planes, armored vehicles or recce troops.

Squarepeg—The Allied code name for the invasion of the Green Islands, February 1944.

Stonk—Concentrated artillery barrage.

Svy. Tp.—Survey troop.

SWPA—South West Pacific Area: A U.S. area of command encompassing New Guinea. Commanded by General Douglas MacArthur.

Tai (Japanese)—Company.

Territorial—A military unit made up of part-time voluntary soldiers (Commonwealth).

TF—Task Force, generally a grouping of naval craft with supporting air and other units for the fulfillment of a particular purpose.

Thirteenth Air Force (13th USAAF)—The USAAF unit that operated in conjunction with the 5th USAAF in the Solomon Islands.

T.O.E—Table of Organization and Equipment.

Toenails—U.S. code name for the invasion of New Georgia, 20 June 1943 to 16 October 1943. A multi-national and multi-service campaign involving USMC, U.S. 13th Corps, 3 NZ Division and 5 Australian Division.

Tokyo Express—U.S. nickname for the attempts by the Imperial Japanese Navy to reinforce their forces on Guadalcanal by convoying troops to the island.

Towpath—A U.S. Army plan for the assault on Rabaul which envisaged the use of 2 U.S. Marine Division and 3 NZ Division. Cancelled in November 1943.

Tps.—Troops; part of a squadron of tanks; part of a battery.

Ultra—Intelligence gained from the interception and decoding of Axis radio communications.

Unholy Four—The nickname given to four U.S. Navy troop transport ships active in the South Pacific in World War II: USS *President Adams* (APA-19), USS *President Monroe*, USS *President Jackson* and USS *President Hayes*. The nickname apparently derived from the fact that when crossing the international date line the ships lost a day, Sunday, and Sunday services were therefore missed. The Troopships were active in transporting troops of 3 NZ Division.

Universal Carrier—A tracked vehicle used by British and Commonwealth forces. Also known as a "Bren gun carrier" due to the ability to mount a Bren machine gun in the forward seat next to the driver. Because they were open topped, they afforded the crew very limited protection. Used mainly for the haulage of ordnance and supplies.

USAAF—United States Army Air Force.

USMC—United States Marine Corps.

USN—United States Navy.

USNR—United States Naval Reserve.

USS—United States Ship.

VAdm—Vice Admiral.

Val—Allied code name for the Japanese Aichi D3A dive bomber.

Veh.—Vehicle.

Vickers machine gun—Medium machine gun used by Commonwealth forces.

VJ Day—Victory over Japan Day, 2 September 1945.

VLR—Very Long Range, in reference to aircraft.

VMF—U.S. acronym "V" signifies fixed wing aircraft, "M" signifies U.S. Marine Corps and "F" signifies a fighter unit.

VT—U.S. prefix for fixed-wing torpedo bomber. The "V" stands for fixed wing aircraft, and the "T" to designate a torpedo carrying aircraft.

War Plan Orange—U.S. operational plan for the defeat of Japan prepared by the U.S. War Plans Division. It envisaged holding part of the Philippines and advanced bases in the Pacific while a U.S. Naval Force fought its way to the relief of U.S. garrisons. This was going to culminate in a Trafalgar-like battle with Japanese forces.

Watchtower—U.S. code name for Guadalcanal-Tulagi landings, 7 August 1942. Wryly nicknamed "Operation Shoestring" by participants because of the lack of resources allocated.

Wharfie—New Zealand slang expression, a dock worker who loads and unloads ships. The American term is "longshoreman."

WIA—Wounded in Action.

Wildcat—Allied code name for Grumman F4F fighter (U.S. Navy).

WO—Warrant Officer.

W/T—Wireless Telegraphy.

Yank—A New Zealand expression referring to all Americans, including those from the Southern states.

YMS—U.S. Navy designation for Yard Mine-Sweeper.

YMCA—Young Men's Christian Association.

Y Service—Specialized Allied unit that intercepted Axis radio signals.

Zeke or Zero—Allied code name for Mitsubishi A6M fighter (IJNAF).

Chapter Notes

Preface

1. John M. Rentz, *Bougainville and the Northern Solomons* (Washington, D.C.: Historical Section, Headquarters, USMC, 1948), p. 130.

Chapter One

1. Archives NZ, EA 86/27/10 Defense Conference, 1939. The Waitomo Caves are a famed tourist attraction in the North Island of New Zealand due to their glow worms.
2. Memo, D.D. Eisenhower to G.C. Marshall, 25 March 1942, cited in George C. Dyer, *The Amphibians Came to Conquer*, Vol. 1 (Washington, D.C.: U.S. Printing Office, 1969), p. 248.
3. Edward S. Miller, *War Plan Orange: The U.S. Strategy to Defeat Japan, 1897–1945* (Annapolis: Naval Institute Press, 1991).
4. Samuel Eliot Morison, *History of United States Naval Operations in World War II: Coral Sea, Midway and Submarine Actions May 1942–August 1942*, Vol. 4 (New Jersey: Castle Books, 2001), p. 246.
5. For Australasian historians there are heated debates whether the Japanese actually intended to invade Australia and New Zealand. Regardless, the perception in both countries in 1942 was that they faced this threat.
6. Dyer, *The Amphibians Came to Conquer*, Vol. 1, p. 250.
7. Nimitz was appointed commander of the Pacific Ocean Area and delegated command of the South Pacific Area to Ghormley.
8. Archives NZ, Air 118, 81f Defense of Pacific, Narrative, p. 97.
9. Archives NZ AD Series 12, 28/3, Vol. 4, NZ Minister in Washington to Prime Minister New Zealand, 8 May 1942.
10. New Zealand Prime Minister Peter Fraser was fearful that an Allied invasion of Europe would result in the Japanese taking advantage of Allied preoccupation with Europe and launching "a wholehearted attack upon the Pacific," Archives NZ, EA 81/1/28, Peter Fraser to Winston Churchill, 22 September 1942.
11. Bruce Gamble, *Fortress Rabaul: The Battle for the Southwest Pacific, January 1942–April 1943* (Minneapolis, MN: Zenith Press, 2010), pp. 64–67.
12. John M. Rentz, *Bougainville and the Northern Solomons* (Washington, D.C.: Historical Section, Headquarters, USMC, 1948), p. 2.
13. John Miller, Jr., *Cartwheel: The Reduction of Rabaul* (Washington: Center of Military History, United States Army 1990), p. 187.
14. Stephen R. Taaffe, *MacArthur's Jungle War: The 1944 New Guinea Campaign* (Lawrence: University Press of Kansas, 1998), p. 28.
15. Rentz, *Bougainville and the Northern Solomons*, p. 6.
16. James Christ, *Mission: Raise Hell—The U.S. Marines on Choiseul, October–November 1943* (Annapolis: Naval Institute Press, 2006).
17. Henry I. Shaw and Douglas T. Kane, *Isolation of Rabaul: History of U.S. Marine Corp Operations in World War II*, Vol. 2 (Washington Historical Branch Headquarters, U.S. Marine Corps, 1963), p. 175.
18. Andrew Roberts, *Masters and Commanders* (London: Allen Lane, 2008), p. 588.
19. New Zealand veterans that I have interviewed have expressed mystification when I asked about their participation in "Operation Goodtime."
20. Samuel Eliot Morison, *History of United States Naval Operations in World War II: Breaking the Bismarck's Barrier*, Vol. 6 (Edison, NJ: Castle Books, 2001), p. 293.
21. Archives NZ, Air, 120 16F Objective Folder Treasury Islands HQ U.S. FTS, pa, updated.
22. Archives NZ, WAII, 1, DAZ 151/9/6, Terrain study Treasury Islands, C-2 PIU, FMAC.
23. Archives NZ, WAII, 1, DAZ 151/9/5 Map Treasury Islands CICSOPAC, 22 June 1943.
24. Gordon Rottman, *World War II Pacific Island Guide* (Westport, CT: Greenwood Press, 2002), pp. 130–132.
25. Lieutenant Commander William J. Perry, USN, in the late 1940s found that notwithstanding this, the Treasury Islands had ten species of mosquito of five genera—Anopheles, Aedes, Culex, Armigeres and Tripteroides. See William J. Perry, "The Mosquitoes and Mosquito-borne Diseases of the Treasury Islands," *American Journal of Tropical Medicine* (1949), pp. 747–758. Perry found 0.7 percent infectivity in the inhabitants of Falamai Village of Wuchereria bancroft, a parasitic filarial nematode worm spread by mosquitoes.

26. Archives NZ, WA II, 1, DAZ 151/9/4, Estimate of the Situation, p. 28.
27. Ibid., p. 28.
28. Eric Bergerud, *Touched with Fire: The Land War in the South Pacific* (New York: Viking Penguin, 1996), pp. 105, 118.
29. David Gegeo and Geoffrey M. White (eds.), *The Big Death: Solomon Islanders Remember World War II* (Solomon Islands: Solomon Islands College of Higher Education and the University of the South Pacific, 1988).
30. Third Division Histories Committee, *Pacific Service: The Story of the New Zealand Army Service Corps Units with the Third Division in the Pacific* (Wellington: A.H. and A.W. Reed, 1948), p. 95.
31. Paul M. Lewis, *Ethnologue: Languages of the World*, 16th Edition (Dallas: SIL International, 2009).
32. William F. Halsey and J. Bryan, *Admiral Halsey's Story* (New York: McGraw-Hill, 1947), p. 176.
33. Shaw and Kane, *Isolation of Rabaul*, p. 175.
34. Bruce F. Meyers, *Swift, Silent and Deadly: Marine Amphibious Reconnaissance in the Pacific, 1942–45* (Annapolis: Naval Institute Press, 2004), pp. 2–3.
35. Charles W. Barlow, correspondence with author, May 2002.
36. Trench had been a district officer in the Solomons 1938–40 and in 1942 had become district officer in Guadalcanal, where he had organized resistance to the Japanese, including a rescue service for Allied airmen. Colonial Office, *Among those Present: The Official Story of the Pacific Islands at War* (London: His Majesty's Stationery Office, 1946), pp. 31–33.
37. Gunner's Mate Adam "Bow Wow" Balwierczak was topside when approximately 26 Marines arrived and went below. Correspondence, George Hinda, 7 May 2002.
38. Correspondence, Charles Barlow, 16 July 2002.
39. Correspondence, Captain Hubert T. Murphy, USNR (Ret.), with author, 27 May 2002.
40. Correspondence George Hinda, 7 May 2002.
41. Department of the Navy, Navy Historical Center, Washington, D.C., NRS 1978-27, *Greenling* (SS-213), World War II.
42. Supplied by Commander Hubert T. Murphy.
43. Meyers, *Swift, Silent and Deadly*, pp. 34–35.
44. Archives NZ, WAII, 1, DAZ 151/9/6 Report on Treasury Islands, 14 September 1943.

Chapter Two

1. Gary Nila and Robert A. Rolfe, *Japanese Special Naval Landing Forces* (Oxford: Osprey Publishing, 2006).
2. Archives NZ, DAZ 151/9/4 Treasury Islands, 1 MAC Estimate of Situation, undated.
3. Archives NZ, WAII, 1, DAZ, 151/9/1/20, Prisoner of War Interrogation Report Number 9 and 10, 13 December 1943.
4. Archives NZ, WAII, 1, DAZ 151/9/1/20, Prisoner of War Interrogation Report Number 2, 4 November 1943.
5. This date was given in a prisoner of war interrogation and is probably incorrect.
6. Archives NZ, WAII, 1, DAZ 151/9/1/20 Prisoner of War Interrogation Report No. 2, 4 November 1943.
7. John N. Rentz, *Bougainville and the Northern Solomons*, p. 93 n.14.

8. Jesse Scott, correspondence with author, 6 November 2001.
9. Cowan interview.
10. Archives NZ, WAII, 1, DAZ 151/9/1/20 Prisoner of War Interrogation Report No. 11, 18 December 1943. See also Archives NZ, WAII, 1, DAZ 113/1/9, War Information Summary No. 2, 6 November 1943. The wounded Japanese seaman was fresh from Japan and had only been on Buin for three days.
11. Archives NZ, WAII, 1, DAZ 151/9/4 Estimate of the Situation, p. 24.
12. Archives NZ, WAII, 1, DAZ 151/9/1/20 Prisoner of War Interrogation Report No. 11, 18 December 1943.
13. Archives NZ, WAII, 1, DAZ 151/9/4 Estimate of the Situation, p. 37.
14. Cowan interviews, Archives NZ, WAII, 1, DAZ 151/9/5 HQ 8 Bde. reports on Treasury Islands, "Recce to Mono," undated, p. 2.
15. Jonathon Lewis and Ben Steele, *Hell in the Pacific* (London: Channel 4 Books 2001), pp. 53–68.
16. John Dower, *War Without Mercy: Race and Power in the Pacific War* (London: Faber and Faber, 1986), p. 26.
17. Archives NZ, Navy, 1, 8/7 Lt. Gen. Edward Puttick to the Naval Secretary, Wellington, 21 October 1942.
18. Archives NZ, WAII, 1, DAZ 121/9/18/1/4A NZ Prisoner of Japanese, Sgt. F. White, HQ Co., 10 October 1943.
19. Meirion and Susie Harries, *Soldiers of the Sun: The Rise and Fall of the Imperial Japanese Army* (New York, Random House, 1991), pp. 475–484.
20. Megan Hutching (ed.), *Against the Rising Sun: New Zealanders Remember the Pacific War* (Auckland: Harper Collins, 2006), p. 97.
21. Mark Felton, *Slaughter at Sea: The Story of Japan's Naval War Crimes* (Barnsley, South Yorkshire: Pen and Sword, 2007), p. 36.
22. Ibid., pp. 34–43.
23. Ibid., pp. 167–180.
24. Archives NZ, WAII, 1, DAZ 151/9/4 Estimate of Situation, p. 35.
25. Archives NZ, WAII, 1, DAZ 151/9/4 Estimate of Situation, p. 27.
26. John Miller, Jr., *Cartwheel: The Reduction of Rabaul* (Washington, D.C.: Center of Military History, United States Army, 1990), p. 238.
27. For land force composition see Appendix B.
28. Diary entry, Robert W. Connor, http://www.Seabees93.netdiary.
29. David Williams interview.
30. Third Division Histories Committee, *The Gunners* (Wellington: A.H. and A.W. Reed, 1952), p. 167.
31. The Japanese had "Setsueitai" or Pioneers and "Kaigun Kenchiku Shisetsu Butai" or Navy Civil Engineering and Construction units. These were under IJN command. *U.S. War Department Handbook on Japanese Military Forces* (London: Greenhill Books, 1991), p. 80.
32. Bureau of Yards and Docks, *Building the Navy's Bases in World War II: History of the Bureau of Yards and Docks and the Civilian Engineer Corps, 1940–1946*, Vol. 1 (Washington, D.C: United States Printing Office, 1947), p. 133.
33. Eric Bergerud, *Fire in the Sky* (Boulder, CO: Westview Press, 2000), pp. 75–76.
34. Bureau of Yards and Docks, *Building the Navy's*

Bases in World War II: History of the Bureau of Yards and Docks and the Civil Engineers Corps, 1940–1946, p. 138.

35. Department of the Navy, Naval Historical Center, Navy Seabee History, www.history.navy.mil/faq.

36. William Bradford Huie, *Can-Do: The Story of the Seabees* (Annapolis, Naval Institute Press, 1997).

37. ONI Combat Narrative, Solomon Islands Campaign.

38. Gordon Rottman said "fewer than 100 Marines participated." Gordon Rottman, *U.S. Marine Corps World War II Order of Battle* (Westport, CT: Greenwood Press, 2002), p. 291.

39. Lyn Crost, *Honor by Fire: Japanese Americans at War in Europe and the Pacific* (Novato, CA: Presido Press, 1994), p. 54.

40. John Lorrelli, *To Foreign Shores: U.S. Amphibious Operations in World War II* (Annapolis: Naval Institute Press, 1995, p. 2.

41. Lt. General Nathan Bedford Forrest, in Peter G. Tsouras (ed.), *The Greenhill Dictionary of Military Quotations* (London: Greenhill Books, 2000). p. 106. A less popular version is, "I always make it a rule to get there first with the most men."

42. Lorelli, *To Foreign Shores*, p. 158.

43. Joseph H. Alexander *Edson's Raiders: The 1st Marine Raider Battalion in World War II* (Annapolis: Naval Institute Press, 2001), pp. 13–17.

44. Archives NZ, WAII, 1, DAZ 151/9/6 General Procedure for Embarked Troops, undated.

45. M.J. Whitley, *Destroyers of World War Two: An International Encyclopaedia* (Annapolis Naval Institute Press, 2002), pp. 279–285.

46. *Ships of the U.S. Navy 1940–5, Transports*.

47. David Gault, "YMS: First In — Last Out: World War II's Wooden Wonders," *Sea Classics*, June 2004.

48. *Dictionary of American Naval Fighting Ships*. http://www.hazegray.org/danfs/.

49. Gordon Rottman, *Landing Ship, Tank (LST) 1942–2002* (Oxford: Osprey, 2005).

50. Rottman, *Landing Ship, Tank*, p. 18.

51. J.D. Ladd, *Assault From the Sea 1939–45: The Craft, The Landings, The Men* (New York: Hippocrene, 1976), p. 217.

52. Rottman, *Landing Ship, Tank*, p. 3.

53. Ladd, *Assault From the Sea*, p. 218.

54. Rottman, *Landing Ship, Tank*, p. 19.

55. Rottman *Landing Ship, Tank*, pp. 23–24.

56. Rottman, *Landing Ship, Tank*, pp. 32–33.

57. Gordon L. Rottman, *Landing Craft, Infantry and Fire Support* (Oxford: Osprey, 2009), p. 4; Ladd, *Assault From the Sea*, p. 190.

58. Ibid.

59. Morison, *History of United States Naval Operations in World War II: Breaking the Bismarck's Barrier*, Vol. 6, p. 295.

60. Archives NZ, AD12, 28/15/1 J.I. Brooke, GS Notes undated.

61. A flightless bird with a long beak — the national bird of New Zealand, endearingly referred to by an American observer as "a short arsed duck." A black kiwi symbol adorned 3 NZ Division vehicles.

62. Major B.H. Pringle, letter, 27 November 1943, author's collection.

63. Third Division Histories Committee, *Communications* (Wellington: A.W. and A.H. Reed, 1945), p. 176.

64. David Williams, correspondence with author, 7 January 2010.

65. Narrative of Gordon Campbell Davie.

66. Archives NZ, WAII, 1, DAZ 155/9/2, Report on Amphibious Training.

67. Interview Harry Bioletti, 2006.

68. Trevor Whaley, correspondence with author, 14 July 2000.

69. Ashley James, correspondence with author, 17 August 2000.

70. Third Division Histories Committee, *Communications*, p. 178.

71. Archives NZ, WA II, 1, DAZ 151/1/21 War Diary, 8 Brigade HQ.

72. Wilmer Easley, "Legend of the Un-holy Four," unpublished manuscript (2004), p. 232.

73. HQ 8 Inf. Bde. War Diary, p. 3.

74. Ian McGibbon (ed.), *The Oxford Companion to New Zealand Military History* (Auckland: Oxford University Press, 2000), p. 273.

75. A bottle green Hessian helmet cover secured by a draw string was used. Barry O'Sullivan and Matthew O'Sullivan, *New Zealand Army Personal Equipment 1910–1945* (Christchurch: Willson Scott, 2005), p. 202.

76. For definitive information on NZ Army clothing in the Pacific, see Barry O'Sullivan and Matthew O'Sullivan, *New Zealand Army Uniforms and Clothing 1910–1945* (Christchurch: Willson Scott, 2005), pp. 25–27.

77. David Williams — correspondence with author, 7 January 2010.

78. Duncan M. Stout, *Medical Services in New Zealand and the Pacific* (Wellington: War History Branch, 1958), p. 68.

79. Stout, *Medical Services in New Zealand and the Pacific*, p. 71.

80. Harry Bioletti interview, 2006.

81. Third Division Histories Committee, *Communications*, p. 178.

82. *Admiral Ghormley's Account of Early History, April–November 1942*. Library of Congress Manuscript Division, Papers of Ernest J. King, Box 2, DA, NHC R.V. Goddard to R.L. Ghormley (August 2, 1942). Fraser bluntly told Ghormley that he did not want another Crete in the Pacific and demanded to be advised of any plans for the proposed use of New Zealand troops. Ghormley unfortunately kept Fraser in the dark and engendered distrust.

83. Nimitz to Ghormley: Notes on Conference held aboard USS *Argonne* at 1300, 2 October 1942, cited in Edwin P. Hoyt, *How They Won the War in The Pacific" Nimitz and his Admirals* (Guildford, CT: Lyons Press, 2002), pp. 151–158.

84. Henry I. Shaw and Douglas T. Kane, *Isolation of Rabaul: History of U.S. Marine Corps Operations in World War*, pp. 35–36.

85. Halsey in his memoir refers to the New Zealanders as "veterans of North Africa, Greece and Crete." William F. Halsey and J. Bryan, *Admiral Halsey's Story* (New York: McGraw-Hill, 1947), p. 175. Even contemporary U.S. Navy intelligence bulletins referred to the New Zealanders in this way. Some later historians have continued to repeat this error.

86. Frank Cooze, *Kiwis in the Pacific* (Wellington: A.H. and A.W. Reed, 1945), p. 37.

87. Mark Felton, *Slaughter at Sea: The Story of Japan's Naval War Crimes*, p. 56.

88. John Dower, *War Without Mercy: Race and Power in the Pacific War* (London, Faber and Faber, 1986), p. 64.
89. Harry Bioletti, correspondence, 2009.
90. Stout, *Medical Services*, pp. 45–46.
91. Correspondence, Padre Baragwanath.
92. Cowan interview, 2001.
93. John Tonkin Covell, recollection of his father.
94. Third Division Histories Committee, *Story of the 34th* (Wellington: A.H. and A.W. Reed 1947), p. 119.
95. Third Division Histories Committee, *Stepping Stones to the Solomons* (Wellington: A.H. and A.W. Reed, 1947), p. 96.

Chapter Three

1. Col. Joseph H. Alexander, USMC (Ret.), *A Fellowship of Valor: The Battle History of the United States Marines* (New York: Harper Collins, 1997), p. 120.
2. James F. Christ, *Mission Raise Hell: The U.S. Marines on Choiseul, October–November 1943* (Annapolis, MD: Naval Institute Press, 2006), p. 8.
3. Rentz, *Bougainville and the Northern Solomons*, p. 119.
4. Rentz, Ibid.
5. William F. Halsey and J. Bryan, *Admiral Halsey's Story*, pp. 175–6.
6. William H. Bartsch, "'Operation Dovetail' Bungled Guadalcanal Rehearsal, July 1943," *Journal of Military History* (April 2002): pp. 443–476.
7. Archives NZ WA II, 1, DAZ 151/1/23 Report on Treasury Islands, November 30 1943.
8. Nigel Steel and Peter Hart, *Defeat at Gallipoli* (London: MacMillan, 1994), pp. 66–67, p. 72.
9. Rentz, *Bougainville and the Northern Solomons*, p. 93.
10. Lorrelli, *To Foreign Shores*, p. 158.
11. The APD USS *Ward* was used to transport the Blissful raiders to Choiseul on 28 October 1943. Christ, *Mission Raise Hell*, p. 15.
12. Archives NZ, WAII, 9, S14 Operations, Row to Barrowclough, 8 October 1943.
13. Harry A. Gailey, *Bougainville: The Forgotten Campaign, 1943–1945* (Lexington: University Press of Kentucky, 1991), p. 41. A similar criticism could be made of the opening phase of Operation Watchtower where an American Marine Corps Division had been used to secure Guadalcanal and Tulagi.
14. Ron Tucker, correspondence with author, 2000.
15. Barrowclough's predecessor, Major General Owen Mead, had found himself in command of New Zealand and American troops on Fiji in 1942.
16. Trent Home, "U.S. Navy Surface Battle Doctrine and Victory in the Pacific," *Naval War College Review* (Winter 2009), Vol. 62, 1, p. 69. Being able to use ships interchangeably meant that a rapid pace of operations could be sustained.
17. Task Force 31, Operation Plan A14-43, 1–3.
18. Samuel Eliot Morison, *History of United States Naval Operations in World War II: Breaking the Bismarck's Barrier, 22 July 1942–1 May 1944*, Vol. 6, p. 282.
19. Ibid., p. 282.
20. Robert B. Asprey, *Once a Marine: The Memoirs of General A.A. Vandegrift* (New York: W.W. Norton, 1964), p. 227.
21. Jeter A. Isely and Philip A. Crowl, *The U.S. Marines and Amphibious War* (Princeton: Princeton University Press, 1951), p. 176.
22. Archives NZ, WAII, 9, S14 Operations, Row to Barrowclough, 8 October 1943.
23. Row Report, para. 13.
24. Row Report, para. 14.
25. Fort Report, p. 13.
26. Row Report, para. 15.
27. Third Division Histories Committee, WAII, 9, S14 Operations, Barrowclough to Row, 18 October 1943.
28. Archives NZ, WAII, 9, S14 Operations, Barrowclough to Row, 22 October 1943.
29. Archives NZ, WAII, 1, DAZ 151/1/23, Appendix 18.
30. Third Division Histories Committee, *Headquarters* (Wellington: A.H and A.W. Reed, 1947), p. 47.
31. Archives NZ, WAII, 1, DAZ 151/9/2, HQ 8 Brigade, Commander in Chief, U.S. Fleet, January 1943.
32. Ibid., Transport Loading-Embarkation 7-A-1.
33. Archives NZ, WAII, 1, DAZ 151/9/6. Letter of Instruction, 28 September 1943.
34. Ibid.
35. Archives NZ, WAII, DAZ 151/1/23 Notes on Planning-Combined Operations, 30 November 1943.
36. David Williams interview.
37. Archives NZ, WAII, DAZ 154/1/24, Appendix 3.
38. Third Division Histories Committee, *The Story of the 34th*, p. 63.
39. Henry I. Shaw, Jr., and Douglas T. Kane, *Isolation of Rabaul: History of U.S. Marine Corps Operations in World War II*, Vol. 2, p. 191.
40. Row Report, p. 13–14.
41. Archives NZ, WAII, 1, DAZ 151/1/23, Combined Operations Notes on Planning, 30 November 1943.
42. Ibid.
43. For a graphic account, see James F. Christ, *Mission Raise Hell*, pp. 1–5.
44. Archives NZ, WA II, 9, S9 Barrowclough to Wilkinson, 3 October 1943.
45. Archives NZ, WA II, 9, S9 Wilkinson to Barrowclough, undated.
46. Archives NZ, WA II, DAZ 128/9/ SLA 38/3 Lessons of Treasury Campaign, 29 Lt. AA Regt., p. 6.
47. Ibid.
48. Southern Force Task Group 31.1, Operation Order No. A16-43, 18 October 1943.
49. Fort Report, p. 14.
50. Fort Report, p. 15.
51. William I. McGee, *Amphibious Operations in the South Pacific in World War II: Vol. 2, The Solomons Campaigns 1942–43* (Santa Barbara, CA: BMC, 2002), p. 473.
52. Stephen Taaffe, *MacArthur's Jungle War: The 1944 New Guinea Campaign* (Lawrence: University of Kansas Press, 1998), pp. 94–95.
53. Archives NZ, WAII, 1, DAZ 151/1/22, Part 1.
54. Archives NZ, WAII, 1, DAZ 151/9/4 Estimate of the Situation, undated, p. 18.
55. Third Division Histories Committee, *Story of the 34th*, p. 62.
56. Archives NZ, WAII, 1, DAZ 151/9/6, Row to all Ranks.
57. Archives NZ, WAII, 1, DAZ 15/1/23 8 (NZ) Bde. Gp. 00, No. 1, 21 October 1943.
58. Third Division Histories Committee, *Story of the 34th*, p. 64.

59. The USS *Ward* had engaged a Japanese submarine at Pearl Harbor shortly before the devastating aerial attack. It therefore had the distinction of being the first Allied ship to fire at a warship of the Imperial Japanese Navy.

60. Narrative of Peter Basil Renshaw, author's collection.

61. Renshaw narrative.

62. Officers were particularly choice targets for Japanese snipers, so it made sense to remove things that could easily identify them as officers. Many elected to carry rifles rather than revolvers for this reason.

63. Renshaw narrative.

64. Renshaw narrative.

65. Third Division Histories Committee, *Pacific Pioneers: The Story of the Engineers of the New Zealand Expeditionary Force in the Pacific* (Wellington: A.H. and A.W. Reed, 1948), p. 39

66. Major B.H. Pringle, letter, 27 November 1943.

67. Third Division Histories Committee, *Pacific Service*, p. 96.

68. Third Division Histories Committee, *Story of the 34th*, p. 64.

69. Diary, Bdr. Gordon T. Thomas, 49 Battery, 38 Field Regt., entry 30 October 1943, author's collection.

70. Archives NZ, WA II, 1, DAZ 139/15/1, Narrative: 7th (NZ) Field Ambulance Historical Record, Treasury Island Landing.

71. Third Division Histories Committee, *The Gunners*, p. 121.

72. Oliver A. Gillespie, *The Pacific* (Wellington: War History Branch, Department of Internal Affairs, 1952), p. 148.

73. USS *Denver*, Deck Log and Diary, October 1943.

74. Fort Report, p. 13.

75. Rentz, *Bougainville and the Northern Solomons*, p. 96.

76. Archives NZ, WAII, 1, DAZ 151, 9/1/20 POW Report No. 11.

77. Barrowclough complained to NZ Army HQ in Wellington about the inadequacies of the radio sets supplied to his forces but the reality was that good quality dependable radio systems able to operate in the tropics would only be available to the late 20th Century.

78. Third Division Histories Committee, *Communications*, p. 211.

79. OP "Goodtime," 21 October 1943.

Chapter Four

1. Correspondence, Jesse Scott with author, 6 November 2001.

2. Archives NZ, WAII, 1, DAZ 151/9/5. Three Successful Emergency Water Landings in the Shortlands, 25 September 1943.

3. Seth Bailey "Stranded! There were 7 Japs and the Sea to Fight."

4. "We were Missing Men," by Lt. (JG) Edward M. Peck, USNR, as told to Will Oursler, Pacific correspondent, *True*, author's collection.

5. Medical report on survivors marooned on a South Pacific island, Lt. John F.W. King, USN. Author's collection.

6. Walter M. Lord, *Lonely Vigil* (Annapolis: Bluejacket Books, 2006), pp. 279–280.

7. Lord, *Lonely Vigil*, p. 279.

8. Jesse Scott, correspondence with author, 11 April 2002.

9. Lord, *Lonely Vigil*, p. 279.

10. Lord, *Lonely Vigil*, p. 280.

11. Jesse Scott, correspondence with author, 6 November 2001.

12. Peck narrative, author's collection.

13. Archives NZ, WAII, 1, DAZ 151/9/6, Log of Lt. E.M. Peck.

14. Jesse Scott, correspondence with author, 12 June 2002.

15. Jesse Scott, correspondence with author, 9 February 2002.

16. Lord, *Lonely Vigil*, p. 281.

17. Cowan interview, 28 August 2001.

18. Chief John Goldie, interview with Maori Television, 2009.

19. "Our Successful Escape from the Japanese, Daily Log, 18 July to 22 October 1943," J.D. Mitchell and C.J. Estep. Author's collection.

20. 'The Pacific,' Maori Television Episode aired 25 April 2010.

21. Mitchell and Estep narrative, p. 12.

22. Mitchell and Estep narrative.

23. William Wolf, *13th Fighter Command in World War II: Air Combat over Guadalcanal and the Solomons* (Atglen, PA: Schiffer Military History, 2004), p. 191.

24. Archives NZ, WAII, 1, DAZ 151/9/15, Three Successful Emergency Water Landings in the Shortlands.

25. Lord, *Lonely Vigil*, p. 282.

26. Peck narrative.

27. Mitchell and Estep narrative.

28. Medical report on U.S. aviators, author's collection.

29. Mitchell and Estep narrative, p. 19.

30. Mitchell and Estep narrative.

31. Eric M. Bergerud, *Fire in the Sky* (Boulder, CO, Westview Press, 2000), pp. 118–120. Also, correspondence, Jesse Scott.

32. Lord, *Lonely Vigil*, p. 282.

33. Mitchell and Estep narrative, p. 16.

34. Jesse Scott, 6 November 2001.

35. On his way back to the United States Mitchell encountered the RNZAF PBO crew Espiritu Santo. They confirmed that they had reported the sighting of the raft to Air Operations.

36. Tefft correspondence with Jesse Scott, undated. Author's collection.

37. Peck narrative.

38. Interrogation report of Peck, Tefft, King and Mitchell, 18 September 1943, author's collection.

39. Wolf, *13th Fighter Command in World War II: Air Combat over Guadalcanal and the Solomons*, pp. 223–4.

40. Estep narrative.

41. Finney County Historical Society, *Those Who Served: Finney County Veterans* (Finney County: Walsworth, 2002), p. 215.

42. Archives NZ, WAII, 1, DAZ 113/1/9 HQ RNZEF-HQ NZEF, War Information Summary No 1.

43. Keith Mulligan, *Kittyhawks and Coconuts* (Raumati Beach, New Zealand: Wings, 1995), pp. 114–119.

Chapter Five

1. Carl von Clausewitz, *On War* (New York: Alfred A. Knopf, 1993), 1: 3, p. 117.
2. Archives NZ, WAII, DAZ 151/9/6, Row to 1 MAC, 11 October 1943.
3. Cowan described how he was interviewed by Rear Admiral Wilkinson for 30 minutes and was very proud of being hand picked for the mission by the U.S. naval commander. Cowan interview, December 2005.
4. Cowan interview, 29 August 2001.
5. Cowan interviews.
6. Ray Starr, "A Jungle Amphibious Training Course for Advanced Landings." *36 Battalion Newsletter*, author's collection.
7. Flight Lieutenant "Robbie" Robinson, RAAF, "Wet Robbie," was "a free spirited, beer drinking old timer who had been a Burns Philip plantation manager before the war." Lord, p. 223. In contrast, Flight Lt. Forbes Robertson was known as "Dry Robbie" because of his abstinence.
8. Cowan interview, 29 August 2001.
9. For example, Row's Report.
10. Correspondence with Ilala and Wickham families.
11. Lord, *Lonely Vigil*, p. 294.
12. Cowan interview.
13. Archives NZ, WAII, 1, DAZ 151/1/23, Appendix 19.
14. Archives NZ, WAII, 1, DAZ 151/9/5, HQ 8 Bde. Reports on Treasury Island. Recce to Mono Island, W.A. Cowan, undated.
15. Cowan interview, 29 August 2001.
16. Cowan interview, 29 August 2001.
17. Cowan correspondence, 10 March 2002.
18. Jesse Scott, correspondence with author, 13 November 2001.
19. Cowan interview, 29 August 2001.
20. Archives NZ, WAII, 1, DAZ 151/9/6 3 Div S0132 to Trinsed Rear, 23 October 1943.
21. Correspondence Jesse Scott, 27 February 2002.
22. Estep narrative.
23. Estep narrative.
24. Archives NZ, WAII, 1, DAZ 151/1/22, Part 2, Appendix 1.
25. Row Report, para. 11.
26. They operated the Coast Watcher system in the Solomons.
27. Row Report, para 9.
28. Cowan interviews.
29. Row Report, para. 11.
30. Archives NZ, WAII, 1, DAZ, 151/1/9/6, 8 Bde. HQ, 25 October 1943.
31. Archives NZ, WAII, 1, DAZ 113/1/9, War Information Summary No. 1.
32. Third Division Histories Committee, *Headquarters*, p. 55.
33. This should not be viewed too harshly. The Americans inserted a covert two man patrol into Torokina, Bougainville, on 27 October 1943 with orders to signal by radio or beacon fire whether the Japanese had reinforced their troops. No signal was received and landing operations were delayed by 15 minutes. Wilkinson ordered debarkation but worried that his men were heading into an ambush. In reality the patrol had simply suffered radio failure and "terrain difficulties." Shaw and Kane, p. 208.
34. Archives NZ, WAII, 1, DAZ, 151/9/1/20, Prisoner of War Interrogation Report No. 8, 19 November 1943.
35. Third Division Histories Committee, *Story of the 34th*, p. 79.
36. George W. Smith, *Carlson's Raid: The Daring Marine Assault on Makin* (Novato, CA: Presido, 2001), pp. 228–9.
37. Taaffe, *MacArthur's Jungle War: The 1944 New Guinea Campaign*, p. 71.
38. Don Dennis, *The Guns of Muschu* (Crow's Nest, NSW: Allen and Unwin, 2006).

Chapter Six

1. Frank Cooze, *Kiwis in the Pacific* (Wellington: A.H. and A.W. Reed, 1945), p. 37.
2. Row Report.
3. Rentz, *Bougainville*, p. 119, note 35.
4. Third Division Histories Committee, *Story of the 34th*, p. 65.
5. Both were Fletcher class destroyers, displacing 2,325 tons, with a length of 376 feet, a speed of up to 38 knots and equipped with five 5-inch guns, four 1.1-inch guns, four 20mm guns and ten 21-inch torpedoes. M.J. Whitley, *Destroyers of World War Two* (Annapolis: Naval Institute Press, 2002), pp. 279–285.
6. "A destroyer whose guns [were] mostly 4.7 inch could lay fire out to 20,000 yards [or] about 11 miles, [and] equated to two batteries of Army Field Artillery." Ian Gooderson, *A Hard Way to Make a War* (London: Conway, 2008), p. 82.
7. Third Division Histories Committee, *Story of the 34th*, p. 65.
8. Third Division Histories Committee, *Story of the 34th*, p. 66.
9. Shaw and Kane, *Isolation of Rabaul: History of the U.S. Marine Corps Operations in World War II*, p. 191.
10. Rentz, *Bougainville and the Northern Solomons*, pp. 96–97; Shaw and Kane, *Isolation of Rabaul: History of the U.S. Marine Corps Operations in World War II*, p. 193.
11. Fort Report, p. 14, para. 32.
12. Cooze, *Kiwis in the Pacific*, p. 37.
13. Archives NZ, WAII, 1, DAZ 151/9/1/20, Prisoner of War Interrogation Report No. 1, 31 October 1943.
14. Ric Oram, "Island of Long Memories," *New Zealand Herald* (1 December 1993).
15. Archives NZ, WAII, 1, DAZ 151/9/1/20, Prisoner of War Interrogation Report No. 8, 19 November 1943.
16. Third Division Histories Committee, *Pacific Service*, p. 97.
17. Barrowclough later took Cowan to task for not detecting this Japanese MG position. Cowan replied that he had not seen it, but if he had been a Japanese defender then Cummings Point is where he would have sited a machine gun. Cowan interview.
18. "Thirty-Six Battalion, Third New Zealand Division: Robert Gordon Dunlop," in Bruce M. Petty, *New Zealand in the Pacific War* (Jefferson, NC: McFarland, 2008), p. 26.
19. Conversation with author, 29 October 2009.
20. Interview, Jeff Tunnicliffe, 18 June 2000.
21. Letter, Major B.H. Pringle, 36 Bn., 27 November 1943, author's collection.
22. Fort Report, p. 6.

23. Shaw and Kane, *Isolation of Rabaul*, p. 192.
24. Pringle.
25. Archives NZ, WAII, 1, DAZ 151/1/23, Report on Operations 30 November 1943.
26. Ibid., p. 97.
27. Rentz, *Bougainville and the Northern Solomons*.
28. Narrative of Private E.A. James, 29 Battalion, author's collection.
29. Army Board, *Guadalcanal to Nissan: With the Third New Zealand Division through the Solomons* (Wellington: 1945), p. 31.
30. Allan Rogers, interview, 20 September 2006.
31. Conversation with author, 29 October 2009.
32. Alec Cruickshank, interview, 19 October 2009.
33. Renshaw narrative.
34. Robert Dunlop, conversation with author, 29 October 2009.
35. Dunlop, in Petty, *New Zealand in the Pacific War*, p. 26.
36. Oliver A. Gillespie, *The Pacific* (Wellington: War History Branch, Department of Internal Affairs, 1952), p. 150.
37. Third Division Histories Committee, *Stepping Stones to the Solomons*, p. 57.
38. "Mono Island: The First Ten Days," From the diary of Les Taylor, 46117 Carrier Platoon, HQ Co. 36 Bn., M.S. 2004/82 Auckland War Memorial Library.
39. Cooze, *Kiwis in the Pacific*, p. 37.
40. Les Taylor diary.
41. "The New Zealand Army conducted tests in 1944 and noted that the Carriers were vulnerable to a grenade attack by a determined enemy and concluded that in the jungle the vehicle has little to recommend it as a fighting vehicle but has distinct possibilities as a load carrier because it can blaze its own trail." Archives NZ, WAII, 1 DAZ 149/1/1, NZ Tank Squadron, Vol. 7, 1 January 1944 to 31 January 1944.
42. George Hodgson recalled that there was a small walking track which went across the mangrove but he would have needed engineers with bridging equipment to get his Carriers across. Interview, 13 June 2001.
43. Interview, Bernie Harris, 2000.
44. Third Division Histories Committee, *Base Wallahs* (Wellington: A.H. and A.W. Reed, 1946), pp. 163–164.
45. Andy Lysaght, correspondence with author, 20 June 2000.
46. Third Division Histories Committee, *Pacific Service*, p. 97.
47. Interview, Thom Sen, 20 June 2000.
48. Gillespie, *The Pacific*, p. 150. The discrepancy in timing may be attributable to the Japanese operating on Tokyo time.
49. USS LCI-334 Action Report A16-3/(81), 29 October 1943, cited in McGee, *The Solomons Campaigns*, pp. 482–3.
50. McGee, *The Solomons Campaigns, 1942–43*, p. 482.
51. "War Anniversaries Commemorated," *Rotorua Review* (1963). Correspondence with author.
52. Third Division Histories Committee, *The Gunners*, p. 290.
53. McGee, *The Solomons Campaigns, 1942–43*, p. 483. Fort Report, p. 8.
54. Fort Report, p. 8.
55. Third Division Histories Committee, *Communications*, p. 213.
56. William Bradford Huie, *Can-Do*, p. 197.
57. George Hodgson interview.
58. John Wasley, correspondence with author.
59. http://freepages.generalogy.rootsweb.ancestry.com/-tqpeiffer/documents.
60. Archives NZ, WAII, 1, EA1, 87/19/7, "Report of the Occupation of the Treasury Islands," 27 October 1943, Wilkinson to Nimitz, 10 November 1943.
61. Rentz, *Bougainville and the Northern Solomons*, p. 98.
62. Naval Staff History, *War with Japan, Vol. 3, The Campaigns in the Solomons and New Guinea* (London: Historical Section, Admiralty, 1956), p. 185.
63. George Hodgson interview.
64. Archives NZ, DAZ 152/1/38, Appendix 2, p. 1.
65. National Library of New Zealand, newspaper cutting undated, *New Zealand Free Lance*, George Luoni Oral History Folder.
66. Gillespie, *The Pacific*, pp. 150–151.
67. Third Division Histories Committee, *The Gunners*, p. 122.
68. Third Division Histories Committee, *Stepping Stones to the Solomons*, pp. 58–59.
69. Third Division Histories Committee, *The Gunners*, p. 163.
70. Conversation, John Foote with author, 27 November 2009.
71. Conversation, John Foote with author, 27 November 2009.
72. Carl W. Ruble, editor in chief, *The Earthmover: A Chronicle of the 87th Seabee Battalion in World War II*, p. 57.
73. Third Division Histories Committee, *Communications*, p. 214.
74. Third Division Histories Committee, *Communications*, p. 216.
75. Dunlop, in Bruce M. Petty, *New Zealand in the Pacific War* (Jefferson, NC: McFarland, 2008), p. 26.
76. Dunlop, conversation with author, 2009.
77. Third Division Histories Committee, *Stepping Stones to the Solomons*, p. 59.
78. *The Evening Post*, "Correspondents Help" (November 2, 1943).
79. Cooze, *Kiwis in the Pacific*, p. 38.
80. Fort Report, p. 8.
81. Cooze, *Kiwis in the Pacific*, p. 38.
82. Cooze, *Kiwis in the Pacific*, p. 38.
83. Third Division Histories Committee, *Pacific Service*, p. 98.
84. Army Board, *Guadalcanal to Nissan*, p. 31.
85. Conversation with author, July 2005, and interview, July 3, 2000.
86. Third Division Histories Committee, *Pacific Pioneers*, p. 96.
87. *The Earthmover*, p. 56.
88. Shaw and Kane, *Isolation of Rabaul*, p. 192.
89. Archives NZ, WAII, Series 1, DA 428/3/2 Lt D.W. Bain, "Jap guns were Red Hot," November 6, 1943.
90. Gillespie, *The Pacific*, p. 152.
91. Third Division Histories Committee, *Headquarters*, p. 48.
92. Third Division Histories Committee, *Pacific Pioneers*, p. 126.
93. Third Division Histories Committee, *Pacific Pioneers*, p. 97.

94. Archives NZ, WAII, 1, DAZ 139/15/1, Lt. G.L. Lynds, "A" Coy. Landing and Action (Mono), October 25–29, 1943. Hereinafter referred to as "Lynds narrative."
95. Third Division Histories Committee, *The Gunners*, p. 229.
96. Gillespie, *The Pacific*, p. 152.
97. Shaw and Kane, *Isolation of Rabaul*, p. 192.
98. Gillespie, *The Pacific*, pp. 152–3.
99. Fort Report, p. 11.
100. Fort Report, p. 11.
101. Archives NZ, WAII, 1, DAZ151, 9/1/20, POW Interrogation Report No. 11, December 18, 1943.
102. Shaw and Kane, *Isolation of Rabaul*, p. 192.
103. Third Division Histories Committee, *Pacific Engineers*, p. 84.
104. Row Report, p. 9.
105. Third Division Histories Committee, *Pacific Service*, p. 98.
106. Third Division Histories Committee, *The Gunners*, p. 124.
107. Ibid.
108. David Williams, Maori Television interview, 2009. He "had a most inadequate foxhole" and very little sleep.
109. Don Taylor (ed.), *Everyone's War* (New Plymouth: Zenith Press, 2004), p. 129.
110. Diary of Les Taylor, 36 Bn.
111. Cooze, *Kiwis in the Pacific*, p. 38.
112. Megan Hutching, *Against the Rising Sun: New Zealanders Remember the Pacific War*, p. 131. Also, Peter Renshaw Oral History, Alexander Turnbull Library.
113. Diary entry, Bombardier G. Thomas, 30 October 1943.
114. Diary entry, Bombardier G. Thomas, 4 November 1943.
115. David Williams interview, Maori Television, 2009.
116. Diary entry, Bombardier G. Thomas, 30 October 1943.
117. Dunlop in Bruce M. Petty, *New Zealand in the Pacific War*, p. 27.
118. Dunlop, correspondence with author, 14 November 2009.
119. Ibid. See also Third Division Histories Committee, *Communications*, p. 186. "In the bush at night small beetles flew about in shoals like animated diamonds, each a pin point of light weaving to and fro."
120. Interview Jeff Tunnicliffe, June 18, 2000.
121. Lynds narrative.
122. Cooze, *Kiwis in the Pacific*, p. 39.
123. Archives NZ, WAII, 1, DA 428/3/2, Lt. D.W. Bain, Message No. 41, 5 November 1943.
124. Ibid.
125. Pringle letter.
126. David Williams, interview with Maori Television, 2010.
127. Row Report, p. 9.
128. Kiwi soldiers often referred to landing craft as "barges."
129. Third Division Histories Committee, *Story of the 34th*, p. 67.
130. Ibid.
131. G. Thomas diary entry, 30 October 1943.
132. Archives NZ, WAII, 1, DAZ 139/15/1 7 (NZ), Field Ambulance Narrative.
133. Third Division Histories Committee, *Story of the 34th*, p. 67.
134. Interview, Trevor Whaley, 2000.
135. Third Division Histories Committee, *Story of the 34th*, p. 67.
136. Trevor Whaley, correspondence, 30 January 1999, author's collection.
137. Third Division Histories Committee, *Story of the 34th*, p. 68.
138. G. Thomas, diary entry, 30 October 1943.
139. Taylor diary entry, 30 October 1943.
140. Diary entry, Bombardier G. Thomas, 30 October 1943.
141. Recollections of Clair Charles, E-mail to author, 1 August 2001.
142. NZ Defense Force Base Records, Personnel File.
143. Third Division Histories Committee, *Communications*, p. 124.
144. *The Earthmover*, p. 57.
145. Recollections of Clair Charles, Seaman, Second Class, 87th CB. Correspondence with Julianne Chester, 1 August 2001.
146. Third Division Histories Committee, *Story of the 34th*, pp. 73–74.
147. Letter, R.P. Townsend to author, 27 May 2001.
148. Cowan interview, 29 August 2001.
149. Third Division Histories Committee, *Stepping Stones to the Solomons*, p. 62.
150. Cowan interview, 29 August 2001.
151. Telephone discussion, George and Jean Luoni, 15 March 2009; Oral History, Alexander Turnbull Library; Archives NZ, AIR 152/4 Report, Flight Sergeant G.I. Luoni, 4 November 1943.
152. "October 27, 1943, Attack on the Cony," http://usscony.com/Chronology/ConyAttack/Attack_10-27-43.html
153. Journal of Stanley Baranowski, http://USSCony.Com/Chronology.
154. Wolf, *13th Fighter Command in World War II*, p. 219.
155. Fort Report, p. 6.
156. http://USSCony.Com/Chronology.
157. Wolf, *13th Fighter Command in World War II*, p. 219.
158. T. Duncan M. Stout, *Medical Services in New Zealand and the Pacific*, p. 49. These figures do not include the casualties suffered by those on the USS *Cony*. The casualty total only refers to units under the command of 8 Brigade.
159. War diary, GOC, 3 NZ Division, 27 October 1943, p. 29.
160. Ray E. Otto, correspondence with author, 26 June 2000.
161. Third Division Histories Committee, *Pacific Service*, p. 102.
162. John Prados, *Combined Fleet Decoded* (New York: Random House, 1995), p. 508.
163. A light cruiser of about 5,000 tons armed with seven 5.5 inch guns and eight torpedo tubes in twin mounts with a maximum speed of 36 knots. Evans and Peattie, *Kaigun*, p. 176.
164. Archives NZ, WAII, 1, DA 438.3/3 Japanese View, Monograph 34, South East Pacific, Area Operations Record, Part II, 17th Army Operations, Vol. 1.
165. T. Duncan M. Stout, *Medical Services in New Zealand and the Pacific*, p. 50.

166. T. Duncan M. Stout, *Medical Services in New Zealand and the Pacific*, p. 50.
167. T. Duncan M. Stout, *Medical Services in New Zealand and the Pacific*, p. 73.
168. Fort Report, p. 11.
169. T. Duncan M. Stout, *Medical Services in New Zealand and the Pacific*, p. 50.
170. Ibid., p. 52.
171. Interview, August 21, 2000.
172. Ibid., p. 53.
173. T. Duncan M. Stout, *Medical Services in New Zealand and the Pacific*, p. 54.
174. Ibid., p. 75.
175. Ibid., p. 54.
176. Ibid., p. 70.

Chapter Seven

1. William Hess, *Pacific Sweep: The 5th and 13th Fighter Commands in World War II* (New York: Doubleday, 1974), pp. 134–5.
2. Archives NZ, WAII, 1 DAZ 151/1/23 Report on Fighter Direction, Treasury Islands, October 27 to November 5.
3. Ibid.
4. Archives NZ, WAII, 1, DAZ 151/1/23.
5. James A. Winnefeld, *Joint Air Operations: Pursuit of Unity in Command and Control 1942–1991* (Santa Monica: Rand, 1993), pp. 33–34.
6. Ibid., p. 35.
7. "Zeke," Allied code name for the Mitsubishi A6M Zero. "Hamp" was a variant with the wingtips clipped for greater maneuverability.
8. J.M.S. Ross, *Royal New Zealand Air Force* (Wellington: War Histories Branch, Department of Internal Affairs, 1955), pp. 204–205.
9. Row Report, para. 37(a).
10. Archives NZ, Air 150, 1, Operations Book 43–44.
11. Diary entry, Bombardier G. Thomas, 30 October 1943.
12. Archives NZ, WA II, 1, DAZ 128/9 SLA 38/3 Lessons of Treasury Campaign 29 Lt. AA Regt.
13. Third Division Histories Committee, *The Gunners*, p. 125.
14. Archives NZ, WAII, 1 DAZ 151/1/23 Report of Fighter Direction, Treasury Island, 4 November to 10 November.
15. Wartime diary of Flight Lieutenant St. John Spicer, RNZAF, entry 28 October 1943, Royal New Zealand Air Force Museum, Christchurch.

Chapter Eight

1. Third Division Histories Committee, *Story of the 34th*, p. 140.
2. Allied troops thought that the Japanese were using signal flares to direct the bombing of their positions.
3. Archives NZ, WAII, 1, DAZ 151/1/23, Prisoner of War Interrogation Reports, Numbers 4 and 5, 6 November 1943.
4. Third Division Histories Committee, *Story of the 34th*, p. 140.
5. Third Division Histories Committee, *Story of the 34th*, p. 74.

6. Third Division Histories Committee, *Stepping Stones to the Solomons*, p. 63.
7. Recollections of Clair Charles. E-mail to author, 1 August 2001.
8. Recollections of Clair Charles.
9. Archives NZ, WAII, 1, DAZ 151/1/23, Appendix 19 and WAII, 1, DAZ 151/9/20, Statement taken from Japanese Prisoner Captured at Malsi, 30 January 1944.
10. Archives NZ, WAII, 1, DAZ 151/9/1/20, Prisoner of War Interrogation Report No. 11, 18 December 1943.
11. Third Division Histories Committee, *Communications*, p. 219.
12. Archives NZ, 1, WAII, DAZ 153/1/37, Appendix G.
13. Third Division Histories Committee, *Communications*, p. 219.
14. Third Division Histories Committee, *The Gunners*, p. 164.
15. Archives NZ, WAII, 1, DAZ 151/9/1/20, Statement taken from Japanese Prisoner Captured at Malsi, 30 January 1944.
16. Archives NZ, WAII, 1 DAZ 151/7/1/1-7, Pacific Broadcast Soanotalu, 25 November 1943, Major G.W. Logan, Logan Force.
17. Third Division Histories Committee, *Story of the 34th*, p. 116.

Chapter Nine

1. Cooze, *Kiwis in the Pacific*, p. 39. This explanation is unlikely. The Japanese survivors were intent on killing Allied soldiers and would not have wasted ammunition "for a lark." It is an interesting commentary, however, on how the Kiwis viewed the Japanese. More likely explanations for the fire would be a sneak airraid, or alternatively jittery "friendly fire" from a neighboring Allied unit.
2. Lynds narrative.
3. Third Division Histories Committee, *Pacific Service*, p. 99.
4. Third Division Histories Committee, *Communications*, p. 216.
5. Third Division Histories Committee, *Communications*, p. 217.
6. Third Division Histories Committee, *Pacific Pioneers*, p. 97.
7. Row Report, p. 9.
8. Basil Renshaw, "Guadalcanal, October 1943." *New Zealand Listener*, May 12–18, 2001, p. 94.
9. Diary, Les Taylor.
10. Bergerud, *Touched With Fire*, pp. 377–80.
11. Diary, Les Taylor.
12. Lynds narrative.
13. Third Division Histories Committee, *Stepping Stones to the Solomons*, p. 63.
14. Arthur N. Talbot, "Medical Doctor with the Third New Zealand Division," in Petty, p. 32.
15. The Row Report, p. 9.
16. Bernie Harris interview, 3 July 2000.
17. Archives NZ, WAII, 1, DA 428/3/2, Lt. D.W. Bain, Message No. 41, 5 November 1943.
18. Lynds narrative.
19. Lynds narrative.
20. Lynds narrative.
21. Ken Treanor, *The Staff, The Serpent and the Sword: 100 Years of the Royal New Zealand Army Medical Corps* (Christchurch: Willson Scott, 2008), p. 149.

22. Third Division Histories Committee, *Pacific Pioneers*, p. 97.
23. Army Board, *Guadalcanal to Nissan*, p. 33.
24. Archives NZ, WAII, 1, DAZ 113/1/9, War Information Summary No. 2, 6 November 1943.
25. Army Board, *Guadalcanal to Nissan*, p. 33.
26. Rentz, *Bougainville and the Northern Solomons*, p. 102.
27. Third Division Histories Committee, *Pacific Pioneers*, p. 98.
28. Row Report, p. 10.
29. Les Taylor diary.
30. Row Report, Appendices 17 and 19.
31. Third Division Histories Committee, *Stepping Stones to the Solomons*, p. 63.
32. Cooze, *Kiwis in the Pacific*, pp. 29–41.
33. Third Division Histories Committee, *The Gunners*, p. 125.
34. Fort Report, p. 12.
35. Third Division Histories Committee, *Story of the 34th*, p. 82.
36. Robert J. Bulkley, *At Close Quarters: PT Boats in the United States Navy* (Washington: Naval History Division, 1962), p. 140.
37. Third Division Histories Committee, *Communications*, p. 217.
38. Third Division Histories Committee, *Story of the 34th*, p. 71.
39. Third Division Histories Committee, *Communications*, p. 218.
40. Third Division Histories Committee, *Story of the 34th*, p. 69.
41. An intelligence officer had told him that the New Zealanders were simply "bait" for the Japanese. Although strictly correct since Goodtime was a diversionary operation, this did little to help the nerves of its participants.
42. Trevor Whaley, correspondence with author, 14 July 2000.
43. Third Division Histories Committee, *Story of the 34th*, p. 71.
44. Diary entry, Bombardier G. Thomas, 4 November 943.
45. Colonial Office, *Among those Present: The Official Story of the Pacific Islands at War* (London: His Majesty's Stationery Office, 1946), pp. 63–64.
46. The Third Division Histories Committee, *The 36th* (Wellington: A.H. and A.W. Reed, 1948), pp. 56–57, p. 108.
47. Third Division Histories Committee, *Story of the 34th*, pp. 80–81.
48. Gillespie, *The Pacific*, p. 158.
49. Third Division Histories Committee, *Stepping Stones to the Solomons*, pp. 63–66.
50. Colonial Office, *Among Those Present*, p. 64.
51. Archives NZ, WAII, 1, DAZ 151/1/23 Intelligence Summary No. 8, 11 November 1943.
52. Archives NZ, WAII, 1, DAZ 151/9/1/20, Prisoner of War Interrogation Report No. 7, 7 November 1943.
53. Third Division Histories Committee, *Story of the 34th*, p. 80.
54. Hocken Collections Archives and Manuscripts, Misc-MS 1644, Translation of Captured Enemy Diary.
55. Row Report, para. 46.
56. Kent Fedorowich, "Understanding the Enemy: Military Intelligence, Political Warfare and Japanese Prisoners of War in Australia 1942–45," in Philip Towle, Margaret Kosuge and Yoichi Kibata (eds.), *Japanese Prisoners of War*, (Hambledon and London: London, 2000), p. 66. A U.S. intelligence officer commented, "There is no shutting them up."
57. Archives NZ, WA II, 1, DAZ 151/9/1/20, Prisoner of War Interrogation Report No. 11, 18 December 1943.
58. Archives NZ, WA II, 1, DAZ 151/9/1/20 Prisoner of War Interrogation Report No. 6.
59. Gillespie, *The Pacific*, p. 158.
60. Fort Report, p. 12.
61. Fort Report, p. 12, para. 26.
62. Third Division Histories Committee, *Pacific Service*, pp. 99–100.
63. Row Report, 8 (NZ) Bde. GP DO No. 2, 12 November 1943.
64. Row reported that by 12 November, 205 Japanese had been killed and 8 taken prisoner. At that point there had been 40 New Zealanders killed and 12 Americans killed. There were 145 New Zealand and 29 American wounded. Row Report, p. 13.
65. Ibid., p. 3.
66. Third Division Histories Committee, *Pacific Pioneers*, p. 32.
67. Third Division Histories Committee, *Story of the 34th*, p. 89.
68. Ibid., p. 82.
69. Third Division Histories Committee, *Headquarters*, p. 49.
70. Third Division Histories Committee, *Pacific Service*, p. 102.
71. Third Division Histories Committee, *Story of the 34th*, p. 81.
72. Third Division Histories Committee, *The Gunners*, p. 166.
73. Ibid., p. 166.
74. Ibid., pp. 168–9.
75. Third Division Histories Committee, *Stepping Stones to the Solomons*, p. 67.
76. Third Division Histories Committee, *Story of the 34th*, p. 91.
77. Diary entry, Bombardier G. Thomas, 14 January 1944.
78. Ibid.
79. Maori Television interviews with islanders.
80. Third Division Histories Committee, *The Gunners*, p. 127.
81. Ibid., p. 169.
82. Forbes Greenfield interview, 16 May 2007.
83. Narrative of Forbes Greenfield, 49th Battery, 38 Field Regiment, author's collection.
84. Third Division Histories Committee, *The Gunners*, p. 127.
85. Third Division Histories Committee, *Stepping Stones to the Solomons*, p. 68.
86. Archives NZ, WA II, 1, DAZ 151/9/1/20, Report, Commander, 34 Battalion, 29 January 1944.
87. Eric Feldt, *The Coast Watchers* (Hawthorn, Australia: Lloyd O'Neil, 1975), p. 14.
88. Third Division Histories Committee, *Story of the 34th*, p. 83.
89. Bob Dunlop Recollection, "Recapture of Mono Island," author's collection.
90. Archives NZ, WAII, 1, DAZ 151/1/23, Intelligence Summary No. 12, 15 November 1943.
91. Ibid., Intelligence Summary No. 17.

92. Ibid., Intelligence Summary No. 18, 29 November 1943.
93. Cowan interview, 29 August 2001.
94. Third Division Histories Committee, *Story of the 34th*, pp. 88–89.
95. Third Division Histories Committee, *Story of the 34th*, p. 84.
96. Ibid., pp. 84–5.
97. Archives NZ, WA II, 1, DAZ 151/9/1/20, Report Lt. R. Turbott, I.O. 34 NZ Bn., 30 January 1944.
98. Third Division Histories Committee, *Story of the 34th*, p. 86.
99. Letter to author, King Whitney, Jr., 7 March 2003.
100. Archives NZ, WA II, 1, DAZ 151/9/1/20, Officer in Charge, 88th Naval Construction Battalion to Intelligence Officer, Island 31 Command, January 1944.
101. Third Division Histories Committee, *Story of the 34th*, p. 86.
102. 3 NZ Division Association Newsletter, "Son of Heaven Slugged by Seabee Cook."
103. Third Division Histories Committee, *Story of the 34th*, p. 85.
104. Ibid., p. 85.
105. Ibid., p. 85.
106. Ibid., p. 95.
107. In his formal report to Wellington, Row commented on the wholehearted and loyal support of American personnel but especially singled out Turnbull and his Seabees for their "splendid work."
108. *The Earthmover*, p. 65.
109. Ibid.
110. *The Earthmover*, p. 63.
111. *The Earthmover*, p. 66.
112. Third Division Histories Committee, *Communications*, p. 220.
113. Ibid., p. 68.
114. Ibid., p. 69.
115. Bureau of Yards and Ships, *Building the Navy's Bases in World War II, Vol. 2, Part III, The Advance Bases*, p. 268.
116. Diary entry, Bombardier G. Thomas, 18 February 1944.
117. Diary entry, Bombardier G. Thomas, 20 November 1943.
118. Gillespie, *The Pacific*, p. 161.
119. Bureau of Yards and Ships, *Building the Navy's Bases in World War II, Vol. 2, Part III, The Advance Bases*, p. 268.
120. Gillespie, *The Pacific*, p. 161.
121. *The Earthmover*, p. 101.
122. Letter to author King Whitney, Jr., 7 March 2003.
123. Third Division Histories Committee, *Story of the 34th*, p. 91.
124. Diary entry, Bombardier Thomas, 2 December 1943.
125. Diary entry, Bombardier Thomas, 18 February 1944.
126. Diary of Maurice Stills, 50th Battery, 38th Field Regiment, 3 NZ Division Association newsletter *Pacific Diary*.
127. Barbara Bolt, "Mail Call: New Zealanders at War in the Pacific." *The New Zealand Genealogist* (March–April 2005), p. 94.
128. Third Division Histories Committee, *Story of the 34th*, p. 90.
129. Ibid., p. 85.
130. Archives NZ, WAII, 1, DAZ 153/14/1 *Spam*, magazine of 34 Battalion.
131. Ibid.
132. Ibid.
133. Ibid., p. 90.
134. Diary entry, Bombardier G. Thomas, 8 December 1943.
135. Third Division Histories Committee, *Communications*, p. 221.
136. Third Division Histories Committee, *The Gunners*, p. 167.
137. Rick Atkinson, *An Army at Dawn* (New York, Henry Holt, 2002), p. 507.
138. Third Division Histories Committee, *Pacific Pioneers*, p. 63.
139. Diary entry, Bombardier G. Thomas, 4 November 1943.
140. Diary entry, Bombardier G. Thomas, 8 December 1943.
141. Third Division Histories Committee, *The Gunners*, p. 166.
142. Third Division Histories Committee, *Communications*, p. 222.
143. Third Division Histories Committee, *Pacific Service*, p. 102.
144. Greenfield narrative, pp. 5–6.
145. Third Division Histories Committee, *Story of the 34th*, p. 91.
146. Third Division Histories Committee, *Stepping Stones to the Solomons*, p. 66.
147. David Williams, correspondence with author, 21 July 2006.
148. Third Division Histories Committee, *Story of the 34th*, p. 90.
149. Third Division Histories Committee, *Story of the 34th*, p. 87.
150. Third Division Histories Committee, *Headquarters*, p. 50.
151. Gillespie, *The Pacific*, p. 161. Air units likewise required huge quantities of Avgas.
152. Third Division Histories Committee, *Story of the 34th*, p. 86.
153. Third Division Histories Committee, *Pacific Service*, p. 102.
154. Doug Eaton, *All in a Day's Work*, author's collection.
155. Third Division Histories Committee, *Story of the 34th*, p. 105.
156. Doug Eaton, *Let's Go to the Movies*, author's collection.
157. 3 NZ Division Association newsletter *Our 3rd Div. Band*.
158. Third Division Histories Committee, *Headquarters*, p. 50.
159. Ibid., p. 51.
160. Third Division Histories Committee, *Communications*, pp. 220–221.
161. Ibid., p. 221.
162. Third Division Histories Committee, *Pacific Pioneers*, p. 57.
163. Gillespie, *The Pacific*, p. 164.
164. Third Division Histories Committee, *Pacific Pioneers*, p. 117.
165. Campbell Davie narrative, author's collection.

166. Third Division Histories Committee, *Story of the 34th*, p. 100.
167. Archives NZ, Puttick Papers, Puttick to Barrowclough, 4 November 1943. Also Archives NZ, Air 118, 81f Salmon to Cos., 8 November 1943.
168. *The Evening Post*, "Treasury Invasion" (2 November 1943).
169. Rentz, *Bougainville and the Northern Solomons*, p. 130.
170. Harry M. Gailey, *Bougainville: A Forgotten Campaign* (Lexington: University of Kentucky Press, 1991).
171. Row had reached the staff corps retirement age, *Headquarters*, p. 50.
172. Archives NZ, AD Series 12, 28/15, Salmon to Puttick, 2 December 1943.
173. Third Division Histories Committee, *Story of the 34th*, p. 84.
174. NZDF Base Records, Trentham. Personnel File, G.W. Logan.
175. Diary entry, Bombardier G. Thomas, 20 November 1943.
176. Ron Tucker, correspondence with the author, 2000.
177. Third Division Histories Committee, *The Gunners*, p. 166.
178. Third Division Histories Committee, *Headquarters*, p. 61.
179. Diary entry, Bombardier G. Thomas, 26 December 1943.
180. Bombardier G. Thomas, diary entry, 1943.
181. Theft of material was endemic in the South West Pacific. "Port battalions and combat troops pressed into unloading duty ruthlessly pilfered holds of their more valuable goods. Even more mundane commodities were not safe." Stephen R. Taaffe, *MacArthur's Jungle War: The 1944 New Guinea Campaign* (Lawrence: University of Kansas Press, 1998), p. 46.
182. Third Division Histories Committee, *The Gunners*, p. 166.
183. Interview, Jeff Tunnicliffe, 18 June 2000.
184. Correspondence, George E. Tschudi, 23 May 2001.
185. Correspondence, David Williams with author, 21 July 2006.
186. Narrative of Forbes Greenfield.
187. Cowan interview, 29 August 2001.

Chapter Ten

1. Alexander, *A Fellowship of Valor*, p. 121.
2. Ibid., p. 122.
3. Captain John C. Chapin, USMCR (Ret.), *Top of the Ladder: Marine Operations in the Northern Solomons* (Washington, D.C.: Marine Corps Historical Center, 1997).
4. Taaffe, *MacArthur's Jungle War*, p. 75.
5. Trevor Whaley, correspondence with author, undated, 2000.
6. Archives NZ, AD 28/15/4, Barrowclough to Fraser, 31 December 1943.
7. Ladd, *Assault From the Sea*, p. 190.
8. Third Division Histories Committee, *Headquarters*, p. 63.
9. Interview with Alec Cruickshank, 19 November 2009.
10. Cowan interview. A similar situation occurred on the Green Islands in February 1944.
11. Interview, Alec Cruickshank, 19 November 2009.
12. Gillespie, *The Pacific*, p. 158.
13. Archives NZ, WAII, 1, DAZ 121/1/11, Appendix 1.
14. Archives NZ, WAII, 1, DAZ 151/9/6 HQ 1 MAC to Row 23, October 1943. Trench was accompanied by Lt. Frederick J. Bentley, BSIDF (British Solomon Islands Defense Force).
15. Archives NZ, WAII, 1, DAZ 154/1/24, Appendix 3.
16. Colonial Office, *Among those Present*, p. 64.
17. Diary entry, Bombardier G. Thomas, 14 March 1944.
18. Third Division Histories Committee, *Stepping Stones to the Solomons*, p. 71.
19. For example, the visit of John McKinnon to Mono, November 2008. October 27 each year is commemorated as "New Zealand Day" in appreciation of the islanders' liberation.
20. Ric Oram, "Island of Long Memories," *New Zealand Herald*, 1 December 1993.
21. Alison Parr, *Silent Casualties: New Zealand's Unspoken Legacy of the Second World War* (Birkenhead: Tandem Press, 1995).
22. *New Zealand Gazette*, 27 January 1944 (immediate award).
23. Discharged 20 July 1944.
24. Family correspondence and material provided to the author by Clint Nash.
25. James Michener, *Tales of the South Pacific* (New York: Fawcett Books, 1993).
26. Rodgers and Hammerstein's *South Pacific*, director Joshua A. Logan, 20th Century–Fox, 1958.
27. James Michener, *The World is My Home: A Memoir* (New York: Random House, 1972), p. 91.
28. Morison, *Breaking the Bismarck's Barrier*, p. 295.
29. Archives NZ, WAII, 1, DAZ 154/1/24, Appendix 3, p. 1.
30. U.S. Combat Narrative Solomon Islands Campaign: 12, p. 19–20.
31. Archives NZ, EA 1, 87/19/7, Barrowclough to Fraser, 31 December 1943.
32. Ibid.
33. Rentz, *Bougainville and the Northern Solomons*, p. 123.

Appendix C

1. Task Group Thirty-one Point One Report of Occupation of the Treasury Islands, 27 October 1943, 10 November 1943.

Appendix G

1. Ian V. Hogg, *British and American Artillery of World War II*, London: Greenhill, 2002.

Bibliography

Primary Sources

Barrowclough, Harold E. War Diary, GOC 3 NZ Division.

Davie, Campbell. Narrative.

Easley, Wilmer. "Legend of the Un-holy Four," unpublished manuscript, 2004. Author's collection.

Estep, Chauncey J., and Mitchell, Joe David. "The Story of Seven American Airmen who were MIA During World II." Author's collection.

James, E.A. Narrative of Private E.A. James, 29 Battalion. Author's collection.

Office of Naval Intelligence. *Combat Narratives, Solomon Islands Campaign, the Bougainville Landing and the Battle of Empress, Augusta Bay, 27 October–2 November 1943.* 1945.

Pringle, Major B.H. Letter, 27 November 1943. Author's collection.

Renshaw, Peter Basil. Narrative of Sgt. P.B. Renshaw, 36 Battalion. Author's collection.

Ruble, Carl W. (editor in chief). *The Earthmover: A Chronicle of the 87th Seabee Battalion in World War II*. Baton Rouge, LA: Army and Navy Pictorial Publishers, 1946.

Spam. Magazine of 34 Battalion.

Taylor, Leslie Noel. "Mono Island: The First Ten Days," Auckland War Memorial Museum Library MS 2004 182.

36 Battalion Newsletter.

Thomas, Gordon. Private diary, Author's collection.

Interviews and Correspondence with Veterans

Charles Barlow
Harry Bioletti
Clair Charles
Bert Cowan
Campbell Davie
Bob Dunlop
Wilmer Easley
Forbes Greenfield
Bernie Harris
George Hodgson
Ashley James
George Luoni
Andy Lysaght
Ray Otto
Basil Renshaw
Allan Rogers
Thom Sen
Jeff Tunnicliffe
David Williams

Secondary Sources

Alexander, Joseph H. *Edson's Raiders: The 1st Marine Raider Battalion in World War II*. Annapolis, MD: Naval Institute Press, 2001.

_____. *A Fellowship of Valor: The Battle History of the United States Marines*. New York: Harper Collins, 1997.

Army Board. *Guadalcanal to Nissan: With the Third New Zealand Division through the Solomons*. Wellington: Army Board, 1945.

Asprey, Robert B. *Once a Marine: The Memoirs of General A.A. Vandegrift*. New York: W.W. Norton, 1964.

Atkinson, Rick. *An Army at Dawn*. New York: Henry Holt, 2002.

Bergerud, Eric. *Fire in the Sky*. Boulder, CO: Westview Press, 2000.

_____. *Touched with Fire: The Land War in the South Pacific*. New York: Viking Penguin, 1996.

Bolt, Barbara. "Mail Call: New Zealanders at War in the Pacific." *The New Zealand Geneologist* (March–April 2005).

Bulkley, Robert J. *At Close Quarters: P.T. Boats in the United States Navy*. Washington: Naval History Division, 1962.

Bureau of Yards and Docks. *Building the Navy's Bases in World War II: History of the Bureau of Yards and Docks and the Civil Engineers Corps, 1940–46*. 2 volumes. Washington, D.C.: United States Government Printing Office, 1947.

Chapin, John C. *Top of the Ladder: Marine Operations in the Northern Solomons*. Washington, D.C.: Marine Corps Historical Center, 1997.

Christ, James F. *Mission Raise Hell: The U.S. Marines on Choiseul, October–November 1943*. Annapolis, MD: Naval Institute Press, 2006.

Clausewitz, Carl Von. *On War*. New York: Alfred A. Knopf, 1993.

Colonial Office, *Among those Present: The Official Story of the Pacific Islands at War*. London: His Majesty's Stationery Office, 1946.

Cooze, Frank. *Kiwis in the Pacific*. Wellington: A.H. and A.W. Reed, 1945.

Crost, Lyn. *Honor by Fire: Japanese-Americans at War in Europe and the Pacific*. Novato, CA: Presido Press, 1994.

Denis, Don. *The Guns of Muschu*. Crow's Nest, NSW: Allen and Unwin, 2006.

Dorny, Louis B. *U.S. Navy PBY Catalina Units of the Pacific War*. Oxford: Osprey, 2007.

Dower, John. *War Without Mercy: Race and Power in the Pacific War*. London: Faber and Faber, 1986.

Dyer, George C. *The Amphibians Came to Conquer, Vol. 1*. Washington, D.C.: U.S. Printing Office, 1969 Collins Publishers Inc, 1997.

Feldt, Eric. *The Coast Watchers*. Hawthorn, Australia: Lloyd O'Neil, 1975.

Felton, Mark. *Slaughter at Sea: The Story of Japan's Naval War Crimes*. Barnsley: South Yorkshire: Pen and Sword Books, 2007.

Gailey, Harry M. *Bougainville: A Forgotten Campaign*. Lexington: University of Kentucky Press, 1991.

Gamble, Bruce. *Fortress Rabaul: The Battle for the Southwest Pacific, January 1942–April 1943*. Minneapolis, MN: Zenith Press, 2010.

Gegeo, David W., and Geoffrey M. White (eds.). *The Big Death: Solomon Islanders Remember World War II*. Solomon Islands: Solomon Islands College of Higher Education and the University of the South Pacific, 1988.

Gillespie, Oliver A. *The Pacific*. Wellington: War History Branch, Department of Internal Affairs, 1952.

Halsey, William F., and J. Bryan. *Admiral Halsey's Story*. New York: McGraw-Hill, 1947.

Harries, Meirion and Susie. *Soldiers of the Sun: The Rise and Fall of the Imperial Japanese Army*. New York: Random House, 1991.

Hensley, Gerald. *Beyond the Battlefield: New Zealand and its Allies 1939–1945*. North Shore, Auckland: Penguin Viking, 2009.

Hess, William. *Pacific Sweep: The 5th and 13th Fighter Commands in World War II*. New York: Doubleday, 1974.

Hogg, Ian V. *British and American Artillery of World War II*. London: Greenhill, 2002.

Hoyt, Edwin P. *How They Won the War in the Pacific: Nimitz and His Admirals*. Guildford C.T: Lyons Press, 2002.

Huie, William Bradford. *Can-Do: The Story of the Seabees*. Annapolis: Naval Institute Press, 1997.

Hutching, Megan (ed.). *Against the Rising Sun: New Zealanders Remember the Pacific War*. Auckland: Harper Collins, 2006.

Isley, Jeter A. and Crowl. *The U.S. Marines and Amphibious War*. Princeton: Princeton University Press, 1951.

Ladd, J.D. *Assault from the Sea 1939–45: The Craft, The Landings, The Men*. New York: Hippocrene, 1976.

Lewis, Jonathon, and Ben Steele. *Hell in the Pacific*. London: Channel 4 Books, 2001.

Lewis, Paul M. *Ethnologue: Languages of the World*. Dallas: SIL International, 2009.

Lord, Walter M. *Lonely Vigil*. Annapolis: Bluejacket Books, 2006.

Lorelli, John. *To Foreign Shores: U.S. Amphibious Operations in World War II*. Annapolis: Naval Institute Press, 1995.

McGee, William I. *Amphibious Operations in the South Pacific in World War II, Vol. 2. The Solomons Campaigns 1942–43*. Santa Barbara, CA: BMC, 2002.

McGibbon, Ian (ed). *The Oxford Companion to New Zealand Military History*. Auckland: Oxford University Press, 2000.

Michener, James. *Tales of the South Pacific*. New York: Fawcett Books, 1993.

_____. *The World Is My Home*. New York: Random House, 1972.

Miller, Edward S. *War Plan Orange: The U.S. Strategy to Defeat Japan, 1897–1945*. Annapolis: Naval Institute Press, 1991.

Miller, John. *Cartwheel: The Reduction of Rabaul*. Washington, D.C.: Center of Military History, United States Army, 1990.

Morison, Samuel Eliot. *History of United States Naval Operations in World War II, Vol. 4, Coral Sea Midway and Submarine Action, May 1942–August 1942*. Edison, NJ: Castle Books, 2001.

_____. *History of United States Naval Operations in World War II, Vol. 6, Breaking the Bismarck's Barrier*. Edison, NJ: Castle Books, 2001.

Mulligan, Keith. *Kittyhawks and Coconuts*. Raumati Beach, New Zealand: Wings, 1947.

Myers, Bruce F. *Swift, Silent and Deadly: Marine Amphibious Reconnaissance in the Pacific 1942–45*. Annapolis, MD: Naval Institute Press, 2004.

Nila, Gary, and Robert A. Rolfe. *Japanese Special Naval Landing Forces*. Oxford: Osprey, 2006.

O'Sullivan, Barry, and Matthew O'Sullivan. *New Zealand Army Personal Equipment 1910–1945*. Willson Scott, 2005.

_____. *New Zealand Army Uniforms and Clothing 1910–1945*. Willson Scott, 2009.

Parr, Alison. *Silent Casualties: New Zealand's Unspoken Legacy of the Second World War*. Birkenhead: Tandem Press, 1995.

Petty, Bruce M. *New Zealand in the Pacific War*. Jefferson, NC: McFarland, 2008.

Prados, John. *Combined Fleet Decoded*. New York: Random House, 1995.

Rentz, John A. *Bougainville and the Northern Solomons*. Washington, D.C.: USMC, 1948.

Roberts, Andrew. *Masters and Commanders*. London: Allen Lane, 2008.

Ross, J.M.S. *Royal New Zealand Air Force*. Wellington: War Histories Branch, Department of Internal Affairs, 1955.

Rottman, Gordon L. *Landing Craft, Infantry and Fire Support*. Oxford: Osprey, 2009.

_____. *Landing Ship, Tank (LST) 1942–2002*. Oxford: Osprey, 2005.

_____. *U.S. Marine Corps World War II Order of Battle, Ground and Air Units in the Pacific War 1939–1945*. Westport, CT: Greenwood Press, 2002.

_____. *World War II Pacific Island Guide*, Westport, CT: Greenwood Press, 2002.

Shaw, Henry I., and Douglas T. Kane. *Isolation of Rabaul: History of U.S. Marine Corps Operations in World War II, Vol. 2*. Washington: Historical Branch, Headquarters, U.S. Marine Corps, 1963.

Smith, George W. *Carlson's Raid: The Daring Marine Assault on Makin*. Novato, CA: Presido Press, 2001.

Stout, Duncan M. *Medical Services in New Zealand and the Pacific*. Wellington, NZ: War History Branch, 1958.

Taaffe, Stephen R. *MacArthur's Jungle War: The 1944 New Guinea Campaign*. Lawrence: University of Kansas Press, 1998.

Taylor, Don. *Everyone's War*. New Plymouth: Zenith Press, 2004.

Third Division Histories Committee. *Base Wallahs*. Wellington: A.H. and A.W. Reed, 1946.

_____. *Communications*. Wellington: A.H. and A.W. Reed, 1945.

_____. *The Gunners*. Wellington: A.H. and A.W. Reed, 1952.

_____. *Headquarters*. Wellington: A.H. and A.W. Reed, 1947.

_____. *Pacific Pioneers: The Story of the Engineers of the New Zealand Expeditionary Force in the Pacific*. Wellington: A.H. and A.W. Reed, 1948.

_____. *Shovel, Sword and Scalpel*. Wellington: A.H. and A.W. Reed, 1945.

_____. *Stepping Stones to the Solomons*. Wellington: A.H. and A.W. Reed, 1947.

_____. *Story of the 34th*. Wellington: A.H. and A.W. Reed, 1947.

_____. *The 36th*. Wellington: A.H. and A.W. Reed, 1948.

Treanor, Ken. *The Staff, The Serpent and the Sword: 100 Years of the Royal New Zealand Army Medical Corps*. Christchurch: Willson Scott, 2008.

Tsouras, Peter G. (ed.). *The Greenhill Dictionary of Military Quotations*. London: Greenhill Books, 2000.

Whitley, M.J. *Destroyers of World War II*. Annapolis, MD: Naval Institute Press, 2002.

Winnefeld, James A. *Joint Air Operations: Pursuit of Unity in Command and Control 1942–1991*. Santa Monica: Rand, 1993.

Wolf, William. *13th Fighter Command in World War II: Air Combat over Guadalcanal and the Solomons*. Atglen, PA: Schiffer Military History, 2004.

Web Sites

Robert W. Connor. http://www.Seabees93.netdiary

USS *Cony*. http://USSCony.Com.Chronology

Dictionary of American Naval Fighting Ships. http://www.hazegray.org/danfs/

NZ Official War Histories. http://www.nzetc.org

Seabees. http://ww.history.navy.mil/faq

Archives New Zealand

Archives New Zealand files are those held at Archives New Zealand Head Office, Wellington, New Zealand.

Index

Numbers in ***bold italics*** indicate pages with photographs.

AA defenses: barrage balloons 157; communications difficulties 142; importance of in planning 57; Million Dollar Barrage 165, 210
AA guns 22–23, 43–44, 48, 89, 166, 173, 186, 200, 206
Adroit 55, 106, 163, 203
advanced dressing station 118–119, 136–138, 155, 211
Ahaesy, John T. 170
Alexander, Joseph (U.S. historian) 41
American–New Zealand relationships 183–186; American generosity 185; culinary tastes 184; pilfering 185; post-war relationship 192; pre-war strategic relationship 4
amphibious operations 2, 5, 16, 19–22, 24, 26, 28, 32, 38, 54, 56, 190–191, 198–200, 207, 214, 217, 223–224, 234
amphibious training 29, 31–32, 58, 83, 215, 223, 226
amphibious warfare 20, 29, 47, 48, 191
ANZAC 2, 4, 40, 211
Apache 22, 133, 203
Arcadia Conference 5
Argus units 19, 49, 57, 140, 202, 208, 212, 217
Armstrong, Corp. F.A. 161
Atabrine 74, 173, 175
Ausburne 62
auxiliary motor minesweepers 22, 55, 96, 106–107, 120
auxiliary personnel destroyer 21, 31, 43, 49, 55–56, 58, 60, 62, 96, 98–99, 101, 105–106, 128, 203, 209, 211, 224

Balzwierczak, Adam (crewman *Greenling*) 11
Banks, Pvt. Cedric 110

Baragwanath, Padre Owen 37, 100, 224
Baranowski, Stanley (crewman *Cony*) 131, 228
Barlow, Charles (crewman *Greenling*) 10, 11, 222, 233
Barrett, Maj. Gen. Charles D. (U.S. Army) 48, 209
Barrowclough, Maj. Gen. Harold Eric 2, 28, 32–33, 36, 39, 45–46, 50–51, 54, 63, 83, 89, 91, 134, 181, 183–185, 188–190, 192, 196, 199, 212, 224, 226, 232–233; AA guns on LSTs 54; attitude towards disposal of Japanese dead 192; Barrowclough's charter 51, 212; concerns over inadequacy of initial landing force on Mono 50–51; desire to have 3NZ Division take part in combat 51; military experience 28; post-war career 196; relationship with Sgt W.A. Cowan 83, 89; removal of Brigadier Row from command of 8 Brigade 182–183; Vella Lavella 134
Battle of Empress Augusta Bay 210, 233
Battle of Midway 4, 16
Battle of the Caves, Mono Island 160–161
Battle of the Coral Sea 4, 221, 234
beach: Emerald 44, 55, 57, 128–129, 140, 208, 212; Orange 44, 49, 57, 100, ***103***, ***104***, 106–107, 120–121, 157, 208, 212; Purple 44, 57–58, 61, 106, 113, 118, 125, ***126***, 127, 136, 159–169, 164, 208, 212
Bergerud, Eric (historian) 9, 152, 222
Black Cat, PBY5A, Squadron 75–77

Blanche Harbor 7, 8, 53, 60, 91, 96, 98, 106–107, 115–116, 131–132, 142, 166, 177, 180, 186, 192
Booth, Lt. L.T.G. 116
Bougainville 1, 6, 8–10, 12, 16–17, 23, 41–44, 46–48, 50, 56, 62, 64, 67, 69, 70, 75–77, 109, 125, 132, 135, 139, 141–142, 145, 150, 152, 157–158, 170–171, 177, 182, 187–189, 197, 199–200, 209–210, 213, 215, 221–222, 224–227, 230, 232–235
boys anti-tank rifle 35, 174, 206
Braithwaite, Maj. J.C. 58, 146
Bren gun carrier *see* universal carrier
Bren guns 35, 105, 110, 205–206, 213, 219
British Protectorate of the Solomon Islands 9
British Solomon Islands Defence Force 85, 232
Brooks, Capt. P.H. 57
Burke, Capt. Arleigh, USN 188

Catalina (flying boat) 75–78, 213, 218, 234
Chandler, E.C. 161
Charles, Clair (seabee) 146, 228–229, 233
Claxton 62
Cleveland 62
Coast Watchers 9, 15, 73, 83–84, 87, 169, 197, 214, 230, 234; Japanese 9, 169
combat loading 29, 52, 214
Compton, Gunner M.J. 110
Conflict 55, 106, 163, 203
Conway 98, 203
Cony 2 55, 131–134, 198, 203, 228, 235
Cooze, Frank 36, 96–97, 103, 114, 122, 124, 150, 156, 223, 226

237

Cowan, Sgt. William Albert (Bert) 3, 39, 82, *83*, *90*; attitude to Japanese 168, 197; "Blokes Patrols" 93–94; communication difficulties 63; contact with U.S. aircrew on Mono 3, 86–87; first patrol 82–89; incorrect signal to Barrowclough 91; knowledge of date of Goodtime 85; knowledge of Flt. Sgt. Luoni 130; military training 83–84; preparation for patrols 85, 89–90; prewar career 82–83; relationship with Maj. Gen. Barrowclough 83, 89; relationship with members of his patrols 86, 90, 92; second patrol 89–93, 145; warning to Mono Islanders of impending invasion 89, 91
crabs, land 121–122, 172, 177

Dahl, Chauncey Dale Verre 70–72, 75, 77, *88*
Daihatsu 120, 189, 207
Daring 55, 106, 163, 203
Davie, Gunner Gordon Campbell 30–31, 223, 231, 233
Davis, Lt. Col. F.L.H. 40
Dimery, Corp. R.S. 148
Dowell, Lt. J.A.H. 145
Duncan, Sapper Jack Keith 118, 223
Dunlop, Pvt. Robert 99–100, 112–113, 123, 167, 226–228, 230, 233
Dyson 62

Eaton 47, 55, 96, 106, 114, 116, 140, 203
Eaton, Doug 178–179, 231
Ellis, Pvt. "Slim" 115
Empress Augusta Bay, Bougainville 6, 16, 21, 41–43, 47–49, 76, 135, 139, 141–142, 157, 187, 189, 210, 213, 233
Estep, Chauncey, J. 69–73, 75, 77–78, 86, *88*
Execise Efate 33, 51, 215
Eyre, Lt. Col. R.J. 40, 56, 183

Fairfax, John of *Sydney Morning Herald* 114
Falamai 7, 15, 26, 42, 44, 48–50, 57–58, 65, 77–78, 88–89, 91, 93–94, 98–100, 102, 104–105, 110–112, 115–116, 118, 120–122, 126, 135, 142, 148, 155–156, 160–161, 164, 168, 179, 186, 191–196, 198, 208, 221
Falamai Village, Mono Island: Church of Remembrance 193–194; destruction of church 115; raising of Union Jack flag *116*
"Ficklefinger," B-25 Mitchell 171, 210
field surgical unit 136–137
Fiji 5; Koro Island 42; *see also* Operation Dovetail
films 56, 169, 179
first echelon 43, 48, 53, 55, 57, 136, 140, 157, 193
1st Marine Amphibious Corp (IMAC) 46, 48, 214–215, 217–218
Flynn, Corp. D.J. 161
Foote 62
Foote, John 111, 115, 130, 227
Fort, RAdm. George H., USN 47–49, 55–56, 96–97, 114, 116, 140, 209, 224–230
Fraser, Peter (prime minister of New Zealand) 36, 190, 199, 221; fear of casualties 36
Freyberg, Gen. Bernard 27, 51, 189, 196

Gage, Lt. Fred, USN 76–77
Gailey, Harry A. (U.S. historian) 44, 224
Gallipoli Campaign, 1915 1, 28, 38, 40, 43, 45, 224
Geissen, Maj. 138
Ghormley, Vice Adm. Robert Lee, USN 4–5, 29, 36, 214, 221, 223
Gilfillan, Corp. William (Bill) *90*, 91–93, 130, 145
Goettge Patrol 37
Goodtime *see* Operation Goodtime
Greenfield, Forbes 166, 186, 230, 231–233
Greenling 9–13, 48, 73, 209, 222
grenades 35, 123, 146–148, 159, 162, 205
Guadalcanal 5–6, 8, 19, 25, 34, 37, 43, 46–47, 50, 52–53, 56, 59, 60–63, 71, 73, 76–77, 79, 83–85, 87, 89–91, 98, 102, 107–108, 120–122, 131, 136, 138, 153, 157, 163, 169–170, 182, 186, 191, 193–194, 199, 209, 213–215, 218–219, 222, 224–225, 227, 229–230, 233, 235

Haig, Gen. Douglas 38
Halsey, Adm. William, USN 5–6, 10, 24, 36, 41–42, 44–45, *46*, 63, 182–184, 190, 192, 200, 209–210, 214, 219, 222–224, 234; attitude towards use of New Zealand soldiers in combat 5, 36, 45; planning of Goodtime 41–42, 44–45; response to removal of Brigadier R.A. Row from command of 8 Brigade 183
Hanson, Pvt. G.W. 148
Harris, Pvt. Bernie 105, 115, 154, 227, 229, 233
Havea, John (Mono Islander) 67, 69
Hodgson, 2nd Lt. George, 8 Brigade 32, 104–5, 110, 122, 171, 227, 233
Holmes, Pvt. "Jungle" 169
Howie, Lt. Samuel (USAAF) 134
Hunter, Lt. S. 136
Hyakutake, Lt. Gen. Haruyoshi, I.J.A. 17, 187

Ilala, Sgt. David, SIDF 85–86, 89–93, 130, 160–161, 197
"Island X" 7

James, Pvt. E.A. (Ashley) 99, 102, 223, 233
Japanese airpower 120, 139, 153; countermeasures by Allied air forces 139, 142; effect on Allied troops 142; effect of threat on planning 139; Washing Machine Charlie 153
Japanese Armed Forces: attitude of Allied soldiers to being captured by Japanese troops 15; attitude towards Allied prisoners 15–16; attitude towards Red Cross and medical personnel 37; attitude towards surrender to Allied forces 163; attitude towards Treasury Islanders 15, 69; deficiencies in medical care 15; Japanese attempts to escape from Mono Island 162, 167–168; Japanese holdouts 169; Japanese strength on Treasury Islands 199, 203; massacre of Goette Patrol on Guadalcanal 37; nightfighting 124; special naval land forces 13–16
Japanese prisoners of war 63, 93, 98, 162, 168, 192, 229, 230; Gosaburo, Seaman First Class Ishiura 98; Mizuno, Superior Seaman Kohei 14, 121, 147, 149
Joint Chiefs of Staff (U.S.) 5–6, 45, 216

Kahili Harbor, Southern Bougainville 69, 71, 79, 80, 142, 204
Khaki drill other ranks 35, 216

King, 2nd Lt. Benjamin Harold (USAAF) 69–70, 73, 197
King, Adm. Ernest, USN 4–5, 214, 216
Kirk, Capt. Les J. 146–147
Kolehe River, Mono Island 91, 102, 112, 121, 156
Krulak, Lt. Col. Victor ("Brute"), USMC 42, 187

Laifa Point, Mono Island 7, 14, 89, 91, 94, 131, 155, 160
landing craft, infantry (LCI) 24, 31–32, 43, 53–54, 58, 60–62, 98–99, 103–107, 110–111, 114, 120, 126, 130, 138, 157, 163, 191, 203–204, 207, 209, 217, 223, 227, 235; LCI-24 25, 106; LCI-67 127; LCI-334 106
landing craft, infantry (gun) LCI (G) 24, 107, 114, 116, 132, 155, 157, 191, 203
landing craft, mechanized (LCM) 25, 55, 60, 128, 204, 217
landing craft, tank (LCT) 25, 32, 43, 48–50, 52, 55, 110, 129, 140, 203–204, 207, 217, 227
landing craft, vehicle and personnel (LCVP) 25–26, *32*, 207, 216–217
landing ship tank (LST) 22–24, 32, 42–44, 48, 52, 54–56, 60–61, 100, 106–109, 111, *113*–116, 120–122, *127*, 132, 134, 136–138, 142, 157, 163–165, 170, 178, 198–199, 203–204, 207, 209, 217; LST 399 105, 107–109, 121, 136; LST 485 107, 113, 121, 127
Leary, Maj. V. 140
Lempriere, Pvt. J. *90*
Lendrum, Lt. J. 110
linesmen 112, 148, 171, 180
Logan, Maj. Gordon White 44, 50, 129, 145, 147- 149, 183, 232
Loganforce 50–51, 57, 62, 82, 128–130, 136, 144, 145–149, 159–160, 183, 200, 210, 217
logistical support 134-5
Lord, Walter (U.S. historian) 66, 68
Lorelli, John (U.S. historian) 1, 20
Louden, Capt. K.E. 102, 160
Lowden, Padre A.H. 169
Luoni, Flt. Sgt. George, RNZAF 79–81, 91, 130, 141, 145, 197, 209, 227–228
Lynds, Lt G.L. 119, 123, 130, 154, 228–229, 233
Lysaght, Pvt. Andy 105, 227, 233

MacArthur, Gen. Douglas, US Army 4, 6, 182; announcement of Goodtime to the media 182; influence on strategy 6; pressure to advance 6
malaria 9, 14–15, 35, 74, 175, 196, 201, 211; Treasury Islands 9; see also Atabrin
Malsi, Mono Island 7, 50, 66, 86, 89, 92–93, 102, 144–145, 148, 155–156, 158, 160–161, 164, 166–169, 178–179, 193, 229
Mannix, Lt. W.E. 170
Maxwell, Lt. W.M. 147
McKean 55, 62, 128, 203
McKenzie-Muirson, Lt. Col. Kenneth Basil 40, 183
Merrill, RAdm., USN 187
Methodist missionaries 9, 69
Michener, James (U.S. author) 197, 232; Bali Hai 198; *South Pacific* 197–198
Million Dollar Barrage 165, 210
Mills bomb *see* grenades
Milne, Lt. H.W. 110
Mitchell, Capt. F.J. 110
Mitchell, Ens. Joe David, USN 70–73, 75, 197, 209
Mitchell, Maj. Gen. 210
Mitchell Bombers 172–173
Mizuno, Superior Seaman Kohei 14, 121, 147, 149
Mono Island 3, 8, 11–12, 14, 16, 42, 44, 49, 70, 80, 82, 85, 87–89, 96, 99, 101, 103–104, 116, 121, 127, 143, 160, 174, 194, 198, 208, 212, 217, 226, 227, 230, 233; dispositions of Japanese forces 14; geography 7; population 7
Mono Islanders *194*; assistance to downed Allied aircrew 67–68, 70, 73, 81; attitude towards Japanese occupiers 15; "Blokes Patrols" 93–94, 168; ethnicity 9; gardens and food sources 193; language 9; religious beliefs 9, 69
morale 36, 105, 109, 151, 153; importance of combat operations for New Zealand soldiers 36
Morison, Samuel Eliot (U.S. historian) 47, 198, 221, 223–224, 232, 234
movie theaters: St. James, Falamai 179; Seabee Bijou, Stirling 179
Munda, New Georgia 64, 69, 85, 96, 134, 142, 170, 194, 204

Nakaseko, Ensign 14, 121, 144
Nash, Corp. Benjamin Franklin (Frank) 84–85, 89–90, 197

Nash, Walter 5
National Patriotic Fund Board 105
Naval Construction Battalion (NCB) 18–19, 108, 129, 140, 175, 185, 202, 210, 217; *see also* Seabees
naval gunfire 21, 26, 44, 49, 53, 89, 91, 98, 101, 191, 214
New Caledonia 5, 7, 22, 29, 40, 50, 52, 138, 152, 173, 180, 185, 191, 209–211, 218
New Georgia 6, 22, 36, 44, 47–48, 64, 70, 139, 179, 190, 209, 218–219
New Guinea 4–6, 16, 35, 45, 56, 69, 95, 105, 135, 182, 191, 200, 213, 215, 219, 221, 224, 226–227, 232, 235
New Zealand Freelance 110
New Zealand units: 2 Field Surgical Unit 136; 2NZ Division 27, 36, 40, 51, 129, 181–182, 189, 191; 3NZ Division 1–2, 5, 8, 28–29, 33, 201, 205, 207, 210, 211–213, 216, 218–219, 223, 228, 231, 233; 4 ASC 134; 4th Motor Transport Co. 163–164, 201; 7(NZ) Field Ambulance 61, 118–119, 123, 125, 129, 136, 150, 154, 201, 225, 228; 8 Brigade 5, 15, 26, 28–29, 31–32, 34–36, 38–40, 45, 48, 51, 56, 58, 62, 82, 83–84, 93, 104, 109, 118, 128–129, 158, 160, 164, 173–174, 180–182, 184, 190–193, 199, 201, 209–210, 213, 223; 23 Field Company 57, 115, 118, 121, 175, 193, 201, 208; 29 Battalion 37, 40, 57, 90, 92–93, 99, 102, 105, 110–113, 118, 151, 153, 155–156, 161, 162, 201, 208, 227, 233; 29 Light Antiaircraft Regiment 31, 52, 126, 157, 201; 34 Battalion 40, 53, 56–58, 60, 93, 125–129, 144–146, 148–149, 158–161, 164–165, 167, 169, 174, 178, 183, 201, 208, 230, 231, 233; 36 Battalion 40, 57–58, 60, 83, 93, 99–100, 102, 112, 115–118, 120, 122–125, 127, 138, 152–155, 160–161, 164, 167, 188, 201, 208, 226, 233; 38 Field Regiment 57, 61, 111, 129, 148, 158, 166, 177, 201, 230; 49th Battery 150, 165, 177, 230; 54 Anti-tank Battery 20, 201, 208; 208 Light AA Battery 107, 153; Graves Registration Unit 191; NZ Corps of Signals 108; Order of Battle 182, 202–203, 208

Newall, Gov. Gen., Sir Cyril 164
Nimitz, Adm. Chester, USN 4, 6, 36, 43, 45–47, 109, 170, 182, 214, 219, 221
Ninamo (village chief, Mono Island) 68, 75
Nisei 20; Shinto, Sgt Harry 20, 168
Norris, Pvt. A.H. 161
North Carolina 47

Operation Blissful 6, 41–44, 187, 209–210, 213, 224
Operation Cartwheel 6, 92, 182, 188, 212–213, 221–222, 234
Operation Cherryblossom 6, 21, 41, 43–44, 46–47, 49, 56, 63, 131, 151, 158, 187, 190, 198, 210
Operation Copper 95
Operation Dovetail 42, 215, 224
Operation Galvanic 17, 21, 199, 210, 216
Operation Goodtime: air cover by Allied planes 139–143; analysis 198–200; choice of codename 7; date of, brought forward 41; diversionary operation 41, 187; effect on Treasury Islanders 192–195; faded from public memory 1, 186; importance for future New Zealand Army operations in the South Pacific 199; importance of conservation of shipping 43, 198; importance of radar 49–50; limited shipping 49, 52; neutralization of Rabaul 5–6, 200; news of 181–182; planning 42–49, 51; risk 41–42; significance of 199–200
Operation "Shoestring 43, 220
Operation Squarepeg 188, 196, 219
Ostman, Seaman Second Class, Edwin 130
Otto, Ray 134, 228, 233
Owens, Ted 110

Pacific Defence Council 3
Papua, New Guinea 4, 16, 35, 191
Pearson, Sgt. W.J. 42–44, 113
Philip 53, 55, 57, 96–97, 114, 120, 131, 157, 203
planning 45–49; naval gunfire support 53, 89, 91
Plummer, Signalman D.E. 159
Port Purvis Anchorage, Florida Island 62, 133
Post Office Unit 174
President Adams 31–32, 44, 219

President Hayes 31–32, 34, 44, 219
President Jackson 31–33, 44, 219
President Monroe 3–32, 44, 210, 219
Pringle 53, 55, 96–98, 131, 157, 203
Pringle, Maj. B.H. 124
PT boats 9, 22, 44, 55, 57, 62, 84, 86–87, 134, 158, 166, 170, 178, 187, 189, 230
Puttick, Lt. Gen. Edward 45, 183, 190, 232

Rabaul: airfields 5; importance as main Japanese base in South Pacific 5–6, 8, 14, 16–17, 41–42, 56, 98, 135, 139, 171–172, 187–188, 196, 198, 200, 204, 209, 213, 215, 219, 221–224, 226–228, 234–235; Japanese defenders 5–6; Japanese HQ 135; objective in Operation Cartwheel 6
radar 9, 14, 19, 25, 41, 43, 48–50, 55, 57, 63, 78, 87, 96, 129–130, 131, 134–135, 140, 142, 144–145, 155, 159, 166, 187, 199–200, 208, 210, 212; establishment plans 49; limitations 142; long range (Type 270) 49; risk if Soanatalu overrun 50; at Soanatalu 130
rations: C & K rations 35; NZ soldiers abhorrence of U.S. rations 184
Red Cross 37
Regional Assistance Mission Solomon Islands (RAMSI) 195
Reidy, Maj. J.M. 127, 160
Renshaw 55, 98, 203
Renshaw, Sgt. Peter Basil 58–60, 101, 151–152, 233
Rentz, John A. (U.S. historian) 1, 46, 200, 203
RNZAF 26, 76, 79, 88, 91, 98, 111, 115, 141–143, 212, 214, 216–218, 225, 229; fighter cover over Treasury Islands 139–143; Hudson patrol bomber 76, 79, 88, 91, 216, 218; P-40 Kittyhawk Fighter 79, 139, 141
Robert C. Grier 167
Robinson, Pat (International News Service) 114
Rogers, Allan 100, 138, 227, 233
Roosevelt, Pres. Franklin Delano 5, 45, 212
Row, Brigadier Robert Amos 28, 36–38, **39**, 40, 43–45, **46**, 48–57, 62–63, 82–83, 89–91, 99, 105, 118, 120–121, 129, 131,
134, 142, 144–145, 154–156, 163–164, 182–184, 190, 198, 200, 209; career 38–39, 182; relationship with Maj. Gen. H.E. Barrowclough 39, 182
Rusden, Pvt. Carl **90**, 91–92, 130, 145

Sargent, Pvt. C.J.
Saufley 55, 107, 120, 157, 203
Saveke River 57, 89, 91, 99–100, 102, 106, 112–115, 117, 119, 121, 151–153, 155–156, 159, 164, 180, **181**, 208, 212
Schwartzwalder, Lt., USAF 171
Scott, Ensign Jesse, USN 3, 64–67, 74–75, 79, 86, **87**, **88**, 222, 225–226
Seabees 17–19, 43, 49, 61, 88, 109, 116, 128–130, 139–140, 144, 146, 148–149, 166, 170–173, 179, 185, 190, 192, 195, 198, 200, 210, 222–223, 231, 234–235; 87th NCB 108; *see also* NCB
second echelon 48, 134, 138, 156–157, 163
2nd Marine Parachute Battalion 41
Sen, Gunner Thom 142, 227, 233
Sherson, Pvt. C.H. 147
shipping 21, 27, 35, 42–44, 47–49, 52–53, 55, 63–64, 71, 76, 131, 134, 136, 138–139, 141–143, 151, 187, 191, 198–199
Shortland Islands 8, 9, 16–17, 42–44, 50, 62, 65, 75–77, 128, 134, 146, 149, 158, 160, 162–163, 165, 168, 170, 189, 199
Singapore, fall of 3, 37, 209
Small Coastal Transports (APc) 21, 55, 157, 163, 203–204, 211
Smith, Pvt. Joe 147–148
snipers 105–106, 114–115, 147, 153–155, 158, 206, 210, 225; effect on morale 153–4; pinning effect 153–4
Soanatalu, Mono Island 7, 43–44, 49–50, 54–55, 57, 62–63, 67, 80, 91–92, 121, 128, 134, 140, 142, 144–146, 148–149, 156, 158–161, 164, 168, 169–170, 178–179, 186, 193
South Pacific 197–8
South West Pacific Area 4, 6, 219
Spam (magazine of 34 Battalion) 174, 233, 231
Special Naval Landing Force (Tokubetsu Rikusentai) 13, 16, 219, 222, 235
Speight, Lt. (34 Battalion intelligence officer) 56

Spence 62
Spicer, Flt. Lt. St. John, RNZAF 143, 229
Starr, Ray 83–84, 226
Steele, Capt. A.G. 57
Stephenson, Warrant Officer E. 113
Stirling Island 8, 14, 42–44, 49, 54, 56–57, 61, 63, 65–66, 75, 91, 9, 96, 98–99, 106, 111, 113, 118, 120, 125–128, 130, 134–136, 140, 143, 148, 153–154, 157–159, 164, 166, 170–174, 176, 195, 208, 210, 212; construction of airstrip 170–173; geography of 7–8; landing beaches 43; Soala Lake 151
strategy: American strategy in South Pacific 3–6, 182, 189, 200; Germany First 5, 212; Japanese strategy in Pacific 16

tactical communications 158
Talbot 99, 157, 203
Talbot, Dr Arthur N. 153, 229
Task Force 39.3 (USN) 62
Tassone, Machinists Mate Aurelio 107–111
Taylor, Les 104, 122, 152, 156, 227–230, 233
third echelon 48, 121, 138, 163, 203, 210
Thomas, Archer (Sydney Telegraph) 104, 114
Thomas, Bdr. Gordon 2, 61, 125, 142, 165, 173, 175–176, 184; observations on Islanders 193

Treasury Islands: British rule 9, 192–193; geography 7–8
Trench, David 10, 193, 222, 232
Tschudi, George E. 185, 232
tugs 22, 128, 159; USS *Apache* 22, 133; USS *Sioux* 22
Tunnicliffe, Jeff 99–100, 123, 185, 226, 228, 232, 233
Turbott, Lt. I.G. 168, 231
Twhigg, Brig. John 28
Twining, Maj. Gen. 77, 139

The Unholy Four 31, 44, 211, 219
uniforms 13, 35, 59, 87, 90, 185, 207, 223, 235; NZ "Lemon Squeezer" hat 34, 36, 207; steel helmet 34, 124, 207; tropical clothing 34–35
United States Marine Corps 19, 48, 53, 62, 95, 109–110, 187, 199, 209–211, 213–215, 219, 221, 224, 232, 235
universal carrier 35, 105, 213, 219

Val (Japanese divebomber) 132, 141, 219
Vella Lavella 8, 15, 20–21, 44, 50, 54, 62, 64–65, 71–72, 75–76, 78, 82, 85, 87, 134, 136, 142, 207, 209; Barakoma 91, 204

W130 Assault Cable 151
Wagner, Herbert 169
Waitomo Caves 3, 221
Waller 132, 157

War Plan Orange 4, 220–221, 234
Ward 55, 58–59, 203, 224–225
Washing Machine Charlie 153
Washington 4–5, 45, 212,
Wasley, Pvt. John 106–107, 109, 227
Watson Island 8, 97, 99, 105, 113, 126, 166, 178
Wayne, John 109
Whaitiri, Pvt. Jackson 116–118
Whaley, Sgt. Trevor 31, 126, 159, 188, 223, 228, 230, 232
Wickham, Sgt. Maj. Frank, SIDF 85, 89, **90**–94, 197
Wilkinson, Vice Adm. Theodore Stark (Ping), USN 43, 46, 47, 49, 51, 54, 82, 109, 163, 184, 190, 198, 200, 209
Williams, David 122–123, 125, 186, 222–224, 228, 231–233
Williams, Capt. H.W. 160
Wilson Island 8, 106, 121
wounded 14, 28, 38, 65, 71, 99, 105–107, 111–114, 118–121, 124–125, 131–134, 136–138, 144, 147–153, 155–156, 161–163, 165, 167, 192, 196, 199, 220, 222, 230
Wynyard, Lt H.C. 158

YMCA secretaries 105, 125

Zero (Japanese fighter) 69–71, 76, 79–80, 135, 141, 143, 220, 229

www.ingramcontent.com/pod-product-compliance
Lightning Source LLC
Chambersburg PA
CBHW081550300426
44116CB00015B/2831